Educational Assessment in an Information Age

Series Editors

Patrick Griffin
Esther Care

This series introduces, defines, describes and explores methods of developing new assessment tools in educational and work environments which are increasingly characterised by use of digital technologies. Digital technologies simultaneously demand, reflect, and build student skills in many areas of learning, old and new. They can and will continue to adapt and facilitate the assessment of both traditional academic disciplines as well as those known as 21st century skills. These skills include creativity, critical thinking and problem solving, collaborative skills, information technology skills, and new forms of literacy, and social, cultural, and metacognitive awareness. The capacity of digital technologies to capture student learning as a process as well as student achievement is vast. New methods need to be developed to harness this capacity in a manner that can produce useful and accurate information to teachers for classroom interventions, and to education systems for policy development. The series includes innovative approaches to assessment in terms of their psychometrics and technology platforms; outcomes of implementation of assessments of generic skills at large scale in the classroom; and use of large scale assessment data to inform policy in education. The series explores the assessment of new and emerging skills required of graduates and how new forms of assessment inform teaching; it projects into the future the kinds of assessment possibility associated with technology and explores the assessment links between education and the workplace.

More information about this series at http://www.springer.com/series/13475

Esther Care • Patrick Griffin • Mark Wilson
Editors

Assessment and Teaching of 21st Century Skills

Research and Applications

Springer

Editors
Esther Care
Brookings Institution
Washington DC, Washington, USA

University of Melbourne
Parkville, VIC, Australia

Patrick Griffin
Melbourne Graduate School of Education
University of Melbourne
Parkville, VIC, Australia

Mark Wilson
University of California
Berkeley, CA, USA

University of Melbourne
Parkville, VIC, Australia

ISSN 2363-5177 ISSN 2363-6025 (electronic)
Educational Assessment in an Information Age
ISBN 978-3-319-65366-2 ISBN 978-3-319-65368-6 (eBook)
DOI 10.1007/978-3-319-65368-6

Library of Congress Control Number: 2017954919

Printed on acid-free paper

This Springer imprint is published by Springer Nature
The registered company is Springer International Publishing AG
The registered company address is: Gewerbestrasse 11, 6330 Cham, Switzerland

Preface

Over the past 8 years, I have had the privilege of leading a truly innovative project. Two previous volumes have reported on the conceptual framework and the research methodology used in this project to develop and calibrate collaborative problem solving and digital literacy tasks engaged in by human beings interacting on the Internet. The international research programme was led by Professor Esther Care, while I had the privilege of leading and directing the project overall. In this volume Professor Care has gathered together a group of researchers who have been exploring areas related to our first two volumes, bringing some closure to the ATC21S research. However, the work in this volume also opens the door to a large group of researchers to make contributions as we achieve a better understanding of the future of education and work within a digital environment.

This volume explores the impact of the global shift towards information- and technology-driven economies and the digital revolution demanding unprecedented shifts in education and learning systems. These shifts impact on curriculum for early childhood, school and further and higher education. Education and learning systems are under pressure to change and to emphasise lifelong learning approaches to education. This change expands upon education provision that occurs within the boundaries of formal age- and profession-related educational institutions that have historically been responsible for the transmission of bodies of knowledge.

The Internet has become a major source of knowledge and is rapidly becoming accessible to all. Information is now available faster than a teacher can tell, more broadly than an encyclopaedia can present and more comprehensively than a community library can provide. Educators want to respond to this change, but their training and employment are based on how much they know and can impart to students; governments want to respond too, but the pace of government policy change is at times debilitating; teacher education will need to review its role, but the loss of esteem and celebrated expertise associated with changing direction is difficult to overcome; parents are bewildered by the changes in schools and cannot recognise their own style of education in their children's classrooms; employers are reorganising their workplaces to alter manufacturing from products to information, but the new positions created by these changes are not being filled with first-job work-ready employees. Relentless waves of change are producing the equivalent of an assault on learning, living and work that is transforming workplaces as we know them. We are moving into an era with new forms of work and new kinds of workplaces that require new training to induct people into them. Yet vocational education is, in many countries, locked into a model that treats workplace competence as a comprehensive set of discrete skills that are rehearsed in training but that struggle to remain relevant in the changing workplace.

In this rapidly changing world, education is, on the one hand, a cause of widespread consternation because of its apparent inertia; on the other hand, it offers salvation through its potential to prepare societies for economic changes in work, life and learning. But can education deliver through a different approach?

Modern education, both formal and informal, needs to prepare citizens for jobs that have not yet been created and for the fact that many jobs will disappear under the wave of technology-based change brought about by robotics and digitisation of the workplace. In the future, there will be technologies that have not yet been invented, and there will be ways of living, thinking and learning that have not yet emerged. Because of the digital revolution, people will leave school and universities with competencies, attitudes and values commensurate with a digital information age. Education must now focus on the preparation of a workforce demanding new ways of thinking and working that involve creativity, critical analysis, problem solving and decision making. Citizens need to be prepared for new ways of working that will call upon their communication and collaboration skills. They will need to be familiar with new tools that include the capacity to recognise and exploit the potential of new technologies. In addition, they will need to learn to live in this multifaceted new world as active and responsible global citizens.

For many countries, it is a formidable economic problem to prepare graduates for the new kind of workforce. Those wishing to be highly rewarded in the workforce of the future will need to be expert at interacting with people to acquire information and to understand what that information means and how to critically evaluate both the sources and the information. They will need to be able to persuade others of implications of information for action. As the world becomes more complex and integrated across national boundaries, individuals will need to be able to cross workplace and national boundaries to collaborate on shared information and emerging knowledge. The more complex the world becomes, the more individuals will need these competencies. The more content knowledge that can be accessed and researched, the more important filters and explainers will become: individuals need to be able to build problem solutions by identifying components and linking these together in ways that make sense to themselves and others.

In this volume, Professor Care and colleagues explore the implications of this digital world and today's dynamic environment for the education issues surrounding assessment and teaching of twenty-first-century skills: a timely and necessary undertaking as the world begins to face the implications of the fourth Industrial Revolution.

Melbourne, VIC, Australia Patrick Griffin

Contents

About the Editors and Contributors

Editors

Esther Care is a Professor at the University of Melbourne and directs the Assessment, Curriculum and Technology Research Centre, funded by the Australian Government to undertake research in the Philippines to inform that country's major K-12 education reform. Esther is also Senior Fellow with the Brookings Institution, Washington, DC, and there leads the Skills for a Changing World project which draws on countries' experiences as they integrate twenty-first-century skills into their education policy and practice and which works with countries to support teaching and assessment of skills in the classroom. From 2017, Esther is leading an initiative with regional centres in Africa and Asia to build assessment capacity in the context of countries monitoring their education progress against the Sustainable Development Goals.

Patrick Griffin held the Chair of education (assessment) at the University of Melbourne for more than 20 years. He was Associate Dean of the Graduate School of Education and the Foundation Director of the Assessment Research Centre as well as the Executive Director of the Assessment and Teaching of 21st Century Skills (ATC21S) project. As Lead Consultant for the UNESCO Future Competencies project, he led the development of competency curriculum and assessment.

Mark Wilson is Professor of education and Director of the Berkeley Evaluation and Assessment Research Center at the University of California and Professor of assessment at the University of Melbourne. He teaches courses on measurement in the social sciences, especially as applied to assessment in education. In 2016, he was elected President of the National Council on Measurement in Education, and in 2012 president of the Psychometric Society. His research interests focus on the development and application of approaches for measurement in education and the social sciences, the development of statistical models suitable for measurement contexts, the creation of instruments to measure new constructs and scholarship on the philosophy of measurement.

Contributors

Raymond J. Adams specialises in psychometrics, educational statistics, large-scale testing and international comparative studies, is an Honorary Senior Fellow at the Assessment Research Centre of the University of Melbourne, and leads the Centre for Global Education Monitoring at the Australian Council for Educational Research. He was the International Project Director for the OECD Programme for International Student Assessment (PISA) – perhaps the world's largest and most significant educational research project – from its inception until 2014 and led its design. His personal research programme is on the extension of fundamental measurement models (Rasch item response models) to deal with performance assessments and on the application of item response methods to international surveys of educational outcomes.

Arto K. Ahonen is a Senior Researcher in the Finnish Institute for Educational Research at the University of Jyväskylä. His current work is related to the PISA 2018 study, in which he holds a position as a National Project Manager. He is also involved in the PREP21 study (Preparing Teacher Students for 21st Century Learning Practices), where his research is related to the assessment of preservice teachers' collaborative problem-solving skills.

María Eugenia Bujanda is an Associate Researcher in the Omar Dengo Foundation, Costa Rica, where for more than 10 years she has held research and management responsibilities, first in the Research Department and then in the National Program of Educational Informatics. Her research is related to the use of digital technologies to promote personal, educational and social development. She has taught in the Universidad Pontificia Comillas of Madrid and the Universidad Estatal a Distancia of Costa Rica. She holds a bachelor's degree in pedagogy (Universidad de Deusto) and a Ph.D. in social education (Universidad Complutense de Madrid).

Imelda Caleon is a Research Scientist at the Centre for Research in Pedagogy and Practice and the Learning Sciences Lab at the National Institute of Education, Nanyang Technological University. Her main research interests are in the areas of positive education and science education. She is currently engaged in several studies focusing on cultivating learners' well-being and resilience. She received her Ph.D. from the Nanyang Technological University.

Kathleen B. Comfort works in the STEM programme at WestEd and is the Director of the Partnership for the Assessment of Standards-Based Science. Previously, she directed science assessment for the California Department of Education, served as Senior Research Associate for Project 2061 of the American Association for the Advancement of Science, was Coordinator of the Shasta County Assessment System and was a Teacher. She has served on National Research

Council committees including the Life Science Design team for the Framework for K-12 Science Education, the Board on Science Education, the Science Education K-12 Committee, the National Science Education Standards Assessment Group and the Addendum on Classroom Assessment.

Andreas Fischer is a Research Associate at the Research Institute for Vocational Education and Training (f-bb) in Nuremberg, Germany. Since 2014, he has been Editor-in-Chief of the *Journal of Dynamic Decision Making*. His research interests include wisdom, vocational competencies and complex problem solving.

Peter W. Foltz is Vice President in Pearson's Advanced Computing and Data Science Laboratory and Professor Adjoint at the University of Colorado's Institute of Cognitive Science. His work covers twenty-first-century skills learning, large-scale data analytics, artificial intelligence and uses of machine learning and natural language processing for educational and clinical assessments. The methods he has pioneered are used by millions of students annually to improve student achievement, expand student access and make learning materials more affordable. Dr. Foltz has served as content lead for framework development for OECD PISA assessments for reading literacy and collaborative problem solving.

Carol Forsyth is an Associate Research Scientist in the Cognitive, Accessibility, and Technology Sciences group at Educational Testing Service. She earned her Ph.D. in cognitive psychology with cognitive science graduate certification at the University of Memphis. Her research interests include discourse processes, theoretically grounded educational data mining, collaboration and serious games. She applies her knowledge of these topics to both learning and assessment. She has published over 30 peer-reviewed publications on these topics.

Joachim Funke is Full Professor of theoretical and cognitive psychology at the Department of Psychology, Heidelberg University, Germany. His primary interests are issues within problem solving and thinking research. He is one of the promoters of the European approach to complex problem solving using computer-simulated microworlds.

Mae-Lynn Germany is a Doctoral Candidate in counselling psychology and the Institute for Intelligent Systems at the University of Memphis. She has worked as a Research Assistant in cognitive science with the Institute for Intelligent Systems for the past 9 years, studying intelligent tutoring systems, question-asking and computational linguistics.

Perman Gochyyev is a Research Psychometrician at the University of California, Berkeley (UC Berkeley), at the Berkeley Evaluation and Assessment Research Center. Perman received his Ph.D. in quantitative methods and evaluation from UC Berkeley in 2015. His research focuses on latent variable and multilevel modelling, multidimensional and ordinal IRT models, latent class models and issues related to causal inference in behavioural statistics.

Arthur C. Graesser is a Professor in the Department of Psychology and the Institute of Intelligent Systems at the University of Memphis, as well as an Honorary Research Fellow at the University of Oxford. His research interests include discourse processing, cognitive science, computational linguistics, artificial intelligence and development of learning technologies with natural language (such as AutoTutor) and those that analyse text on multiple levels of language and discourse (Coh-Metrix and QUAID). He has served on expert panels on problem solving for OECD, including PISA 2015 Collaborative Problem Solving (Cochair).

Samuel Greiff is Associate Professor at the Institute of Cognitive Sciences and Assessment and Head of the research group Computer-Based Assessment at the University of Luxembourg. His current research interests cover large-scale assessment; cross-curricular skills such as problem solving, collaboration and adaptivity; and their assessment, validity and facilitation.

Päivi Häkkinen is a Professor of educational technology at the Finnish Institute for Educational Research, University of Jyväskylä. She has led research projects on technology-enhanced learning and computer-supported collaborative learning (CSCL). Together with her research group, she has conducted research related to processes, outcomes and contexts of CSCL. Her current research interests are related to the progression of twenty-first-century skills (skills for learning, problem solving and collaboration, as well as ability to use ICT in teaching and learning), particularly in the context of teacher education.

Daniel V. Holt is a Lecturer in theoretical and cognitive psychology at the Department of Psychology, Heidelberg University, Germany. His research interests include problem solving, executive functions and self-regulation.

Helyn Kim is a post-doctoral Fellow at the Center for Universal Education at the Brookings Institution. Her research focuses on understanding and assessing a broad range of skills that contribute to learning and development. She works on the Skills for a Changing World project, which seeks to ensure that all children have high-quality learning opportunities that build the breadth of skills necessary to succeed in the global economy. She received her Ph.D. in education from the University of Virginia. Her doctoral work provided a multidimensional approach to understanding the nature of and interplay between the foundations of learning.

Elizabeth Koh is Assistant Dean (research translation) and Research Scientist at the Learning Sciences Lab, Office of Education Research, at the National Institute of Education, Nanyang Technological University, Singapore. Her research interests are in education and IT, particularly the twenty-first-century competency of teamwork in technology-mediated environments, computer-supported collaborative learning and learning analytics. She received her Ph.D. in information systems from the National University of Singapore.

Katarina Krkovic is a Research Assistant and a Doctoral Student at the Institute for Psychology, Clinical Psychology and Psychotherapy at Universität Hamburg, Germany. Her current research interests cover emotion regulation processes and stress reactivity in psychopathology, as well as cognitive performance, including complex and collaborative problem solving.

Maida Mustafic is a Research Associate and Postdoctoral Research Fellow at the Institute of Cognitive Sciences and Assessment and a member of the research group Computer-Based Assessment at the University of Luxembourg. Her current research interests cover the understanding of the determinants and assessment of complex problem solving and collaborative problem-solving skills.

Hui Leng Ng is the Lead Research Specialist in international benchmarking and research at the Ministry of Education, Singapore. She received her B.Sc. and M.Sc. in mathematics from Imperial College of Science, Technology and Medicine; her M.Ed. in general education from the National Institute of Education, Nanyang Technological University; and her Ed.D. in quantitative policy analysis in education from Harvard University. She is involved in large-scale international studies such as TIMSS, ATC21S and other evaluation studies that inform educational policymaking and practice in Singapore. She is currently Singapore's National Research Coordinator for TIMSS.

Chew Leng Poon is Divisional Director for the Research and Management Information Division at the Ministry of Education, Singapore. She is also a Principal Specialist in research and curriculum. She earned her master's degree in curricular studies at the Ohio State University, USA, and her Ph.D. from the National Institute of Education, Nanyang Technological University, specialising in science inquiry pedagogy. She currently directs Singapore's efforts in various international benchmarking studies and was Singapore's National Project Manager for the ATC21S project.

Leda Muñoz is the Executive Director of the Omar Dengo Foundation and Full Professor at the Faculty of Medicine of the University of Costa Rica. She holds a B.Sc. in biology (University of Costa Rica), an M.Sc. in physiology (California State University), a Ph.D. in human nutrition (University of California) and a post-doctorate in nutritional epidemiology (Cornell University). Her research is focussed on improving opportunities for the development of children and youth through education and health. She has engaged in the design and implementation of large-scale sustainable projects in these areas, focusing on educational interventions that support the development of skills and talents among youth.

Nienke Nieveen is Associate Professor at Eindhoven University of Technology, Netherlands, and Senior Researcher at the Netherlands Institute for Curriculum Development (SLO). Her work focuses on teacher professional learning in relation to school-based curriculum development, educational design research and curriculum design approaches and tools. Her doctoral dissertation (1997) was based on a design research project in the field of curriculum design and evaluation. She chairs the Curriculum Division of VOR (Netherlands Educational Research Association) and the Curriculum Network of EERA (European Educational Research Association) and is a member of the international advisory group of the Stirling Network for Curriculum Studies.

Tjeerd Plomp is Professor Emeritus at the University of Twente, Enschede, Netherlands. He has an M.Sc. in mathematics (1964) and a Ph.D. in education (1974) from the Free University Amsterdam. From 1989 to 1999, he was the chair of the IEA (International Association for the Evaluation of Educational Achievement), which conducts international comparative assessments, including TIMSS and PIRLS. He has received honorary doctorates from the Universities of Ghent, Belgium and Pretoria, South Africa. His research interests are educational design research, information technology in the curriculum and twenty-first-century skills in education. His most recent book is *Educational Design Research* (2013), coedited with Nienke Nieveen and freely downloadable from http://international.slo.nl/edr.

Johanna Pöysä-Tarhonen is a Senior Researcher at the Finnish Institute for Educational Research at the University of Jyväskylä. She obtained her Ph.D. in educational sciences in 2006 at Katholieke Universiteit Leuven, Belgium, and the title of docent in 2016 at the University of Eastern Finland. Her research interests include computer-supported collaborative learning, learning environments and technology-enhanced assessment of collaboration and collaborative problem solving.

Dara Ramalingam is a Senior Research Fellow in the Assessment and Psychometric Division of the Australian Council for Educational Research. She is part of a test development team that specialises in constructing, describing and validating developmental continua. Dara played a leading role in test development for reading literacy in the Programme for International Student Assessment (PISA) 2009 and led test development for the computer-based assessment of problem solving that was included in PISA 2012. Her Ph.D. focussed on how the data resulting from computer-delivered assessments can be used to improve construct validity and measurement precision.

Yigal Rosen is a Senior Research Scientist at Harvard University. He leads a research and development group that advances data analytics, learning and assessment initiatives across digital learning platforms such as HarvardX and Canvas. Dr. Rosen teaches design and development of technology-enhanced assessments at the Harvard Graduate School of Education. He obtained his Ph.D. in educational assessment from the University of Haifa, Israel. He was a Postdoctoral Fellow at Harvard University and at Tel Aviv University. Prior to joining Harvard, he was a Senior

Research Scientist at Pearson, leading innovative learning and assessment technology research.

Kathleen Scalise is Associate Professor at the University of Oregon and Director of the National Assessment of Educational Progress (NAEP) Science for ETS. Her areas of research are technology-enhanced assessments in science and mathematics education, item response models with innovative item types, computer-adaptive approaches and applications to equity studies. Her recent research projects include work on twenty-first-century skills assessments with Cisco, Intel and Microsoft; virtual performance assessments with Harvard University; and technology-enhanced assessments in the USA and with OECD and IEA projects.

Claire Scoular is a Research Fellow at the Assessment Research Centre, University of Melbourne, and the Australian Council for Educational Research. Her work focuses on the improvement of assessment practices in education, drawing on applications of psychological measurement. Her recent research has focused on measurements of twenty-first-century skills. Her doctoral work at the University of Melbourne identified a measurement methodology for assessing collaboration in online problem-solving environments. She has worked in psychometric assessment, intervention and research in the UK, the USA, New Zealand, Australia, the Philippines and Vietnam.

Jennifer Pei-Ling Tan is Senior Research Scientist (Learning Sciences Lab) and Assistant Dean (knowledge mobilisation) at the Office of Education Research, National Institute of Education, Singapore. She specialises in technology-mediated pedagogical innovations aimed at assessing and fostering twenty-first-century skills and dispositions in learners. She leads a number of competitively funded research projects, working closely with schools and policymakers to design, implement and evaluate web-based collaborative learning and formative learning analytics initiatives to promote collaborative creativity and criticality in young people. She holds doctoral and master's degrees in philosophy, education and business.

Michael Timms is Director of Assessment and Psychometric Research at the Australian Council for Educational Research. His research interests are in how technology can support the process of assessment by providing learners and teachers with feedback that enables them to advance their learning.

Sascha Wüstenberg works at TWT GmbH Science & Innovation. He received his Ph.D. at Heidelberg University, Germany, in 2013. His dissertation "Nature and Validity of Complex Problem Solving" considerably advanced research on CPS. He held a postdoctoral appointment at the University of Luxembourg from 2013 to 2015. His main research interests lie in educational measurement of problem-solving competency. He developed computer-based assessment of the interactive problem-solving tasks that were included in the assessment of interactive problem solving in the Programme for International Student Assessment (PISA) in 2012.

Magaly Zúñiga is the Director of the Research and Evaluation Department in the Omar Dengo Foundation, Costa Rica. She currently leads the evaluation of learning outcomes of the National Program of Educational Informatics from a formative perspective, the development of tools to evaluate the professional development of educators regarding the educational use of digital technologies and the development of a test to evaluate computational thinking in students aged between 12 and 15 years.

Part I
Introduction

Chapter 1
Twenty-First Century Skills: From Theory to Action

Esther Care

Abstract This chapter provides a general introduction to issues and initiatives in the assessment of twenty-first century skills, the implications of assessment for the teacher and teacher training, the role played by technologies not only for demonstration of skills but for their measurement, and a look to the future. Frameworks that have informed a gradual shift in the aspirations of education systems for their students are described, followed by evidence of implementations globally and regionally. The role of the Assessment and Teaching of 21st Century Skills (ATC21S; Griffin et al. (Eds.) (2012), Assessment and teaching of 21st century skills. Springer, Dordrecht) in reflecting and acting on a call by global consortia is outlined. This provides the context for the book contents, with the chapters briefly described within their thematic parts. The chapters provide a clear picture of the complexities of the introduction of teaching and assessment strategies based on skills rather than content.

The Assessment and Teaching of 21st Century Skills (ATC21S; Griffin et al. 2012) initiative was stimulated by a coalition of global commercial organisations and engaged in by six countries in its research phase. Reflecting concerns about generating future workforces with the "21st century" skills that their workplaces required, Kozma (2011) discussed an aspiration for education reform which was information communications and technology-centric. The global discourse has moved toward a broader concern around global citizenship and global competence, but underpinning these concepts are the myriad twenty-first century skills identified in seminal frameworks of human characteristics. Each framework approaches the question of what people need to function effectively in society, and takes a variety of perspectives from high-level to detailed, and from inclusion of a vast array of human characteristics to skills or competencies alone. This is the context for the assessment and teaching of twenty-first century skills.

E. Care (✉)
Brookings Institution, Washington, DC, USA
e-mail: ecare@brookings.edu

E. Care et al. (eds.), *Assessment and Teaching of 21st Century Skills*, Educational Assessment in an Information Age,
DOI 10.1007/978-3-319-65368-6_1

Frameworks

The frameworks, notwithstanding similarities (Voogt and Roblin 2012), also reveal very different ways of conceptualising human characteristics and the human condition. There are more differences across ways of framing these than there are in identifying the actual skills themselves. For example, some frameworks (e.g. Delors et al. 1996) take a very high-level perspective, echoing generic human learning targets – to know, to do, to be, to live together. Others such as OECD's DeSeCo Report (Rychen and Salganik 2001) take into account the twenty-first century context more explicitly and provide more detail in identification of competencies. Similarly Partnerships 21 (www.p21.org) and the European Commission (Gordon et al. 2009) comprehend both the high-level concepts as well as specific competencies. The ATC21S framework (Binkley et al. 2012) follows this model but explicitly acknowledges competencies beyond skills, identifying knowledge, and the cluster set of attitudes, values and ethics. This perspective was prescient given the growing emphasis on global competency (OECD 2016) and global citizenship which clearly tap cognitive and social skills as well as morals, ethics, attitudes and values. Another influential framework, focussed on skills and abilities, was presented by Pellegrino and Hilton through the US National Research Council (2012). More recently, at the 2015 World Economic Forum core twenty-first century capabilities were again confirmed across the categories of foundational literacies (how students apply core skills to everyday tasks – e.g. literacy, ICT literacy), competencies (how students approach complex challenges – e.g. problem solving, communication), and character qualities (how students approach their environment – e.g. persistence, leadership).

In terms of the particular competencies that populate these frameworks, and that are identified as salient to twenty-first century education, there is strong consistency across global organisations and research groups. The majority of identified competencies generally fall within the cognitive and social domains, although a variety of classification systems is used. Since release of the aspirations that are the Sustainable Development Goals (UNESCO 2015a), a solid platform for consideration of a broader curricular approach has been established. Of particular interest in this context, Sustainable Development Goal 4 calls for skills beyond literacy and numeracy – including readiness for primary education (4.2), technical and vocational skills (4.4), and skills needed to promote global citizenship and sustainable development (4.7). These targets signal an emphasis on the breadth of skills necessary to prepare children, youth and adults comprehensively for twenty-first century citizenship and life. In order to capture an indication of how regions or countries, as opposed to global consortia and academia, are investing in a breadth-of-skills perspective in considering education reform, three initiatives illuminate the current state.

Movement at Regional and Global Levels

The Learning Metrics Task Force (2013a, b) was convened in 2012 to investigate how learning progress can be tracked at a global level and to "improve the learning outcomes of all children and youth by strengthening assessment systems and the use of assessment data". The Task Force was coordinated by the UNESCO Institute for Statistics and the Brookings Institution. It conducted two phases of research work. In the first phase the task force completed several rounds of global consultation and technical development involving 1700 people from 118 countries. Through this consultation process, a series of recommendations for improving learning outcomes and measurement at the global level was put forward. A significant output of the consultation was the Global Framework of Learning Domains, which described seven domains of learning that should be available to all children: physical well-being, social and emotional, culture and the arts, literacy and communication, learning approaches and cognition, numeracy and mathematics, and science and technology. The focus on competencies across the domains of learning took a curricular approach to twenty-first century skills. The penetration of the LMTF initiative is in large part due to the strong engagement by countries as well as global partners.

Since 2013, the UNESCO-supported ERI-NET and NEQMAP groups have been exploring the status and reach of transversal competencies in the Asia Pacific region. The first report (UNESCO 2015b) describes transversal competencies arrived at through an ERI-NET consensus process. Ten countries (Australia, Shanghai [China], China, Hong Kong, Republic of Korea, Japan, Malaysia, Mongolia, Philippines, and Thailand) in the Asia-Pacific region participated in the study which documented the variety of approaches to transversal competencies that these countries took at policy and practice levels. The list represented core sets of skills (critical and innovative thinking, inter-personal skills, intra-personal skills, global citizenship) as well as allowing for national and cultural differences across countries in the region. The report concluded that "the ten education systems… have all recently introduced or moved to strengthen existing dimensions of transversal competencies in their education policies and curricula" (p. 21). The second study in the series (UNESCO 2016) addressed the links between policy and practice. The emergence of teaching practices which emphasised student-centred practical tasks was documented, as was also the lack of teacher training to support these practices. The majority of participating systems were of the view that existing mechanisms could be used for assessment of transversal competencies. This finding hinted at lack of deep understanding of the implications of introduction of competencies to the education process. This finding was supported in the fourth study supported by UNESCO through NEQMAP (Care and Luo 2016) which explored implementation of assessment of these skills. Across the nine participating countries in the fourth study, there was strong evidence of awareness at policy and school levels of the drive for assessment, but its implementation was hampered by lack of teacher understanding about the skills and relevant materials and resources.

In the third initiative, and taking an individual countries perspective, a scan of online national education websites representing 102 countries by the Brookings Institution (Care et al. 2016) demonstrated that 86% of sampled countries include twenty-first century skills in some aspect of their educational aspirations. The most frequently named skills drawn from the global scan were communication, creativity, critical thinking and problem solving. The congruence of these country-nominated skills with those identified in the global frameworks and elsewhere (e.g., Voogt and Roblin 2012; UNESCO 2016) is striking, and provides strong support for the stability of attitudes about what qualities are to be valued in twenty-first century education.

The second decade of the twenty-first century has thus seen evidence of increasing emphasis on twenty-first century skills, demonstrating that the conversations are not confined to global organisations or academic consortia, but are being addressed at regional and country levels.

Both the UNESCO NEQMAP initiative and the Brookings Institution global scan surface the big issue – implementation. The scan of the 102 countries represented information available in the second half of 2016, and is dynamically updated (www.skills.brookings.edu). It does not represent the total population of such information – merely that which is accessible through online search. The data were analysed across four levels. The first level explored vision or mission statements. Where these include a reference to a goal that is explicit concerning twenty-first century skills, or implicit by virtue of referring to a quality that requires such skills, this is taken as evidence of endorsement of the importance of twenty-first century skills. The second level explored whether a country identifies particular skills. The third level sought for evidence that would clarify that skills are a part of the curriculum; and the fourth sought for evidence of awareness that skills in their own right follow a learning progression and will therefore be taught and learnt at different stages and through different discipline areas. Meeting this final level would imply that the notion of development of skills as part of a sequence of learning is accepted. This would be a pre-requisite for adaptive integration of skills in the curriculum, in pedagogy and assessment.

The data demonstrate that most countries identify twenty-first century skills as part of their educational goals, while fewer countries identify skills development progressions and their integration through the curriculum (Fig. 1.1). In some cases, the commitments of national education authorities are to specific skills or competencies, and how these are included in the curriculum without information about learning progressions. In other cases, just mission or vision statements make explicit the valuing of the competencies.

In cases where the mission is not supported by information at all the levels, it may well be due to natural lag between intention and action. Notwithstanding, it is clear from the patterns of penetration of the "skills agenda", as well as from the richer information derived from the ERI-NET and NEQMAP studies (2015, 2016), that some national systems face challenges in addressing what amounts to a considerable education reform. The challenges can be ascribed to many factors that play into reform generally – political, procedural, and technical. Beyond these are factors

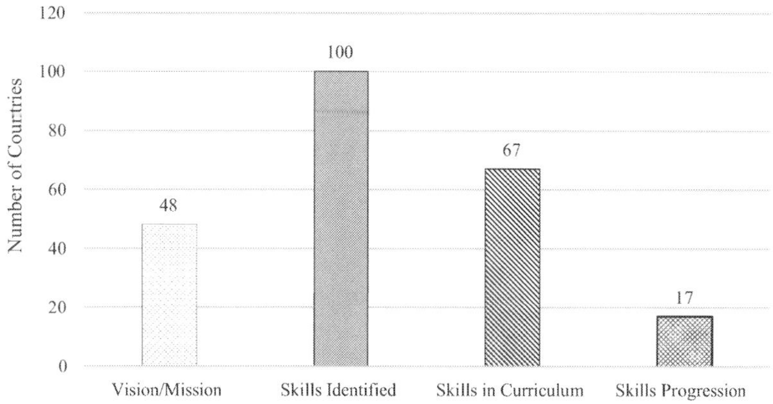

Fig. 1.1 Skills across layers of country documentation (Adapted and updated from Care et al. 2016)

associated with this particular reform. Introduction of a competencies focus in education requires a shift from the content focus that characterises many national curricula. This shift relies not only on curriculum reform, but also changed approaches to pedagogy and assessment. What is to be taught dictates best methods for teaching and best methods for assessment. And this is the area which currently challenges us.

The Assessment and Teaching of 21st Century Skills Project

The ATC21S project was sited very much in this space, of establishing frameworks within which to link assessment and teaching. The project closed formally in 2012 with the development and delivery of a conceptual framework for twenty-first century skills (Griffin et al. 2012); a focus on two skills areas – collaborative problem solving and ICT literacy in digital networks; an approach to formative assessment; and teacher professional development modules (Griffin and Care 2015). Since that time, interest has peaked in collaborative problem solving, mainly as a result of the 2015 PISA study in which collaborative problem solving was assessed in up to 65 countries.

ATC21S provided an approach to assess students as they engaged with tasks online and collaborated. Student navigation of digital networks and problem solving behaviour was captured electronically in activity log files for synchronous scoring and reporting against developmental progressions. The progressions provided guidelines for teachers about how students might demonstrate the skills at increasing levels of sophistication and competence such that these could be integrated into their teaching. How the insights into these complex twenty-first century skills might be translated into classroom practice is the challenge for national education systems globally.

Technology permeates our living and working. If education is to prepare students for the future, technology is an integral component. If, however, technology is to realise its potential, it needs to be better integrated at the classroom level, as part of instructional delivery, formative assessment, and appropriate intervention and tracking of outcomes and learning. At the system level, technology can be embedded into the broader educational policy decisions that align standards and objectives with twenty-first century skills.

A great deal of current research and system monitoring programs focus on basic skills such as reading comprehension, writing, mathematics, and scientific literacy, which are taught in schools under pressure of traditional curriculum demands. Little progress in terms of international comparative studies that examine the processes by which cognitive and social skills are developed had been made either at the student or the system level until 2015 when the OECD through its PISA project measured student performance in collaborative problem solving. Building on the ATC21S research across six countries on collaborative problem solving and digital literacy in social networks, the measurement and identification of collaborative problem solving assumes an important status in twenty-first century skills education. Collaborative problem solving (Hesse et al. 2015) incorporates the cognitive skills of task analysis (problem analysis, goal setting resource management, flexibility and ambiguity, collecting information and systematicity), and problem resolution (representing and formulating relationships, forming rules and generalisation and testing hypotheses), as well as interpersonal skills such as participation (action, interaction and perseverance), perspective taking (adaptive responsiveness, and audience awareness [mutual modelling]) and social regulation (negotiation, meta-memory, transactive memory, and responsibility initiative). These non-cognitive skills are increasingly important and the identification of ways to focus attention on them in terms of their measurement and development at student and system level is becoming increasingly urgent.

An Explicit Shift in Education

What we are seeing is not a revolution in education. It is better understood as a shift in how we recognize the importance of developing generic skills and competencies during basic and secondary education. We are making explicit our expectations of education in terms of these generic outcomes. The point of education has always been to equip students to function effectively in society. As our society has changed, we are re-visiting this expectation, and focusing more explicitly on the particular skills and competencies that have been highlighted as essential for functioning in our technological world.

Intrinsic to this move toward the explicit, countries are including twenty-first century skills in their curricula, looking at the implications for teaching, and exploring assessment approaches that might both capture and support the skills. There is clearly major interest in twenty-first century skills at country, regional and global levels. Lagging behind the interest is knowledge about how to assess and teach the skills. In this volume we see initiatives to redress this balance.

Description of This Volume

The chapters in this volume are organised within three main themes. These are assessment of twenty-first century skills, country initiatives with a focus on implications of the twenty-first century skills agenda for teachers and teacher education, and the measurement and applications of information technologies. The final chapter provides a comprehensive systemic view on the phenomenon.

Part 1, Assessment of 21st Century Skills, opens with this chapter, and is followed by a chapter exploring the authenticity of assessments of twenty-first century skills. Care and Kim (2018) highlight the challenges associated with the measurement of skills in a general education context. Taking the position that assessment should reflect as closely as possible the way in which the object of that assessment will be demonstrated, they highlight the consequences of the nature of twenty-first century skills for assessment. The practical and adaptive nature of skills is identified as a primary challenge to their assessment, since it is the capacity to respond to different situations and non-routine scenarios that is the goal, while the nature of assessment typically requires that a situation is known and that there is a finite number of responses to ensure objective evaluation. To illustrate their argument Care and Kim use Gulikers et al. (2004) principles of authenticity as a framework to review a selection of assessments of twenty-first century skills. They conclude on a note of major concern about lack of progress in the assessment of complex constructs, thereby raising challenges which authors of the subsequent chapters explore from different perspectives.

The following three papers delve into the history of technology-supported problem solving and its move into complex and collaborative variants. The perspective of these papers distinguishes the concerns of assessment specialists rather than practitioners, and traverse terrain far removed from assessment in the classroom.

Funke et al. (2018) focus on complexity. Rather than seeing problem solving as a simple model in which a number of processes combine to facilitate a desired outcome, their approach considers the role played by non-cognitive factors such as motivation and self-regulation. This moves the discussion past recent views which have focussed on problem solving solely as a cognitive set of processes. Constructs such as collaborative problem solving have considered the additional role of social processes but primarily due to the need to make interactive processes explicit as part of group approaches to problem solving. The authors express some impatience with the slowness of technical progress in assessment of problem solving, dare to refer to the invisible elephant, "g", although without resolution of its role, and suggest expansion of the computer-simulated microworlds approach to assess their postulated "systems competence". Although this may provide the potential to capture communication as well as the cognitive processes in problem solving, social characteristics such as self-regulation or motivation, initially identified as clearly important by the authors, remain to be addressed. As researchers struggle to theorise and measure increasing complexity as knowledge about that complexity increases, this chapter raises questions about whether systems competence is merely about acting on a complex problem space that requires a multiplicity of different problem solving processes, or whether it is something qualitatively different.

Krkovic et al. (2018) follow the iterations in online assessment of problem solving. They introduce their work with reference to the ambiguous and non-routine nature of complex and collaborative problem solving. Grounding much of their discussion in the MicroDYN tasks designed as minimal complex systems (Funke 2010) where respondents manipulate input variables and monitor effects on outcome variables, the authors move from assessment of the individual to the collaborative. Noting the challenges inherent in trying to capture both social and cognitive processes in online assessment environments, the authors contrast the PISA human-to-agent approach with the ATC21S human-to-human approach. Krkovic et al. point out that large scale assessments of problem solving processes have now been implemented for over 15 years. The history of these processes makes clear the early progress in online capture through dynamic systems, and the complexities that arise as our understanding of the cognitive and social competencies becomes successively more comprehensive.

Graesser et al. (2018) identify differences between problem solving and collaborative problem solving as based primarily in need for multiple resources, division of labour, and diverse perspectives. Their focus is on these needs rather than on what characterises the two sets of activities – to wit, that collaborative problem solving requires the processes to be explicit due to the need to communicate. Their approach leads directly to the issue of whether the team or the individual needs to be the focus of assessment. Aligned with OECD's PISA (2013) approach to assessment of the construct, Graesser et al. provide a comprehensive justification for assessment of the individual within the collaborative dynamic – primarily on logistic grounds. Notwithstanding a matrix approach of 12 skills to identify the structure of the construct for PISA, the authors describe the main task as working toward a unidimensional scale for collaborative problem solving. This tension between complexity and the desire for simplicity is reflected more broadly in other efforts in measurement of skills – for example in OECD's efforts to measure global competency (2016), or current attempts to determine a universal global metric for education. Graesser et al. describe the approach taken by the PISA Collaborative Problem Solving Expert Group and following the ATC21S method of initially identifying three levels of functioning to guide task development and measurement. Issues of interdependence and symmetry are also highlighted although the human-agent nature of the PISA approach nullifies some of the measurement issues associated with these (Scoular et al. 2017). Moving to the challenges in assessment and measurement of complex skills, Graesser et al. highlight discourse management, group composition, and the use of computer agents in assessments. An extensive discussion of the complexities of communication makes clear the huge challenge in attempting to capture this phenomenon in a standard and automated way. This challenge of course is inextricably linked to decisions concerning use of agents in online assessment platforms, an issue that Graesser et al. inform.

Both the circumscribing of capacity to stimulate human processes and collect the emanating data, as well as the potential of that data capture, are highlighted. Notwithstanding aspirations to identify sets of complex processes as unidimensional constructs, it is not yet clear that our methods or data can support these. These chapters reflect concern with assessment issues in a space far from the use of results by teachers to enhance student skills.

The chapters in Part 2 illustrate applications and exploration of assessment of twenty-first century skills from founder countries in ATC21S. From the focus on assessment which characterised the original project, these chapters reflect transition to deeper exploration of skills and their implications for teaching and learning. The authors respond to the global uptake of the notion of skills education, and focus on how implementation of these complex constructs might be seen, monitored, and enhanced in the classroom.

Tan et al. (2018) jump right into this conundrum, hypothesising associations between collective creativity and collaborative problem solving with a focus on students. Using Assessment and Teaching of twenty-first Century Skills (ATC21S) project data, Tan and colleagues argue that creativity is central to problem solving, implicitly drawing on creativity's cognitive dimensions such as divergent thinking, and explore the degree to which the assessment data support the association. Tan et al.'s definition of collective creativity identifies dimensions similar to those that were hypothesized by Hesse et al. (2015) as contributing to collaborative problem solving, thereby providing a rationale for associations between the two constructs. The complexity of the model proposed highlights the challenge of assessment of interactive problem solving behaviour. The authors' finding of lack of impact of metacognition needs to be considered within the wider question of whether knowledge-building necessarily has immediate impact on the learning task itself, as opposed to longer-term impact. Tan et al.'s contribution confirms the value of deconstruction of complex constructs to components that can be brought to the attention of teachers for instructional purposes.

Ahonen et al. (2018) reflect upon the demand for better assessment of twenty-first century skills as a result of Finland's emphasis on interdisciplinary and generic skills and competencies. Introduction of more inquiry-based learning approaches and reliance on small group learning and teaching assumes teachers' own understanding of these approaches and their own skills. Ahonen et al. seek in particular to understand teachers' teamwork and collaborative dispositions given the centrality of these to Finland's vision for inquiry-based learning approaches that rely on collaborative as well as technology-enhanced modes of working. Within a large scale study of training needs of pre-service teachers, the authors focus on a small group of pre-service teachers, and analyse self-report across components of collaboration, such as negotiation and cooperation, as well as their performance on ATC21S tasks. Lack of consistency across the data sources raises both methodological and substantive questions. Do collaborative skills necessarily contribute to outcomes in a collaborative problem solving context? To what extent are self evaluations valid forms of assessment of characteristics such as collaborative dispositions? The PREP21 project provides a valuable context through which to understand the preparation needed to ensure that teachers can shift from their own learning experiences to a twenty-first century learning and teaching environment.

Comfort and Timms (2018) introduce their concerns about twenty-first century learning by alluding to the transmission model, through which teachers transmit factual knowledge to students but which does not necessarily facilitate students' capacity to understand and apply. They postulate that twenty-first century skills are not learnt unless explicitly taught. Comfort and Timms hold that despite large scale twenty-first century initiatives such as Partnerships21 and ATC21S, as well as development of the US-specific Common Core State Standards, teaching and assessment of twenty-first century skills in the US is minimal. Taking a particular interest in Next Generation Science Standards, the authors consider how learning activities in the classroom might be structured through the use of games, drawing on collaborative skills and focussed on inquiry, explanation, argumentation and evaluation. Expanding on a study by Bressler (2014), Comfort and Timms highlight the specific opportunities needed by teachers in order to develop the skills to model the learning that needs to take place in the twenty-first century classroom.

Scoular and Care (2018) focus on how systems might facilitate the teaching of twenty-first century skills, through looking at Australian approaches to teacher development. They draw attention to the issues generated by lack of understanding of the nature of the skills, and how and when the various skills might differentially be brought to bear across school subjects. Notwithstanding the Australian Curriculum, Assessment and Reporting Authority's (ACARA) development of the General Capabilities (ACARA 2013) which is accompanied by extensive online resources for teachers, the gap between policy and implementation is noted. With trans-disciplinary skills needing a coherent messaging across different teaching staff, school approaches rather than individual professional development for teachers need to be considered. Looking specifically at collaborative problem solving, Scoular and Care present three case studies which focus on preparation of teachers themselves, teacher resources, and higher education responsibilities. The diversity of the case studies across these topics is testament to the complexity of this education shift and the need for a systemic perspective.

Bujanda et al. (2018) position Costa Rica's education initiatives in the country's decision to prioritise needs and opportunities associated with technologies and technology-based learning since the 1980s. The National Program of Educational Informatics established in 1988 has moved from a learning-by-doing orientation to a learning-by-making approach. Its constructivist approach draws attention to evidence of learning, often enabled through technologies. Costa Rica's current curriculum emphasises project-based learning, and assessment is increasingly influenced by its formative purpose. Bujanda et al. identify the contributions of ATC21S to the country's increasing expertise through initiatives such as the National Program's assessment of Citizenship and Communication, Productivity and Research and Problem Solving. The 2017 announcement of Costa Rica's new curriculum identifies the ATC21S framework as inspiring expected learning outcomes. The authors make clear the country's continuing emphasis on technologies and their use as an intrinsic component of twenty-first century education provision.

Together, the perspectives contributed by these authors who participated in the research active phase of ATC21S, demonstrate an increasing concern for translation of the theory into approaches to implementation. It is clear that despite varied performance in international large scale assessments across the countries, there is concensus at the actual delivery level to students for education systems to explore how to deliver opportunities to their students for acquisition of skills above and beyond traditional discipline achievements.

The chapters in Part 3 witness the multiple implications of information and communications technologies – for measurement and within the classroom. We follow the technical path taken by Wilson and colleagues in the context of the skills themselves, to insights from Ramalingam and Adams about how capture of process data further informs our understanding of the skills. Scalise follows with examples of student activities at differing levels of proficiency within an information literacy environment.

Wilson et al. (2018a) present a historical account of development of concepts of ICT literacy over the past two decades which form the framework for their work on ICT literacy in networks. In describing this framework Wilson et al. also provide contextual information about the ATC21S project at large providing a picture of the drivers for the project and its goals. From this base, Wilson et al. (2018b) raise some fascinating issues around complementarity of the measurement approach taken by Wilson et al. (2015) with learning analytics. They describe four principles that good assessment and measurement should adhere to: to be based on a developmental paradigm, to be aligned with instructional goals, to produce valid and reliable evidence, and to provide information useful to teachers and students. Wilson et al. (2018b) argue that a learning analytics approach can be used to explore data that remain inaccessible to most automated scoring methods, such as may be used in text analysis. Their "sentiment analysis" demonstrates reasonably strong alignment with handscoring methods, prompting their conclusion that learning analytics modules might reasonably be embedded within measurement models. Wilson et al. (2018b) also approach a vexed issue in the assessment of individuals operating within groups. Where individuals' responses cannot be regarded as independent, there are both measurement and substantive concerns. From modelling of results from ATC21S using both unidimensional and multidimensional item response models, and with and without random effects for groups, the authors propose that a combined measure of group and individual level performance provides the best estimates of ability. How these findings are to be explored in the context of the four principles of good assessment and measurement is part of the new vista for assessment.

Ramalingam and Adams (2018) explore the nature of and the opportunities provided by data captured as part of online assessment of complex constructs. Drawing on the traditional item format also used by Graesser et al. (2018) – multiple choice items – Ramalingam and Adams interrogate PISA digital reading data to determine the extent to which the logstream or "process" data can inform more accurate measurement. Whereas Graesser et al. describe decisions taken due to the limitations of online data capture, Ramalingam and Adams describe the opportunities provided by the medium. Their approach firmly aligns the potential of automated assessment with the nature of the target through focus on processes. In so doing, they identify the capacity of the medium to explore the nature of the target in ways not previously accessible. Since the focus on skills development and assessment is primarily a focus on processes rather than solutions, tracking of navigation behaviour for example can demonstrate that a task respondent is, or is not, activating certain processes. In turn, this demonstration can be recognised and valued, regardless of whether the process meets with success in terms of achieving a "correct" result.

Scalise (2018) brings together classroom based digital and collaboration skills to demonstrate the implications of the theoretical frameworks developed in ATC21S for practice. She demonstrates how teachers can use review of student work to evaluate patterns in student learning and link these with the strands of digital literacy. Through the process, teachers can develop strategies to guide their teaching and evaluation of impact. Using student work examples, Scalise identifies correspondence with skill levels across the *learning through digital networks* construct. Drawing on student responses to the ATC21S Arctic Trek task, Scalise mines the rich data from students working in an online collaborative learning environment. She traces student progress across Wilson et al.'s (2018a) four strands of literacy through the eyes of Roblyer's (2006) technology integration grid, providing strong links between the theoretical frameworks, the measurement, and the practice.

In the concluding Part 4, Nieveen and Plomp (2018) provide a model-based discussion of the elements to be considered in educations systems' change processes with a primary focus on the curriculum and the implications of its changes for pedagogies and system coherence. With particular reference to the ATC21S Binkley et al. (2012) framework, they explore implications at classroom, school, and system levels. Outlining different models for implementation of skills in curriculum – adding to existing curriculum, integration as cross-curricular competencies, or introducing new curricula – the authors adopt integration as the basis for their discussion. Implications of changes to one aspect of the curriculum for others is highlighted, as is the need for new approaches to assessment, to pedagogy, to the role of teachers, and the nature and use of information. The need to move from a group focus in terms of pedagogical strategies is elucidated with consequences for teacher beliefs. This leads to the intersections of curriculum development, teacher development and the organisation of the school. Reflecting the nature of the skills themselves, the mechanics of implementing the change are described as inherently collaborative and dynamic, in contrast to the view of teachers as silos within classrooms. Nieveen and Plomp then move to the wider context, and describe bottom-up and top-down models situating the levels of system, school, and classroom which in turn draws attention to the intended, implemented and achieved curriculum story. The critical theme of interdependence between layers of the system, between curriculum, assessment and pedagogy, and their dynamic nature runs strongly through the discussion, providing a coherent overview of the landscape of the twenty-first century skills change phenomenon.

Conclusion

This volume, reflecting the concerns and questions of researchers and practitioners highlights five points: that the shift towards twenty-first century skills in national education systems is occurring; that the shift is raising implementation issues in terms of teacher education and strategies; that the opportunities provided by technologies also provide challenges; that the measurement world is engaging with new approaches; and that transfer of these new approaches remain to transition into the classroom. It is unrealistic to assume that curricular shift, and innovation in assessment to reflect current teaching and learning associated with that shift, will all happen at once. As this volume demonstrates, there is movement in classrooms and some higher education contexts. This presents researchers with a situation of some urgency in moving beyond the theoretical and conceptual toward pragmatic solutions to the teaching and assessment of twenty-first century skills that will enhance student growth.

References

Ahonen, A. K., Häkkinen, P., & Pöysä-Tarhonen, J. (2018). Collaborative problem solving in Finnish pre-service teacher education: A case study. In E. Care, P. Griffin, & M. Wilson (Eds.), *Assessment and teaching of 21st century skills: Research and applications*. Dordrecht: Springer.

Australian Curriculum, Assessment and Reporting Authority (ACARA). (2013). *General capabilities in the Australian curriculum.* Retrieved from http://www.australiancurriculum.edu.au/GeneralCapabilities/Pdf/Overview.

Binkley, M., Erstad, O., Herman, J., Raizen, S., & Ripley, M. (2012). Defining 21st century skills. In P. Griffin, B. McGaw, & E. Care (Eds.), *The assessment and teaching of 21st century skills*. Dordrecht: Springer.

Bressler, D. (2014). Better than business-as-usual: Improving scientific practices during discourse and writing by playing a collaborative mystery game. *Double Helix, 2*, 1–13.

Bujanda, M. E., Muñoz, L., & Zúñiga, M. (2018). Initiatives and implementation of 21st century skills teaching and assessment in Costa Rica. In E. Care, P. Griffin, & M. Wilson (Eds.), *Assessment and teaching of 21st century skills: Research and applications*. Dordrecht: Springer.

Care, E., & Kim, H. (2018). Assessment of 21st century skills: The issue of authenticity. In E. Care, P. Griffin, & M. Wilson (Eds.), *Assessment and teaching of 21st century skills: Research and applications*. Dordrecht: Springer.

Care, E., & Luo, R. (2016). *Assessment of transversal competencies: Policy and practice in the Asia-Pacific Region*. Bangkok: UNESCO.

Care, E., Anderson, K., & Kim, H. (2016). *Visualizing the breadth of skills movement across education systems, Skills for a Changing World.* Washington, DC: The Brookings Institution.

Comfort, K., & Timms, M. (2018). A 21st skills lens on the common core standards and the next generation science standards. In E. Care, P. Griffin, & M. Wilson (Eds.), *Assessment and teaching of 21st century skills: Research and applications*. Dordrecht: Springer.

Delors, J., Al Mufti, I., Amagai, I. A., Carneiro, R., Chung, F., Geremek, B., et al. (1996). *Learning: The treasure within*. Paris: UNESCO.

Funke, J. (2010). Complex problem solving: A case for complex cognition? *Cognitive Process, 11*, 133–142.

Funke, J., Fischer, A., & Holt, D. V. (2018). Competencies for complexity: Problem solving in the 21st century. In E. Care, P. Griffin, & M. Wilson (Eds.), *Assessment and teaching of 21st century skills: Research and applications*. Dordrecht: Springer.

Gordon, J., Halasz, G., Krawczyk, M., Leney, T., Michel, A., Pepper, D., Putkiewicz, E., & Wisniewski, J. (2009). *Key competences in Europe: Opening doors for lifelong learners across the school curriculum and teacher education*. Warsaw: Center for Social and Economic Research.

Graesser, A., Foltz, P. W., Rosen, Y., Shaffer, D. W., Forsyth, C., & Germany, M. (2018). Challenges of assessing collaborative problem-solving. In E. Care, P. Griffin, & M. Wilson (Eds.), *Assessment and teaching of 21st century skills: Research and applications*. Dordrecht: Springer.

Griffin, P., & Care, E. (Eds.). (2015). *Assessment and teaching of 21st century skills: Methods and approach*. Dordrecht: Springer.

Griffin, P., McGaw, B., & Care, E. (Eds.). (2012). *Assessment and teaching of 21st Century Skills*. Dordrecht: Springer.

Gulikers, J. T. M., Bastiaens, T. J., & Kirschner, P. A. (2004). A five-dimensional framework for authentic assessment. *Educational Technology Research and Development, 52*, 67–86.

Hesse, F., Care, E., Buder, J., Sassenberg, K., & Griffin, P. (2015). A framework for teachable collaborative problem solving skills. In P. Griffin & E. Care (Eds.), *Assessment and teaching of 21st century skills: Methods and approach*. Dordrecht: Springer.

Kozma, R. B. (2011). A framework for ICT policies to transform education. In *Transforming education: The power of ICT policies*. Paris: UNESCO.

Krkovic, K., Mustafic, M., Wüstenberg, S., & Greiff, S. (2018). Shifts in the assessment of problem solving. In E. Care, P. Griffin, & M. Wilson (Eds.), *Assessment and teaching of 21st century skills: Research and applications*. Dordrecht: Springer.

Learning Metrics Task Force. (2013a). *Toward universal learning: What every child should learn*. Montreal: UNESCO Institute for Statistics and Brookings Institution.

Learning Metrics Task Force. (2013b). *Toward universal learning: Recommendations from the Learning Metrics Task Force*. Montreal: UNESCO Institute for Statistics and Brookings Institution.

Nieveen, N., & Plomp, T. (2018). Curricular and implementation challenges in introducing 21st century skills education. In E. Care, P. Griffin, & M. Wilson (Eds.), *Assessment and teaching of 21st century skills: Research and applications*. Dordrecht: Springer.

OECD. (2013). *Draft PISA collaborative problem solving framework*. Paris, France: OECD Publishing.

OECD. (2016). *Global competency for an inclusive world*. Paris: OECD Publishing.

Pellegrino, J. W., & Hilton, M. L. (Eds.). (2012). *Education for life and work: Developing transferable knowledge and skills in the 21st century*. Washington, DC: The National Academies Press.

Ramalingam, D., & Adams, R. J. (2018). How can use of data from computer-delivered assessments improve measurement? In E. Care, P. Griffin, & M. Wilson (Eds.), *Assessment and teaching of 21st century skills: Research and applications*. Dordrecht: Springer.

Roblyer, M. D. (2006). *Integrating educational technology into teaching*. Upper Saddle River: Pearson.

Rychen, D. S., & Salganik, L. H. (Eds.). (2001). *Defining and selecting key competencies*. Göttingen: Hogrefe & Huber.

Scalise, K. (2018). Next wave for integration of educational technology into the classroom: Collaborative technology integration planning practices. In E. Care, P. Griffin, & M. Wilson (Eds.), *Assessment and teaching of 21st century skills: Research and applications*. Dordrecht: Springer.

Scoular, C., & Care, E. (2018). Teaching 21st century skills: Implications at system levels in Australia. In E. Care, P. Griffin, & M. Wilson (Eds.), *Assessment and teaching of 21st century skills: Research and applications*. Dordrecht: Springer.

Scoular, C., Care, E., & Hesse, F. (2018). Designs for operationalizing collaborative problem solving for automated assessment. *Journal of Educational Measurement, 54*(1), 12–35.

Tan, J. P., Caleon, I., Koh, E., Poon, C. L., & Ng, H. L. (2018). Collective creativity and collaborative problem-solving among Singapore secondary school students. In E. Care, P. Griffin, & M. Wilson (Eds.), *Assessment and teaching of 21st century skills: Research and applications*. Dordrecht: Springer.

UNESCO. (2015a). *Sustainable development goals: 17 goals to transform our world*. http://www.un.org/sustainabledevelopment/sustainable-development-goals/. Paris: UNESCO.

UNESCO. (2015b). *2013 Asia-Pacific Education Research Institutes Network (ERI-Net) regional study on transversal competencies in education policy & practice (phase I)*. Paris: UNESCO.

UNESCO. (2016). *2014 Asia-Pacific Education Research Institutes Network (ERI-Net) regional study on transversal competencies in education policy & practice (phase II): School and teaching practices for twenty-first century challenges: Lessons from the Asia-Pacific Region*. Paris: UNESCO.

Voogt, J., & Roblin, N. P. (2012). A comparative analysis of international frameworks for 21st century competences: Implications for national curriculum policies. *Journal of Curriculum Studies, 44*(3), 299–321.

Wilson, M., Scalise, K., & Gochyyev, P. (2015). Rethinking ICT literacy: From computer skills to social network settings. *Thinking Skills and Creativity, 18*, 65–80.

Wilson, M., Scalise, K., & Gochyyev, P. (2018a). Learning in digital networks as a modern approach to ICT Literacy. In E. Care, P. Griffin, & M. Wilson (Eds.), *Assessment and teaching of 21st century skills: Research and applications*. Dordrecht: Springer.

Wilson, M., Scalise, K., & Gochyyev, P. (2018b). Intersecting learning analytics and measurement science in the context of ICT literacy assessment. In E. Care, P. Griffin, & M. Wilson (Eds.), *Assessment and teaching of 21st century skills: Research and applications*. Dordrecht: Springer.

Part II
Assessment of Twenty-First Century Skills

Chapter 2
Assessment of Twenty-First Century Skills: The Issue of Authenticity

Esther Care and Helyn Kim

Abstract Writing skills are assessed through writing tests, typing skills are assessed through typing; how do we assess critical thinking or collaboration? As interest in twenty-first century skills increases globally, and as skills goals are explicitly adopted into curricula, the inadequacy of our knowledge of how these skills develop becomes increasingly problematic. These goals reflect human processes, both cognitive and social, and this challenges many current assessment approaches. To highlight some of the issues associated with assessment of twenty-first century skills, a review of a sample of assessment tools was undertaken. The review provides some insights both into how far we have come as well as how far we have to go. The diversity of the tools and evaluation of these against authenticity dimensions highlights the challenges not only in design of assessment but in how teachers might design classroom learning experiences that facilitate development of twenty-first century skills.

Introduction

There is global recognition of the need for students to develop a broader set of skills during the years of formal education than has traditionally been the case. Although recognition of importance of work-ready skills has long been endorsed, it is relatively recent that calls for their development have moved from a strongly vocational stance (e.g., Brewer 2013) to an education for both work and life perspective (e.g., Pellegrino and Hilton 2012).

In many countries, education ministries commit to goals such as developing "the whole person", characterised by sets of values, ethics, and attitudes aligned with national identity, as well as developing students' social-emotional characteristics and cognitive skills. Introduction of twenty-first century curricula requires knowledge and understanding of how the aspirations in mission statements

E. Care (✉) • H. Kim
Brookings Institution, Washington, DC, USA
e-mail: ecare@brookings.edu

E. Care et al. (eds.), *Assessment and Teaching of 21st Century Skills*,
Educational Assessment in an Information Age,
DOI 10.1007/978-3-319-65368-6_2

translate into the particulars of what students need to learn and know how to do, and of what teachers need to teach and know how to assess. Given that a primary justification for assessment is to improve student educational outcomes, information from assessment must be aligned with the purposes to which it will be applied (Almond 2010).

Assessment is often dichotomised across summative and formative functions. Another function is as a driver of teaching and learning. For example, the fact of assessing particular domains is sometimes seen as signalling that the domain is valued by the system (Schwartz et al. 2011) particularly to teachers. Where the main interest is in stimulating learning and competency development (Birenbaum 1996), authenticity of the assessment is pre-eminent since we are interested in predictive capacity of results. Taking four "21st century skills" that have recently been identified by country education systems as valued (Care and Luo 2016; Care et al. 2016a), in this chapter we highlight authenticity issues associated with their assessment through exploration of tools designed to measure them. The four skills are problem solving, collaborative problem solving, computer and information literacy, and global citizenship.

Complex Nature of Skills

Some skills, such as problem solving, might be seen as uni-dimensional in the sense that just one main type of contributing factor – cognitive skills – describes them, although multiple processes contribute to them. Other skills are clearly multi-dimensional by virtue of drawing on qualitatively different skills. Collaborative problem solving is a case in point. It combines the two broad domains of social and cognitive skills, and within these, calls on the skills of collaboration and problem solving. In turn, each of these is comprised of more finely delineated subskills such as responding, organising information, and so on. Such skills might be referred to as complex skillsets (Care et al. 2016a; Scoular et al. 2017) or complex constructs (Ercikan and Oliveri 2016). Another complex skillset is global citizenship, which is hypothesised to draw on social and cognitive capacities as well as values, knowledge and attitudes. Such complex skillsets pose additional challenges for measurement due to the difficulty of identifying the degree to which each subskill might contribute unique variance, or the degree to which demonstration of one subskill might depend on reaching some hurdle level of competence in another.

The research phase of the Assessment and Teaching of 21st Century Skills (ATC21S) project highlighted two complex skillsets – collaborative problem solving and digital literacy in social networks. Through its exploration of these, one of the project's major contributions was clarification of our understandings of these skills. This understanding culminated in the development of tools for assessment and consideration of curricular and pedagogical implications. The research contributed in particular to global perceptions of the nature of collaborative problem solving (OECD 2013), as well as to discussion about innovative forms of assessment.

The assessment approach taken by ATC21S was decided upon in response both to the nature of the complex skillsets of interest, and the affordances of online data capture. The use of the ATC21S tools has been largely confined to research studies and has provided valuable insights about the degree to which online data capture of student action can inform estimates of student performance across both social and cognitive activities (Care and Griffin 2017).

The Assessment Challenge for Twenty-First Century Skills

Demonstration of skills or competencies is through behaviours which we hypothesise are accounted for by latent traits. ATC21S therefore targeted behaviours for capture in order to draw inferences about these traits. This approach is quite different from targeting individual's perceptions about their latent traits (as demonstrated through self-report techniques), or knowledge or reasoning capacities (as demonstrated through correct/incorrect responses to test items). And here lies one of the challenges for assessment.

In comparison to the educational assessment of content-based knowledge, assessment of twenty-first century skills is in its infancy. To date, there has been little attention paid to construct validation of assessments in the classroom, or to predictive validity based on evidence of the generalisability of skills-based learning. Challenges in assessing twenty-first century skills lie in our lack of comprehensive understanding of the nature and development of the skills, about their multidimensionality, and about how to partition variance in behaviour that is attributable to knowledge, or attributable to skill.

These issues are key for psychometricians in developing standardised instruments as well as for classroom teachers in developing classroom based tasks. Critical to skills domains is the assumption of developmental trajectories (Gee 2010). Knowledge of the skills requires not only identification of contributing subskills, but also evidence of how these individually and together progress, from simple to advanced. This explains the need to design tasks that require demonstration of skills at increasing difficulty levels.

An issue in design of assessments of twenty-first century skills is the degree to which assessment tasks actually stimulate the processes that indicate the targeted construct and provide a facility for their capture. To stimulate them, it is essential that the assessment design, as much as possible, mirrors the authentic demands of the situation that provoke behaviors associated with the targeted skill (Care et al. 2016a, b). Ercikan and Oliveri (2016) address this challenge by proposing to acknowledge the complexity of the construct and systematically align tasks with different elements of the construct. This raises questions about whether the construct itself is being assessed, or merely some of its components. Of interest is whether an assessment takes a form that can capture the true nature of the skills and report on this in a way that represents the skill in varying degrees of competency.

A Focus on Authenticity

There has been a rapid spread in the twenty-first century skills phenomenon in formal education (Care and Luo 2016). The intention of explicit focus on twenty-first century skills in education is that students will develop the capacity to apply these skills to real life situations. Hence, assessment tasks should be authentic (Gulikers et al. 2004) – that is, reflect the characteristics of long-term professional work and life behaviours. This means that assessment tools must be designed to capture the cognitive and social processes rather than factual knowledge. Authenticity does not guarantee construct validity – whether an assessment actually measures what it purports to measure – but can contribute evidence to support it. This evidence may be derived from tasks that reflect the competency of interest, represent a realistic application of the competency, and reflect the cognitive and social processes that contribute to the behaviour in real life.

In 1996, USA's National Research Council (NRC) called for assessment to support educational reform for the twenty-first century. The NRC proposed more focus on learning processes as opposed to learning outcomes; more targeted assessment as implied by a focus on what learners understand and can do; and rich or authentic knowledge and skills. These goals are aligned not only with a competencies approach in education, but to principles of formative assessment. Student-centred pedagogies that rest on formative assessment are well aligned with concepts of skills development. A majority of twenty-first century skills are demonstrated through actions, and therefore require an interactive style of pedagogy as opposed to transmission paradigms. Accordingly, assessment needs to attend to actions and behaviours, or enable inferences to be drawn from these. Central to the rationale for twenty-first century skills education is the degree to which students can develop skills that can be applied across different contexts (Blomeke et al. 2015); the whole point is to develop in students the capacity to generalise, to adapt and to apply. How can assessment capture these applications?

This brief review examines the degree to which selected tools are consistent with five characteristics of authentic assessment defined by Gulikers et al. (2004). This in no way competes with current views on validity as represented in standards for educational and psychological assessment (e.g. AERA/APA/NCME 2014), but is complementary. As pointed out by Pellegrino et al. (2016) "an assessment is a tool designed to observe students' behavior and produce data that can be used to draw reasonable inferences about what students know" (p. 5). This definition clearly addresses tools designed for educational purposes. Pellegrino et al.'s (2016) interest in instructional validity is consistent with concerns about authentic assessment (e.g., Wiggins 1989; Gulikers et al. 2004).

Review of Selected Tools

Gulikers et al. (2004) state that authenticity lies in "an assessment requiring students to use the same competencies, or combinations of knowledge, skills, and attitudes, that they need to apply in the criterion situation in professional life. The level of authenticity of an assessment is thus defined by its degree of resemblance to the criterion situation" (p. 69). Authenticity also needs to reflect a learning approach from students' early basic skills through to those in final years of secondary school where behaviours are displayed that are more recognisable as the mature skills. Assessments need to reflect this progression.

Gulikers et al.'s (2004) five dimensions of authentic assessment are:

(a) An authentic task presents as a set of activities that emulate professional practice
(b) The physical context reflects the way the competencies will be applied in professional practice
(c) The social processes (if these are relevant) will reflect those applied in the real situation
(d) The product or performance mirrors a real life one, permits inferences about the underlying construct, includes multiple indicators, and is available to others for review
(e) Criteria identify what is valued, and standards indicate levels of performance expected.

One aspect of Gulikers et al. (2004) model is including the student perspective on relevance of task. Although this information might well be collected during development of assessments, through cognitive laboratories or interviews, it is rarely included in test manuals of large scale assessments. Evidence addressing this in the review is therefore slight.

For the four selected twenty-first century skills (problem solving, collaborative problem solving, communication and information literacy, and global citizenship), one measure of each was chosen to illustrate and consider the authenticity of current assessments from the perspective of these five dimensions. The search for example assessments was conducted systematically. First, specific key words and phrases were entered into search engines (google, google scholar, bing). These key words and phrases included: "assessments of 21st century skills", "21st century skills", "large scale assessments", "key competencies", "collaboration", "problem solving", "information and communication literacy", "technology", "global citizenship", or some combinations of these words and phrases. Based on these searches, reports and articles were accessed and explored to gather a pool of assessments of twenty-first century skills.

In order to select just one assessment tool of each skill, the database of tools was successively refined. Initially, two criteria were used: intended for use at large scale for school populations; and availability of technical and/or research information. Tools were then filtered out if discontinued as of October 2016; if in fact were second or third party rating tools; or were measures that assess course knowledge for academic qualifications or those that are part of program-based toolkits or badged programs. For example, the Pearson Edexcel International GCSE Global Citizenship[1] exam comprises an externally-assessed paper, which is given after

[1] http://qualifications.pearson.com/en/qualifications/edexcel-international-gcses-and-edexcel-certificates/international-gcse-global-citizenship-2017.html.

Table 1.1 Tools in the context of five dimensions of authenticity

		Five-dimensional framework for authentic assessment				
21st century skill	Tool	Assessment task	Physical context	Social context	Assessment result or form	Assessment criteria
Problem solving	MicroDYN (Funke 2001; Greiff and Funke 2009)	Items require participants to control dynamic and interactive simulated systems, which are designed to mirror what may occur in real-life, and require the integration of knowledge, skills, and attitudes to complete the task. Example task is the virtual chemical laboratory, where students have to understand causal relations among chemical substances and elements and build models and make predictions based on knowledge gathered while exploring the system.	Participants receive 8–12 items lasting about 6 min each, totalling roughly 1 h. There is high fidelity in terms of how close the system imitates reality, in terms of the underlying processes (e.g., retrieve information and apply it to make predictions and build models).	Not specifically mentioned; but task is completed individually.	Participants generate solutions through a performance-based task; Includes items with different underlying structures and difficulty levels.	Criteria are embedded within items based on characteristics valued and used in real life; some expectations are made explicit, whereas others are not.
Collaborative problem solving	ATC 21 collaborative problem solving (Care and Griffin 2014)	Task requires collaborative effort and integration of cognitive and social skills to reach a solution, resembling the complex nature of the construct. Students' ownership of task and processes are rewarded, rather than the solution. Example is Olive Oil task, which reflects Tower of Hanoi-like problem.	Tasks simulate scenarios within a technology context and mimic the resources and tools available in real-life, as well as the asymmetric nature of solving problems.	Students have differing resources, tools, and information, and must work together to establish the series of steps to solve a problem (not face to face interactions).	Result relies on actions and processes captured in logfiles; multiple tasks are available to be "bundled", in order to capture the construct comprehensively.	Criteria and standards are pre-determined and task-specific. Logfiles are coded and mapped onto cognitive and social dimensions that are linked to specific competence levels.

Computer and Information Literacy	IEA International Computer and Literacy Study (Fraillon et al. 2015)	Tasks require integration of knowledge and skills in a simulated environment that mirrors real life situations. Example is working with collaborators to plan a design of a new garden for their school. Final product is an information sheet that explains the design and convinces peers to vote to use that design.	Computer-based task simulates real-life situations; Estimated time component for each module is between 20 and 30 min.	Incorporates social processes due to requirement for collaboration, which occurs entirely within the test platform (not face to face interactions).	Results are in the form of product and performance, such as creating a design plan.	Criteria and standards are in the form of an achievement scale that maps onto proficiency levels, which describe skills and knowledge that are expected at each level.
Global citizenship	Southeast Asian primary learning metrics global citizenship domain (Parker and Fraillon 2016)	Items are student self-reports on attitudes and values, and to a certain extent, behaviours and skills related to global citizenship issues.	Student questionnaire does not capture how knowledge, skills, and attitudes are used in real-life situations; low fidelity since environment (self-rating) does not imitate reality; 20–30 min to complete the assesment	Not specifically mentioned	Items assess attitudes and values in the form of a student questionnaire.	Criteria and standards are not specified.

completion of a 2-year course for teaching in international schools or undertaking community action on a global issue. Despite the focus on global citizenship (Pearson 2017), such a tool would not be included in the review.

The four large scale assessments selected were developed for summative purposes in the first instance. As shown in Table 1.1, they are assessments of: problem solving (MicroDYN; Greiff and Funke 2009); collaborative problem solving (ATC21S; Care and Griffin 2014); communication and information literacy (IEA International Computer and Literacy Study [ICILS]; Fraillon et al. 2015); and global citizenship (South East Asian Primary Learning Metrics; Parker and Fraillon 2016).

Problem Solving

Problem solving involves being able to negotiate complex and dynamically changing environments and situations successfully by drawing on behavioural patterns to reach a desired goal (Funke 2003; Greiff et al. 2013). More specifically, dynamic or complex problem solving has been defined as "the successful interaction with task environments that are dynamic (i.e., change as a function of user's intervention and/or as a function of time) and in which some, if not all, of the environment's regularities can only be revealed by successful exploration and integration of the information gained in that process" (Buchner 1995, p. 14). Therefore, someone who is successful at problem solving is able to interact with the task environment and adapt to the dynamic nature of these environments in order to collect information; integrate and structure information in a meaningful way; and effectively apply the acquired knowledge to make predictions and solve the problem at hand (Dörner 1986; Mayer and Wittrock 2006).

Due to the complexity of the construct, measuring problem solving is also complex. Assessments of problem solving depend on the flexibility of tools and platforms to capture problem solving abilities in dynamically changing contexts (Greiff et al. 2013). Hence, computer-based performance assessments are well equipped to capture the acquisition and application of knowledge to solve complex problems. MicroDYN (Funke 2001; Greiff and Funke 2009), a computer-based assessment of complex problem solving was chosen as an example to examine authenticity. MicroDYN is based on a framework (Funke 2001) in which inputs affect outputs. For instance, increasing an input variable might result in a decrease or an increase in one or more output variables in the system (Greiff et al. 2012). The user interacts with and navigates through an unfamiliar system or situation which mirrors problem solving in real-life settings. Participants are prompted to detect causal relations and control systems that are presented. There are three stages underlying each MicroDYN item that align with three aspects of problem solving: (1) exploration, where participants can explore the system freely with no restrictions, and use strategies to retrieve information about the system; (2) drawing mental models, where participants draw the assumed connections between variables as they understand it to be; and (3) forecasting phase, where participants attempt to achieve target values in the output variables by entering correct values in the input variables within a fixed number of steps. This is the stage where practical application of acquired knowledge from the previous stages is assessed. Eight to twelve independent items are presented to the participants in dynamic and interactive situations.

The assessment task is authentic in that it confronts students with situations that mirror what occurs in professional practice – meaningful and relevant and requires the knowledge, skills, and attitudes to complete the task. For example, one MicroDYN test is composed of 11 independent tasks and 2 trial tasks that are embedded in the context of a virtual chemical laboratory. The students are presented with chemical substances and elements and need to understand their interrelations to build models and forecast. In addition, there appears to be autonomy in the exploration phase where students can explore the system freely. The fact that items are designed to activate minimal prior knowledge provides support for authenticity – only the specific knowledge gathered during the task is relevant. When problems rely on prior knowledge and specific content, solutions tend to be routinely available, which detracts from the essence of complex problem solving, to which dynamic interaction with an unknown environment is key (Greiff et al. 2012).

The physical context of the MicroDYN items is authentic in that it reflects the way knowledge, skills, and attitudes will be used in real-life situations, although it can be argued that the physical context is less authentic – being a test platform. Regardless, students need to use strategies to retrieve information about the system, and then integrate and apply that information to draw connections between variables in the model, and finally achieve target values based on hypotheses about how inputs and outputs are related. There is high fidelity in terms of how the MicroDYN systems imitate reality. The time limit of five to six minutes per item may seem counter to the amount of time that is available to solve problems in real life; however, according to the developers of the MicroDYN approach, "a short time on task is ecologically valid because successful interaction with unknown task environments in real life seldom lasts longer than a few minutes (e.g., buying a ticket at a new vending machine)" (Greiff et al. 2012, p. 193). In terms of the social processes of the MicroDYN approach, there is no specific mention of the social context; the test is designed for individual completion rather than in collaboration with others, reflecting many real-life situations. The assessment result is in the form of information retrieval through exploring the simulated systems, building models by drawing connections between variables, and then applying the acquired knowledge by controlling and meeting target values. Authenticity of assessment result lies with students demonstrating their competencies by generating solutions through a performance-based task and by engaging with items with different underlying structures and difficulty levels.

Finally, the criteria for an authentic assessment are referred to the dimensions of the framework. Embedded within the items are characteristics valued and used in real life, including "the ability to use knowledge, to plan actions, and to react to dynamic changes" (Greiff et al. 2012, p. 195). Some expectations are made transparent and explicit beforehand. For instance, during the information retrieval and model building stages, students are explicitly told that they do not have to achieve specific target values as they are navigating and gathering knowledge about the system but that they will be asked to do so later on. How items are scored varies and is not made explicit to students beforehand.

Collaborative Problem Solving

Collaborative problem solving (CPS) is defined as a complex skill that requires both cognitive and social processes (Care and Griffin 2014). CPS has been hypothesised as consisting of five strands of participation, perspective taking, social and task regulation, and knowledge building, and is brought to bear when the ability or resources of a single person is not enough to solve a problem. Individuals need to be able to combine various resources and skills when confronted with a complex problem (Hesse et al. 2015).

Putting aside arguments (Scoular et al. 2017; Rosen and Foltz 2014; Rosen 2015) concerning authenticity of assessment of collaborative problem solving that involves agents as opposed to people, of interest in this discussion is the degree to which the problem solving environment mirrors real life freedom of movement in the exercise of cognitive and social competencies by a pair of problem solvers. Any online platform imposes constraints on freedom of movement, but can vary through presentation of well-defined versus ill-defined problems.

The ATC21S Collaborative Problem Solving environment (Care et al. 2015, 2016a, b) was used to examine the authenticity of the assessment. The assessment is online with eleven tasks that are designed to capture human to human collaborative problem solving. Some tasks are asymmetric, meaning that each student engaging with the tasks has access to different, but critical, information to solve the problem, and exemplified by the Olive Oil task which reflects the Tower of Hanoi style of problem. As the students work on solving the problem, actions, chat events, and combinations of both are captured in a logstream file for coding and scoring of CPS competence based on the hypothesised cognitive and social underpinnings. The scores are then used to indicate the student's level of CPS competence.

ATC21S CPS presents an authentic assessment task that requires the integration of cognitive and social skills. For example, one indicator is that the student "uses understanding of cause and effect to develop a plan", which corresponds to the element of knowing the "if-then" rule, which in turn, captures the broader strand of knowledge building (Care and Griffin 2014). The task illustrates the complexity of the construct, involving unstructured exploration of the problem space, as well as arriving at a solution in multiple ways. The assessment rewards processes enacted rather than the actual solution (Adams et al. 2015). The CPS tasks allow students to take ownership of the process of reaching a solution and are designed to capture the transferable or generalizable skills involved in the types of problems that require real life collaborative effort. No pathways are pre-defined except insofar as students must move forward from one screen to another to complete the tasks.

The CPS tasks are intended to simulate scenarios that may occur in learning and teaching environments as students work together to solve complex problems. The physical context is a technology context but does not detract from the fact that the tasks elicit the cognitive and social processes involved in CPS, including problem analysis, planning and executing, and awareness of and ability to adapt to whoever is the partner. The task context mimics the resources and tools available in real-life situations; and the way skills will be used in professional settings. The fact that some tasks are asymmetric in nature, with each student coming to the problem with different resources, is similar to real life problems. The social context supports the authenticity of the assessment as students who are provided with different resources, tools, and information, must work together to establish how the tools function, whether they are necessary to solve the problem, and the series of steps to follow. Assessment result and form rely on the actions and processes of the students, which are captured using logfiles. This type of result and form are analogous to those which occur in real life in that it depicts the processes and actions that are undertaken to solve complex problems in professional capacities. The developers recognise that any one task may not necessarily capture the construct in a comprehensive way (Care et al. 2016b). Therefore, multiple tasks are available that can be bundled to "provide a comprehensive sampling across the construct, as well as the capacity to assess students at different levels of competence" (p. 14). The tasks do not require students to defend their solution, as may occur in real-life settings, although the free form chat could promote that activity. Finally, the criteria and standards are predetermined and task-specific. The coded indicators based on the actions and chat events gathered from logfiles are mapped onto cognitive and social dimensions, which are identified across competency levels.

Although ATC21S CPS has received major psychometric attention, the challenge of capturing this complex multi-dimensional construct remains. Technical information is presented in Scoular et al. (2017). Primary issues relate to lack of evidence of construct validity evidence beyond model-fitting techniques, difficulty in capturing social processes in an online environment, and capacity of an online platform to provide a sufficiently unstructured environment in which sophisticated levels of the skill might be demonstrated.

Computer and Information Literacy

As global economies seek to maintain productivity and embrace technological advances, equipping students with information and communication technology (ICT) and digital literacy skills is important for their full participation and success in today's information-rich, technology-driven society (Kozma 2011). From the basic ability to use computers and other technology devices individuals need to process, evaluate, and retrieve information (Catts and Lau 2008), participate in social networks to create and share knowledge, and to use and produce digital media.

The International Association of the Evaluation of Educational Achievement's (IEA) International Computer and Information Literacy Study (ICILS) (Fraillon et al. 2015) is used as an example to consider authenticity of assessment. Computer and information literacy (CIL) comprises two overarching categories or strands. The first strand focuses on collecting and managing information. The second strand focuses on producing and exchanging information, including transforming, creating, sharing, and using. CIL is assessed through four computer-based assessment modules that follow a linear narrative structure using a combination of purpose-built applications and existing software. Students navigate the system, as well as complete questions and tasks which are delivered in 30-minute modules. Students complete two of four available modules, with each module including a series of smaller five to eight tasks with a total task time of 15–20 min. Three task types include: (1) information-based response tasks, which use computer technology to deliver pencil-and-paper-like questions using multiple-choice, constructed-response, or drag-and-drop- response formats; (2) interactive simulations or universal applications to complete an action, such as navigating through a menu structure, and capturing "correct" responses; and (3) authoring tasks, in which students modify or create information products using software applications. The test items are automatically scored, and the score is placed on a CIL achievement scale corresponding to proficiency levels (Fraillon et al. 2014).

Specifically, ICILS defines CIL as "an individual's ability to use computers to investigate, create, and communicate in order to participate effectively at home, at school, in the workplace, and in society" (Fraillon et al. 2015, p. 17). ICILS provides authentic assessment tasks that require students to integrate their knowledge and skills in a simulated environment that mirrors the kinds of tasks they may face in real-life situations. For example, one module requires students to work with a group of collaborators to plan the design of a new garden area for their school. The final product is a student-generated information sheet that explains the garden design, as well as creates support for that particular design, so that their classmates will vote to use the design. Attitudes are assessed separately through a student questionnaire. The physical context of the test is authentic in that the computer-based task simulates real-life scenarios. The garden design example simulates computer-based professional landscape design technologies to communicate information. However, there is an estimated time component for each of the modules of about 20–30 min, whereas in professional activities, this assignment would presumably involve a longer period. To this extent, the task may not reflect the real-life complexity. As for the social context, the tasks incorporate the social processes that are drawn upon in practice. In real life, architects and designers may work individually; but more often than not, a larger project would require multiple people with differing expertise working together to create the final design product. In ICILS, the collaboration occurs entirely within the test platform rather than through face-to-face interactions. Assessment result and form rely on products and performance by students, which are similar in nature to the kinds of products that professionals may be asked to generate in professional settings (i.e., a design plan). Finally, the criteria and standards are specified in the form of an achievement scale that maps onto proficiency levels. The proficiency levels describe the kinds of skills and knowledge that are valued and expected at the various levels. The criteria are pre-determined but it is unclear whether students have access to the descriptions beforehand to guide their learning (Sluijsmans 2002). How the scoring of the items locates where the student may fall along the achievement scale is similarly unclear.

Global Citizenship

The significance of global citizenship education (GCED) in promoting sustainable development, equity, and inclusive societies is well-recognized (United Nations Educational, Scientific and Cultural Organization, UNESCO 2014). Global citizenship can be broadly described as a sense of collective identity, belonging to a global community, with the implication that people are connected in multiple ways to each other and to their environments (UNESCO 2014).

The Southeast Asian Primary Learning Metrics (SEA-PLM) Global Citizenship Domain Assessment (Parker and Fraillon 2016), an assessment of the attitudes and values related to global citizenship, is provided as an example to examine authenticity. SEA-PLM focuses on the attitudes and values (e.g., feeling, sensing, valuing, believing) related to global citizenship and "reflects the dispositions that can lead to deeper engagement with global citizenship in the later years of schooling" (p. 6). A student questionnaire, adopting Likert scale response options, addresses attitudes toward global citizenship systems, issues and dynamics; citizenship awareness and identity; and global citizenship engagement. A few items also ask about students' experience of activities related to global citizenship, such as presenting ideas or leadership, to capture behavioural aspects of the construct. Items target awareness of diversity in society, knowledge of concepts of citizenship including "good citizens" and "global citizens", knowledge of benefits and consequences of personal and collective civic engagement, attitudes toward the value of learning about global citizenship, self-reported behaviour associated with global citizenship, and attitude and behavioural intentions with regard to protecting the environment (Parker and Fraillon 2016). A teacher questionnaire is forthcoming.

The development of the SEA-PLM Global Citizenship Domain assessment is grounded in the following working definition of global citizenship:

> *Global citizens appreciate and understand the interconnectedness of all life on the planet. They act and relate to others with this understanding to make the world a more peaceful, just, safe and sustainable place* (Parker and Fraillon 2016, p. 5).

The authenticity of the assessment task as it currently stands is questionable, first and foremost because a self-rating student questionnaire is used. Research suggests there are three major competencies related to global citizenship: cognitive aspects (i.e., knowledge acquired about global structures, systems, and issues); attitudes and values about global citizenship concepts (e.g., appreciation of diversity, equity, non-violence, social justice); and behaviours and skills involved in participating in activities that create "positive change and foster social participation" (Parker and Fraillon 2016, p. 5). The student SEA-PLM global citizenship assessment focuses primarily on the dimensions of attitudes and values, and less on behaviours and skills. An important dimension of authenticity is that assessments are not atomistic (Gulikers et al. 2006), and that tasks reflect underlying dimensions according to performance, as opposed to what respondents *think* about what they would do, or about their own traits. According to the developers of the assessment, factors including time, age and grade level, contributed to decisions upon which components to focus. The initial targeting of Grade 5 students for the field trial, as well as the limited time available for the assessment, influenced the decision to focus mainly on attitudes and values. As a result, the complexity of the construct is not captured, nor is ownership of the task reflected for students as they are not engaging in global citizenship-related activities.

Although the context of the assessment is not specifically identified, the student questionnaire format means that the physical context does not reflect the way knowledge, skills, and attitudes will be used in real-life settings. The assessment has low fidelity, since the environment does not closely imitate reality (Alessi 1988). The method itself of assessing global citizenship detracts from the capacity of the tool to capture student ability to use global citizenship competencies. Relatedly, the assessment is given in 20–30 min. Whether global citizenship responses could be generated within such a restricted time period is questionable. Similar to the physical context, the social context is not mentioned. Global citizenship includes a sense of interconnectedness of citizens around the globe. This implies the importance of the social context that fosters a sense of belonging to the global community. This is not captured by the assessment. In terms of the assessment form and result, indicators tap attitudes and values rather than the full construct. Although questionnaire items ask about opportunities students have had for active participatory engagement, this cannot reflect a competency; other methods such as a product or performance may be required to demonstrate mastery (Darling-Hammond and Snyder 2000). Finally, criteria and standards are not specified. To note, the SEA-PLM global citizenship domain survey remains under development, having gone through field trials in 2015–2016 (Parker and Fraillon 2016).

The approach adopted by SEA-PLM reflects traditional methods of measuring attitudes and values through self-rating surveys. Taking into consideration the frameworks for global competence specifying that knowledge, skills, attitudes and values lead to competencies and action (Ramos and Schleicher 2016), it is clear that SEA-PLM has followed the line that assessment of global competence and citizenship can be achieved by measurement of these predictors, rather than targeting the competencies and actions. To date, although knowledge and attitudes are clearly targeted, attention to skills is not so clear.

Perhaps reflecting this state of the art and perspective, PISA 2018 global competency measurement will rely on cognitive items that reflect knowledge, perspective-taking and analytical and critical thinking components. Along with multiple choice items, OECD proposes use of critical incident case studies which prompt open-ended responses to be scored with use of rubrics. Self-report on skills and attitudes will be used for reporting at country or sub-population level. These decisions are the clearest communication by the OECD assessment community that authentic assessment of social competencies underpinned by values, attitudes, and beliefs, still eludes us (Ramos and Schleicher 2016).

Discussion

Authenticity informs validity. The emphasis on authenticity in this chapter is to draw attention to how modern assessments stimulate, capture, score and evaluate in ways that might contribute supporting evidence to validity. Although the focus of the chapter is assessment, the authenticity demand within the classroom teaching and learning context is analogous – and equally demanding. The sample of assessment tools demonstrates both traditional and innovative approaches to assessment of twenty-first century skills. They range from Likert scale self-ratings of attitudes and values to rich computer-based task environments where students can display a repertoire of skills. Are we actually capturing indications of the skills of interest? The majority of published technical information on the tools reviewed consists of explorations of the internal structures of the tools. This is not sufficient to inform judgements about the degree to which we can rely on assessment data to understand student capabilities or readiness to learn.

The ICT literacy tasks stand out in the authenticity stakes, given that the assessment mode is firmly situated within the operating environment required for real life enactment of the skills. The examples demonstrate use of rich task environments, concentrating on how the individual accesses and uses technology-based artefacts.

Assessment of problem solving illustrates innovative approaches to measurement of the skills through capturing processes using twenty-first century technologies. With strong reliance on online facilities, assessment of problem solving still uses traditional multiple choice options, but has also moved into logging student progress through rich online tasks, and attempting to interpret the activity data trail left by the student through engaging with the task environments. Capturing student activity, coding it, and trying to make sense of it, is the state of the art.

The main skill area in which boundaries have been pushed is collaborative problem solving. The lure of the cognitive, or problem solving, aspects of the construct, with which much progress has been made, makes both closer and more tantalising the challenge of capturing the social processes that are brought to bear in a collaborative environment (e.g. von Davier et al. 2017).

The area that is not associated with state of the art assessment approaches is global citizenship. Although often referred to as a skill, in fact this includes (1) processes brought to bear in decision-making, critical thinking, and problem solving; (2) social processes including communication, which are intrinsic to resolving wicked problems; and (3) values and attitudes. Approaches to assessment of these latter continue to rely on approaches derived from psychological measures including self-rating of characteristics, attitudes or values. Lundberg's (2015) characterisation of 'metrics' of non-cognitive skills as falling across three categories – self-assessments, parent/teacher reports, and extrinsic administrative indicators holds true for this competency.

The defining characteristic of a twenty-first century skill is that an individual or group of individuals can bring that competency to bear in and across new situations including those associated with or within technology environments. This very characteristic is what challenges assessment. How to measure the non-routine is what confronts us. With well-known skills such as literacy, assessment tools are able to capture both early and more developed competencies. With complex skills that are less well-known, our current assessment technologies also appear to be able to capture some early subskills, but are less capable of capturing the more developed competencies since these latter are exercised in free ranging ways and in environments that do not offer the opportunity for reliable data capture, coding or scoring given our current technological progress. For the early forms of competencies, we make assumptions that the behaviours sampled are predicted by the complex skill which will account for the individual's performance in real-life situations. Our inability to capture the more developed competencies puts at question our capacity to measure the full range of skill. This is a crucial validity threat to instruments. Another important consideration concerns the degree to which what is measured reflects all aspects of the competency (Soland et al. 2013). For example, measurement of collaborative problem solving, both by PISA OECD and by ATC21S, has found eliciting objective measurement of subskills of the social domains elusive while other aspects of the construct are captured reliably.

Against a backdrop of consensus globally about the importance of twenty-first century skills for equipping future generations to live constructively, implementation by education systems through reformed curricula, dynamic pedagogies, and innovative and aligned forms of assessment lags behind. The findings from the Network on Education Quality Monitoring in the Asia-Pacific (NEQMAP) study of the assessment of transversal competencies (Care and Luo 2016) across nine countries in Asia Pacific demonstrates that classroom assessment tools are no more sophisticated or prolific than are large scale assessment tools. Lack of clear guidelines about how to assess from national system level is reflected at school level, and signified by calls from teachers for more guidance about the nature of twenty-first century skills, how to teach, and how to assess them. Recent mapping of national education mission statements with a focus on twenty-first century skills (Care et al. 2016a) demonstrates the lag across aspiration and implementation in the actual curriculum. From the brief review in this chapter, similarly is seen a scattering of assessments that are intended to measure these skills but vary from reliance on traditional methods to testing the possibilities of innovative methods of data capture, interpretation, and use.

As pointed out by Csapó et al. (2012), an issue that has confronted assessment experts is the constraint placed on capturing a construct where paper and pencil is the major capture medium. Notwithstanding that electronic media expand the opportunities for capture, they do not solve the other major issue – that of ensuring that what is captured is interpretable. The issue is well demonstrated by this review of the assessment tools – that the capture medium has expanded widely, but still falls short of providing an authentic environment in which the skills can be freely exercised yet reliably captured. In addition, the majority of effort has been dedicated to crafting the opportunities, and checking internal indications of psychometric robustness, rather than looking to concurrent or face validation opportunities. Ercigan and Oliveri (2016) consider three sets of factors that relate to validity in the consideration of assessment of twenty-first century skills: construct complexity and how this influences task design in the context of generalisability; the use of empirical data that can provide evidence that relates to student performance in real life; and cross-cultural and context issues. Blomeke et al. (2015) focus on two validation approaches: first, a model fitting approach comprising hypothesis, followed by analysis to see if the data fit; and second, a "real-life" approach in which the effort is to obtain measures as closely related to criterion performance as possible. The four tools reviewed here demonstrate varied levels of authenticity, which go some way to addressing criterion performance, but as of yet, their predictive capacity is not evident.

There is no doubt that our capacity for data capture of assessment transactions has taken great strides. The challenge remains first, to provide stimulus environments for the transactions that are themselves aligned with the nature of what is to be measured; and second, to capture the indicators of skills in a reliable manner that is interpretable in terms of competence levels. These challenges have clear implications for the demands on the teaching and learning environment, and the degree to which the teacher can create the context in which the same skills can be nurtured.

Acknowledgement The authors wish to thank Scott Paris of the Australian Council for Educational Research for extensive and constructive comments to earlier versions of this manuscript.

References

Adams, R., Vista, A., Scoular, C., Awwal, N., Griffin, P., & Care, E. (2015). Automatic coding procedures. In P. Griffin & E. Care (Eds.), *Assessment and teaching of 21st century skills: Methods and approach*. Dordrecht: Springer.

Alessi, S. M. (1988). Fidelity in the design of instructional simulations. *Journal of Computer-Based Instruction, 15*, 40–47.

Almond, R. G. (2010). Using evidence centered design to think about assessments. In V. J. Shute & B. J. Becker (Eds.), *Innovative assessment for the 21st century* (pp. 75–100). Boston: Springer Science+Business Media. doi:10.1007/978-1-4419-6530-1_3.

American Educational Research Association, American Psychological Association, & National Council on Measurement in Education. (2014). *Standards for educational and psychological testing*. Washington, DC: American Educational Research Association.

Birenbaum, M. (1996). Assessment 2000: Towards a pluralistic approach to assessment. In M. Birenbaum & F. J. R. C. Docy (Eds.), *Alternatives in assessment of achievements, learning processes and prior knowledge* (pp. 3–30). Boston: Kluwer.

Blomeke, S., Gustafsson, J., & Shavelson, R. J. (2015). Beyond dichotomies: Competence viewed as a continuum. *Zeitschrift fur Psychologie, 223*(1), 3–13.

Brewer, L. (2013). *Enhancing the employability of disadvantaged youth: What? Why? and How? Guide to core work skills*. Geneva: International Labour Organization.

Buchner, A. (1995). Basic topics and approaches to the study of complex problem solving. In P. A. Frensch & J. Funke (Eds.), *Complex problem solving: The European perspective* (pp. 27–63). Hillsdale: Erlbaum.

Care, E., & Griffin, P. (2014). An approach to assessment of collaborative problem solving. *Research and Practice in Technology Enhanced Learning, 9*(3), 367–388.

Care, E., & Griffin, P. (2017). Collaborative problem solving processes. In B. Csapó & J. Funke (Eds.), *The nature of problem solving. Using research to inspire 21st century learning* (p. 227–243). Paris: OECD Publishing.

Care, E., Griffin, P., Scoular, C., Awwal, N., & Zoanetti, N. (2015). Collaborative problem solving tasks. In P. Griffin & E. Care (Eds.), *Assessment and teaching of 21st century skills: Methods and approach* (pp. 85–104). Dordrecht: Springer.

Care, E., & Luo, R. (2016). *Assessment of transversal competencies: Policy and practice in the Asia-Pacific Region*. Bangkok: UNESCO.

Care, E., Anderson, K., & Kim, H. (2016a). *Visualizing the breadth of skills movement across education systems. Skills for a changing world.* Washington, DC: The Brookings Institution.

Care, E., Scoular, C., & Griffin, P. (2016b). Assessment of collaborative problem solving in education environments. *Applied Measurement in Education, 29*(4), 250–264.

Catts, R., & Lau, J. (2008). *Towards information literacy indicators: Conceptual framework paper*. Paris: UNESCO.

Csapó, B., Lörincz, A., & Molnár, G. (2012). Technological issues for computer-based assessment. In P. Griffin & E. Care (Eds.), *Assessment and teaching of 21st century skills* (pp. 143–230). Dordrecht: Springer.

Darling-Hammond, L., & Snyder, J. (2000). Authentic assessment in teaching in context. *Teaching and Teacher Education, 16*, 523–545.

Dörner, D. (1986). Diagnostik der operativen Intelligenz [Diagnostics of operative intelligence]. *Diagnostica, 32*, 290–308.

Ercikan, K., & Oliveri, M. E. (2016). In search of validity evidence in support of the interpretation and use of assessments of complex constructs: Discussion of research on assessing 21st century skills. *Applied Measurement in Education, 29*(4), 310–318.

Fraillon, J., Ainley, J., Schulz, W., Friedman, T., & Gebhardt, E. (2014). *Preparing for life in a digital age: The IEA International Computer and Information Literacy Study international report*. Cham: Springer.

Fraillon, J., Schulz, W., Friedman, T., Ainley, J., & Gebhardt, E. (2015). *ICILS 2013 technical report*. Amsterdam: IEA.

Funke, J. (2001). Dynamic systems as tools for analysing human judgement. *Thinking & Reasoning, 7*, 69–89.

Funke, J. (2003). *Problemlösendes Denken [Problem solving and thinking]*. Stuttgart: Kohlhammer.

Gee, J. P. (2010). Human action and social groups as the natural home of assessment. In V. J. Shute & B. J. Becker (Eds.) (2010), *Innovative assessment for the 21st century* (pp. 13–40). Boston, MA: Springer Science+Business Media. doi:10.1007/978-1-4419-6530-1_3

Greiff, S., & Funke, J. (2009). Measuring complex problem solving: The MicroDYN approach. In F. Scheuermann & J. Björnsson (Eds.), *The transition to computer-based assessment: Lessons learned from large-scale surveys and implications for testing* (pp. 157–163). Luxembourg: Office for Official Publications of the European Communities.

Greiff, S., Wüstenberg, S., & Funke, J. (2012). Dynamic problem solving: A new assessment perspective. *Applied Psychological Measurement, 36*, 189–213.

Greiff, S., Wustenberg, S., Holt, D. V., Goldhammer, F., & Funke, J. (2013). Computer-based assessment of complex problem solving: Concept, implementation, and application. *Educational Technology Research and Development, 61*, 407–421.

Gulikers, J. T. M., Bastiaens, T. J., & Kirschner, P. A. (2004). A five-dimensional framework for authentic assessment. *Educational Technology Research and Development, 52*, 67–86.

Gulikers, J. T. M., Bastiaens, T. J., Kirschner, P. A., & Kester, L. (2006). Relations between student perceptions of assessment authenticity, study approaches and learning outcome. *Studies in Educational Evaluation, 32*, 381–400.
Hesse, F., Care, E., Buder, J., Sassenberg, K., & Griffin, P. (2015). A framework for teachable collaborative problem solving skills. In P. Griffin & E. Care (Eds.), *Assessment and teaching of 21st century skills: Methods and approach* (pp. 37–56). Dordrecht: Springer.
Kozma, R. B. (2011). A framework for ICT policies to transform education. In *Transforming education: the power of ICT policies* (pp. 19–36). Paris: UNESCO.
Lundberg, S. (2015). *Non-cognitive skills as human capital*. NBER/CRIW Conference on Education, Skills, and Technical Change.
Mayer, R. E., & Wittrock, M. C. (2006). Problem solving. In P. A. Alexander & P. H. Winne (Eds.), *Handbook of educational psychology* (pp. 287–303). Mahwah: Erlbaum.
OECD. (2013). *PISA 2015 draft collaborative problem solving framework*. Paris: OECD. https://www.oecd.org/pisa/pisaproducts/Draft%20PISA%202015%20Collaborative%20Problem%20Solving%20Framework%20.pdf
Parker, R., & Fraillon, J. (2016). *Southeast Asia Primary Learning Metrics (SEA-PLM): Global citizenship domain assessment framework*. Melbourne: Australian Council For Educational Research. http://research.acer.edu.au/ar_misc/20.
Pearson. (2017). *Edexcel International GCSE Global Citizenship (2017)*. Retrieved from http://qualifications.pearson.com/en/qualifications/edexcel-international-gcses-and-edexcel-certificates/international-gcse-global-citizenship-2017.html
Pellegrino, J. W., & Hilton, M. L. (2012). *Education for life and work: Developing transferable knowledge and skills in the 21st century*. Washington, DC: National Research Council, National Academies Press. http://nap.edu/13398.
Pellegrino, J. W., DiBello, L. V., & Goldman, S. R. (2016). A framework for conceptualizing and evaluating the validity of instructionally relevant assessments. *Educational Psychologist, 0*(0), 1–23.
Ramos, G., & Schleicher, A. (2016). *Global competency for an inclusive world*. Paris: OECD.
Rosen, Y. (2015). Computer-based assessment of collaborative problem solving: Exploring the feasibility of human-to-agent approach. *International Journal of Artificial Intelligence in Education, 25*, 380–406.
Rosen, Y., & Foltz, P. (2014). Assessing collaborative problem solving through automated technologies. *Research and Practice in Technology Enhanced Learning, 3*(9), 389–410.
Schwartz, H., Hamilton, L. S., Stecher, B. M., & Steele, J. L. (2011). *Expanded measures of school performance*. Santa Monica: RAND Corporation.
Scoular, C., Care, E., & Hesse, F. (2017). Designs for operationalizing collaborative problem solving for automated assessment. *Journal of Educational Measurement, 54*(1), 12–35.
Sluijsmans, D. M. A. (2002). *Student involvement in assessment. The training of peer assessment skills*. Unpublished doctoral dissertation Heerlen, The Netherlands: Open University of the Netherlands.
Soland, J., Hamilton, L. S., & Stecher, B. M. (2013). *Measuring 21st century competencies: Guidance for educators*. New York: RAND Corporation/Asia Society/Global Cities Education Network.
UNESCO. (2014). *Global citizenship education: Preparing learners for the challenges of the 21st century*. Paris: UNESCO.
von Davier, A. A., Zhu, M., & Kyllonen, P. (Eds.). (2017). *Innovative assessment of collaboration*. Cham: Springer International.
Wiggins, G. (1989). A true test: Toward more authentic and equitable assessment. *Phi Delta Kappan, 70*(9), 730–713.

Chapter 3
Competencies for Complexity: Problem Solving in the Twenty-First Century

Joachim Funke, Andreas Fischer, and Daniel V. Holt

Abstract In this chapter, we present a view of problem solving as a bundle of skills, knowledge and abilities that are required to deal effectively with complex non-routine situations in different domains. This includes cognitive aspects of problem solving, such as causal reasoning, model building, rule induction, and information integration. These abilities are comparatively well covered by existing tests and relate to existing theories. However, non-cognitive components, such as motivation, self-regulation and social skills, which are clearly important for real-life problem solving have only just begun to be covered in assessment. We conclude that currently there is no single assessment instrument that captures problem solving competency in a comprehensive way and that a number of challenges must be overcome to cover a construct of this breadth effectively. Research on some important components of problem solving is still underdeveloped and will need to be expanded before we can claim a thorough, scientifically backed understanding of real-world problem solving. We suggest that a focus on handling and acting within complex systems (systems competency) may be a suitable starting point for such an integrative approach.

Introduction

Problem solving is a key competency for the twenty-first century with its increasing complexity in many areas of life. This requires a new type of problem solving that involves a high degree of systems thinking, taking into account connectedness, complex dynamics and sometimes also fragility of the systems we live with. In recent years a shift away from well-defined analytical forms of problem solving, such as text book problems, towards more complex problems involving dynamic

J. Funke (✉) • D.V. Holt
Department of Psychology, Heidelberg University, Heidelberg, Germany
e-mail: joachim.funke@psychologie.uni-heidelberg.de

A. Fischer
Research Institute for Vocational Education and Training, Nürnberg, Germany

E. Care et al. (eds.), *Assessment and Teaching of 21st Century Skills*,
Educational Assessment in an Information Age,
DOI 10.1007/978-3-319-65368-6_3

interaction with the task or collaborative elements can be observed in problem solving research. However, theoretical and conceptual progress in the field seems out of step with the recent proliferation of empirical data. What is required is a theoretical foundation for the application of problem solving assessments in educational contexts and a careful selection of tools to adequately measure this ability.

In this chapter, we present a view of problem solving competency as a bundle of skills, knowledge and abilities that are required to deal effectively with complex and dynamic non-routine situations in different domains (Fischer and Neubert 2015). We consider this change of perspective important to move away from the relatively narrow conception of problem solving ability based on a conventional psychometric perspective which has become prominent in recent years (Funke 2014a, b; Funke et al. 2017; Schoppek and Fischer 2015). The components of this competency do not necessarily need to be correlated, which is often implied in the psychometric view on problem solving. Instead, problem solving competency may be understood as a formative construct (Fischer and Neubert 2015; Schoppek and Fischer 2015), where successful performance can arise from a range of different factors. The components of problem solving competency may also vary in their degree of generalizability. For example, content knowledge is highly domain specific, while self-regulatory abilities are very general, with generic problem solving strategies occupying the middle ground.

According to Duncker (1935) problem solving simply is what is needed when an organism pursues a goal and does not know how to reach that goal. This classical definition provides three fundamental elements: a given state, a goal state, and some obstacles between them that make it impossible to reach the goal state in an immediate and obvious way. Subsequently, Newell and Simon (1972) elaborated the information processing perspective on problem solving, describing it as an activity that relies on states of knowledge, operators for changing one state into another, and constraints on applying the operators. Moving beyond the well-defined problems studied by Newell and Simon, Donald Broadbent in Great Britain and Dietrich Dörner in Germany, independently started new lines of research dealing with complex and dynamic systems (Broadbent and Aston 1978; Dörner and Reither 1978). Broadbent was interested in the implicit understanding of complex rules; Dörner wanted to understand how ordinary people (as opposed to experts) cope with complexity and dynamics in the context of everyday decision-making and problem solving. At the same time, MacKinnon and Wearing (1980) from Australia proposed to look deeper into "dynamic decision making" (Edwards 1962). The subject of this new field of research was soon labelled "complex problem solving" and it found a place in two anthologies (Frensch and Funke 1995b; Sternberg and Frensch 1991) which emphasised that problems in the real world differ markedly from simple problems and entertaining brain-teasers. This development resembled a similar change in research focus in the field of decision making, where it was recognised that experts' "naturalistic decision making" (Klein 2008) or "risky decision making" (Huber 2012) differs fundamentally from decision making within gambling situations commonly used in laboratory-based decision making research.

In their review of the first 20 years of complex problem solving (CPS) research, Frensch and Funke (1995a) summarize a wide range of different views about the topic in the following definition: "CPS occurs to overcome barriers between a given state and a desired goal state by means of behavioral and/or cognitive, multistep activities. The given state, goal state, and barriers between given state and goal state are complex, change dynamically during problem solving, and are intransparent. The exact properties of the given state, goal state, and barriers are unknown to the solver at the outset. CPS implies the efficient interaction between a solver and the situational requirements of the task, and involves a solver's cognitive, emotional, personal, and social abilities and knowledge" (p. 18). If one compares that CPS definition with the understanding of Newell and Simon (1972), a new emphasis on complexity, dynamics, and on non-cognitive factors becomes apparent.

Taxonomic Aspects

Over the last 30 years, many new terms have been coined like "complex" problem solving (Sternberg and Frensch 1991), "interactive" problem solving (Greiff et al. 2013a, b), or "analytical" problem solving (Leutner et al. 2012). At the same time, there has been research exploring "everyday" problem solving (Willis 1996), "creative" problem solving (Treffinger et al. 1994), "social" problem solving (Chang et al. 2004), "collaborative" problem solving (O'Neil et al. 2003) or simply "applied" problem solving (Heppner 2008).

This collection of labels for problem solving shows that there is no obvious boundary between the different labels or the constructs they represent. For example, complex problems usually involve analytical problem solving, among other kinds (Dörner 1997; Fischer et al. 2015; Funke 2010). Additionally, one can easily imagine combinations, e.g., "social creative" problem solving for group collaboration, which in turn could be "interactive". In the recent literature, the labelling seems to be largely arbitrary. For example, the OECD (OECD 2014) decided to label the task group including analytic and interactive problems within PISA 2012 as "creative problem solving" and even constructs using identical assessment methods are sometimes labelled differently in different publications.

Beyond simple and complex the literature reveals several criteria that can be used to distinguish different types of problems: content domain (a mathematical problem in algebra is different from a problem of how to find a good apartment), time scale (how to cope with a dangerous traffic situation, compared to the question of how to make a good living), high vs. low stake problem situations (a problem in a computer game vs. admission to a prestigious university), static vs. dynamic problems, and so on. Relating to CPS, well-defined and ill-defined problems have been differentiated according to the nature of the clarity of the goal (originally introduced by McCarthy 1956). In another context, Rittel and Webber (1973) introduced a class of "inherently wicked" planning problems which they opposed to "tame" problems. Some attributes of "wicked" problems according to Rittel and Webber (1973) are as

Table 3.1 Typology of problems according to the three dimensions "availability of data", "awareness of methods", and "precision of outcome criteria" together with appropriate skill descriptions

Type	Data needed	Methods for solution	Outcome criteria	Skills required
1	Given	Familiar	Given	Recall of algorithm
2			Open	Decision about appropriate goals; exploration of knowledge networks
3		Unfamiliar	Given	Looking for parallels to known methods
4			Open	Decision about goals and choice of appropriate methods; exploration of knowledge and technique networks
5	Incomplete	Familiar	Given	Analysis of problems to decide what further data are required
6			Open	Once goals have been specified by the student, they are seen to be incomplete
7		Unfamiliar	Given	Weighing up possible methods and deciding on data required
8			Open	Suggestions of goals and methods to get there

From Wood (2006), p. 99

follows: (1) that there is no definitive formulation of a wicked problem, (2) that solutions to wicked problems are not true-or-false but good-or-bad, (3) that every solution to a wicked problem is a "one-shot operation" (because there is no opportunity to learn by trial-and-error, every attempt counts significantly), and (4) that wicked problems do not have an enumerable (or an exhaustively describable) set of potential solutions, nor is there a well-described set of permissible operations that may be incorporated into the plan in which they arise.

Similarly, Dörner (1975) characterized complex problems as involving dynamic systems that people must deal with under conditions of uncertainty. These systems can be described by their (1) complexity (number of interconnected elements; requires *complexity reduction*), (2) interconnectedness (relations between the elements; requires *model building*), (3) intransparency (availability and accessibility to relevant information; requires *information retrieval* and *information management*), (4) dynamics (system changes over time – either slow or fast; requires *prediction* of future developments), and (5) whether they involve competing goals (polytelic goal structure; requires *balancing* of competing interests).

A recent typology of problems based on formal aspects of the problem situation proposed by Wood (2006) seems especially useful for demonstrating the wide range of problems that could be (but is not yet) involved in the assessment of problem solving competency. According to his approach (Table 3.1), the three dichotomous dimensions "availability of data" (given or incomplete), "awareness of methods" (familiar or unfamiliar), and "precision of outcome criteria" (given or open) produce eight different types of problems. These types also differ in terms of the skills required to solve them.

Obviously, there is no simple consensus about the best classification of problems. Which aspects of problem solving competency are most required depends heavily on the set of problem situations selected (Fischer 2015). Therefore, from an assessment point of view, one needs to carefully select the types of stimuli that are used for measuring the construct: what you present to participants determines what is measured.

Problem Solving as a Competency

Some people think of problem solving as a competency; others talk about the (cognitive) abilities involved; another group conceives of problem solving as a skill, e.g., with respect to applying particular strategies (also see Griffin and Care 2015, p. 5). We prefer the term 'competency' as it emphasizes that a range of different cognitive and non-cognitive resources may contribute to successful problem solving and implies that this competency may have changed through training. In contrast, the term ability usually refers to something more static and innate (although in some papers, ability is used as a neutral alternative to competency). Expertise refers to the endpoint in the development some skill or competency, and is opposite to the novice situation.

The long tradition in measuring general intelligence has produced some of the most reliable assessment instruments, which are among the best predictors of job performance (Schmidt and Hunter 1998). However, problem solving and not intelligence has been chosen in many frameworks (e.g., within PISA and other large-scale assessments) as a central skill with high importance for the twenty-first century. One reason for this might be that the still increasing complexity and interconnectivity of social and economic life requires a change in thinking style. Instead of simple and mechanistic cause-effect assumptions (i.e., stimulus-response associations or input-output relations), a more holistic kind of systems thinking is required to consider the dynamics of the relevant processes and the feedback (see, e.g., Brehmer 1996, 2005). A combination of analytic, creative, and pragmatic thinking is needed for the identification of goals, the creation of solution paths, and the practical realization of planned actions in the light of obstacles. But it also becomes evident that problem solvers need to do more if they want to solve problems in the real world: they need to build models of dynamic processes, make predictions about changes in the future, and identify side-effects of their dynamic decision making (Selten et al. 2012).

Problem solving can be contrasted with routine behaviour. Routine behaviour (e.g., Betsch and Haberstroh 2005) makes life easy, but some events are more complicated and call for higher cognitive activities – not only to adjust known routines to a given situation but also to create new courses of action to overcome barriers on the way to a goal. In these cases, heuristics and strategies come into play as tools for the solution process; sometimes trial-and-error and other heuristics (simple ones as well as more sophisticated ones) do the job; sometimes effort is needed for problem solving. There is not a single method for problem solving (Fleck and Weisberg 2013).

Problem solving is strongly bound to knowledge. We may recognize a distinction between knowledge-lean and knowledge-rich problems, but on that scale a completely knowledge-free problem does exist. Problems cannot be defined without reference to the knowledge of the problem solver. The status of a specific situation as a problem depends on the absence or presence of solution-relevant knowledge. The simple question "What is the result of 7+9?" is not a problem at all for most adults, but for a pre-schooler, it might be unsolvable because of missing knowledge. For assessment, this has the implication of controlling previous knowledge in order to see if a given situation really is a problem. Because of the difficulties of knowledge assessment, researchers prefer knowledge-lean tasks to reduce the effect of prior knowledge.

To summarize, problem solving is a goal-oriented and high-level cognitive process. This implies that, for a problem to be solved, many elementary cognitive operations like attention, perception, learning, memory use, etc. need to be coordinated effectively. Indeed, problem solving can be seen as a regulation process – one that regulates not only cognitive but also non-cognitive factors (Zelazo et al. 1997).

The inclusion of non-cognitive factors can be understood as a shift in the historical paradigm of problem solving research, in which problem solving was seen as a purely cognitive activity. It is important to recognize that every problem-solving situation potentially produces a negative feeling for the problem solver. Frustration is a natural result of unforeseen obstacles between one's goal and one's current state, and there are more and less competent ways to deal with feelings of frustration. This connection between cognition and emotion is closely related to the definition of problems, but there are more non-cognitive factors to take into account. The class of "non-cognitive" skills in this context is a kind of residual category: it is everything but cognition!

Some researchers suggest that positive and negative affect trigger different styles of information processing (Fiedler 2001). Positive affect promotes a heuristic, top-down processing style in which individuals refer to pre-existing knowledge structures. Negative affect, in contrast, leads to an analytic, bottom-up processing style through the consideration of new information. Positive affect facilitates creative problem solving (Isen et al. 1987); negative affect enhances the performance of tasks that require a systematic and analytic approach (Forgas 2007). Even if there is not much research on the influence of affect on complex problem solving, evidence suggests that this may be an interesting line of research for the future (Barth and Funke 2010; Spering et al. 2005). Especially in economic contexts, the role of non-cognitive factors (e.g., motivation, trustworthiness, tenacity and perseverance) has been highlighted as important for success in life (e.g., Heckman and Rubinstein 2001).

Further insights about non-cognitive aspects of problem solving come from personality research. Assumptions about influences from the "big five" personality dimensions have not been supported up to now (e.g., Greiff and Neubert 2014), but perhaps more process-oriented research will reveal the influences of such traits as "conscientiousness" or – in collaborative contexts – "agreeableness". The role of motivation in problem solving is also evident but not often demonstrated. In the context of dynamic systems, Vollmeyer and Rheinberg (2000) showed that the motivational state of subjects affected their knowledge acquisition and encouraged them to stay with the instructed systematic strategy. For assessment situations, the motivation of participants therefore seems important for showing their real performance level. Toy, or simple, problems (low-stakes situations, as compared to high-stakes ones) might therefore not be able to measure the real capacity in a proper way (Alison et al. 2013).

Systems Competency as a Focus for Future Assessments

To integrate the different facets of problem solving competency that have been proposed so far (e.g., Fischer et al. 2015) we propose a focus on what might be termed *systems competency*. Systems competency implies the ability to construct mental models of systems, to form and test hypotheses, and to develop strategies for system identification and control. The idea of focusing on systems competency as an important construct in the area of problem solving within dynamic systems is not new (see, e.g., Kriz 2003, 2008), but we think the value of this concept has not been fully realized in the context of assessment. Systems competency is more specific than CPS in that it explicitly emphasizes system dynamics aspects. However, it is also more generic in so far as it also covers routine controls of systems. Small disturbances from outside need to be compensated, shifts of the system into certain directions are made smoothly and without producing system crashes. In contrast, CPS is required only in situations where novel states are given, where a new system is encountered into play, or unusual goals have been set.

A focus on systems competency requires to reconsider the value of existing measurement approaches for CPS. Funke (2014b, p. 495) emphasized the importance of task selection in the context of problem solving assessment: According to his view, an emphasis on psychometric qualities (e.g., increasing reliability by repeating similar tasks; Greiff et al. 2015) has led to a loss of variety and validity (see also Dörner and Funke 2017). For example, in the minimally complex systems (MCS) approach the problem solver is confronted with a larger set of unknown problems, each of them lasting for about 5 min only. To achieve such short testing times per item, the simulations of the MCS approach need to be less complex than traditional microworlds. While interacting with the problem, participants need to generate and test hypotheses and plans based on feedback from a series of interventions. To ensure a sufficient amount of commonality between different problems, each problem is formulated in a certain formal framework (see Greiff et al. 2015) such as the framework of linear equation systems (MicroDYN) or the framework of finite state. However, Funke (2014b) argues that systems thinking requires more than analyzing models with two or three linear equations. Inherent features of complex problems like nonlinearity, cyclicity, rebound effects, etc. should show up in at least *some* of the problems used for research and assessment purposes. Minimal complex systems run the danger of becoming minimally valid systems. To increase the validity of assessments, we do not need more of the *same*, but *different* types of task requirements (see also Funke et al. 2017).

With respect to the process-oriented nature of the construct, we need a broad scope of indicators to assess the portfolio of person's problem solving competencies. Within the PISA 2012 Problem Solving Framework (OECD 2013; see also Csapó and Funke 2017), four dyads of cognitive processes have been differentiated that follow the assumed processes of PS: *exploring and understanding, representing and formulating, planning and executing*, and *monitoring and reflecting*. Assessment instruments need to tap different competencies and their interplay: analytic problem solving, creative problem solving, scientific reasoning, complex problem solving, model building and hypothesis testing, to name just a few. In the tradition of Dörner (1975), we summarize these different concepts under the heading of systems competency (Kriz 2003, 2008) as a global construct that describes the competency to handle all types of systems in different respects, such as constructing, understanding, controlling or predicting.

To move towards a comprehensive assessment of the skills and abilities involved in systems competency, existing assessment approaches could be expanded in several respects. Rather than a revolution, we suggest a gradual evolution to cover additional facets of the problem solving process and to make increasing use of technology-based assessment. Below, we will outline two routes for further development in the assessment of problem solving and systems competency.

The first route is to extend the line of work that started with classical microworld scenarios and has recently been continued with minimally complex systems (MCS; Greiff et al. 2015). While MCS improved efficient delivery and reliability of assessment compared to classical microworlds, the approach is limited in terms of the variability of scenarios that can be constructed, which does not allow the assessment of a broadly-based competency. Thus, we suggest a systematic expansion of MCS in the direction of the original microworlds approach (e.g., Dörner 1997; Vester 2007) making use of complex systems for assessment purposes. Slightly increasing number of variables and/or relations (especially feedback loops) as well as with the inclusion of nonlinear relations, we argue that it should be possible to approximate some of the most interesting aspects of traditional CPS simulations. These include, for instance, limits-to-growth problems (e.g., EcoPolicy; Vester 2007), unstable homeostasis (e.g., Moroland; Strohschneider and Güss 1999), and interaction of variables (e.g., Tailorshop; Danner et al. 2011). Systems with such a moderate degree of complexity allow to obtain information about a broad palette of a person's competencies in dealing with complexity (dealing with information, use of different strategies, proactive or reactive style of dealing with system events, etc.) within an acceptable amount of testing time. In this way, it may be possible to combine the variety of demands inherent in different microworld simulations with the psychometric benefits of minimal complex systems.

A second route of development focuses on the role of communication and collaboration in problem solving. Many complex problems in the real world are not tackled by individuals but by people collaborating in teams. Collaboration brings certain benefits, e.g., sharing knowledge, combining specialist skills, or distributing work, but also introduces difficulties through miscommunication, coordination losses, and potential goal conflicts. Given that collaborative problem solving (CoPS) is a key skill for the twenty-first century, as for example identified by the World Economic Forum or the OECD, the question arises how it could be measured appropriately. CoPS is a complex activity with closely intertwined cognitive, social and self-regulatory aspects, which may require new approaches to measurement and the development of a suitable theoretical framework.

Currently, several approaches are being piloted by different research groups and it is still too early to say what is likely to work in the long run. We suggest to build on existing approaches using computer-simulated microworlds, which can be systematically expanded towards interactive CoPS assessments. One advantage of these microworlds is that they already are computer-implemented, which makes it easy to integrate electronic communication mechanisms into the scenarios. Furthermore, in many of these scenarios social interactions and communication can be made a natural part of the simulation. Finally, there are established procedures for administering and scoring microworld scenarios in assessment, which makes them a convenient starting point for further developments.

The scoring of CoPS performance could be conducted along an "individual problem solving" axis (e.g., information search or strategic activities), drawing on existing scoring criteria for simulation scenarios, and a "collaboration" axis (e.g., effective communication, organization, or knowledge sharing). The framework proposed by the OECD for the Programme for International Student Assessment 2015 (PISA) provides a good illustration of what a competency matrix with these two main dimensions could look like. One of the main challenges in devising CoPS assessments will be to devise problem solving situations with suitable communication demands and to define appropriate scoring criteria for analysing communication behavior. Another challenge will be the validation of the derived scores against relevant external criteria such as performance in real-world collaborative problem solving activities. Standardized computer-based CoPS tests would fill an important niche in assessing systems competency, particularly with respect to one of the central non-cognitive factors – communication – that so far has been largely neglected in problem solving assessment.

Conclusion

In the twentieth century, skilled routine behaviour was a key to success. The challenges of the twenty-first century require humans' problem solving competency more than ever. To assess this competency, we need knowledge-rich test situations that represent the full order of complexity in a diversity of domains. To measure system competency, the interaction between those diverse environments on the one side and the person with his or her abilities and skills on the other side needs to be carefully analyzed. Assessment of transversal (in educational contexts, cross-curricular) competencies cannot be achieved with one or two types of assessment. The plurality of skills and abilities requires a plurality of assessment instruments. Think of a good orchestra: if there are only violins playing, it is not the full sound that you will hear. And even if the triangle is played for only 1 min in a 60-min performance, we do not want to miss it. To reduce a complete orchestra to the most frequently used instruments might be a proposal made by business consultants but would hopefully never be realized. For a realistic assessment of problem solving competency that offers a realistic valuation of persons we, too, need tools that tap a wide range of contributors – of relevant cognitive and non-cognitive components. Systems competency may be fundamental for successfully dealing with the uncertainties of the twenty-first century – we have to be able to assess it!

Acknowledgment The authors wish to thank Bruce Beswick, Esther Care, and Mark Wilson for extensive and helpful comments to earlier versions of this manuscript. The authors declare that the research was conducted in the absence of any commercial or financial relationships that could be constructed as a potential conflict of interest. The research was supported by a grant from the German Research Foundation (DFG) to the first author (Az. Fu 173/14).

References

Alison, L., van den Heuvel, C., Waring, S., Power, N., Long, A., O'Hara, T., & Crego, J. (2013). Immersive simulated learning environments for researching critical incidents: A knowledge synthesis of the literature and experiences of studying high-risk strategic decision making. *Journal of Cognitive Engineering and Decision Making, 7*(3), 255–272. doi:10.1177/1555343412468113.

Barth, C. M., & Funke, J. (2010). Negative affective environments improve complex solving performance. *Cognition & Emotion, 24*, 1259–1268. doi:10.1080/02699930903223766.

Betsch, T., & Haberstroh, S. (Eds.). (2005). *The routines of decision making*. Mahwah: Erlbaum.

Brehmer, B. (1996). Man as a stabiliser of systems: From static snapshots of judgment processes to dynamic decision making. *Thinking and Reasoning, 2*, 225–238. doi:10.1080/135467896394528.

Brehmer, B. (2005). Micro-worlds and the circular relation between people and their environment. *Theoretical Issues in Ergonomics Science, 6(1)*, 73–93. doi:10.1080/14639220512331311580.

Broadbent, D. E., & Aston, B. (1978). Human control of a simulated economic system. *Ergonomics, 21*, 1035–1043.

Chang, E. C., D'Zurilla, T. J., & Sanna, L. J. (Eds.). (2004). *Social problem solving: Theory, research, and training*. Washington, DC: APA.

Csapó, B., & Funke, J. (Eds.). (2017). *The nature of problem solving. Using research to inspire 21st centurylearning*. Paris: OECD Publishing. doi:10.1787/9789264273955-en.

Danner, D., Hagemann, D., Holt, D. V., Hager, M., Schankin, A., Wüstenberg, S., & Funke, J. (2011). Measuring performance in a complex problem solving task: Reliability and validity of the tailorshop simulation. *Journal of Individual Differences, 32*, 225–233. doi:10.1027/1614-0001/a000055.

Dörner, D. (1975). Wie Menschen eine Welt verbessern wollten [How people wanted to improve a world]. *Bild der Wissenschaft, 12*, 48–53.

Dörner, D. (1997). *The logic of failure. Recognizing and avoiding error in complex situations.* New York: Basic Books.
Dörner, D., & Reither, F. (1978). Über das Problemlösen in sehr komplexen Realitätsbereichen [On problem solving in very complex domains of reality]. *Zeitschrift für Experimentelle und Angewandte Psychologie, 25*, 527–551.
Dörner, D., & Funke, J. (2017). Complex problem solving: What it is and what it is not. *Frontiers in Psychology, 8*,1153. doi:10.3389/fpsyg.2017.01153.
Duncker, K. (1935). *Zur Psychologie des produktiven Denkens [On the psychology of productive thinking]*. Berlin: Julius Springer.
Edwards, W. (1962). Dynamic decision theory and probabilistic information processing. *Human Factors, 4*, 59–73.
Fiedler, K. (2001). Affective states trigger processes of assimilation and accomodation. In L. L. Martin & G. L. Clore (Eds.), *Theories of mood and cognition: A user's guidebook* (pp. 85–98). Mahwah: Erlbaum.
Fischer, A. (2015). *Assessment of problem solving skills by means of multiple complex systems – Validity of finite automata and linear dynamic systems.* Dissertation, Heidelberg: Heidelberg University.
Fischer, A., & Neubert, J. C. (2015). The multiple faces of complex problems: A model of problem solving competency and its implications for training and assessment. *Journal of Dynamic Decision Making, 1*(6), 1–14. https://doi.org/10.11588/jddm.2015.1.23945.
Fischer, A., Greiff, S., Wuestenberg, S., Fleischer, J., Buchwald, F., & Funke, J. (2015). Assessing analytic and interactive aspects of problem solving competency. *Learning and Individual Differences, 39*, 172–179. doi:10.1016/j.lindif.2015.02.008.
Fleck, J. I., & Weisberg, R. W. (2013). Insight versus analysis: Evidence for diverse methods in problem solving. *Journal of Cognitive Psychology, 25*, 436–463. doi:10.1080/20445911.2013.779248.
Forgas, J. P. (2007). When sad is better than happy: Negative affect can improve the quality and effectiveness of persuasive messages and social influence strategies. *Journal of Experimental Social Psychology, 43*, 513–528. doi:10.1016/j.jesp.2006.05.006.
Frensch, P. A., & Funke, J. (1995a). Definitions, traditions, and a general framework for understanding complex problem solving. In P. A. Frensch & J. Funke (Eds.), *Complex problem solving: The European perspective* (pp. 3–25). Hillsdale: Erlbaum.
Frensch, P. A., & Funke, J. (Eds.). (1995b). *Complex problem solving: The european perspective.* Hillsdale: Erlbaum.
Funke, J. (2010). Complex problem solving: A case for complex cognition? *Cognitive Processing, 11*(2), 133–142. doi:10.1007/s10339-009-0345-0.
Funke, J. (2014a). Analysis of minimal complex systems and complex problem solving require different forms of causal cognition. *Frontiers in Psychology, 5*, 739. doi:10.3389/fpsyg.2014.00739.
Funke, J. (2014b). Problem solving: What are the important questions? In P. Bello, M. Guarini, M. McShane, & B. Scassellati (Eds.), *Proceedings of the 36th annual conference of the cognitive science society* (pp. 493–498). Austin: Cognitive Science Society.
Funke, J., Fischer, A., & Holt, D. V. (2017). When less is less: Solving multiple simple problems is not complex problem solving – A comment on Greiff et al. (2015). *Journal of Intelligence, 5*(1), 5. doi:10.3390/jintelligence5010005.
Greiff, S., & Neubert, J. C. (2014). On the relation of complex problem solving, personality, fluid intelligence, and academic achievement. *Learning and Individual Differences, 36*, 37–48. doi:10.1016/j.lindif.2014.08.003.
Greiff, S., Fischer, A., Wüstenberg, S., Sonnleitner, P., Brunner, M., & Martin, R. (2013a). A multitrait-multimethod study of assessment instruments for complex problem solving. *Intelligence, 41*, 579–596. doi:10.1016/j.intell.2013.07.012.

Greiff, S., Holt, D. V., & Funke, J. (2013b). Perspectives on problem solving in educational assessment: Analytical, interactive, and collaborative problem solving. *Journal of Problem Solving, 6*, 71–91. doi:10.7771/1932-6246.1153.

Greiff, S., Fischer, A., Stadler, M., & Wüstenberg, S. (2015). Assessing complex problem-solving skills with multiple complex systems. *Thinking & Reasoning, 21*(3), 356–382. https://doi.org/10.1080/13546783.2014.989263.

Griffin, P., & Care, E. (2015). The ATC21S method. In P. Griffin & E. Care (Eds.), *Assessment and teaching of 21st century skills: Methods and approach* (pp. 3–33). Dordrecht: Springer.

Heckman, J. J., & Rubinstein, Y. (2001). The importance of noncognitice skills: Lessons from the GED testing program. *American Economic Review, 91*(2), 145–149.

Heppner, P. P. (2008). Expanding the conceptualization and measurement of applied problem solving and coping: From stages to dimensions to the almost forgotten cultural context. *American Psychologist, 63*, 803–805. doi:10.1037/0003-066X.63.8.805.

Huber, O. (2012). Risky decisions: Active risk management. *Current Directions in Psychological Science, 21*(1), 26–30. doi:10.1177/0963721411422055.

Isen, A. M., Daubman, K. A., & Nowicki, G. P. (1987). Positive affect facilitates creative problem solving. *Journal of Personality and Social Psychology, 52*, 1122–1131.

Klein, G. (2008). Naturalistic decision making. *Human Factors, 50*, 456–460. doi:10.1518/001872008X288385.

Kriz, W. C. (2003). Creating effective learning environments and learning organizations through gaming simulation design. *Simulation & Gaming, 34*(4), 495–511. doi:10.1177/1046878103258201.

Kriz, W. C. (2008). A systemic-constructivist approach to the facilitation and debriefing of simulations and games. *Simulation & Gaming, 41*, 663–680. doi:10.1177/1046878108319867.

Leutner, D., Fleischer, J., Wirth, J., Greiff, S., & Funke, J. (2012). Analytische und dynamische Problemlösekompetenz im Lichte internationaler Schulleistungsvergleichsstudien: Untersuchungen zur Dimensionalität [Analytical and dynamic problem-solving competence from an international educational studies perspective. Analysis of dimensionality]. *Psychologische Rundschau, 63*, 34–42. doi:10.1026/0033-3042/a000108.

MacKinnon, A. J., & Wearing, A. J. (1980). Complexity and decision making. *Behavioral Science, 25*, 285–296.

McCarthy, J. (1956). The inversion of functions defined by Turing machines. In C. E. Shannon & J. McCarthy (Eds.), *Automata studies (AM-34)*. Princeton: Princeton University Press.

Newell, A., & Simon, H. A. (1972). *Human problem solving*. Englewood Cliffs: Prentice-Hall.

O'Neil, H. F., Chuang, S., & Chung, G. K. W. K. (2003). Issues in the computer-based assessment of collaborative problem solving. *Assessment in Education: Principles, Policy & Practice, 10*(3), 361–373. doi:10.1080/0969594032000148190.

OECD. (2013). *PISA 2012 assessment and analytical framework. Mathematics, reading, science, problem solving and financial literacy*. Paris: OECD.

OECD. (2014). *PISA 2012 results: Creative problem solving: Students' skills in tackling real-life problems* (Vol. V). Paris: OECD Publishing.

Rittel, H. W. J., & Webber, M. M. (1973). Dilemmas in a general theory of planning. *Policy Sciences, 4*, 155–169.

Schmidt, F. L., & Hunter, J. E. (1998). The validity and utility of selection methods in personnel psychology: Practical and theoretical implications of 85 years of research findings. *Psychological Bulletin, 124*(2), 262–274. doi:10.1037/0033-2909.124.2.262.

Schoppek, W., & Fischer, A. (2015). Complex problem solving – single ability or complex phenomenon? *Frontiers in Psychology, 6*(1669), 1 4. https://doi.org/10.3389/fpsyg.2015.01669.

Selten, R., Pittnauer, S., & Hohnisch, M. (2012). Dealing with dynamic decision problems when knowledge of the environment is limited: An approach based on goal systems. *Journal of Behavioral Decision Making, 25*(5), 443–457. doi:10.1002/bdm.738.

Spering, M., Wagener, D., & Funke, J. (2005). The role of emotions in complex problem-solving. *Cognition & Emotion, 19*(8), 1252–1261. doi:10.1080/02699930500304886.

Sternberg, R. J., & Frensch, P. A. (Eds.). (1991). *Complex problem solving: Principles and mechanisms*. Hillsdale: Erlbaum.

Strohschneider, S., & Güss, D. (1999). The fate of the Moros: A cross-cultural exploration of strategies in complex and dynamic decision making. *International Journal of Psychology, 34*, 235–252.

Treffinger, D. J., Isaksen, S. G., & Dorval, K. B. (1994). Creative problem solving: An overview. In M. A. Runco (Ed.), *Problem finding, problem solving and creativity* (pp. 223–236). Norwood: Ablex.

Vester, F. (2007). *The art of interconnected thinking. Ideas and tools for tackling complexity*. Munich: MCB-Verlag.

Vollmeyer, R., & Rheinberg, F. (2000). Does motivation affect performance via persistence? *Learning and Instruction, 10*, 293–309. doi:10.1016/S0959-4752(99)00031-6.

Willis, S. L. (1996). Everyday problem solving. In J. E. Birren, K. W. Schaie, et al. (Eds.), *Handbook of the psychology of aging* (4th ed., pp. 287–307). San Diego: Academic.

Wood, C. (2006). The development of creative problem solving in chemistry. *Chemistry Education Research and Practice, 7*(2), 96–113. doi:10.1039/b6rp90003h.

Zelazo, P. D., Carter, A., Reznick, J. S., & Frye, D. (1997). Early development of executive function: A problem-solving framework. *Review of General Psychology, 1*(2), 198–226.

Chapter 4
Shifts in the Assessment of Problem Solving

Katarina Krkovic, Maida Mustafic, Sascha Wüstenberg, and Samuel Greiff

Abstract In recent decades, the types of problems encountered in daily life have changed considerably. In particular, the technology-based society of today increasingly requires people to deal with dynamically changing, intransparent, and complex problems that cannot be solved only by applying factual knowledge. Moreover, in education and at work, such complex problems often need to be addressed collaboratively. Problem solving skills belong to the skills needed to successfully master such problems and are therefore considered to be crucial in the twenty-first century, but we can differentiate between problem solving on an individual level and collaborative problem solving. In the first part of this chapter, we provide insight into individual complex problem solving (CPS) research, with a special focus on its assessment. Specifically, we elaborate on different computer-based approaches to the measurement of CPS and their benefits and limitations. On the basis of the results of various empirical studies, we describe to which extent the CPS assessment has an added value in explaining the scholastic achievement and offer insights into a particular development of the assessment of this skill in large-scale educational contexts. Specifically, we elaborate on the assessment of CPS in the most influential large-scale project worldwide – the Programme for International Student Assessment (PISA) – and illustrate the process by describing example tasks. Further, we elaborate on how research on CPS has expanded towards the conceptually related skill of collaborative problem solving (ColPS) and discuss specific challenges in its assessment. With respect to the recent inclusion of ColPS in large-scale assessments, we present the assessment approach of another large-scale worldwide project – The Assessment and Teaching of Twenty-first Century Skills (ATC21S) – and describe

---

Statement by the Authors
SG and SW are the authors of the commercially available COMPRO-test that is based on the multiple complex systems approach and that employs the same assessment principle as MicroDYN. However, for any research and educational purpose, a free version of MicroDYN is available. SG and SW receive royalty fees for COMPRO.

K. Krkovic (✉)
Universität Hamburg, Hamburg, Germany
e-mail: katarina.krkovic@uni-hamburg.de

M. Mustafic • S. Wüstenberg • S. Greiff
University of Luxembourg, Luxembourg, Germany

E. Care et al. (eds.), *Assessment and Teaching of 21st Century Skills*,
Educational Assessment in an Information Age,
DOI 10.1007/978-3-319-65368-6_4

how ColPS was assessed in the PISA 2015 cycle. Finally, we outline the importance of problem solving concepts in general and CPS specifically for future research, and discuss open research questions in this field.

Introduction

What makes a person successful in the twenty-first century? This question has become a central topic of discussion across the world. A search for the answer to this question across major Internet search engines currently produces over 85 million pages that refer to workforce skills, preparing students for the twenty-first century workplace, transforming the workplace, tips and tricks on how to fulfill the requirements of twenty-first century schools and workplaces, and similar topics. These results, in turn, raise the question of what makes the twenty-first century student or worker different from an individual of the twentieth, nineteenth, or any other century. To answer this question we need to look at the primary innovation of the twenty-first century – information technology – and how it has influenced the development of society. Although information technology began developing across the second half of the twentieth century, it is only in recent decades that we find information technology in every sector of our lives. From complex devices that accompany us in our everyday lives, such as smartphones, tablets, and diverse automated machines in public and in our homes, to various digitalized processes at work and in school, the new ways of functioning in everyday life triggered by information technologies require people to possess very sophisticated and complex skills. Examples of such skills, better known as twenty-first century skills, are information literacy, divergent thinking ("thinking out of the box"), and problem solving (on both an individual and a collaborative level). Autor and colleagues' (2003) metastudy, which investigated changes in requirements over time, showed how the nature of tasks has changed in the twenty-first century. Specifically, routine, repetitive tasks (e.g., assembly line work) were common in the past. Nowadays, such tasks are mostly automated and therefore outdated as forms of human employment. In turn, people who possess very complex skills are required to perform non-routine, complex tasks – for instance, to program the machines that perform the automated tasks, optimize the production, and manage and monitor the quality of products. For this reason, in education instructional methods are increasingly incorporating complex problem solving skills. For instance, in the domains of the natural sciences and information technology, the guided discovery learning is often applied, where students need to discover the path to the solution by exploring possibilities by themselves (e.g., laboratory experiments, programming tasks), triggering complex problem solving skills. Moreover, such complex problem solving tasks frequently require people to work collaboratively (e.g., in schoolwork, such as preparing a joint presentation on a specific topic or working in a group on a science project), which places another conceptually related twenty-first century skill at the forefront – collaborative problem solving (Binkley et al. 2012).

Hence, complex problem solving, which represents successful interaction with ambiguous, interactive and dynamic tasks (Buchner 1995), may occur individually or collaboratively. Since the beginning of research on the constructs of individual and collaborative complex problem solving, the focus has shifted from experimental simulation studies in labs (for an overview see Funke 1995) to large-scale empirical studies. This is because, over the last couple of decades, both individual complex and collaborative problem solving have been acknowledged as core competencies in today's economy, and this in turn has led to the necessity for the global assessment and facilitation of these skills (cf. Von Davier and Halpin 2013). This is especially the case in the education sector, where different experts and institutions from around the world work on implementing individual and collaborative complex problem solving in educational systems. For instance, in 2002, The Partnership for Twenty-First Century Skills was founded with the goal of incorporating a readiness for twenty-first century skills into the core curricula of primary and secondary (K-12) education in the United States. In that project, individual complex problem solving and collaboration, among other skills, were identified as central topics (P21 Framework 2009). In response to this development, this chapter places a special emphasis on the conceptualization and measurement of individual and collaborative complex problem solving in a large-scale context, and provides some specific examples of assessment solutions. Considering the fact that computer-based large-scale assessments (LSAs) comprise a relatively new field within the larger new domain of twenty-first century skills, we outline the benefits and constraints that come along with this approach. Finally, the chapter provides an outlook on where the computer-based large-scale assessment of individual and collaborative complex problem solving skills is headed and what we can expect from future research and practice.

Defining Complex Problem Solving

The core of complex problem solving lies in the problem situation. A situation can be understood as a problem when a goal state needs to be reached but the path between the initial state and the goal state is ambiguous and nonroutine activities need to be undertaken to approach the solution (Mayer 1990). In line with this, problem solving is defined as "cognitive processing directed at achieving a goal when no solution method is obvious to the problem solver" (Mayer and Wittrock 2006, p. 287). However, not all problems are the same, and problem solving research differentiates between static (simple) and interactive (complex) problem solving (cf. Funke 2003, p. 107).

In static problem solving, the problems are well-defined meaning that the initial state and goal state are transparent, and all the components necessary to solve the problem are available from the very beginning (Greiff 2012, p. 24). For instance, putting together a piece of furniture without any instructions is a classic example of static problem solving. From the beginning, the problem solver has all the necessary parts and tools and has knowledge of what the furniture should look like when put together. The main problem is to find the best way to put the pieces together – where to start, what the best order of actions is, which parts fit together, and which tools to use for which parts. However, in complex problem solving, the problem solver deals with ill-defined problems, where the initial state and the goal state are intransparent, and the problem solver needs to actively engage with the problem to acquire knowledge about it in order to manage the problem situation (Funke 2003). A good example of such a complex problem solving task is the process of repairing a car with highly interdependent parts. Here, the problem solver needs to explore several possible reasons that could account for why the car is not running, make changes to its parts, monitor how these changes influence the functioning of other parts and the general functioning of the vehicle, and on the basis of the information that is gathered, make subsequent repairs and reevaluate the progress. The focus of the investigation may shift as a result of the problem solver's interaction with the car or the interdependency of the parts of the vehicle. Thus, complex problem solving according to Buchner (as cited in Frensch and Funke) can be understood as "the successful interaction with task environments that are dynamic (i.e., change as a function of user's intervention and/or as a function of time) and in which some, if not all, of the environment's regularities can only be revealed by successful exploration and integration of the information gained in that process" (Frensch and Funke, p. 14). Hence, in contrast to static problem solving, where the beginning and goal state are transparent and do not change in the course of problem solving, complex problem solving requires, on the one hand, the acquisition of relevant knowledge by interactive exploration of a situation which can dynamically change in the course of the problem solving process (e.g., trying out the functioning of the different parts of the car), and, on the other hand, the subsequent goal-oriented use of the acquired knowledge (e.g., making specific repairs on the selected sources of the problem in the car). In line with this, the literature on complex problem solving suggests that knowledge acquisition and knowledge application are two distinct dimensions of complex problem solving (e.g., Kröner et al. 2005; Wüstenberg et al. 2012).

Given that complex problem solving has been recognized as a core competency of the twenty-first century, important questions have emerged in complex problem solving research in recent decades, including how to best operationalize and assess complex problem solving and its facets. In order to offer the reader the first insights into the measurement of complex problem solving skills on the individual and collaborative level, especially in the context of LSAs, some of the available operationalizations will be discussed in the following pages.

Operationalization of Individual Complex Problem Solving

In order to offer an operationalization that can fulfill the requirements of educational large-scale studies with respect to psychometric qualities such as objectivity, reliability, validity, and fairness, attempts to operationalize individual complex problem solving have rapidly shifted from experimental research to empirical studies.

Over the course of this shift many different approaches to operationalizing the construct have been introduced. All of them have been based on computer-supported scenarios. These interactive scenarios simulate a complex problem situation and make it possible to capture the entire processes of complex problem solving of an individual. For instance, the complex problem solving example discussed above – repairing a car – may be converted into a computer simulation, where a problem solver needs to explore the car virtually, make changes, monitor the outcomes and changes on the car system, and finally find the right way to make the repair.

The tools applied to assess individual complex problem solving can differ in their structure and also in their semantic cover (i.e., in their "cover story"). On the one hand, there are "realistic" scenarios that are structured by deliberately chosen relations between variables in the system (i.e., ad hoc systems), which are commonly based on one face-valid task; and on the other hand, there are so called formal systems that are based on a priori set structural equations, which are characterized by multiple short tasks (Funke 2003). Moreover, scenarios can be embedded into specific contexts that require either previous knowledge or domain overarching skills. In the following pages, we discuss differences between "realistic" systems and formal systems and elaborate on the semantic covers of different scenarios for the assessment of individual complex problem solving.

"Realistic" Assessment Scenarios

The "realistic" systems were the first assessment scenarios that appeared in research on individual complex problem solving. A typical example of such a system is Lohhausen (Dörner 1997). Lohhausen is a scenario that is comprised of a single task that simulates the functioning of a fictional village. The problem solver's goal is to act as the mayor of this fictional village and make sure that the community is content with its living situation. The problem solver can structure the village according to his or her own vision, and manipulate many different variables that have influence on the outcome variables, such as capital, satisfaction of the population, productivity and percentage of unemployment. One of the most important benefits of scenarios such as Lohhausen is their face validity, because the scenarios are commonly semantically rich and therefore able to simulate the complexity of the real world. Nevertheless, they come with some limitations, especially regarding their psychometric properties – low objectivity due to unclear achievement criteria or questionable reliability, as reported in previous reliability studies (e.g., low reliability coefficients and retest reliability suggesting learning effects, Greiff 2012). However, some researchers (e.g., Greiff 2012) doubt the face validity of the so-called "realistic" scenarios and have suggested that the complexity of these scenarios does not adequately represent the complexity of the real world. Specifically, in the example of Lohhausen, it is questionable whether the scenario can depict realistic structures of a typical village and the actual factors of the successful functioning of a village (since, for example, these structures might differ internationally, or the factors might change in reality due to developments in urban planning, culture, or life style), so that the face validity of the measurement can be called into question along with the questionable generalizability of such assessments.

Formal System-Based Scenarios

Formal scenarios originated as a reaction to the above-mentioned limitations of the "realistic" scenarios. The development of formal-based scenarios had a strong impact on including complex problem solving in LSAs, since the new approach offered better psychometrical properties of the tasks, as necessary in a large-scale context.

In particular, the formal systems are usually based on multiple items that have a specific underlying structure, the goal of which is to enable more reliable and valid assessment. Since Funke (1985, 1999) first introduced the use of formal systems in the task development, a number of individual complex problem solving scenarios have been based on them, for instance, Multiflux (Kröner 2001), Genetics Lab (Sonnleitner et al. 2012), MicroDYN (Wüstenberg et al. 2012), and MicroFIN (Neubert et al. 2015).

The formal-based scenarios differ according to the structure of the system they are based on. Consequently, the formal systems can be categorized as two different types – linear structural equation (LSE) systems and finite state automata (FSA). The main difference between these two approaches is that whereas the LSE systems tend to be rather homogeneous in their structure, the FSA systems are heterogeneously structured. This, in turn, determines how broadly aspects of complex problem solving may be captured, depending on the instrument used. In the following sections we will outline the main characteristics of these two systems using specific assessment examples and discuss how the introduction of LSE and FSA represents a substantial development of the psychometric qualities of complex problem solving simulations.

Linear Structural Equation Systems

In LSE systems, each problem simulation consists of a specific number of so-called input and output variables. The input variables (X_1, X_2, and X_3 in Fig. 4.1) can be manipulated by the problem solver, whereas the output variables (Y_1, Y_2, and Y_3 in

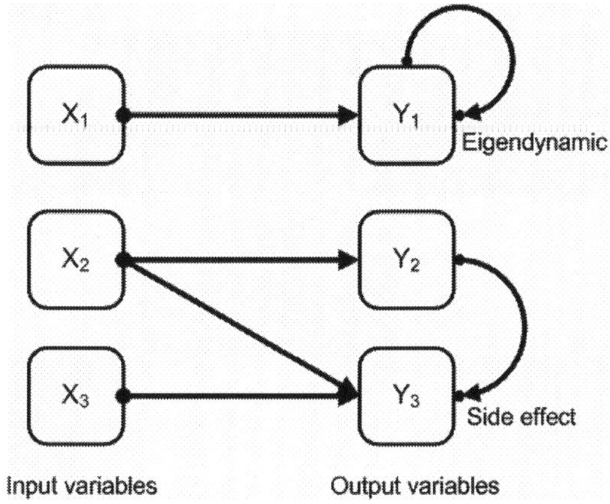

Fig. 4.1 Example of the structure of a typical LSE system displaying three input (X_1, X_2, X_3) and three output (Y_1, Y_2, Y_3) variables (From Greiff et al. 2012. Reprinted with permission from SAGE Publications)

Fig. 4.1) are the variables that are affected by the manipulation of the input variables (e.g., Greiff et al. 2012). In addition, in LSE systems, an output variable can change on its own as a function of time (eigendynamic of Y_1 in Fig. 4.1), or the change in one output variable can impact the change in another output variable (side effect from Y_2 to Y_3 in Fig. 4.1). In contrast to "realistic" scenarios, where the connections between variables are not necessarily linear and there are many interdependencies between a large number of variables, the LSEs make it possible to mathematically structure the connections between input and output variables whereby one equation describes one output variable. This makes it relatively easy for researchers to structure a set of items to cover a wide range of difficulty (e.g., by adding more direct connections or eigendynamics; see Greiff et al. 2014). In addition, the clear structure of the items in formal systems, which is not present in "realistic" systems, enables researchers to develop a number of parallel items that can keep the same LSE structure and at the same time to vary only the semantic covers.

One example of an individual complex problem solving assessment that is based on LSEs is MicroDYN. MicroDYN tasks are normally comprised of two to three input variables and two to three output variables with a range of connections between them that are represented by linear structural equations. Thus, each task consists of two parts that are designed to assess two dimensions of individual complex problem solving – knowledge acquisition and knowledge application. As described by Wüstenberg and colleagues (2012), in the knowledge acquisition phase (see Fig. 4.2a), the participant needs to explore the problem scenario by manipulating the input variables, and by monitoring their effects on the outcome variables. For instance, in Fig. 4.2, the problem solver needs to explore how the amount of different (fictive) types of flowers – wild tendrils, pale leaf, and sun grass – influences the number of three different sorts of butterflies (red, blue, or green). Furthermore, in the first phase of the task, the problem solver is asked to graphically present his or her knowledge in a model by drawing the connections between the

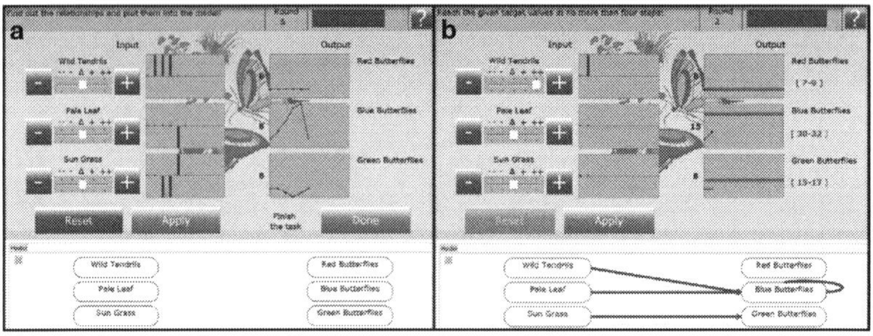

Fig. 4.2 (**a**) The knowledge-acquisition phase in MicroDYN on the *left*. (**b**) The knowledge-application phase in MicroDYN on the *right*

input and output variables as presented in the lower part of Fig. 4.2. In the knowledge application phase, illustrated in Fig. 4.2b, the problem solver is required to apply his or her knowledge by using the correct model that is presented in the lower part of the screen in this phase. In the "Butterfly" example in Fig. 4.2b, the problem solver needs to manipulate the input variables in so that he or she reaches the goal of 7–9 red, 30–32 blue, and 15–17 green butterflies (see Fig. 4.2b).

There are several aspects of LSE systems that are particularly advantageous when their tasks are used as assessments, especially in a large-scale context. As noted above, LSE based items can easily be varied in their difficulty, and the construction of parallel items is relatively simple. In addition, LSE based tasks are commonly short time-on-task assessments. For instance, in MicroDYN, the knowledge acquisition phase of each scenario lasts a maximum of around 180 s and the knowledge application phase a maximum of around 90 s. Hence, in contrast to the "realistic" scenarios, formal based LSE scenarios such as MicroDYN require the test taker to spend only a small amount of time on each task. This further makes it possible to include multiple items in one test session, which is an important contributor to a reliable assessment. MicroDYN tests, for example, commonly include eight to task tasks, allowing reliable estimation of individual complex problem solving ability levels (Wüstenberg et al. 2012).

Overall, the combination of the discussed benefits of LSE based formal systems such as MicroDYN – short time on tasks, multiple-item tests, and allowing for a wide range of difficulties – makes such assessments well suited for application in large scale contexts.

Finite State Automata

Tasks based on FSA differ from LSE-based tasks in their structure. Specifically, the structure of LSE systems is homogeneous in that it always follows a pattern of linear quantitative relations (cf. Neubert et al. 2015). In contrast to LSEs, FSAs do not need to follow such a pattern and can include various nonlinear features (e.g.,

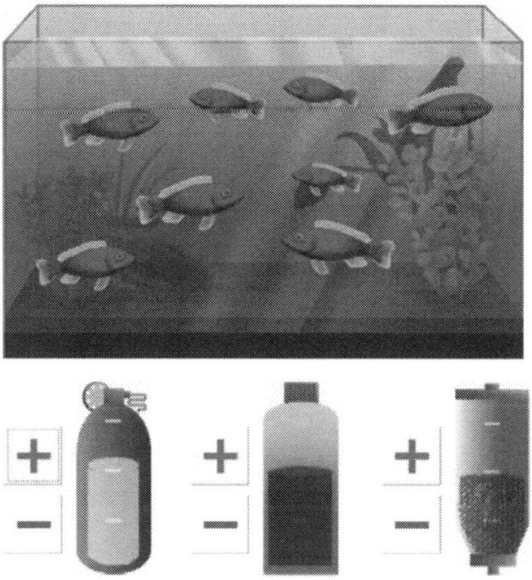

Fig. 4.3 Screenshot of the MicroFIN task "Fish-o-mat" (From Neubert et al. 2015. Reprinted with permission from Hogrefe Publishing, www.hogrefe.com, DOI: 10.1027/1015-5759/a000224)

cut-off values, where a specific variable has an influence on the outcome from only a specific value onwards). The presence of more heterogeneous relations between the input and output variables requires the problem solver to approach the exploration of the problem differently than in LSE-based scenarios, triggering different aspects of complex problem solving skills. To demonstrate this, let us look at an example of a task that is based on FSA – MicroFIN (see Neubert et al. 2015). In the MicroFIN task example "Fish-o-mat," shown in Fig. 4.3, three different bottles represent the input variables, whereas the number and color of fish in the aquarium represent the output state. A specific combination of the amounts of the contents of the bottles results in a specific output state for the fish. After exploring the scenario, the problem solver needs to reach specific goal states. This differs from LSE based scenarios in that there is not necessarily a linear relation between the input and output variables. Moreover, the FSA enables the implementation of more heterogeneous relations between variables, which in turn may result in broader complex problem solving assessment (Neubert et al. 2015). For instance, in "Fish-o-mat", the number and color of fish as depicted in Fig. 4.3 can be achieved only when the three inputs are set to exactly the same levels. Hence, the positive change in the state of the fish can be achieved only if all three bottles are simultaneously set to the same level. This in turn means that only a specific interaction of the three input variables leads to a positive change in the output state, which is never the case in formal systems based on LSE.

In summary, there are two sorts of systems that can serve as a base for individual complex problem assessment – "realistic" systems and formal systems. The latter can be further divided into linear system equation based systems, and finite state automata. Especially in the application of assessments on a large-scale, the assessment approach based upon formal systems may have opened the door for more reliable and valid assessment of individual complex problem solving.

Semantic Covers of Assessment Scenarios

With respect to similarities and differences across the different scenarios that can be applied for the assessment of individual complex problem solving, apart from the structure, another aspect that can differ is the semantic cover of assessment scenarios in general. Whereas some scenarios for the assessment of individual complex problem solving may be domain-specific and rely on the problem solver's previous knowledge of the topic, scenarios that are based on formal systems, for instance LSEs, may easily be constructed such that they are independent of previous knowledge and therefore require more domain-general skills. The exemplary MicroDYN task "Butterflies", illustrated in Fig. 4.2, is such a task. This means that specific knowledge about and a real understanding of butterfly breeding will not help a person solve this task. Hence, exploration of the particular task is the only way to discover the influence of these three types of flowers on the red, blue, and green butterflies (see Fig. 4.2). Designing tasks that do not rely on previous content knowledge is useful when the research goal is to investigate skills independent of the domains. For example, in the Lohhausen scenario outlined above, it may be the case that knowledge of urban planning or job markets would be beneficial for the success of the problem solver. This makes it difficult to differentiate to what extent the performance relies on prior knowledge, and to what extent it relies on the actual complex problem solving skills. In domain independent tasks, the success of the problem solver will not depend on how much the person knows about the specific topic in which the scenario is embedded, but will rather rely exclusively on the individual's complex problem solving skills.

The Added Value of Measuring Individual Complex Problem Solving

Apart from the fact that complex problem solving is a skill needed in everyday life of individuals in the twenty-first century, the question arises whether the abilities that have been commonly measured by now as indicators of individuals' capacities are sufficient, or whether an additional measure of complex problem solving skills would be beneficial to understanding and evaluating the individual's cognitive profile. Recent empirical studies have investigated to what extent the measurement of individual complex problem solving can explain the variance in students' scholastic achievement measured by their grade point average (GPA). For instance, a study by

Wüstenberg and colleagues (2012) illustrated the incremental validity of complex problem solving by showing how individual complex problem solving measured with MicroDYN contributes to the prediction of grade point average (GPA) over and above reasoning. Similarly, Greiff et al. (2013) demonstrated how, in some grades, adding complex problem solving as a predictor of GPA in addition to g increased the amount of explained variance, indicating the unique contribution of the individual complex problem solving assessment to the explanation of students' achievement. In the light of these findings it seems that measurement of individual complex problem solving may offer some added value over other exlanatory constructs and that the inclusion of measurement of this skills in large-scale contexts could be useful for better understanding the scholastic success of students across the world.

Individual Problem Solving in Large-Scale Assessments

Problem solving on an individual level has been included in large-scale assessments for about a decade now. This came about as a reaction to various initiatives across countries and educational systems to incorporate twenty-first century skills in curricula, such as the Partnership for Twenty-First Century Skills (P21 Framework 2009). In 2003, for the first time, non-curricular skills (i.e., problem solving skills) were included in arguably the most influential worldwide large-scale student assessment – the Programme for International Student Assessment, run by the Organisation for Economic Cooperation and Development (OECD). The OECD stated that "rather than focusing on the extent to which these students have mastered a specific school curriculum, [the assessment] looks at their ability to use their knowledge and skills to meet real-life challenges. This orientation reflects a change in curricular goals and objectives, which are increasingly concerned with what students can do with what they learn at school" (OECD 2005b). Since then, several international large-scale studies such as the Programme for the International Assessment of Adult Competencies (PIAAC), and ATC21S have included problem-solving skills in their surveys.

Individual Problem Solving in PISA

Since 2000, in 3-year cycles, 15-year-olds from across the world have been representatively chosen to participate in PISA, the largest worldwide educational study that has ever been conducted. From the very beginning, PISA recognized reading, mathematics, and science as the core subjects for the evaluation of student competencies. As early as the second cycle, in the year 2003, problem solving on an individual level was integrated into the assessment as a skill that is curriculum-general rather than connected to a specific domain but that contributes to school performance (OECD 2005a). In the 2003 PISA cycle, all of the material was administered as a paper-pencil test, so the individual problem solving tasks included were the

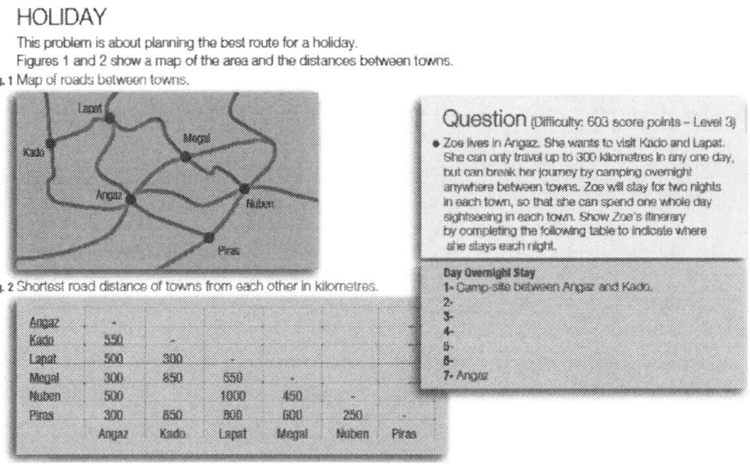

Fig. 4.4 A static problem solving task in PISA 2003 (OECD 2005a)

conventional, static ones. A typical example was the planning of the best route for a holiday (see Fig. 4.4). The participant was given a map with six cities as well as a table with the shortest distances between towns in kilometers. Under specific given constraints, the problem solver was required to plan the optimum route.

In 2012, PISA cycle included a computer-based assessment of both static and interactive problem solving on an individual level. Among others, the MicroDYN tasks described in this chapter were included to assess individual (interactive) complex problem solving.

Results and Implications of CPS Assessment in PISA

The results of the assessments of CPS in PISA offer new insights into the type of skills students possess across the world. For instance, the results of the 2012 PISA cycle show that students from Singapore, Korea, and Japan seem to be extraordinarily good problem solvers, in line with their performances in scholastic tests. Moreover, a very high percentage of students (21.4 %) across the OECD countries displayed surprisingly low proficiency levels and were able to solve only very basic problems. This may indicate that students in high performing countries are taught, through their curriculum or independently of it, to apply complex problem solving skills on cross-curricular problems.

Interestingly, in the 2012 PISA cycle, boys outperformed girls in complex problem solving and showed, at the same time, greater variance in their achievement than girls. Girls, on the other hand, seemed to be more successful in knowledge application than in knowledge acquisition. The OECD further reported smaller effects of socioeconomic status on performance in problem solving than on performance in mathematics, reading, and science (OECD 2013). Moreover, the results painted an interesting picture in which individual complex problem solving was distinguished from curriculum-based achievements. Specifically, in some countries (e.g., the U.S., Serbia, Macao-China, and Australia), students showed considerably higher achievement in problem solving than on scholastic tests.

Considering such heterogeneous results of CPS assessment across the world, the ongoing goal of the research on CPS is to gain an understanding of why such differences in performance can be found. For example, does it make a difference if society or the school system teaches these twenty-first century skills? And how can the teaching of CPS skills be further implemented in countries where students seem to be rather poor problem solvers?

From Individual to Collaborative Problem Solving

To incorporate the shift from individual to collaborative tasks that is accompanying educational and occupational changes in the twenty-first century, individual complex problem solving research has expanded towards collaborative problem solving (e.g., Von Davier and Halpin 2013). This development is a response to the reality that work environments increasingly rely on successful problem solving in collaborative settings. Simply put, the ability to work and solve problems in teams has become more important (e.g., National Research Council 2011).

Although collaboration has been a topic of different research strands such as social, educational, and experimental psychology for some time, collaborative problem solving as a construct is still relatively new. It has been described as the ability to "effectively engage in a process whereby two or more agents attempt to solve a problem by sharing the understanding and effort required to come to a solution and pooling their knowledge, skills and efforts to reach that solution" (OECD 2013). More precisely, Griffin and colleagues have defined collaborative problem solving as "the capacity of an individual to: recognise the perspective of other persons in a group; participate as a member of the group by contributing their knowledge, experience and expertise in a constructive way; recognise the need for contributions and how to manage them; identify structure and procedure involved in resolving a problem; and, as a member of the collaborative group, build and develop knowledge and understanding" (Griffin et al. 2012, p. 7). Under descriptions like these, collaborative problem solving has found its way into large-scale educational assessments.

However, research on collaborative problem solving is challenging. This is partly because the construct is comprised of both social (i.e., collaborative) and cognitive (i.e., problem solving) aspects, and also because these two aspects are not easy to separate, neither conceptually nor empirically (OECD 2013). The presence of the behavioral, collaborative aspects makes the operationalization and measurement of collaborative problem solving exceptionally challenging. Here, not only do we need to capture processes and achievement in complex problem solving, but also behavioral aspects. For instance, the matrix of collaborative problem solving skills provided by the PISA expert group on collaborative problem solving (OECD 2013) incorporates subskills such as discovering perspectives and abilities of team members, communicating about actions, describing roles and team organization, and monitoring and providing feedback. All these subskills are gaining importance in educational and work contexts and should therefore find their way into the large-scale assessment of collaborative problem solving.

The main challenge in the operationalization of collaborative problem solving is to include all the relevant subskills and at the same time maintain the important psychometric criteria, such as objectivity, reliability, validity, and scalability. For example, one question that arises in the operationalization of collaborative problem solving is whether the frequency of collaborative acts can be used as an indicator of the quality of collaborative work. In particular, does a larger number of collaborative acts indicate greater collaboration, or is a lower number an indicator of more efficient and therefore more effective collaboration? Further, are there specific styles of collaboration that rely on personality traits that need to be considered in the operationalization? Can we even make judgments of collaboration on an individual level when, in reality, the person will always need to deal with different team members and may act differently according to the situation? The measurement of collaborative problem solving is not only challenging with regard to such questions of conceptualization and operationalization but also with regard to the very design of the assessment. The main question facing researchers who try to assess collaborative problem solving is whether to use human-to-human settings or human-to-agent settings when designing a collaborative problem-solving computer-based assessment instrument.

Whereas the human-to-human setting offers a more natural way to assess collaborative problem solving and is considered by many researchers to be the only face-valid way to measure collaboration, the less face-valid human-to-agent setting simulates a collaborator by using a computer agent and thereby ensures a standardized assessment setting (cf. Rosen and Tager 2013). To find the optimum solution for collaborative problem solving, researchers are currently investigating whether these two settings, human-to-human and human-to-agent, are equivalent. Rosen and Tager (2013) implemented one of the first empirical studies on the equivalence of the two approaches and concluded that absolute equivalence could not be found. Despite employing the same tasks, using identical communication methods, and ensuring that the same resources were available in both settings, they found achievement differences: the students who worked in a human-to-agent setting achieved results that indicated stronger performance. They also observed differences in, for example, how students behaved with respect to discussions and disagreements. Authors concluded that human-to-human and human-to-agent settings can be useful for different assessment purposes – human-to-human for formative assessments, due to their face validity, and human-to-agent for summative assessments, due to the standardized setting that only the use of a computer collaborator can ensure.

The methodological issues illustrated above represent an immense challenge for the assessment of collaborative problem solving. This is especially the case in large-scale contexts, which require that assessment instruments have an extraordinarily high level of psychometric quality.

The First Large-Scale Assessment of Collaborative Problem Solving in ATC21S

In contrast to individual complex problem solving, which has now been investigated in various empirical studies and in worldwide large-scale assessments, there are not as many empirical findings on collaborative problem solving. In the assessment of collaborative problem solving in a large-scale context, the first and most important project to date is the ATC21S, the large-scale project that is specifically focused on the teaching and assessing of twenty-first century skills – collaborative problem solving and information and communication technology (ICT) literacy. The assessment of collaborative problem solving in ATC21S relies on human-to-human, computer-supported collaboration, where students are randomly matched to work together in various problem situations. The problems that are used differ strongly in their content, but they all challenge participants to use the cognitive skills that are necessary for complex problem solving, and the tasks also require collaborative work. In order to illustrate the structure of ATC21S collaborative problem solving tasks, the balance beam task is shown in Fig. 4.5. Here, two participants work on a typical problem solving task – bringing the scale into balance by using different weights. To do so, participants need to collaborate by exchanging tools back and forth, communicating their ideas, and discussing plans. Thus, the task collects information about students' collaborative skills and how they apply these skills in

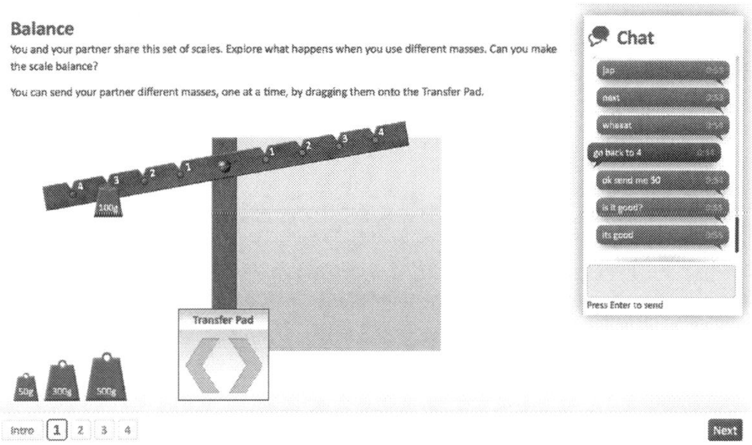

Fig. 4.5 ATC21S task example: The balance beam task (From Care et al. 2015)

complex problem solving contexts. The ATC21S project pursues both formative and summative assessment goals. It brings students together, potentially even from different countries, and provides them not only with the opportunity to use dyadic engagement to exhibit their collaborative problem solving skills, but also to use the assessment tool to learn how to perform better. The project provides students and teachers with an instant report, thus further strengthening its formative purpose.

The ATC21S project pioneered the use of real collaboration in the assessment of collaborative problem solving in large-scale settings and is therefore the most advanced project yet developed for exploiting the qualitative information that comes from the interactions of collaborating dyads.

Collaborative Problem Solving in PISA 2015

In the 2015 cycle of PISA, collaborative problem solving was assessed. Because one of the main goals of the PISA study is international comparison of educational systems, this assessment needed to be highly standardized. Specifically, a student's performance cannot depend on the other group members, an outcome that would be unavoidable in the human-to-human setting described above. For this reason, PISA implemented human-to-agent collaboration in which a student worked with computer-simulated agents. Students collaborated with two to three computer agents on various types of tasks that require collaborative problem solving. The use of this approach not only allowed for the standardization of the assessment environment, but also standardized the way in which the items are scored. This comes from the fact that the agent's behavior is always predictable, and students had a limited number of options for reacting to the agent's behavior. For instance, in the exemplary PISA collaborative problem solving task "Aquarium", presented in Fig. 4.6, each student received exactly the same message from computer agent Abby asking "What should we do now?", and each student was able to answer to this question by using one of the three predefined messages that can be seen in Fig. 4.6. Furthermore, students worked on tasks with different types of agents (e.g., helpful agents, agents who are not interested in collaborating), thereby presenting greater variety of stimuli that are necessary for students to be able to show their full potential for collaborating.

Hence, a human-to-agent approach, such as the one explained here as an example of the PISA 2015 assessment, can be very useful in LSA, where a high level of control over the assessment environment and scoring procedures is needed. Nevertheless it remains to be investigated to which extent the two approaches – human-to-human and human-to-agent – are comparable with regard to the skills that they are aiming to measure.

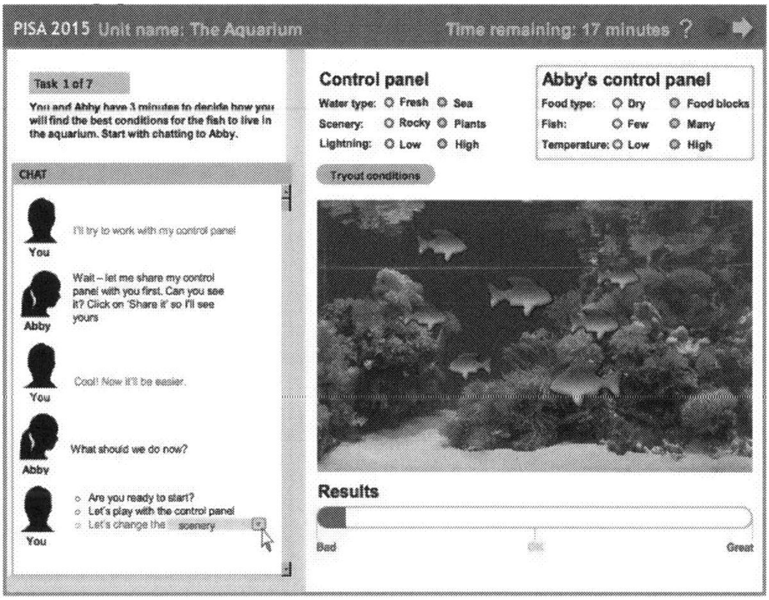

Fig. 4.6 Exemplary PISA 2015 task "Aquarium" (From OECD 2013)

Outlook

Successful problem solvers – individuals and collaborators – are vital human capital in the twenty-first century. Innovations are brought to the market place every day, new job positions are rapidly being created, and twenty-first century students and workers need to be able to adapt to these changes. The challenges facing education and educational assessment are to keep up with these changes and to prepare students and citizens in the twenty-first century to fulfill the expectations that are placed on them. One way to approach this goal is to use the large-scale assessments that have become common tools in education to assess not only scholastic achievements but also twenty-first century skills such as individual complex and collaborative problem solving, creativity, time management, and ICT literacy.

The future research on complex (collaborative) problem solving assessment is strongly oriented toward understanding the processes involved in complex and collaborative problem solving as well as toward optimizing the assessment of these skills. In particular, computer-based assessment and the application of formal systems for the assessment of complex problem solving is opening the door to analyze various aspects of the problem solving process – how fast or slow are the problem solvers; how efficiently do they interact with the problem; how much time passes before the problem solvers start to act in a goal-oriented way; or how often do the problem-solvers repeat unsuccessful strategies. For instance, in the MicroDYN tasks, research has shown that there is one highly efficient strategy that leads to success in most tasks: the so-called VOTAT (vary-one-thing-at-a-time; Rollett 2008) strategy. The use of the VOTAT strategy is positively related to scores on MicroDYN tasks. As mentioned above, the newly developed MicroFIN tasks allow for the tracking of an even wider range of strategies.

In the context of collaborative problem solving the future research of strategic behavior seems to be more complex and challenging. In particular, further insights are needed in how problem solvers share their knowledge during collaborative problem solving by investigating the turn-taking in the course of conversation and the extent to which problem solvers use specific strategies in communication (e.g., the use of specific speech acts, such as questioning and requesting in order to acquire knowledge, or asserting for purposes of sharing knowledge).

Only by fully understanding these processes and skills, their measurement, and students' performance levels will researchers be able to provide a plan to facilitate twenty-first century skills in individuals and to prepare people for the world in which we now live. In the long run, the overarching goal of twenty-first century skills research is to develop interventions or training programs that will help individuals to become better problem solvers.

References

Autor, D. H., Levy, F., & Murnane, R. J. (2003). The skill content of recent technological change: An empirical exploration. *Quarterly Journal of Economics, 118*, 1279-1333.

Binkley, M., Erstad, O., Herman, J., Raizen, S., Ripley, M., & Rumble, M. (2012). Defining 21st century skills. In P. Griffin, B. McGaw, & E. Care (Eds.), *Assessment and teaching 21st century skills* (pp. 17–66). Dordrecht: Springer.

Buchner, A. (1995). Basic topics and approaches to the study of complex problem solving. In P. A. French & J. Funke (Eds.), *Complex problem solving: The European perspective* (pp. 27–63). Hillsdale: Erlbaum.

Care, E., Griffin, P., Scoular, C., Awwal, N., & Zoanetti, N. (2015). Collaborative problem solving tasks. In P. Griffin & E. Care (Eds.), *Assessment and teaching of 21st century skills: Methods and approach* (pp. 85–104). Dordrecht: Springer.

Dörner, D. (1997). *The logic of failure. Recognizing and avoiding error in complex situations*. New York: Basic Books.

Frensch, P., & Funke, J. (1995). Definitions, traditions, and general framework for understanding complex problem solving. In P. A. Frensch & J. Funke (Eds.), *Complex problem solving: The European perspective* (pp. 4–23). Hillsdale: Erlbaum.

Funke, J. (1985). Steuerung dynamischer Systeme durch Aufbau und Anwendung subjektiver Kausalmodelle [Control of dynamic systems via construction and application of subjective causal models]. *Zeitschrift für Psychologie, 193*, 443–465.

Funke, J. (1995). Experimental research on complex problem solving. In P. A. Frensch & J. Funke (Eds.), *Complex problem solving: The European perspective* (pp. 243–268). Hillsdale: Erlbaum.

Funke, J. (2003). *Problemlösendes Denken [Problem solving thinking]*. Stuttgart: Kohl-hammer.

Greiff, S. (2012). *Individualdiagnostik komplexer Problemlösefähigkeit [Individual diagnostics of problem solving competency]*. Münster: Waxmann.

Greiff, S., Wüstenberg, S., & Funke, J. (2012). Dynamic problem solving: A new measurement perspective. *Applied Psychological Measurement, 36*, 189–213.
Greiff, S., Wüstenberg, S., Molnár, G., Fischer, A., Funke, J., & Csapó, B. (2013). Complex problem solving in educational contexts—Something beyond g: Concept, assessment, measurement invariance, and construct validity. *Journal of Educational Psychology, 105*, 364–379.
Greiff, S., Krkovic, K., & Nagy, G. (2014). Systematic variation of task characteristics facilitates understanding of task difficulty. A cognitive diagnostic modeling approach towards complex problem solving. *Psychological Test and Assessment Modeling, 56*, 83–103.
Griffin, P., Care, E., & McGaw, B. (2012). The changing role of education and schools. In P. Griffin, B. McGaw, & E. Care (Eds.), *Assessment and teaching of 21st century skills* (pp. 1–16). Dordrecht: Springer.
Kröner, S. (2001). *Intelligenzdiagnostik per Computersimulation [Intelligence assessment via computer simulation]*. Münster: Waxmann.
Kröner, S., Plass, J. L., & Leutner, D. (2005). Intelligence assessment with computer simulations. *Intelligence, 33*, 347–368.
Mayer, R. E. (1990). Problem solving. In M. W. Eysenck (Ed.), *The Blackwell dictionary of cognitive psychology*. Oxford: Blackwell.
Mayer, R. E., & Wittrock, M. C. (2006). Problem solving. In P. A. Alexander & P. H. Winne (Eds.), *Handbook of educational psychology* (pp. 287–303). Mahwah: Lawrence Erlbaum.
National Research Council. (2011). *Assessing 21st century skills*. Washington, DC: National Academies Press.
Neubert, J., Kretschmar, A., Wüstenberg, S., & Greiff, S. (2015). Extending the assessment of complex problem solving to finite state automata: Embracing heterogeneity. *European Journal of Psychological Assessment, 31*, 181–194.
Organisation for Economic Co-operation and Development. (2005a). *First results from PISA 2003*. Executive summary. Paris: OECD. Retrieved from: http://www.oecd.org/education/school/programmeforinternationalstudentassessmentpisa/34002454.pdf
Organisation for Economic Co-operation and Development. (2005b). *PISA 2003*. Technical report. Paris: OECD. Retrieved from: http://www.oecd.org/edu/school/programmeforinternationalstudentassessmentpisa/35188570.pdf
Organisation for Economic Co-operation and Development. (2013). *PISA 2015 draft collaborative problem solving framework*. Paris: OECD.
Partnership for 21st Century Skills. (2009). *P21 framework definitions*. Retrieved from: http://www.p21.org/storage/documents/P21_Framework_Definitions.pdf
Rollett, W. (2008). *Strategieeinsatz, erzeugte Information und Informationsnutzung bei der Exploration und Steuerung komplexer dynamischer Systeme [Use of strategy, acquisition and application of information, and control of complex dynamic systems]*. Münster: LIT.
Rosen, Y., & Tager, M. (2013). *Computer-based assessment of collaborative problem solving skills: Human-to-agent versus human-to-human approach*. Retrieved from: http://researchnetwork.pearson.com/wp-content/uploads/collaborativeproblemsolvingresearchreport.pdf
Sonnleitner, P., Brunner, M., Greiff, S., Funke, J., Keller, U., Martin, R., Hazotte, C., Mayer, H., & Latour, T. (2012). The genetics lab: Acceptance and psychometric characteristics of a computer based microworld to assess complex problem solving. *Psychological Test and Assessment Modeling, 54*, 54–72.
Von Davier, A. A., & Halpin, P. F. (2013). *Collaborative problem solving and the assessment of cognitive skills: Psychometric consideration, ETS Report No. RR-13-41*. Princeton: Educational Testing Service.
Wüstenberg, S., Greiff, S., & Funke, J. (2012). Complex problem solving. More than reasoning? *Intelligence, 40*, 1–14.

Chapter 5
Challenges of Assessing Collaborative Problem Solving

Arthur C. Graesser, Peter W. Foltz, Yigal Rosen, David Williamson Shaffer, Carol Forsyth, and Mae-Lynn Germany

Abstract An assessment of Collaborative Problem Solving (CPS) proficiency was developed by an expert group for the PISA 2015 international evaluation of student skills and knowledge. The assessment framework defined CPS skills by crossing three major CPS *competencies* with four problem solving *processes* that were adopted from PISA 2012 Complex Problem Solving to form a matrix of 12 specific *skills*. The three CPS competencies are (1) establishing and maintaining shared understanding, (2) taking appropriate action, and (3) establishing and maintaining team organization. For the assessment, computer-based agents provide the means to assess students by varying group composition and discourse across multiple collaborative situations within a short period of time. Student proficiency is then measured by the extent to which students respond to requests and initiate actions or communications to advance the group goals. This chapter identifies considerations and challenges in the design of a collaborative problem solving assessment for large-scale testing.

A.C. Graesser (✉) • C. Forsyth • M.-L. Germany
University of Memphis, Memphis, TN, USA
e-mail: graesser@memphis.edu

P.W. Foltz
University of Colorado, Boulder, and Pearson, Boulder, CO, USA

Y. Rosen
Harvard University, Cambridge, MA, USA

D.W. Shaffer
University of Wisconsin, Madison, WI, USA

E. Care et al. (eds.), *Assessment and Teaching of 21st Century Skills*,
Educational Assessment in an Information Age,
DOI 10.1007/978-3-319-65368-6_5

Introduction

Collaborative problem solving (CPS) was selected by the Organisation for Economic Co-operation and Development (OECD) as a new development for the Programme for International Student Assessment (PISA) for the 2015 international survey of student skills and knowledge (OECD 2013). There are excellent reasons for focusing on CPS. It is widely acknowledged that CPS is an essential skill in the home, the workforce, and the community. Indeed, much of the planning, problem solving, and decision making in the modern world is performed by teams (National Research Council 2011). The success of a team can be threatened by an uncooperative member or a counterproductive alliance, but can be strongly facilitated by a strong leader that insures that team members are all contributing. Skilled collaboration and social communication facilitate productivity in the workplace (Klein et al. 2006; Salas et al. 2008), engineering and software development (Sonnentag and Lange 2002), mission control in aviation (Fiore et al. 2014), and interdisciplinary research among scientists (Nash et al. 2003). Consequently, there is a growing discussion in national education systems for including more group-based project-based learning as well as the teaching and assessment of collaboration as part of twenty-first century skills (Brannick and Prince 1997; Griffin et al. 2012; National Research Council 2011).

One issue that repeatedly surfaces is how CPS differs from individual problem solving. Collaboration allegedly has advantages over individual problem solving because (a) there is a more effective division of labor, (b) the solutions incorporate information from multiple sources of knowledge, perspectives, and experiences, and (c) the quality of solutions is stimulated by ideas of other group members. However, the literature is mixed on whether the quality of solutions is better in a group versus a collection of individuals working independently. Problem solving solutions by a group are sometimes better than the sum of the solutions of the individual members (Aronson and Patnoe 1997; Dillenbourg 1999; Schwartz 1995; Stasser and Titus 2003; Theiner and O'Connor 2010). However, this positive emergence does not always occur when one person dominates the team or there is wasted effort in non-germane communication. Better solutions can sometimes emerge when there are differences in points of view, disagreements, conflicts, and other forms of social disequilibrium in order to minimize inferior solutions via group think (Dillenbourg 1999; Rosen and Rimor 2009). However, chronic discord may have serious negative repercussions. Success in problem solving as a group is therefore dependent on knowing how best to apply the skills at the right times. For example, the ground rules of the collaborative situation need to be understood by the group members in order to optimize group interactions and final solutions. The awareness and ability to convey to students when, why, and which aspects of collaboration are fruitful for the type of knowledge being sought may improve the quality of collaborative efforts (Mullins et al. 2011).

A core focus of CPS assessment is on the quality of the solution. In order to assess student performance in collaborative exercises, a central issue is whether the unit of assessment should be the group versus an individual within a group. That is, should the unit of statistical analyses be one individual within a particular group, the set of individuals in a group, or the solution of the group as a whole? Focus on the individual may be better for tracking individual learning and providing directed feedback. However, focus on the group can assess the more holistic emergence of the processes across the group. Researchers and practitioners undoubtedly need to consider all of these, as well as whether characteristics of the individuals in a group can predict processes and outcomes of CPS as a whole.

A major factor that contributes to the success of CPS and further differentiates it from individual problem solving is the role of communication among team members (Dillenbourg and Traum 2006; Fiore et al. 2010; Fiore and Schooler 2004). Communication is essential for organizing the team, establishing a common ground and vision, assigning tasks, tracking progress, building consensus, managing conflict, and a host of other activities in CPS. Communication further provides a window into the individual processes and team processes. Thus, communication skills are fundamental in the assessments of CPS discussed in this chapter.

Developing an assessment of CPS skills can be quite complex and multifaceted, drawing information and techniques from such fields as individual problem solving, computer-mediated collaborative work, individual and team cognition, and discourse and communication theory. This presented several challenges to the Collaborative Problem Solving Expert Group (CPEG) that developed the framework for the assessment of CPS in PISA 2015. Since this was the first time such an assessment had been developed for a large scale international test of these skills, the expert group had to incorporate facets from an emerging complex and diverse literature rather than modifying a previous assessment. This chapter provides some highlights of aspects of the CPS Framework (OECD 2013) and then focuses on particular assessment considerations and challenges.

Snapshot of Collaborative Problem Solving in PISA 2015

The following definition of CPS was articulated in the PISA 2015 framework for CPS: *Collaborative problem solving competency is the capacity of an individual to effectively engage in a process whereby two or more agents attempt to solve a problem by sharing the understanding and effort required to come to a solution by pooling their knowledge, skills and efforts to reach that solution.* The unit of analysis for the competency is the individual in a group rather than the group as a whole. The competency is an assessment on how well the individual interacts with agents during the course of problem solving; this includes achieving a shared understanding of the goals and activities as well as efforts to solve the problem and pooling resources. An agent could be considered either a human or a computer agent that interacts with the student. In both cases, an agent has the capability of generating goals, performing actions, communicating messages, sensing its environment, adapting to changing environments, and learning (Franklin and Graesser 1997).

Table 5.1 Matrix of collaborative problem solving skills for PISA 2015

	(1) Establishing and maintaining shared understanding	(2) Taking appropriate action to solve the problem	(3) Establishing and maintaining team organisation
(A) Exploring and understanding	(A1) Discovering perspectives and abilities of team members	(A2) Discovering the type of collaborative interaction to solve the problem, along with goals	(A3) Understanding roles to solve the problem
(B) Representing and formulating	(B1) Building a shared representation and negotiating the meaning of the problem (common ground)	(B2) Identifying and describing tasks to be completed	(B3) Describing roles and team organisation (communication protocol/rules of engagement)
(C) Planning and executing	(C1) Communicating with team members about the actions to be/being performed	(C2) Enacting plans	(C3) Following rules of engagement (*e.g.*, prompting other team members to perform their tasks.)
(D) Monitoring and reflecting	(D1) Monitoring and repairing the shared understanding	(D2) Monitoring results of actions and evaluating success in solving the problem	(D3) Monitoring, providing feedback and adapting the team organisation and roles

It is beyond the scope of this chapter to articulate the details of the entire framework but we provide a background on the major competencies, skills, and levels of proficiency that define CPS within the context of PISA. Three major CPS *competencies* are crossed with the four major individual problem solving *processes* to form a matrix of 12 specific *skills*. There are three levels of *proficiency* (below, at, or above standard) for each of these 12 skills; there are associated actions, communications, cognitive and social processes, and strategies that define what it means for the student to be proficient.

Table 5.1 presents the skills of the 3 × 4 CPS Framework (see OECD 2013). The dimension of problem solving processes contains the same four components as the PISA 2012 Problem Solving Framework for individual problem solving (OECD 2010). The dimension of CPS competencies, as well as the associated skills, attempt to incorporate the CPS skills identified in other CPS frameworks, such as the CRESST teamwork processing model (O'Neil et al. 2010), the teamwork model of Salas, Fiore, and colleagues (Fiore et al. 2008, 2010; Salas et al. 2008), and ATC21S (Griffin et al. 2012).

Three CPS Competencies

The three CPS competencies are (1) establishing and maintaining shared understanding, (2) taking appropriate action, and (3) establishing and maintaining team organization.

1. *Establishing and maintaining shared understanding.* Students must have an ability to identify the mutual knowledge (what each other knows about the problem) or what is often called common ground (Clark 1996; Clark and Brennan 1991), to identify the perspectives of other agents in the collaboration, and to establish a shared vision of the problem states and activities (Dillenbourg 1999; Dillenbourg and Traum 2006; Fiore and Schooler 2004). Students must be able to establish, monitor, and maintain the shared understanding throughout the problem solving task by responding to requests for information, sending important information to agents about tasks completed, establishing or negotiating shared meanings, verifying what each other knows, and taking actions to repair deficits in shared knowledge. One important way to maintain a shared understanding is to have a *transactive memory*, a shared knowledge system for acquiring, storing, and retrieving information. Transactive memory facilitates group performance, learning, and transfer (Austin 2003; Lewis et al. 2005) in addition to keeping the group on task and assigning tasks to individuals with the best expertise (Littlepage et al. 2008).
2. *Taking appropriate action to solve the problem.* Students must be able to identify the type of CPS activities that are needed to solve the problem and to follow the appropriate steps to achieve a solution. These include taking actions that solve the main substantive problem and also communication acts, such as explaining, justifying, negotiating, debating, and arguing.
3. *Establishing and maintaining group organisation.* Students must be able to help organize the group to solve the problem, consider the talents and resources of group members, understand their own role and the roles of the other agents, follow the rules of engagement for their role, monitor the group organisation, reflect on the success of the group organisation, and help handle communication breakdowns, conflicts, and obstacles. Students need to take steps to make sure that agents are completing tasks and communicating important information.

Problem Solving Processes

The problem solving processes were incorporated from the PISA 2012 Problem Solving Framework that targeted individual problem solving (Funke 2010; OECD 2010). The four cognitive processes comprise:

(A) *Exploring and understanding*. This includes interpreting the initial information about the problem and any information that is uncovered during exploration and interactions with the problem.
(B) *Representing and formulating*. Information is selected, organized, and integrated with prior knowledge. This may include the use of graphs, tables, symbols, or words. Students formulate hypotheses by identifying the relevant factors of the problem and then critically evaluate the hypotheses.
(C) *Planning and executing*. This includes identifying the goal of the problem, setting any sub-goals, developing a plan to reach the goal state, and executing the plan.
(D) *Monitoring and reflecting*. The student monitors steps in the plan to reach the goal state, marks progress, and reflects on the quality of the solutions.

Matrix of 12 CPS Skills and Proficiencies

The 12 skills in the matrix thus represent the competencies of CPS and the processes required to solve problems. A satisfactory assessment of CPS would assess the skill levels of students for each of these 12 cells. Some of these skills are reflected in actions that the student performs, such as making a decision by choosing an item on the screen, selecting values of parameters in a simulation, or preparing a requested report. Other skills require acts of communication, such as asking other group members questions, answering questions, making claims, issuing requests, giving feedback on other agents' actions, and so on. These acts of communication are needed to monitor shared understanding and team organization.

The CPEG identified various actions and communications that are associated with different levels of proficiency for each of the 12 skills. However, the main task was to specify a unidimensional scale of CPS. There needed to be a reduction in capturing the complexity of the mechanism and a focus on a robust construct that could reasonably handle a broad spectrum of problems, cultures, and students. The CPEG converged on the following three levels of proficiency for each skill: *below*, *at*, and *above* standard. However, it is important to emphasize that these levels of proficiency are being revised after item development, field testing phases, and the 2015 assessments among nations. These three categories reflect the initial theoretical framework on the CPS proficiency construct.

Below Standard of Proficiency The student is ineffective in advancing group goals and CPS. The student does not respond to requests for information and to prompts for them to take action. The student does not take actions that contribute to achieving group goals because they perform random or irrelevant actions.

At Standard of Proficiency The student is a good responsive team member, but does not assertively take the initiative and solve difficult barriers in collaboration. The student responds to requests for information and prompts for action, and selects actions that help achieve group goals. However, the student does not proactively take the initiative in requesting information from the agents, performing unprompted actions, and effectively responding to conflicts, changes in the problem situation, and new obstacles to goals.

Above Standard of Proficiency The student proactively takes the initiative and solves difficult barriers in collaboration. In addition to responding to other agents' requests and prompts, the student proactively requests information from the agents and performs unprompted actions. The student effectively responds to conflicts, changes in the problem situation, and new obstacles to goals.

Additional Components in the CPS Framework

The CPEG recognized that there are dimensions of CPS to consider other than the initiative and responsiveness of the group member. Group members are undoubtedly influenced by their psychological dispositions, cognitive skills, and traits. The complete CPS Framework acknowledged the importance of the students' prior knowledge (math, literacy, science, computer literacy) and psychological characteristics (cognitive abilities, attitudes, motivation, personality). Some of these components are assessed as part of the PISA student survey as well as part of other PISA assessments. The nature of the problem solving context (personal, social, workplace, technology, in versus out of school) and ground-rules of the problem scenario (hidden profile, consensus, negotiation, collaborative work) clearly constrain the sorts of social interactions that contribute to effective solutions. Aside from these obvious contextual influences on CPS, there are two salient dimensions of context that merit considerable attention. They are the team composition and the characteristics of the tasks.

Team composition can have a profound impact on the CPS of a group (Kreijns et al. 2003; Rosen and Rimor 2009; Wildman et al. 2012). Very little can be accomplished if no team member takes initiative or if all are fighting over control. Ideally, the members will identify who has talents or a willingness to take on a subtask, will achieve the subgoals, and will communicate progress to other members in a judicious fashion. CPS performance is compromised to the extent that the division of labour is unintelligent, subgoals are not achieved, the group goals are blocked, and there are communication breakdowns. A meaningful collaborative interaction rarely emerges spontaneously, but requires careful structuring of the collaboration to promote constructive interactions. For example, many types of collaboration have a symmetrical structure with respect to knowledge, status, and goals (Dillenbourg 1999), but the roles and tasks of the different group members may be very different. Symmetry of knowledge occurs when all participants have roughly the same level of knowledge, although they may have different perspectives. Symmetry of status involves collaboration among peers rather than interactions involving status differentials, boss-subordinate relationships, and teacher-student interactions. Finally, symmetry of goals involves common group goals rather than individual goals that may conflict.

Task characteristics impose particularly specific constraints on the solution space. *Interdependency* is a central property of tasks that are desired for assessing collaborative problem solving, as opposed to a collection of independent individual problem solvers. A task has higher interdependency to the extent that student A cannot solve a problem without actions of student B. A simple concrete example is carrying a large table across the room, a problem that cannot be accomplished by one student but rather a collection of students acting in a coordinated manner in time and space. Another example consists of jigsaw problems where a group goal requires the accomplishment of a set of tasks (A, B, and C), each of which is taken up by a particular student, and each student has limited access to the other students' knowledge (Aronson and Patnoe 1997; Stasser and Titus 2003); the puzzle can only be solved when the products of the tasks are pooled and coordinated. Tasks with high interdependency require an organization among team members that assigns tasks to team members and insures that each member is making adequate progress. Communication is essential to achieve such collaboration. The medium in which tasks take place also can have a great effect on the degree to which collaboration can be performed. A shared workspace that every team member can view provides a common ground for members to inspect progress on each other's tasks. However, in hidden profile tasks, team members have different information, so they need to explicitly ask questions and volunteer information through acts of communication in order to facilitate team members having a common understanding.

The difficulty of the problems varies in addition to challenges in collaboration. The PISA 2012 Complex Problem Solving framework and assessment defined many task characteristics that determined problem difficulty (OECD 2010) and also the extent to which assessment was domain-specific versus domain-general (Greiff et al. 2014). It is beyond the scope of this chapter to define the dimensions of problem difficulty. It suffices to say that problem difficulty increases for ill-defined problems over well-defined problems; dynamic problems (that change during the course of problem solving) over static problems; problems that are a long versus a short distance from the given state to the goal state; a large problem space over a small space; the novelty of the solution; and so on. Difficulty also should increase as a function of the number of agents involved in the collaboration and the symmetry of their roles. It is conceivable that the need for effective collaboration would increase as a function of the problem difficulty.

Challenges in Assessment of Collaborative Problem Solving

This section identifies some of the challenges in the assessment of CPS that surfaced in the discussions of the CPEG and in our coverage of the literature. The challenges focus on three issues: discourse management, group composition, and the use of computer agents in assessments.

Discourse Management

Because collaboration requires communication, an assessment of collaborative problem solving requires a suitable design of discourse management. Discourse management is the control of the communication within a task, such as turn-taking and conveying information and topics at the appropriate times. In developing items for CPS assessment, a key goal is to manage the discourse among the student and agents so that the CPS skills can be assessed in a minimal amount of time. This is a new skill for item developers who typically do not have a background in discourse processing theories (Clark 1996; Graesser et al. 2003).

Part of the challenge to students completing CPS tasks lies in creating and maintaining a shared understanding (competency 1) and team organization (competency 3), whereas another part involves taking action (competency 2) to advance a solution and handle conflict or change. Performance increases as a function of common ground of group members (Cannon-Bowers and Salas 2001; Fiore and Schooler 2004; Foltz and Martin 2008; Salas et al. 2008). When systemic group conflicts stem from fouled communication patterns, there is a need to take direct steps to intervene and to do so persistently (Dillenbourg and Traum 2006; Rice 2008). Less conflict occurs when groups have worked together previously and begin a new task (Hsu and Chou 2009). Interestingly, Asterhan and Schwarz (2009) have proposed that argumentation can be an effective means to reaching a deep level of understanding and shared vision. After the group goes through this difficult phase of conflict, which can be associated with negative affect (Barth and Funke 2010), a productive team moves forward with a better solution than if no arguments occur. That is, some amount of social-cognitive dissonance and clashes in common ground forces one to sort out facts and converge on better conclusions and solutions. This is very different from pseudo polite convergence and "group think," where the group quickly agrees with other team members instead of investing time in the task at a deep level (Stewart et al. 2007).

It is widely accepted that the core elements of collaboration (shared understanding, action, and team organization) are all related to one another and need to be coordinated rather than being exhibited in isolation. There is the standard tension between dividing the components into separate assessment modules and integrating them in ways that illuminate nontrivial mechanisms. Moreover, the particular coordination of these skills is to some extent context-dependent and could benefit from sophisticated computational models of discourse processing to assess collaborative competency (Graesser et al. 2011; Rosé et al. 2008; Shaffer and Gee 2012).

Discourse mechanisms of establishing common ground in communication have been investigated in human-human interactions and human-computer interactions (Clark 1996; Clark and Brennan 1991). Common ground is accomplished by making appropriate assumptions on what each other already knows ("old" or "given" knowledge in the common ground) and by performing acts of communication (verbal or nonverbal) about new information and business that is properly *coordinated*. People normally assume that knowledge is in the common ground if it (a) is physically co-present and salient (all parties in the communication can perceive it), (b) has been verbally expressed and understood in the discourse space, in front of the sender, recipients, and any side audience, and/or (c) is common knowledge for members of a group, culture, or target community. If a group member does not respond to a question or request for information, then the member is not taking responsibility for maintaining common ground and fails CPS competency 1. A leader manifests above average competency by taking the initiative in maintaining common ground. The student can ask questions to inquire about the status of the recipient agent with respect to levels of responsiveness and understanding: Are you there? Are you listening? Do you understand? Did you do something? Could you recap/summarize?

Turn-taking conventions facilitate the coordination of communication. For example, backchannel feedback ("uh huh," "okay," head nod) from the recipient acknowledges the sender's message and helps maintain shared understanding. There are adjacent pairs of turns between sender and recipient (Sacks et al. 1974), such as question-answer, request-acceptance, request-denial, command-promise, greeting-greeting, and so on. In dialogues with referential grounding between a leader and follower, there often are four-step handshaking sequences: Leader: "You lift the red bar." Follower: "The red bar?" Leader: "Yes, that bar." Follower: "Okay, the red bar" (Clark et al. 1986). This 4-step frame can be more economically expressed in face-to-face interaction by pointing gestures, directing a person's gaze, and other non-verbal channels (Van der Sluis and Krahmer 2007).

From the standpoint of CPS assessment, it is critical to design tasks that put students in situations that exercise collaboration through communication. It is possible to measure many of the skills related to discourse management by observing the degree to which the student responds to questions and requests for information, acknowledges other team members' actions, and initiates discourse to move the group forward. Within the PISA 2015 assessment, if a student tends to respond but does not initiate questions and requests for information, then the student could be considered as meeting minimal standards of proficiency. However, if the student initiates questions and requests, then the student would be considered as being above the standard of proficiency. Tasks need to be set up to assess both of these situations, as well as students being random or capricious. The design of every discourse episode in a task needs to be mindful of the alternative physical and discourse actions of the student. How does each alternative action map onto the skills in each of the 12 cells in Table 5.1?

Group Composition

CPS tasks with high interdependency are very sensitive to group composition. One team member who has low competency can dramatically decrease the performance of the entire team and force other team members to compensate in order to achieve team goals. An overly strong leader can prevent other team members from manifesting their talents. A team can flounder when leadership is required and no one steps up. When group-think occurs, the team politely agrees and settles for an inferior solution. When group disequilibrium occurs, the team can become dispirited and collapse. Thus, there are a large number of ways that a group can fail in CPS. These failures can be attributed to an individual or to the group process as a whole.

As mentioned early in this chapter, one question that was raised in the development of the PISA assessment was whether to measure the collaborative problem solving ability of the group as a whole or for particular individuals within the group. The CPEG decided on the latter because PISA focuses on measurement of individual skills. This decision has nontrivial consequences on the measurement logistics. In particular, it is necessary to expose each 15-year old student to multiple tasks with different team compositions, to partners with varying collaborative skills, and to multiple phases within a task that afford a broad array of situations. It is important for there to be challenges and barriers in the tasks so that an assessment can be made of the different CPS skills. With students working in teams, there is no guarantee that a particular student will be teamed up with the right combination to arrive at a sensitive measurement of any individual student's CPS skills. Consequently, there was a need to turn to technology to deliver a systematic assessment environment that is attuned to the dynamics of CPS (Griffin et al. 2012; Shaffer 2012).

Computer Agents as a Means to Assessment

The constraints of PISA required a computer-based assessment that measures CPS skills of individual students in a short assessment time window of an hour for four to five problem solving scenarios. Consequently, there was considerable discussion in the CPEG about whether to use computer agents in the assessments rather than other humans collaborating with the student through computer mediated communication (CMC). The CPEG determined that the computer agents provided more control over the interaction and could provide sufficiently valid assessments within the time constraints. Agents also provide control over logistical problems that stem from (a) assembling groups of humans (via CMC) in a timely manner within school systems that have rigid time constraints, (b) the necessity of having multiple teams per student to obtain reliable assessments, and (c) measurement error when a student is paired with humans who do not collaborate. A systematic design of computer agents could be arranged that provides control, many activities and interactions per unit time, and multiple groups of agents. These are all needed to fulfill valid measurement of relevant constructs in a short amount of time. In summary, the logistical constraints of the assessment specification lead the group to decide on the conversational agent option.

Questions have periodically been expressed on the use of computer agents in the assessments. Nevertheless, agents were used for PISA after careful consideration of various costs and benefits of human-human versus human-agent interactions. This decision is compatible with many other high stakes assessments. For example, the

Communicating and Collaborating dimension of the National Assessment of Educational Progress (NAEP 2014) will employ virtual agents, which measures skills such as, "exchange data and information with virtual peers and experts", "provide and integrate feedback from virtual peers and experts", and "debate with a virtual team member."

The amount of time available to assess CPS is very short, namely 60 min in two 30 min sessions. This requires efficiency in data collection. Agents allow a sufficient control over the interaction to get a sufficient number of assessment events that fit these time constraints and that cover the constructs that are essential to measure (Table 5.1). It often takes 5 min or more for a new group of humans to get acquainted in computer-mediated conversation before any of the actual problem solving processes begin. In contrast, agent environments can cut this time dramatically with strategic dialogue management and rapid immersion in the collaborative context. Finally, it is possible to measure a student's CPS competencies in multiple teams, with multiple tasks, and multiple phases in a controlled interaction. This would be logistically impossible with human-human interaction.

There is a broad spectrum of computer agents that have been used in tasks that involve tutoring, collaborating learning, co-construction of knowledge, and collaborative problem solving. At one extreme are fully embodied conversational agents in a virtual environment with speech recognition (*e.g.*, the *Tactical Language and Culture System*, see Johnson and Valente 2008) and tutorial learning environments that hold conversations with the student with talking heads, such as *AutoTutor* (Graesser et al. 2014; Lehman et al. 2013), *Betty's Brain* (Biswas et al. 2010), *Operation ARIES/ARA* (Halpern et al. 2012; Millis et al. 2011), and *iSTART* (Jackson and McNamara 2013). Such environments are motivating to 15-year old students, but the solution is impractical. There would be major challenges in technology, costs, and cultural variations in language and discourse. The more appropriate solution for assessments like PISA is minimalist agents that consist of printed messages in windows on the computer display, such as email messages, chat facilities, print in bubbles besides icons, and documents in various social communication media (Rouet 2006). These forms of agent-based social communication media have already been implemented in PIAAC (OECD 2009) on problem solving in electronically rich environments.

An assessment requires the human to pay attention to the agent when the agent communicates, just as a human does who takes the floor when speaking. This can also be accomplished with a minimalist agent by chat, by dynamic highlighting of messages and windows through colour or flash, and by coordination of messages with auditory signals (Mayer 2009). Humans can communicate with computer agents through a variety of channels. The simplest interface requires the student to click an alternative on a menu of optional speech acts and for there to be a limited number of options (two to seven). An advantage of this approach is that it focuses on the student's ability to know what kind of communication is required to complete the task without requiring the student to generate that communication. Other possibilities are open-ended responses that range from typing (or speaking) a single word, to articulating sentences, and composing lengthier essays.

Practical assessment of CPS can benefit from the use of agent technologies combined with communication and conventional computer technologies. Technology allows investigators to place humans in realistic orchestrated situations and observe their behavior and reactions. For example, many technological environments are based on naturalistic decision making (NDM) (Klein 2008; Lipshitz et al. 2001) in which each individual has his or her own goals, identity, and expertise that must be aligned in decisions and action in order to reach the end goal that affects both the individual and the group as a whole. Fan et al. (2010) have explored the prospects of artificial agents as collaborators during complex problem solving.

In order to validate the approach of using minimalist agents, a focused study has been conducted to investigate possible differences in student performance in human-to-agent (HA) versus human-to-human (HH) PISA-like CPS assessment tasks (Rosen 2014; Rosen and Foltz 2014). The participants were 179 14-year old students from the United States, Singapore, and Israel; there were 136 students assigned to the HA group and 43 students in the HH group. HH students were randomly assigned into pairs to work on the CPS task. The students were informed prior to their participation in the study whether they would collaborate with a computer agent or a classmate. In a case of HH setting, the students were able to see the true name of their partner. Students were exposed to identical collaborative problem solving assessment tasks and were able to collaborate and communicate by using identical methods and resources. However, while in the HA mode students collaborated with a simulated computer-driven partner, and in the HH mode students collaborated with another student to solve a problem. The findings showed that students assessed in HA mode outperformed their peers in HH mode in their collaborative skills. Collaborative problem solving with a computer agent involved significantly higher levels of shared understanding, progress monitoring, and feedback. The results further showed no significant differences in other student performance measures to solve the problem with a computer agent or a human partner, although on average students in HA mode applied more attempts to solve the problem, compared to the HH mode. A process analysis of the chats and actions of the students during the CPS task showed that in the HA group the students encountered significantly more conflict situations than in the human-to-human group. The study provided initial validity evidence for HA approach in assessing CPS skills, although further research is needed to establish more comprehensive evidence. Specifically, there needs to be a systematic analysis of the extent to which the various cells in Table 5.1 are captured with reliability and validity.

These results suggest that each mode of CPS assessment can be differentially effective for different educational purposes. Non-availability of students with particular CPS skill levels in a class may limit the fulfilment of assessment needs, but technology with computer agents can fill the gaps. Thus, in many cases using simulated computer agents, instead of relying on peers, is not merely a replacement with limitations, but an enhancement of the capabilities that makes independent assessment possible. On the other hand, HH interactions may uncover natural patterns of communication and CPS that do not occur in the HA modes.

In closing, CPS is a new field for large-scale assessment. It brings new challenges and considerations for the design of effective assessment approaches because it moves the field beyond standard item design tasks. The assessment must incorporate concepts of how humans solve problems in situations where information must be shared and considerations of how to control the collaborative environment in ways sufficient for valid measurement of individual and team skills. Communication is an integral part of successful CPS in addition to the problem solving mechanisms. Group members must achieve common ground that provides a shared understanding of the task at hand, role assignments, and the contributions of team members as the problem solving evolves. In order to achieve the group goal, there needs to be adequate discourse management, group organization, and subgoal achievement. Such an assessment of CPS proficiency requires computer agents to insure that a human interacts with multiple individuals (agents) in multiple groups with different barriers and impasses. An agent-based assessment system therefore permits the development of an optimal assessment that can be administered for multiple tasks within a short time period.

References

Aronson, E., & Patnoe, S. (1997). *The jigsaw classroom: Building cooperation in the classroom*. New York: Addison Wesley Longman.

Asterhan, C. S., & Schwarz, B. B. (2009). Argumentation and explanation in conceptual change: Indications from protocol analyses of peer-to-peer dialog. *Cognitive Science, 33*, 374–400.

Austin, J. R. (2003). Transactive memory in organizational groups: The effects of content, consensus, specialization, and accuracy on group performance. *Journal of Applied Psychology, 88*, 866–878.

Barth, C. M., & Funke, J. (2010). Negative affective environments improve complex solving performance. *Cognition and Emotion, 24*, 1259–1268.

Biswas, G., Jeong, H., Kinnebrew, J., Sulcer, B., & Roscoe, R. (2010). Measuring self-regulated learning skills through social interactions in a teachable agent environment. *Research and Practice in Technology Enhanced Learning, 5*, 123–152.

Brannick, M. T., & Prince, C. (1997). An overview of team performance measurement. In M. T. Brannick, E. Salas, & C. Prince (Eds.), *Team performance assessment and measurement: Theory methods and applications* (pp. 3–16). Mahwah: Lawrence Erlbaum Associates.

Cannon-Bowers, J. A., & Salas, E. (2001). Reflections on shared cognition. *Journal of Organizational Behavior, 22*, 195–202.

Clark, H. H. (1996). *Using language*. Cambridge: Cambridge University Press.

Clark, H. H., & Brennan, S. E. (1991). Grounding in communication. In L. B. Resnick, J. M. Levine, & S. D. Teasley (Eds.), *Perspectives on socially shared cognition* (pp. 127–149). Washington, DC: American Psychological Association.

Clark, H. H., & Wilkes-Gibbs, D. (1986). Referring as a collaborative process. *Cognition, 22*, 221–239.

Dillenbourg, P. (1999). *Collaborative learning: Cognitive and computational approaches. Advances in learning and instruction series*. New York: Elsevier Science.

Dillenbourg, P., & Traum, D. (2006). Sharing solutions: Persistence and grounding in multi-modal collaborative problem solving. *The Journal of the Learning Sciences, 15*, 121–151.

Fan, X., McNeese, M., & Yen, J. (2010). NDM-based cognitive agents for supporting decision-making teams. *Human Computer Interaction, 25*, 195–234.

Fiore, S., & Schooler, J. W. (2004). Process mapping and shared cognition: Teamwork and the development of shared problem models. In E. Salas & S. M. Fiore (Eds.), *Team cognition: Understanding the factors that drive process and performance* (pp. 133–152). Washington, DC: American Psychological Association.

Fiore, S. M., Rosen, M., Salas, E., Burke, S., & Jentsch, F. (2008). Processes in complex team problem solving: Parsing and defining the theoretical problem space. In M. Letsky, N. Warner, S. M. Fiore, & C. Smith (Eds.), *Macrocognition in teams: Theories and methodologies* (pp. 143–163). London: Ashgate Publishers.

Fiore, S. M., Rosen, M. A., Smith-Jentsch, K. A., Salas, E., Letsky, M., & Warner, N. (2010). Toward an understanding of macrocognition in teams: Predicting processes in complex collaborative contexts. *Human Factors, 52*, 203–224.

Fiore, S. M., Wiltshire, T. J., Oglesby, J. M., O'Keefe, W. S., & Salas, E. (2014). Complex collaborative problem solving in mission control. *Aviation, Space, and Environmental Medicine, 85*, 456–461.

Foltz, P. W., & Martin, M. J. (2008). Automated communication analysis of teams. In E. Salas, G. F. Goodwin, & S. Burke (Eds.), *Team effectiveness in complex organisations and systems: Cross-disciplinary perspectives and approaches* (pp. 411–431). New York: Routledge.

Franklin, S., & Graesser, A. (1997). Is it an agent, or just a program? A taxonomy for autonomous agents. In*Proceedings of the agent theories, architectures, and languages workshop* (pp. 21–35). Berlin: Springer-Verlag.

Funke, J. (2010). Complex problem solving: A case for complex cognition? *Cognitive Processing, 11*, 133–142.

Graesser, A. C., Gernsbacher, M. A., & Goldman, S. (Eds.). (2003). *Handbook of discourse processes*. Mahwah: Erlbaum.

Graesser, A. C., McNamara, D. S., & Rus, V. (2011). Computational modeling of discourse and conversation. In M. Spivey, M. Joanisse, & K. McRae (Eds.), *The Cambridge handbook of psycholinguistics* (pp. 558–572). Cambridge: Cambridge University Press.

Graesser, A. C., Li, H., & Forsyth, C. (2014). Learning by communicating in natural language with conversational agents. *Current Directions in Psychological Science, 23*, 374–380.

Greiff, S., Würstenburg, S., Csapó, B., Demetriou, A., Hautamäki, J., Graesser, A. C., & Martin, R. (2014). Domain-general problem solving skills and education in the 21st century. *Educational Research Review, 13*, 74–83.

Griffin, P., Care, E., & McGaw, B. (2012). The changing role of education and schools. In P. Griffin, B. McGaw, & E. Care (Eds.), *Assessment and teaching 21st century skills* (pp. 1–15). Heidelberg: Springer.

Halpern, D. F., Millis, K., Graesser, A. C., Butler, H., Forsyth, C., & Cai, Z. (2012). Operation ARA: A computerized learning game that teaches critical thinking and scientific reasoning. *Thinking Skills and Creativity, 7*, 93–100.

Hsu, J. L., & Chou, H. W. (2009). The effects of communicative genres on intra-group conflict in virtual student teams. *International Journal of Distance Education Technologies, 7*, 1–22.

Jackson, G. T., & McNamara, D. S. (2013). Motivation and performance in a game-based intelligent tutoring system. *Journal of Educational Psychology, 105*, 1036–1049.

Johnson, L. W., & Valente, A. (2008). Tactical language and culture training systems: Using artificial intelligence to teach foreign languages and cultures. In M. Goker & K. Haigh (Eds.), *Proceedings of the twentieth conference on innovative applications of artificial intelligence* (pp. 1632–1639). Menlo Park: AAAI Press.

Klein, G. (2008). Naturalistic decision making. *Human Factors: The Journal of the Human Factors and Ergonomics Society, 50*, 456–460.

Klein, C., DeRouin, R. E., & Salas, E. (2006). Uncovering workplace interpersonal skills: A review, framework, and research agenda. In G. P. Hodgkinson & J. K. Ford (Eds.), *International review of industrial and organisational psychology* (pp. 80–126). New York: Wiley.

Kreijns, K., Kirschner, P. A., & Jochems, W. (2003). Identifying the pitfalls for social interaction in computer-supported collaborative learning environments: A review of the research. *Computers in Human Behavior, 19*, 335–353.

Lehman, B., D'Mello, S. K., Strain, A., Mills, C., Gross, M., Dobbins, A., Wallace, P., Millis, K., & Graesser, A. C. (2013). Inducing and tracking confusion with contradictions during complex learning. *International Journal of Artificial Intelligence in Education, 22*, 85–105.

Lewis, K., Lange, D., & Gillis, L. (2005). Transactive memory systems, learning, and learning transfer. *Organization Science, 16*, 581–598.

Lipshitz, R., Klein, G., Orasanu, J., & Salas, E. (2001). Taking stock of naturalistic decision making. *Journal of Behavioral Decision Making, 14*, 331–352.

Littlepage, G. E., Hollingshead, A. B., Drake, L. R., & Littlepage, A. M. (2008). Transactive memory and performance in work groups: Specificity, communication, ability differences, and work allocation. *Group Dynamics: Theory, Research, and Practice, 12*, 223–241.

Mayer, R. E. (2009). *Multimedia learning* (2nd ed.). New York: Cambridge University Press.

Millis, K., Forsyth, C., Butler, H., Wallace, P., Graesser, A., & Halpern, D. (2011). Operation ARIES!: A serious game for teaching scientific inquiry. In M. Ma, A. Oikonomou, & J. Lakhmi (Eds.), *Serious games and edutainment applications* (pp. 169–195). London: Springer.

Mullins, D., Rummel, N., & Spada, H. (2011). Are two heads always better than one? Differential effects of collaboration on students' computer-supported learning in mathematics. *International Journal of Computer-Supported Collaborative Learning, 6*, 421–443.

Nash, J. M., Collins, B. N., Loughlin, S. E., Solbrig, M., Harvey, R., Krishnan-Sarin, S., Unger, J., Miner, C., Rukstalis, M., Shenassa, E., Dube, C., & Spirito, A. (2003). Training the transdisciplinary scientist: A general framework applied to tobacco use behavior. *Nicotine & Tobacco Research, 5*, 41–53.

National Assessment of Educational Progress. (2014). *Abridged technology and engineering literacy framework for the national assessment of educational progress*. Washington, DC: National Academies Press.

National Research Council. (2011). *Assessing 21st century skills*. Washington, DC: National Academies Press.

O'Neil, H. F., Chuang, S. H., & Baker, E. L. (2010). Computer-based feedback for computer-based collaborative problem-solving. In D. Ifenthaler, P. Pirnay-Dummer, & N. M. Seel (Eds.), *Computer-based diagnostics and systematic analysis of knowledge* (pp. 261–279). New York: Springer-Verlag.

OECD. (2009). *Problem solving in technology-rich environments: A conceptual framework*. OECD Education Working Papers, 36, OECD Publishing. Retrieved from http://search.oecd.org/officialdocuments/displaydocumentpdf/?doclanguage=en&cote=edu/wkp(2009)15

OECD. (2010). *PISA 2012 field trial problem solving framework*. Paris: OECD. Retrieved from http://www.oecd.org/dataoecd/8/42/46962005.pdf.

OECD (2013). PISA 2015 collaborative problem solving framework. Paris: OECD. Retrieved from http://www.oecd.org/pisa/pisaproducts/Draft%20PISA%202015%20 Collaborative%20 Problem%20Solving%20Framework%20.pdf.

Rice, R. E. (2008). Unusual routines: Organizational (non)sensemaking. *Journal of Communication, 58*, 1–19.

Rosé, C., Wang, Y. C., Cui, Y., Arguello, J., Stegmann, K., Weinberger, A., & Fischer, F. (2008). Analyzing collaborative learning processes automatically: Exploiting the advances of computational linguistics in computer-supported collaborative learning. *International Journal of Computer-Supported Collaborative Learning, 3*, 237–271.

Rosen, Y. (2014). Comparability of conflict opportunities in human-to-human and human-to-agent online collaborative problem solving. *Technology, Knowledge and Learning, 19*, 147–174.

Rosen, Y., & Foltz, P. (2014). Assessing collaborative problem solving through automated technologies. *Research and Practice in Technology Enhanced Learning, 9*, 389–410.

Rosen, Y., & Rimor, R. (2009). Using a collaborative database to enhance students' knowledge construction. *Interdisciplinary Journal of E-Learning and Learning Objects, 5*, 187–195.

Rouet, J.-F. (2006). *The skills of document use*. Mahwah: Erlbaum.

Sacks, H., Schegloff, E. A., & Jefferson, G. (1974). A simplest systematics for the organization of turn-taking for conversation. *Language, 50*, 696–735.

Salas, E., Cooke, N. J., & Rosen, M. A. (2008). On teams, teamwork, and team performance: Discoveries and developments. *Human Factors: The Journal of the Human Factors and Ergonomics Society, 50*, 540–547.

Schwartz, D. L. (1995). The emergence of abstract representations in dyad problem solving. *The Journal of the Learning Sciences, 4*, 321–354.

Shaffer, D. W. (2012). Models of situated action: Computer games and the problem of transfer. In C. Steinkuehler, K. Squire, & S. Barab (Eds.), *Games, learning, and society: Learning and meaning in the digital age* (pp. 403–433). Cambridge: Cambridge University Press.

Shaffer, D. W., & Gee, J. P. (2012). The right kind of GATE: Computer games and the future of assessment. In M. Mayrath, D. Robinson, & J. Clarke-Midura (Eds.), *Technology-based assessments for 21st century skills: Theoretical and practical implications from modern research*. Charlotte: Information Age Publishing.

Sonnentag, S., & Lange, I. (2002). The relationship between high performance and knowledge about how to master cooperation situations. *Applied Cognitive Psychology, 16*, 491–508.

Stasser, G., & Titus, W. (2003). Hidden profiles: A brief history. *Psychological Inquiry, 14*, 304–313.

Stewart, C. O., Setlock, L. D., & Fussell, S. R. (2007). Conversational argumentation in decision making: Chinese and US participants in face-to-face and instant-messaging interactions. *Discourse Processes, 44*, 113–139.

Theiner, G., & O'Connor, T. (2010). The emergence of group cognition. In A. Corradini & T. O'Connor (Eds.), *Emergence in science and philosophy* (pp. 79–117). New York: Routledge.

Van der Sluis, I., & Krahmer, E. (2007). Generating multimodal references. *Discourse Processes, 44*, 145–174.

Wildman, J. L., Shuffler, M. L., Lazzara, E. H., Fiore, S. M., Burke, C. S., Salas, E., & Garven, S. (2012). Trust development in swift starting action teams: A multilevel framework. *Group & Organization Management, 37*, 137–170.

Part III
Country Applications and Initiatives

Chapter 6
Collective Creativity Competencies and Collaborative Problem-Solving Outcomes: Insights from the Dialogic Interactions of Singapore Student Teams

Jennifer Pei-Ling Tan, Imelda Caleon, Hui Leng Ng, Chew Leng Poon, and Elizabeth Koh

Abstract The dynamic and non linear nature of twenty-first century skills and their constitutive interactional processes are posing significant challenges to conventional practices of teaching and assessment today. Despite notable international efforts in the teaching, learning and assessment of collaborative and creative problem-solving skills in recent years, clear empirical insights that illuminate the relationships between students' creative competencies and their problem-solving success on ill-defined collaborative tasks remain elusive. Our chapter aims to address this knowledge gap by turning the lens of inquiry towards the interactional dialogic processes through which Singapore secondary school students accomplish their collaborative and creative problem-solving tasks. Using data generated from the ATC21S Singapore school trials, and drawing from theoretical and methodological advancements in the fields of creativity and collaborative problem-solving (CPS), we seek to explore the empirical relationships between collective creativity (CC) and CPS. This chapter outlines our conceptualisation and operationalisation of CC as a suite of metacognitive, cognitive and socio-communicative competencies, made manifest in the 'talk-in-interaction' of student teams as they engage in and accomplish their CPS tasks. We then use the proposed CC discourse-analytic framework and coding scheme to empirically examine how the features and patterns of dialogic interactions reflecting CC competencies statistically differ between successful and unsuccessful CPS student teams. In conclusion, we reflect on these findings in light of Singapore's curricular innovation efforts over the past decade that reflect its commitment to providing high quality and future-relevant educational

J.P.-L. Tan (✉) • I. Caleon • E. Koh
National Institute of Education, Nanyang Technological University, Singapore
e-mail: jen.tan@nie.edu.sg

H.L. Ng • C.L. Poon
Ministry of Education, Singapore

E. Care et al. (eds.), *Assessment and Teaching of 21st Century Skills*, Educational Assessment in an Information Age,
DOI 10.1007/978-3-319-65368-6_6

experiences, outcomes and social trajectories for its young people. We hope this chapter will provide readers with more intricate understandings of the empirical associations between creative competencies and CPS outcomes, and of Singapore's students and its national education social system at large.

Introduction

The Singapore education landscape defies simplistic stereotypes. On the one hand, some critics are quick to attribute its consistent strong performance in international benchmarking studies, such as the Programme for International Student Assessment (PISA) and the Trends in International Mathematics and Science Study (TIMSS), to a highly-structured, teacher-centric, and content-focused system (see Deng and Gopinathan 2016, for a review). These critiques are often accompanied by claims that such an education system tends to produce students who may do well in memorising and reproducing factual content, who are prolific in providing accurate answers to structured exam questions but weak in exercising creative and critical faculties in a flexible manner to solve ill-defined complex problems. On the other hand, results of the 2012 PISA assessment of students' creative problem-solving abilities served to confound clichéd understandings of Singapore's public education terrain when its 15-year-olds again outperformed many of their international peers on assessment tasks that required flexible and innovative thinking, and the transfer and application of learning to unfamiliar and complex problem contexts (OECD 2014).

Our interest here is to push beyond simple binary formulations and broad generalisations of Singapore's education system, by taking a closer look at the interactional dialogic processes of Singapore secondary school students as they exercise their collaborative and creative faculties to solve ill-defined problem tasks in dyadic teams. While extant literature alludes to close associations among creativity and collaboration competencies in the context of solving ill-structured problems, clear empirical insights on the nature of these associations remain limited. Through this chapter, we make an effort to address this knowledge gap by (i) outlining a theoretically- and empirically-grounded framework and coding scheme for analysing students' collective creativity (CC) competencies made manifest in their 'talk-in-interaction' (Hutchby and Wooffitt 2008; Stahl 2011; Weatherall 2015); (ii) applying this CC discourse-analytic framework and coding scheme to a subset of ATC21S Singapore school trials' student log file data to generate empirical profiles of student teams' CC competencies in terms of their features and patterns of CC dialogic interactions throughout their collaborative problem-solving (CPS) process; (iii) examining if and how successful and unsuccessful CPS student teams differ in their CC competencies; and (iv) discussing the implications of our findings for pedagogical research and practice that aspire to foster essential twenty-first century skills and dispositions in our learners so they may better thrive in and beyond school.

Why Study Collective Creativity Competencies in Collaborative Problem-Solving?

From Individual to Collective Creativity in Collaborative Problem-Solving

Individual problem-solving and creativity are inextricably linked: that is, generating solutions to a problem requires some degree of creativity (Drapeau 2014; Treffinger et al. 2006; Weisberg 2006). By the same token, CPS also requires collective creativity (CC). CC occurs when individuals work together to generate innovative solutions to ill-defined problems through sharing of ideas and understanding (Chaharbaghi and Cripps 2007; Saye and Brush 2002; Tan et al. 2014). Moreover, it was found that CC and individual creativity co-occur, with CC requiring some degree of individual creativity (Chaharbaghi and Cripps 2007). As a key element of CPS, CC requires social and cognitive competencies, which include processes such as generative and critical thinking, problem solving, decision making, perspective taking, social and task regulation, collaboration, and knowledge sharing (Care and Griffin 2014; Hesse et al. 2015; Rosen and Foltz 2014).

CC is receiving burgeoning research attention, particularly from those who are interested in the organizational and adult learning contexts, as well as those who are concerned with the social interactions of dyads, groups, organisations and communities (Chiu 2008; Mamykina et al. 2002; Sannino and Ellis 2013). To date, however, only a few studies have focused on CC in school contexts. One of such studies provided empirical support to the view that micro-creativity (i.e., quantity of ideas produced during an argumentation process conducted within a group) is positively associated with successful completion of CPS tasks, particularly for a sample of secondary school students (Chiu 2008). Another study by Cheng and Yang (2011) indicated that collective creative efficacy, which refers to the shared belief in the team's ability to collectively engage in a creative process to co-generate new and useful outcomes, is positively correlated with better task performance of university students. A more recent study by Tan et al. (2014) showed indications of positive associations between students' collaborative creative dispositions (e.g., reflexivity, divergent production, convergent production and prosocial communication) and their performance on CPS tasks. The aforementioned studies highlight the importance of CC for CPS, as well as the need to go beyond measuring limited components of creativity towards more holistic components of CC. The current study augments the extant literature by generating additional empirical support for the proposition that CC competencies are associated with students' performance in solving ill-defined collaborative tasks.

Defining, Conceptualising and Operationalising CC: A Dialogic Framework and Coding Scheme

Drawing from the extant literature on group or team-based creativity (Chaharbaghi and Cripps 2007; Saye and Brush 2002; Tan et al. 2014; Treffinger et al. 2006), we define CC as the *generation, evaluation and application of innovative solutions to ill-defined problems through a process of mutual grounding and collaborative negotiation within a group*. Guided by this definition, which is augmented by a systematic review of theoretical and empirical studies in the field of creativity, including creative problem-solving, we conceptualize CC as a multi-dimensional suite of competencies encompassing metacognitive, cognitive, and socio-communicative skills and sub-skills, namely:

- *reflexivity* (Cunningham 2009; Jonassen 1997; Treffinger et al. 2006; Wang et al. 2010);
- *divergent production* and *convergent production* (Beghetto and Kaufman 2007; Chiu 2008; Cho et al. 2011; Cropley and Cropley 2008; Ferreira and Lacerda dos Santos 2009); and
- *prosocial interaction* (Dillenbourg and Traum 2006; Saye and Brush 2002; Wegerif 2010).

Figure 6.1 provides a visual representation of the suite of metacognitive, cognitive and socio-communicative CC skills and components (sub-skills) in our conceptualisation. We further operationalised this suite of skills and subskills into 21 distinct dialogic categories and indicators (Table 6.1). A comprehensive discussion and justification for our conceptualisation of CC and our dialogic approach to operationalising CC is detailed in our precursory paper (Tan et al. 2014).

In brief, our dialogic approach to characterising CC is premised on a Vygotskian socio-cultural and dialogic perspective of learning, which sees language to be entwined with cognitive processes, where "talk and social interaction are not just the means by which people learn to think, but also how they engage in thinking", that is, "discourse is cognition is discourse, [where] one is unimaginable without the other" (Resnick et al. 1997, p. 2). In the same way, researchers in computer-supported collaborative learning have increasingly appropriated the types and quality of peer discourse and interactions as both indicators and predictors of productive cognitive, social and motivational learning processes and outcomes (e.g., Cho et al. 2011; Tan et al. 2011; Wegerif 2010; Weinberger and Fischer 2006). Analysing dialogic interactions between learners throughout their CPS endeavours can therefore provide useful insights into the cognitive and social processes (e.g., formulation of problem solutions, collective identification of goals, evaluation of progress towards goals, creation of common ground, forging consensus and dealing with conflicts) that differentiate successful and unsuccessful CPS teams (Rosen and Foltz 2014).

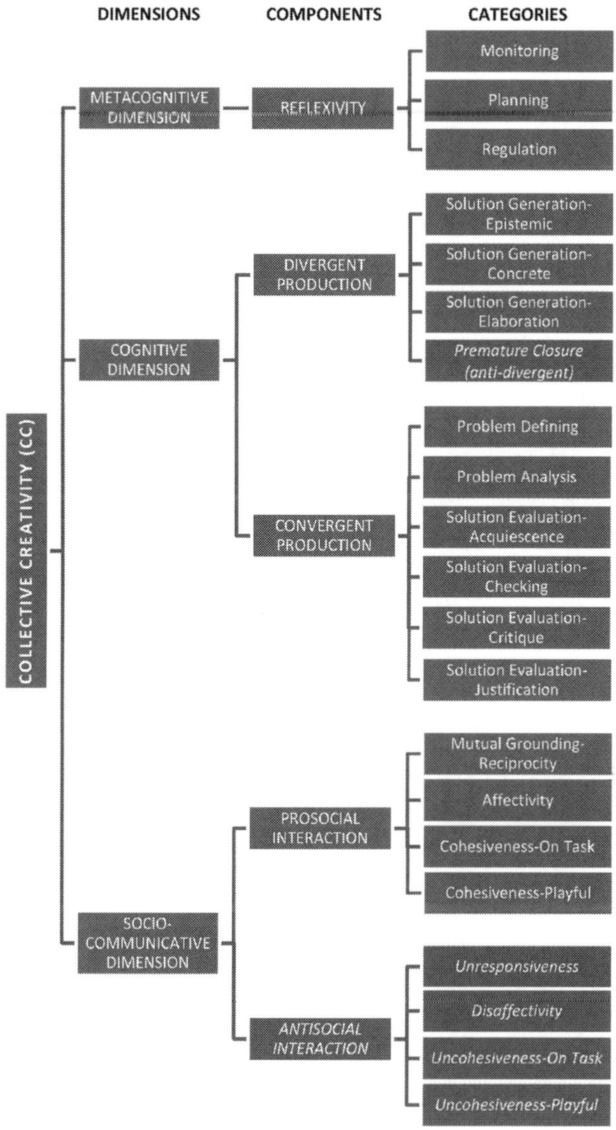

Fig. 6.1 Collective Creativity (CC) skill dimensions, components and dialogic categories

Table 6.1 CC dialogic framework and coding scheme

CC competencies	Codes	Description
Metacognitive dimension		
Reflexive dialogue	***RFD***	***Dialogue moves demonstrating the group's ability to collectively self-examine, reflect on and repurpose group objectives, strategies, processes and solutions***
Monitoring	RFD1	Dialogue moves that indicate evaluative awareness or reflective judgments of self and partner's progress in, or experience of, the problem-solving process
Planning	RFD2	Dialogue moves that indicate planning together for future activity in the problem-solving process, e.g., sequencing of activities or choice of strategies
Regulation	RFD3	Dialogue moves that indicate regulation processes directed to influence the partner's cognition, motivation or action
Cognitive dimension		
Divergent production dialogue	***DPD***	***Dialogue moves demonstrating the group's ability to generate a variety of ideas, options, alternatives, methods to address the problem at hand***
Solution generation-epistemic	DPD1	Dialogue moves that indicate new ideas and possible solutions that are rules-based or criteria-related in nature, or concern general parameters for decision-making.
Solution generation-concrete	DPD2	Dialogue moves that indicate new ideas and possible solutions that are concrete or specific in nature.
Solution generation-elaboration	DPD3	Dialogue moves that provide further information, explanation or justification on a previously stated idea and/or make associations across different ideas.
Anti-divergent production dialogue	***DPDA***	***Dialogue moves demonstrating the group's resistance to the generation of ideas, options, alternatives, methods to address the problem at hand.***
Premature closure	DPDA1	Dialogue moves that indicate the desire to bail out or not vwanting to think further about possible solutions.
Convergent production dialogue	***CPD***	***Dialogue moves demonstrating the group's ability to evaluate and narrow diverse opinions into one by reaching consensus on the best idea or integrating solutions***
Problem defining	CPD1	Dialogue moves that describe the problem and seek to establish a joint problem space (e.g., describing one's screen view to the partner in order to establish if both have the same information).
Problem analysis	CPD2	Dialogue moves that attempt to define, ascertain, make sense of the causes or rules behind the problem.
Solution evaluation-acquiescence	CPD3	Dialogue moves that indicate simple agreement with criteria development or solution suggestion statements.

(continued)

Table 6.1 (continued)

CC competencies	Codes	Description
Solution evaluation-checking	CPD4	Dialogue moves that indicate checking or evaluating criteria development or solution suggestion statements (e.g., asking for confirmation from partner of the suggested solution or decision).
Solution evaluation-critique	CPD5	Dialogue moves that dispute, doubt or probe criteria development or solution suggestion statements.
Solution evaluation-justification	CPD6	Dialogue moves that evaluate alternatives to the proposed criteria development or solution suggestion statements, and give reasons, explicit or implicit, for the evaluations.
Socio-communicative dimension		
Prosocial interaction dialogue	***PID***	***Dialogue moves demonstrating the group's ability to engage in reciprocal and productive communicative interactions, including mutual grounding, that enable (rather than hinder) the preceding metacognitive and cognitive processes***
Mutual grounding-reciprocity	PID1	Dialogue moves that represent attempts to establish shared understandings with partner through (i) the use of questions (e.g., clarifying what is meant by the preceding statement; whether it be related to the problem task, proposed solution or strategy/future activity), followed by (ii) the use of an 'adjacency pair' response that corresponds to the preceding question statement raised by partner (e.g., providing answer or information to question).
Affectivity	PID2	Dialogue moves that express positive affect or emotion. Includes repetitious punctuation, conspicuous capitalization, emoticons, humor, teasing, thanks, apologies, empathy.
Cohesiveness-on task	PID3	Dialogue moves that indicate team-directed positive affect that is related to the task at hand. These include consulting and valuing partner's perspective and contribution (e.g., referencing others, acknowledgment, polite markers, encouragement, addressing the group using we, us, our).
Cohesiveness-playful (off task)	PID4	Dialogue moves that indicate team-directed positive affect, but is off-task and playful in nature. Includes off-topic jokes and statements that serve a purely social function: greetings, salutations, phatics, closures (rather than actually conveying information).
Antisocial interaction dialogue	***PIDA***	***Dialogue moves demonstrating the group's propensity to engage in non-reciprocal, uncommunicative and negative interactions that hinder the preceding cognitive and metacognitive processes.***

(continued)

Table 6.1 (continued)

CC competencies	Codes	Description
Unresponsiveness	PIDA1	Dialogue moves that reflect a lack of responsiveness or failure to reciprocate attempts made by the partner at establishing shared understandings through the use of questions (e.g., no response nor answer/information provided to the preceding question statement raised by partner, whether it be related to the problem task, proposed solution or strategy/future activity).
Disaffectivity	PIDA2	Dialogue moves that express negative affect or emotion, including disengagement from task.
Uncohesiveness-on task	PIDA3	Dialogue moves that indicate team-directed negative affect that is related to the task at hand (e.g., disruptive, rude, messages that indicate lack of respect, blaming or invalidating).
Uncohesiveness-playful (off task)	PIDA4	Dialogue moves that indicate team-directed negative affect, but is off-task and playful in nature (e.g., disruptive, rude, messages that indicate lack of respect, blaming or invalidating).

Exploring the Relationships Between CC Competencies and CPS Success

Setting the Context

ATC21S School Trials

The ATC21S research program was established in 2009 with the core objective of developing new computer-based assessment tasks to evaluate and foster 21C skills in learners. This multi-stakeholder endeavour coordinated by the Assessment and Research Centre (ARC) at the University of Melbourne commenced with seed funding from four founding countries (Australia, Finland, Singapore and US) and three industry partners (Cisco, Intel and Microsoft). To date, ATC21S has developed a number of computer-based CPS formative assessment tasks that were piloted and trialled in schools across multiple countries in 2012 (ATC21S 2014).

In these school trials which lasted approximately 90 minutes per session, students were required to work on individual computers with a randomly-paired anonymous peer (i.e., in student dyads) to solve a series of ill-defined CPS tasks together, using an online synchronous chat tool as their only form of communication. Despite some design variations, the ATC21S CPS tasks could be categorized as ill-structured rather than well-structured problem tasks. This is because the rules and goal states are often not explicitly defined and not easily resolved with any degree of certainty. Two CPS tasks—*Small Pyramids* and *Warehouse*—serve as the focus of analysis in this chapter. Brief descriptions of both these tasks are provided in Section 'Small Pyramids and Warehouse CPS Formative Assessment Tasks'.

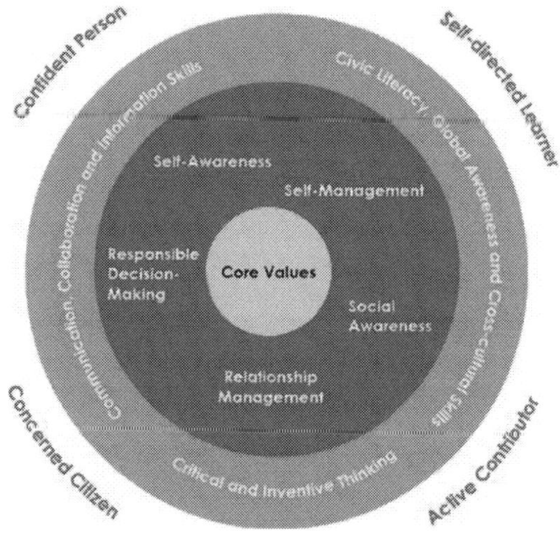

Fig. 6.2 Framework for 21CC and student outcomes, by the Ministry of Education, Singapore, 2015, https://www.moe.gov.sg/education/education-system/21st-century-competencies. Copyright 2017 by the Ministry of Education, Singapore (Reproduced with permission)

CC and CPS in the Singapore Education Context

As one of the founding members, Singapore participated in the ATC21S school trials in 2012. Singapore highly values education as a key means to develop its human capital. The Singapore Ministry of Education (MOE) regularly reviews and updates its policies and curriculum to improve the quality of education provided to the students, in line with evolving trends in broader national and international contexts so as to ensure that graduates from its education system at all levels will have the necessary values, knowledge, skills, and attitudes to thrive in the future. *Thinking Schools, Learning Nation* was launched in 1997 to transform the Singapore education system into one that will—among other things—cultivate a deeper thinking and inquiring mindset among Singapore students (Ng 2004; Sharpe and Gopinathan 2002). A twenty-first century competency (21CC) framework (Fig. 6.2) was developed in 2009 to better articulate the competencies that would enable students to grow into confident and concerned citizens, and self-directed and active contributors. The inner rung highlights the socio-emotional values/skills while the outer rung emphasises three sets of twenty-first century skills: (i) civic literacy, global awareness and cross-cultural skills; (ii) critical and inventive thinking; and (iii) communication, collaboration and information skills (Poon et al. 2015).

Over the past decade, Singapore has been making consistent and progressive efforts through its education policy and curriculum reforms to foster CC and CPS in students as part of achieving the student outcomes set out in the 21CC framework (Tan et al. 2017). In the primary education sector, for instance, curricular initiatives were progressively introduced to develop in students the essential values and skills—especially curiosity, confidence, communication and collaboration—that will enable them to thrive in a dynamic and changing world. To this end, engaging pedagogies were developed to teach skills and values. Teachers adopted a holistic assessment approach as a formative process to better support student learning. More emphasis was given to non-academic programmes within the curriculum, such as the Programme for Active Learning, and Physical Education, Arts and Music, to cultivate creative capacities and personal, cultural and social identities in students (MOE 2009). Similarly, in the secondary education sector, curriculum reviews and changes were enacted in specific domain areas, including Mathematics, Science and English Language, with increasing and more overt emphasis being placed on critical thinking and analytical skills, as well as the transfer and application of knowledge in authentic problem contexts (e.g., Tan and Nie 2015; Poon et al. 2015).

Small Pyramids and Warehouse CPS Formative Assessment Tasks

As highlighted in Section 'ATC21S School Trials', we analysed student log file data drawn from two ATC21S CPS formative assessment tasks: *Small Pyramids* and *Warehouse*. Both tasks are designed so that the two players have different roles and access to different pieces of critical information, and must thus communicate, share resources, and collaborate well to successfully accomplish the task at hand.

In the *Small Pyramids* task, players have to utilize their problem-solving abilities and understanding of number series to figure out the rules of a number pyramid. The task begins with each dyad exploring a three-tiered pyramid in order to determine the rules of the pyramid, that is, how the number they key into the red box at the bottom left of the pyramid is associated with the number that appears in the black box at the top of the pyramid (ATC21S 2012). Each player has access to different pieces of information and must work collaboratively to solve the problem (e.g., only player A can key numbers into the red box while only player B can see the number in the black box). *Small Pyramids* comprises three sub-tasks that can and have been scored by ATC21S, in terms of whether students achieved accurate solutions: (i) sub-task 1 requires players to find the number in the black box when the red box is '6'. Only player A can type '6' in the red box, and once he has done so, only player B (but not player A) can see the answer on his screen. To complete sub-task 1, both players A and B have to negotiate these differential information and concur on the right answer to the sub-task; (ii) sub-task 2 requires them to find the number in the black box when the red box is '20', which entails deriving the answer from the rules of the pyramid as they can only type single-digit numbers into the red box; and (iii) in sub-task 3, both players can see the number in the red box of a two-tiered pyramid and have to use the same rules as before to find the number in the black box (Figs. 6.3 and 6.4).

In the *Warehouse* task, the goal is to 'secure' a warehouse by correctly positioning security cameras to achieve maximum coverage of the warehouse with as few cameras as possible, while catering to the presence of tall boxes in various positions

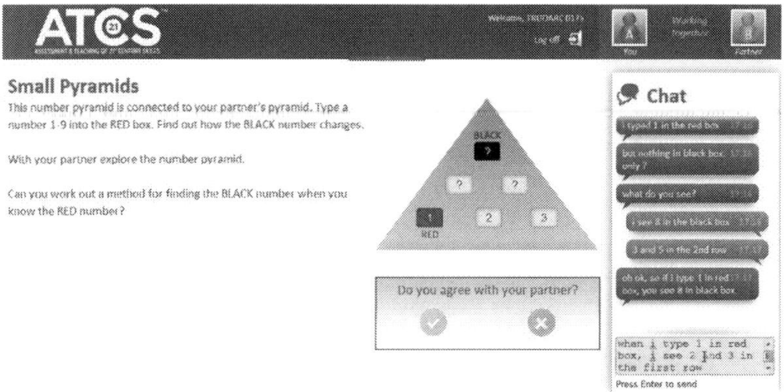

Fig. 6.3 Screenshot of small pyramids (sub-task 1): Player A view

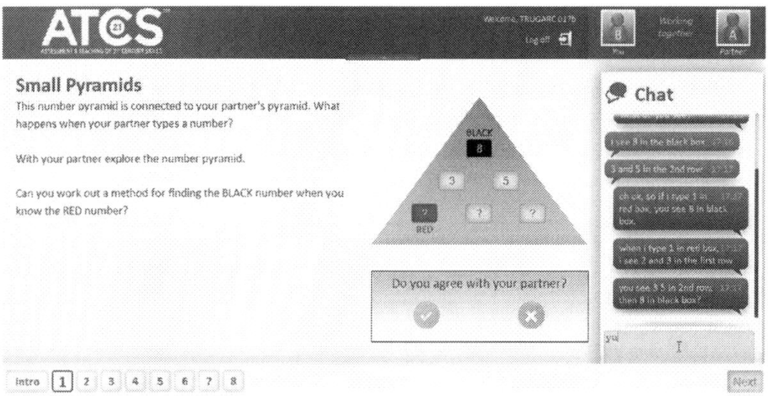

Fig. 6.4 Screenshot of small pyramids (sub-task 1): Player B view

that block the security cameras' view or line of coverage (ATC21S 2012). Similar to the *Small Pyramids* task, there are also three sub-tasks in *Warehouse* that can and have been scored by ATC21S in terms of whether students achieved accurate solutions (i.e., achieving complete coverage of the warehouse with the minimal acceptable number of security cameras). The problem task and rules remain the same across these sub-tasks, but the number of boxes and available cameras increase with each sub-task: (i) sub-task 1 has 6 (3 by 2) stacks of boxes that block the cameras' views, with 7 available cameras for placement in the warehouse; (ii) sub-task 2 has 9 (3 by 3) stacks of boxes, with 8 available cameras; and (iii) sub-task 3 has 12 (4 by 3) stacks of boxes, with 9 available cameras. As with the *Small Pyramids* task, the players have differential roles and information on their screens, and have to negotiate and share these various resources in order to accomplish the task successfully, e.g., only player A can move and place cameras with different angles of coverage in the warehouse (without seeing/knowing the effect of the cameras' placements), while only player B can see the lines of coverage on his screen but without any knowledge of how and which cameras have been placed by the partner (Figs. 6.5 and 6.6).

CPS Success in Small Pyramids and Warehouse Tasks

For the *Small Pyramids* and *Warehouse* CPS tasks, the Singapore dataset comprised a total of 290 dyadic teams of secondary students ($N = 580$ students). Of these, 141 student dyads completed the former task and another 149 student dyads completed the latter task. The student dyads that completed each of the CPS tasks were independent of each other.

We draw on the ATC21S indicators of whether each individual participating student achieved accurate solutions on each of the three sub-tasks in *Small Pyramids* or *Warehouse*, to operationalise the measure of team performance on task as the composite of accuracy and consensus. In line with this approach, a team (student dyad) can be considered as having a "correct solution" to a CPS sub-task when the accurate solution to the CPS sub-task was *jointly* achieved. This is consistent with our interest in *collective*—as opposed to individual—creativity. Student dyads that

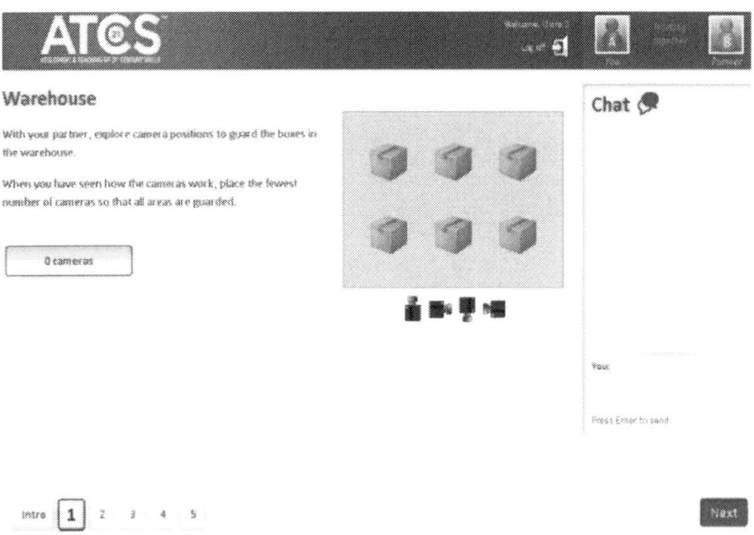

Fig. 6.5 Screenshot of warehouse (sub-task 2): Player A view

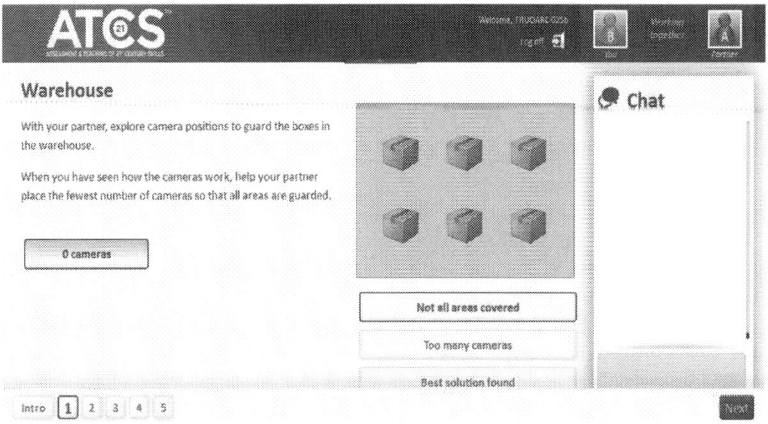

Fig. 6.6 Screenshot of warehouse (sub-task 2): Player B view

provided correct solutions to all three sub-tasks in either *Small Pyramids* or *Warehouse* received a CPS task performance score of three and were deemed to be successful student dyads. On the other hand, student dyads who did not jointly achieve accurate answers to all the 3 sub-tasks, even though one of the students in the dyad could have achieved accurate sub-task solutions at an individual level, received a score of 0, and were deemed to be unsuccessful CPS teams. Student dyads who jointly achieved accurate solutions for 1 or 2 sub-tasks achieved a team CPS task performance score of 1 or 2 respectively, and were correspondingly deemed to be moderately successful student dyads.

Table 6.2 presents the total number of student dyadic teams that completed the *Small Pyramids* or *Warehouse* tasks, grouped according to their degrees of CPS success (i.e., Successful, Unsuccessful, Moderately Successful) and year levels.

Analytic Sample of CPS Student Teams

Of the 290 student dyadic teams who completed *Warehouse* and *Small Pyramids*, we purposively selected a smaller analytic sample for our study. The selection of the analytic sample was informed by considerations of (i) allowing for the highest potential degree of diversity across the dimensions of interest via maximum variation sample (Palinkas et al. 2015; Patton 2005), and (ii) allowing for, where possible, comparably-sized yet naturally-occurring groups with different degrees of CPS success for further statistical comparative analysis (Liu 2012). To this end, we focused on the Successful (3-scorers) and Unsuccessful (0-scorers) teams on both CPS tasks. Table 6.3 reports the 135 student dyadic teams that formed the analytic

Table 6.2 Number of student dyadic teams by degrees of CPS task success and grade levels

	Small pyramids			Warehouse			
CPS Task success *(Team solution score)*	Sec 1/ Year 7	Sec 3/ Year 9	Subtotal	Sec 1/ Year 7	Sec 3/ Year 9	Subtotal	Total teams
Successful *(3-scorers)*	24	21	45	2	26	28	73
Unsuccessful *(0-scorers)*	25	13	38	58	26	84	122
Moderately successful *(1 & 2-scorers)*	30	28	58	13	24	37	95
Total teams	79	62	141	73	76	149	290

Table 6.3 Analytic sample by CPS task and degree of success

CPS Task success *(Team solution score)*	Small pyramids	Warehouse	Total teams (by CPS success)
Successful *(3-scorers)*	45	26	71
Unsuccessful *(0-scorers)*	38	26	64
Total teams (by task)	83	52	135

sample for our study. We excluded Secondary One student teams who completed the *Warehouse* task from our analytic sample because of the substantial imbalance in the number of student dyads that were successful and unsuccessful in solving the task.

Coding

We analysed the content of student dyads' talk-in-interaction message stream generated via the synchronous chat tool throughout their CPS process on the *Small Pyramids* and *Warehouse* tasks that were captured in the raw log file. These were categorised using the CC dialogic framework and coding scheme set out in Table 6.1. Each CC dialogic category (see Table 6.1) was coded as a binary variable (1 if present, otherwise 0).

As recommended by Poole et al. (2000), in order to describe processes in a reliable manner, content analysis of electronic dialogue messages or transcripts should involve segmenting the data stream into meaningful units, and using a theoretically-informed coding scheme to categorise these units. For our purposes, each individual message was considered one meaningful unit as a general rule because most of the synchronous chat messages produced by the students on task were short and usually contained a single communicative function or intention (Strijbos et al. 2006). However, when a single message contained compound functions, it was segmented for analysis and coding. Following Chiu and Hsiao (2010), punctuation and connectives were used as indicative markers to segment compound messages if the utterances prior and subsequent to these markers were deemed to be meaningful. Also, incomplete messages (i.e., statements that stop abruptly and/or where the intended meaning or communicative functions are evidently unfinished) that were completed by successive messages were coded as a consolidated unit.

This quantitative content analysis involved a coding approach that has been explicated and validated by the authors in an earlier publication (Tan et al. 2014). Following this approach, the transcripts of the talk-in-interaction of the student dyads across both *Small Pyramids* and *Warehouse* tasks were coded by two trained researchers independently, without any information on whether the transcripts being coded pertained to successful or unsuccessful CPS teams.

Inter-coder reliability was assessed across all the CC dialogic categories using a multi-method approach comprising percentage joint agreement, Cohen's kappa ($C\kappa$), and Krippendorff's alpha ($K\alpha$) formula for binary data with two observers and no missing data (Krippendorff 2011). Following Strijbos and Stahl's (2007) widely-used reliability criteria for Cκ and Kα in content analysis,[1] the application of our CC dialogic framework and coding scheme achieved very strong inter-coder reliability results across all 21 CC dialogic categories, with (i) percentage joint agreement that ranged from 96 to 99.9%, and (ii) $C\kappa$ and $K\alpha$ reliability coefficients that ranged from .85 to .96. These results foreground the framework's affordances for analysing CC competencies in successful and unsuccessful CPS student dyads.

Analysing Associations Between CC and CPS

Subsequent to the application of our analytic framework and coding scheme to determine the CC competencies profiles of student dyads as reflected in their dialogic features and patterns, chi-square analyses were conducted to determine the associations between each *CC skill dimension*—metacognitive (reflexive dialogue), cognitive (divergent and convergent production dialogue), and socio-communicative (prosocial and antisocial interaction dialogue)—and the *degree of CPS success* (successful and unsuccessful). Besides providing empirical insights into whether CC competency profiles differ between successful and unsuccessful CPS teams (Compton et al. 2012; Sharpe 2015), such a comparative analysis can also serve as an indication of the predictive validity of our CC dialogic framework and coding scheme (Agresti and Kateri 2010; Messick 1995).

Considering the theoretical underpinnings of our CC dialogic framework and coding scheme, we postulated that CPS success is associated with CC skills dimensions. We determined this association by examining the differences in dialogic patterns across and within the five CC dialogic components (i.e., reflexive dialogue, divergent production dialogue, convergent production dialogue, prosocial and antisocial interaction dialogue). We anticipated that successful CPS teams, relative to unsuccessful CPS teams, are more likely to:

[1] Where (i) $C\kappa < .20$ is poor, .20 to .39 is acceptable, .40 to .59 is moderate, .60 to .79 is good, and .80 and above is very good; and (ii) $K\alpha < .45$ is low, .45 to .59 is moderate, and .60 and above is high.

(i) engage in *proportionately more* reflexive dialogue (i.e., monitoring, planning and regulation talk categories), pro-divergent dialogue (i.e., solution generation-epistemic, concrete and elaboration talk categories), convergent dialogue (i.e., problem establishing and analysis, solution evaluation: acquiescence, checking, critique and justification talk categories), and prosocial dialogue (mutual grounding-reciprocity, affective, cohesive-task and cohesive-playful talk categories); and

(ii) engage in *proportionately less* anti-divergent and anti-social dialogue (i.e., premature closure talk, unresponsive talk, disaffective and uncohesive talk).

Results and Discussion

The results of our analyses largely concurred with our postulations set out in section 'Analysing Associations Between CC and CPS'. In Table 6.4, we display these results, including the frequency and relative frequency (i.e., proportion of total coded units of talk) of each CC dialogic category that successful and unsuccessful teams engaged in throughout their CPS process, from task commencement to completion.

At the macro level, we found that successful CPS teams engaged in about twice as much CC dialogue or talk-in-interaction as their unsuccessful peers in the process of accomplishing their CPS task ($p < .001$).

A closer examination of the results showed that, as we had postulated, successful CPS teams differed significantly from unsuccessful teams in the nature of their dialogic interactions, both in terms of (i) the five CC dialogic components (i.e., reflexive dialogue, divergent production dialogue, convergent production dialogue, prosocial interaction dialogue, and antisocial interaction dialogue), as well as (ii) the CC dialogic categories within four of these five components (i.e., all except reflexive dialogue). Specifically, an omnibus chi-square test across the five CC dialogic components indicated that successful and unsuccessful CPS teams engaged in significantly different patterns of reflexive, divergent, convergent, prosocial and antisocial CC dialogue (χ^2 (4, $N = 135$) = 124.90, $p < .001$). Furthermore, successful and unsuccessful CPS teams demonstrated significantly different talk patterns within four of the five CC dialogic components, namely, divergent production dialogue, χ^2 (3, $N = 135$) = 180.89, $p < .001$, convergent production dialogue (χ^2 (5, $N = 135$) = 104.04, $p < .001$), prosocial interaction dialogue (χ^2 (3, $N = 135$) = 89.38, $p < .001$), and antisocial interaction dialogue (χ^2 (3, $N = 135$) = 48.60, $p < .001$). However, contrary to our expectation, there was insufficient evidence to conclude that successful and unsuccessful teams demonstrated distinctly different patterns of CC reflexive dialogue—that is, monitoring, planning, and regulation talk (χ^2 (2, $N = 135$) = 5.20, $p > .05$).

On the whole, the findings aggregated across both tasks reported here largely concurred with the results on one task (*Small Pyramids*) reported in our precursory paper (Tan et al. 2014), thereby foregrounding the importance of the nature of CC for successful CPS teams.

Table 6.4 CC dialogic patterns of successful and unsuccessful CPS teams

CC dialogic dimensions/categories	Successful teams (N = 71) <a>	Unsuccessful teams (N = 64) <b>	Difference < a > – < b>	Chi-square results
	Frequency (proportion) of coded occurrences			
Metacognitive dimension				
Reflexive dialogue component	***2105 (22.5%)***	***949 (21.9%)***	***+1156 (+0.6%)***	**χ^2 (2, N = 135) = 5.20, p = .0742**
RFD1 monitoring	299 (3.2%)	130 (3.0%)	+169 (+0.2%)	
RFD2 planning	1562 (16.7%)	681 (15.7%)	+881 (+1.0%)	
RFD3 regulation	244 (2.6%)	138 (3.2%)	+106 (−0.6%)	
Cognitive dimension				
Divergent production dialogue component	***1047 (11.2%)***	***499 (11.5%)***	***+548 (−0.3%)***	**χ^2 (3, N = 135) = 180.89, p < .001**
Pro-divergent production dialogue	**985 (10.5%)**	**351 (8.1%)**	**+634 (+2.4%)**	
DPD1 solution generation-epistemic	134 (1.4%)	30 (0.7%)	+104 (+0.7%)	
DPD2 solution generation-concrete	667 (7.1%)	283 (6.5%)	+384 (+0.6%)	
DPD3 solution generation-elaboration	184 (2.0%)	38 (0.9%)	+146 (+1.1%)	
Anti-divergent production dialogue	**62 (0.7%)**	**148 (3.4%)**	**- 86 (−2.8%)**	
DPDA1 premature closure	62 (0.7%)	148 (3.4%)	- 86 (−2.8%)	
Convergent production dialogue component	***2546 (27.3%)***	***875 (20.2%)***	***+1671 (+7.1%)***	**χ^2 (5, N = 135) = 104.04, p < .001**
CPD1 problem defining	1214 (13.0%)	447 (10.3%)	+767 (+2.7%)	
CPD2 problem analysis	432 (4.6%)	99 (2.3%)	+333 (+2.3%)	
CPD3 solution evaluation-acquiescence	313 (3.4%)	87 (2.0%)	+226 (+1.3%)	
CPD4 solution evaluation-checking	251 (2.7%)	99 (2.3%)	+152 (+0.4%)	
CPD5 solution evaluation-critique	285 (3.1%)	130 (3.0%)	+155 (+0.0%)	
CPD6 solution evaluation-justification	51 (0.5%)	13 (0.3%)	+ 38 (+0.2%)	

(continued)

Table 6.4 (continued)

CC dialogic dimensions/categories	Successful teams (N = 71) <a>	Unsuccessful teams (N = 64) <b>	Difference < a > − < b>	Chi-square results
	Frequency (proportion) of coded occurrences			
Socio-communicative dimension				
Prosocial interaction dialogue component	***2843 (30.5%)***	***1449 (33.5%)***	***+1394 (−3.0%)***	**χ^2 (3, N = 135) = 89.38, p < .001**
PID1 mutual grounding-reciprocity	1084 (11.6%)	460 (10.6%)	+624 (+1.0%)	
PID2 affectivity	497 (5.3%)	267 (6.2%)	+230 (−0.8%)	
PID3 cohesiveness-on task	1025 (11.0%)	465 (10.7%)	+560 (+0.2%)	
PID4 cohesiveness-playful (off-task)	237 (2.5%)	257 (5.9%)	- 20 (−3.4%)	
Antisocial interaction dialogue component	***793 (8.5%)***	***556 (12.9%)***	***+237 (−4.4%)***	**χ^2 (3, N = 135) = 48.60, p < .001**
PIDA1 unresponsiveness	370 (4.0%)	237 (5.5%)	+133 (−1.5%)	
PIDA2 Disaffectivity	321 (3.4%)	214 (4.9%)	+107 (−1.5%)	
PIDA3 Uncohesiveness-on task	91 (1.0%)	52 (1.2%)	+ 39 (−0.2%)	
PIDA4 Uncohesiveness-playful (off-task)	11 (0.1%)	53 (1.2%)	- 42 (−1.1%)	
Total coded units of talk	**9334 (100%)**	**4328 (100%)**		

For the CC components (i.e., divergent and convergent production dialogue, and prosocial and antisocial interaction dialogue) that were found to be significantly associated with CPS task success in our analytic sample, the results of our preliminary exploratory analysis of the distribution of successful and unsuccessful teams' CC dialogic profiles point to several interesting variations in their CC talk categories (i.e., CC sub-skills) that warrant further investigation:

(i) In terms of divergent production dialogue, (a) the anti-divergent category of premature closure talk was observed to account for the largest proportion difference between successful and unsuccessful CPS teams, with the unsuccessful group engaging in substantially more of such talk, and (b) although successful teams engaged in more of all three categories of solution generation talk (i.e., epistemic, concrete and elaboration), solution elaboration was observed to account for the largest proportion difference between successful and unsuccessful teams;

(ii) In terms of convergent production dialogue, the importance of problem defining and analysis was underscored, while another interesting point of note is that among the four solution evaluation categories of talk (i.e., acquiescence, checking, critique, justification), the proportion of acquiescence talk (i.e., simple agreement with partner's solution statement) was observed to be substantially higher for successful teams than unsuccessful teams;

(iii) In terms of antisocial interaction dialogue, the successful teams engaged in lower levels of unresponsive, disaffective, and uncohesive talk (both on-task and playful off-task).

(iv) In terms of prosocial interaction dialogue, as a proportion of overall prosocial talk, successful teams were noted to engage in higher levels of reciprocal (i.e., mutual grounding-reciprocity) and cohesive on-task talk, but substantially lower levels of off-task talk albeit of a cohesive nature (i.e., cohesive-playful talk), and marginally lower levels of affective talk. We note that both cohesive-playful talk and affective talk were present in successful teams, just that these were proportionately less when compared to unsuccessful teams. This presents somewhat of a mixed finding, which is further explicated below.

Past literature has offered differing views on the CC prosocial dialogic categories pertinent to our research. Some studies have taken the stance of excluding them on the premise that they are off-task in nature and therefore, considered irrelevant to the learning at hand (e.g. Kapur 2011; Weinberger and Fischer 2006), while more recently, others have argued for its importance to students' group-level creative learning processes and performance and called for more empirical research into these forms of talk (Kangas 2010; Wegerif 2010, 2013). Given the nature of CC as our core construct of interest, we have made the purposive choice to conceptualise CC as informed by the latter school of thought (i.e., playful off-task talk being of potential value to collaborative learning and problem-solving). Earlier findings reported in our precursory study (Tan et al. 2014) indicated that off-task playful talk has the potential to contribute positively to both team cohesiveness and creativity, but disproportionate or excessive use may result in unsuccessful CPS task outcomes.

From our current study, it seems that successful teams engaged in cohesive-playful (off-task) talk but did so to a much lesser extent (as a proportion of overall prosocial interaction dialogue) than their unsuccessful peers. In other words, such playful off-task talk are not unprofitable in and of themselves and should therefore not be unequivocally written-off in terms of its value to group learning, but there appears to be a relative ratio when such talk amongst group members becomes counter-productive to CPS task success. The question of where this optimal point resides, therefore, constitutes an area for further examination.

Another area that warrants further examination is the CC metacognitive dimension. Contrary to our earlier postulation, no statistically significant association was found between the CC metacognitive dimension and CPS task success, with only a 0.6% difference in overall proportion of reflective dialogue observed for the successful and unsuccessful teams. Our preliminary exploratory examination of the metacognitive dialogic categories also reveals very similar patterns of monitoring, planning and regulation talk, as a proportion of overall reflexive dialogue. While extant research has pointed to the importance of metacognition in the collaborative and creative problem solving of ill-structured tasks (e.g., Cunningham 2009; Goos et al. 2002; Henri 1992; Larkin 2010), clear and direct empirical associations between metacognitive skills and CPS task performance appear to be more elusive, with variations in the significance of this relationship being mediated by task characteristics, such as task complexity (Stahl et al. 2006) and domain generality/specificity (Veenman and Spaans 2005). At the same time, it has been observed that many early- to middle-school students often struggle to demonstrate metacognitive proficiency skills in formal schooling contexts, even to the extent of being described as "meta-cognitively impoverished", with these "deficiencies" being largely attributed to the fact that young learners are often not encouraged to be "strategic, organised and planful in their early development" (Borkowski and Turner 1990, p. 2). In a similar vein, the absence of any significant associations between CC metacognitive dimensions and CPS success in our study may in part be related to the nature of the CPS tasks from which we drew our analytic sample, being arguably domain-general (with *Warehouse* more so than *Small Pyramids*), and less complex than authentic rich tasks involving larger teams and multiple complex solution pathways. These, however, are postulations at best and remain compelling empirical questions that warrant further research and examination.

Implications and Concluding Remarks

Our findings point to the nuanced nature of CC prosocial interaction and metacognitive skills associated with CPS success, which reveal some useful insights in relation to collaborative team-based problem solving that may be relevant to educational practice in Singapore and beyond. For example, with regard to prosocial interaction, it would be worthwhile for teachers to not simply shut down or write off the potential affordances of off-task or playful talk among students as constructive for collaborative and creative learning and problem-solving, especially if they are of a cohesive nature. Rather, it is perhaps more important to help students learn how to appropriate these forms of talk in a productive and purposeful manner, while refraining from excessive engagement in such dialogic interactions on team tasks that become imperative. In relation to metacognitive skills, we suggest that teachers may do well in being more deliberate in designing for thinking spaces within formal learning time, and scaffolding students towards more strategic planning and reflection of their learning behaviours, processes and outcomes, not only as individuals but also, importantly, as collective teams.

As empirically demonstrated by social economist Carlotta Perez in her seminal work on techno-economic paradigms and socio-institutional innovations (Perez 2010, 2012), it often takes two to three decades for policy reforms to result in observable structural shifts in the social and cultural spheres of practice. In the same way, curricular and structural reforms in education, including teacher preparation and professional learning, as well as strong articulations between rigorous research and practice, often take on complex and nonlinear trajectories and therefore require ample time, patience and commitment to the cause, before systemic shifts may be witnessed in the pedagogical and learning landscapes in schools and classrooms (Tan and Koh 2017). To this end, it is our hope that by (a) clearly articulating a dialogic framework for analysing the constitutive elements of collaborative creative capacities, and (b) providing new empirical understandings of the relationship between these CC capacities and CPS success among students, this chapter has made a modest contribution to the challenging yet compelling endeavour for our collective educational community—that of providing high quality and future-relevant educational experiences, outcomes and social trajectories for our young people, locally and globally.

Acknowledgements This paper refers to data and analysis from the research project OER59/12TPL, funded by Education Research Funding Programme, National Institute of Education, Singapore. The views expressed in this paper are the authors' and do not necessarily represent the views of the National Institute of Education, Singapore. The authors also thank Miss Christin Jonathan for her contributions as research assistant on this project.

References

Agresti, A., & Kateri, M. (2010). Categorical data analysis. In N. J. Salkind (Ed.), *Encyclopedia of research design* (pp. 206–208). Thousand Oaks: SAGE.

ATC21S. (2012). *ATC21S launch: Project background.* Melbourne: University of Melbourne. Retrieved 17 November, 2012, from http://atc21s.org/wp-content/uploads/2012/07/ATC21S-launch-PG-atc21s-background.pdf

ATC21S. (2014). *Collaborative problem-solving skills report: Singapore.* Melbourne: Assessment Research Centre.

Beghetto, R. A., & Kaufman, J. C. (2007). Toward a broader conception of creativity: A case for "mini-c" creativity. *Psychology of Aesthetics, Creativity, and the Arts, 1*(2), 73–79. https://doi.org/10.1037/1931-3896.1.2.73.

Borkowski, J. G., & Turner, L. A. (1990). Transsituational characteristics of metacognition. In*Interactions among aptitudes, strategies, and knowledge in cognitive performance* (pp. 159–176). New York: Springer.
Care, E., & Griffin, P. (2014). An approach to assessment of collaborative problem solving. *Research and Practice in Technology Enhanced Learning, 9*(3), 367–388.
Chaharbaghi, K., & Cripps, S. (2007). Collective creativity: Wisdom or oxymoron? *Journal of European Industrial Training, 31*(8), 626–638. https://doi.org/10.1108/03090590710833679.
Cheng, H. H., & Yang, H. L. (2011). Student team projects in information systems development: Measuring collective creative efficacy. *Australasian Journal of Educational Technology, 27*(6), 881–895.
Chiu, M. M. (2008). Effects of argumentation on group micro-creativity: Statistical discourse analyses of algebra students' collaborative problem solving. *Contemporary Educational Psychology, 33*(3), 382–402. https://doi.org/10.1016/j.cedpsych.2008.05.001.
Chiu, C. H., & Hsiao, H. F. (2010). Group differences in computer supported collaborative learning: Evidence from patterns of Taiwanese students' online communication. *Computers & Education, 54*(2), 427–435. https://doi.org/10.1016/j.compedu.2009.08.026.
Cho, Y. H., Lee, J., & Jonassen, D. H. (2011). The role of tasks and epistemological beliefs in online peer questioning. *Computers & Education, 56*(1), 112–126. https://doi.org/10.1016/j.compedu.2010.08.014.
Compton, D. L., Fuchs, L. S., Fuchs, D., Lambert, W., & Hamlett, C. (2012). The cognitive and academic profiles of reading and mathematics learning disabilities. *Journal of Learning Disabilities, 45*(1), 79–95. https://doi.org/10.1177/0022219410393012.
Cropley, A. J., & Cropley, D. H. (2008). Resolving the paradoxes of creativity: An extended phase model. *Cambridge Journal of Education, 38*(3), 355–373.
Cunningham, D. (2009). *Using ill-structured problems to develop metacognitive strategies*. Paper presented at the 39th Annual Conference of the International Society for Exploring Teaching and Learning (ISETL), Philadelphia, PA. Retrieved from http://citeseerx.ist.psu.edu/viewdoc/download?doi=10.1.1.552.1229&rep=rep1&type=pdf
Deng, Z., & Gopinathan, S. (2016). PISA and high-performing education systems: Explaining Singapore's education success. *Comparative Education, 52*(4), 449–472.
Dillenbourg, P., & Traum, D. (2006). Sharing solutions: Persistence and grounding in multimodal collaborative problem solving. *The Journal of the Learning Sciences, 15*(1), 121–151. https://doi.org/10.1207/s15327809jls1501_9.
Drapeau, P. (2014). *Sparking student creativity: Practical ways to promote innovative thinking and problem solving*. Alexandria: Association for Supervision & Curriculum Development.
Ferreira, D. J., & Lacerda dos Santos, G. (2009). Scaffolding online discourse in collaborative ill-structured problem-solving for innovation. *Informatics in Education-An International Journal, 8*(2), 173–190.
Goos, M., Galbraith, P., & Renshaw, P. (2002). Socially mediated metacognition: Creating collaborative zones of proximal development in small group problem solving. *Educational Studies in Mathematics, 49*(2), 193–223. https://doi.org/10.1023/A:1016209010120.
Henri, F. (1992). Computer conferencing and content analysis. In A. R. Kaye (Ed.), *Collaborative learning through computer conferencing: The Najaden papers* (pp. 117–136). Berlin: Springer-Verlag.
Hesse, F., Care, E., Buder, J., Sassenberg, K., & Griffin, P. (2015). A framework for teachable collaborative problem solving skills. In P. Griffin & E. Care (Eds.), *Assessment and teaching of 21st century skills* (pp. 37–56). Dordrecht: Springer.
Hutchby, I., & Wooffitt, R. (2008). *Conversation analysis*. Cambridge: Polity.
Jonassen, D. H. (1997). Instructional design models for well-structured and ill-structured problem-solving learning outcomes. *Educational Technology Research & Development, 45*(1), 65–94. https://doi.org/10.1007/BF02299613.
Kangas, M. (2010). Creative and playful learning: Learning through game co-creation and games in a playful learning environment. *Thinking Skills and Creativity, 5*(1), 1–15. https://doi.org/10.1016/j.tsc.2009.11.001.

Kapur, M. (2011). Temporality matters: Advancing a method for analyzing problem-solving processes in a computer-supported collaborative environment. *International Journal of Computer-Supported Collaborative Learning, 6*(1), 39–56. https://doi.org/10.1007/s11412-011-9109-9.

Krippendorff, K. (2011). *Computing Krippendorff's alpha-reliability*. Retrieved from http://repository.upenn.edu/asc_papers/43

Larkin, S. (2010). *Metacognition in young children*. Abingdon: Routledge.

Liu, M. (2012). *Power and sample size for some chi-square goodness of fit tests*. Master's thesis. Retrieved from https://esirc.emporia.edu/handle/123456789/1002

Mamykina, L., Candy, L., & Edmonds, E. (2002). Collaborative creativity. *Communications of the ACM, 45*(10), 96–99. https://doi.org/10.1145/570907.570940.

Messick, S. (1995). Standards of validity and the validity of standards in performance assessment. *Educational Measurement: Issues and Practice, 14*(4), 5–8. https://doi.org/10.1111/j.1745-3992.1995.tb00881.x.

Ministry of Education Singapore. (2009). *Government accepts recommendations on primary education- changes to be implemented progressively over the next few years*. Retrieved 22 July, 2015, from: http://www.moe.gov.sg/media/press/2009/04/government-accepts-recommendat.php

Ministry of Education Singapore. (2015). *Framework for 21CC and student outcomes*. Retrieved from https://www.moe.gov.sg/education/education-system/21st-century-competencies

Ng, P. T. (2004). Innovation and enterprise in Singapore schools. *Educational Research for Policy and Practice, 3*, 183–198. https://doi.org/10.1007/s10671-004-8240-z.

OECD. (2014). PISA 2012 results: Creative problem solving: *Students' skills in tackling real-life problems (volume V)*. Paris: OECD Publishing. https://doi.org/10.1787/9789264208070-en

Palinkas, L. A., Horwitz, S. M., Green, C. A., Wisdom, J. P., Duan, N., & Hoagwood, K. (2015). Purposeful sampling for qualitative data collection and analysis in mixed method implementation research. *Administration and Policy in Mental Health and Mental Health Services Research, 42*(5), 533–544. https://doi.org/10.1007/s10488-013-0528-y.

Patton, M. Q. (2005). Qualitative research. In B. S. Everitt & D. C. Howell (Eds.), *Encyclopedia of statistics in behavioral science* (Vol. 3). New York: Wiley.

Perez, C. (2010). Technological revolutions and techno-economic paradigms. *Cambridge Journal of Economics, 34*(1), 185–202. https://doi.org/10.1093/cje/bep05.

Perez, C. (2012). Technological revolutions and the role of government in unleashing golden ages. In L. Grinin, T. Devezas, & A. Korotayev (Eds.), *Kondratieff waves: Dimensions and prospects at the dawn of the 21st century* (pp. 211–218). Volgograd: 'Uchitel' Publishing House.

Poole, M. S., Van de Ven, A. H., Dooley, K., & Holmes, M. E. (2000). *Organizational change and innovation processes: Theory and methods for research*. New York: Oxford University Press.

Poon, C. L., Tan, S., Cheah, H. M., Lim, P. Y., & Ng, H. L. (2015). Student and teacher responses across collaborative problem solving and learning through digital networks in Singapore. In P. Griffin & E. Care (Eds.), *Assessment and teaching of 21st century skills: Methods and approach* (pp. 199–212). Dordrecht: Springer.

Resnick, L. B., Pontecorvo, C., & Säljö, R. (1997). Discourse, tools and reasoning. In L. Resnick, R. Säljö, C. Pontecorvo, & B. Burge (Eds.), *Discourse, tools and reasoning: Essays on situated cognition* (pp. 1–20). Berlin/Heidelberg: Springer.

Rosen, Y., & Foltz, P. W. (2014). Assessing collaborative problem solving through automated technologies. *Research and Practice in Technology Enhanced Learning*,, *9*(3), 389–410.

Sannino, A., & Ellis, V. (Eds.). (2013). *Learning and collective creativity: Activity-theoretical and sociocultural studies* (Vol. 101). Abingdon: Routledge.

Saye, J. W., & Brush, T. (2002). Scaffolding critical reasoning about history and social issues in multimedia-supported learning environments. *Educational Technology Research and Development, 50*(3), 77–96.

Sharpe, D. (2015). Your chi-square test is statistically significant: Now what? *Practical Assessment, Research & Evaluation, 20*(8), 1–10.

Sharpe, L., & Gopinathan, S. (2002). After effectiveness: New directions in the Singapore school system? *Journal of Education Policy, 17*(2), 151–166. https://doi.org/10.1080/02680930110116507.

Stahl, G. (2011). How a virtual math team structured its problem solving. In H. Spada, G. Stahl, N. Miyake, & N. Law (Eds.), *Connecting Computer-Supported Collaborative Learning to Policy and Practice: CSCL2011 Conference Proceedings* (Long Papers, Vol. I, pp. 256–263). International Society of the Learning Sciences.

Stahl, E., Pieschl, S., & Bromme, R. (2006). Task complexity, epistemological beliefs and metacognitive calibration: An exploratory study. *Journal of Educational Computing Research, 35*(4), 319–338. https://doi.org/10.2190/1266-0413-387K-7J51.

Strijbos, J. W., & Stahl, G. (2007). Methodological issues in developing a multi-dimensional coding procedure for small-group chat communication. *Learning and Instruction, 17*(4), 394–404.

Strijbos, J. W., Martens, R. L., Prins, F. J., & Jochems, W. M. (2006). Content analysis: What are they talking about? *Computers & Education, 46*(1), 29–48. https://doi.org/10.1016/j.compedu.2005.04.002.

Tan, J. P.-L., & Koh, E. (2017). Situating learning analytics pedagogically: Towards an ecological lens. *Learning: Research and Practice, 3*(1), 1–11. https://doi.org/10.1080/23735082.2017.1305661.

Tan, J. P.-L., & Nie, Y. Y. (2015). The role of authentic tasks in promoting 21st century learning dispositions in mathematics. In Y. H. Cho, I. S. Caleon, & M. Kapur (Eds.), *Authentic problem solving and learning in the 21st century* (pp. 19–39). Singapore: Springer.

Tan, J. P.-L., Caleon, I. S., Jonathan, C. R., & Koh, E. (2014). A dialogic framework for assessing collective creativity in computer-supported collaborative problem-solving tasks. *Research and Practice in Technology Enhanced Learning, 9*(3), 411–437.

Tan, J. P.-L., Koh, E., Chan, M., Costes-Onishi, P., & Hung, D. (2017). *Advancing 21st century competencies in Singapore*. Asia Society: Center for Global Education. Available: http://asiasociety.org/files/21st-century-competencies-singapore.pdf

Tan, S. C., So, H. J., & Chai, C. S. (2011). Methodological considerations for quantitative content analysis of online interactions. In B. K. Daniel (Ed.), *Handbook of research on methods and techniques for studying virtual communities: Paradigms and phenomena* (pp. 611–630). Hershey: IGI Global. https://doi.org/10.4018/978-1-60960-040-2.ch037.

Treffinger, D. J., Isaksen, S. G., & Stead-Dorval, K. B. (2006). *Creative problem solving: An introduction* (4th ed.). Austin: Prufrock Press Inc.

Veenman, M. V. J., & Spaans, M. A. (2005). Relation between intellectual and metacognitive skills: Age and task differences. *Learning and Individual Differences, 15*(2), 159–176. https://doi.org/10.1016/j.lindif.2004.12.001.

Wang, J., Farooq, U., & Carroll, J. M. (2010). *Creative collective efficacy in scientific communities*. In *Proceedings of COOP 2010* (pp. 331-351). London: Springer.

Weatherall, A. (2015). Sexism in language and talk-in-interaction. *Journal of Language and Social Psychology, 34*(4), 410–426. https://doi.org/10.1177/0261927x15586574.

Wegerif, R. (2010). *Dialogic education and technology: Expanding the space of learning*. New York: Springer.

Wegerif, R. (2013). *Dialogic: Education for the internet age*. London: Routledge.

Weinberger, A., & Fischer, F. (2006). A framework to analyze argumentative knowledge construction in computer-supported collaborative learning. *Computers & Education, 46*(1), 71–95. https://doi.org/10.1016/j.compedu.2005.04.003.

Weisberg, R. W. (2006). *Creativity: Understanding innovation in problem solving, science, invention, and the arts*. New York: Wiley.

Chapter 7
Collaborative Problem Solving in Finnish Pre-service Teacher Education: A Case Study

Arto K. Ahonen, Päivi Häkkinen, and Johanna Pöysä-Tarhonen

Abstract This chapter provides results from a case study utilising tasks from the ATC21S™ assessment portal in the context of pre-service teacher education in Finland. The results from the portal are combined with a questionnaire regarding dispositions towards teamwork and collaboration. Twenty-four pre-service teachers completed both these measures. The students of this study were following two divergent teacher education programs that had different profiles in terms of their study contents and methods. The participants of both groups tended to be highly disposed to collaborate and work in teams, and their collaborative problem solving skills can be described as very good. The participants' measured social skills and self-assessed disposition to negotiate in the collaborative processes were strongly associated.

Introduction

Finnish teachers are highly educated professionals. Whereas the traditional lecturing role of a teacher is still seen as essential, there are also many other roles, such as guidance and collaboration with other professionals, that are coming to be seen as more important parts of the teachers' profession in Finland (Krokfors et al. 2010). However, as noted in the ITL (Innovative Teaching and Learning) study (Norrena 2013), even though twenty-first century skills are recognised and mentioned in the curricula of Finnish comprehensive schools, the schools and, especially, individual teachers vary greatly in their ability to facilitate the development of twenty-first century skills. The teachers consider teaching twenty-first century skills to be difficult (e.g. Niemi 2012) and it is generally up to individual teachers' discretion whether they include elements of innovative teaching and learning in their instruction. Therefore, teacher education units have a central role in contributing to this pedagogical evolution. Teacher education focused on developing twenty-first century skills has the potential, with a research-based curriculum and carefully designed

---

A.K. Ahonen (✉) • P. Häkkinen • J. Pöysä-Tarhonen
Finnish Institute for Educational Research, University of Jyväskylä, Jyväskylä, Finland
e-mail: arto.k.ahonen@jyu.fi

E. Care et al. (eds.), *Assessment and Teaching of 21st Century Skills*,
Educational Assessment in an Information Age,
DOI 10.1007/978-3-319-65368-6_7

learning practices, to provide new teachers entering schools with a better foundation to meet the many challenges of twenty-first century learning environments (see Kong et al. 2013).

The Finnish national interest in fostering twenty-first century skills has highlighted a need for – and interest in the development of – tools and methods for teaching and assessing such skills. Assessment in Finland is often formative, based on constant evaluation of an individual student's development in different subjects. In addition, the changes in the Finnish school curriculum in August 2016 towards phenomenon-based instruction with an emphasis on more interdisciplinary and generic skills and competencies have created a need for new forms of assessment. In this regard, technology-enhanced systems that enable formative assessment of complex performances involving collaboration are becoming more essential (Binkley et al. 2012; Van Aalst 2013).

Finland's participation in the ATC21S project was a step towards better understanding of the assessment of more complex skills. While today's international and national standards primarily measure core subject performance (in math, science and reading), ATC21S designed new assessment prototypes to help education systems include the twenty-first century skills that are essential to performing better in those core subjects. Finding technical solutions to meet schools' everyday pedagogical goals is an interesting and ongoing challenge. The work done in the ATC21S project continued as part of the "Preparing teacher students for 21st century learning practices", PREP21 project (Häkkinen et al. 2017; PREP21 2015; Pöysä-Tarhonen et al. 2016). The purposes of this study are, firstly, to acquire better understanding about the Finnish early stage pre-service teachers' dispositions towards teamwork and collaboration and, secondly, to assess their existing level of collaborative problem solving skills by using the novel technology-enhanced assessment system of the ATC21S portal.

By linking the students' dispositions and self-assessments to objectively measured levels on learning progressions of collaborative problem solving, the aim is to investigate existing connections and disconnections between these measures and answer the following research questions:

1. What is the current level of collaborative problem solving skill among the two selected groups of pre-service teachers?
2. What kind of relation exists between teacher education students' collaboration and teamwork dispositions and assessed collaborative problem solving skills?

Method

Participants and Context of Study

The participants of the study were second-year teacher education students (n = 24, 21 female, 3 male) from one Finnish University. The teacher training program of this university follows phenomenon- and inquiry-based learning approaches. The phenomenon-based curriculum integrates, for example, the study of educational science and research methods into inquiry-based study projects. In addition to the phenomenon-based approach, all the students study in home groups. Different home groups have different profiles in terms of their study contents and methods. The students of this study were following two divergent teacher education programs in their home groups. Common for both of these programs was that they apply phenomenon-based, collaborative modes of studying and their students are, hence, supposed to be experienced in engaging in productive collaborative activities, including collaborative problem-solving activities. Study projects with schools are also included in both of these study programs. Active agency for own learning is emphasized in these study programs in terms of both students' own studying and in promoting pupils' learning at school.

Group A consisted of 12 students from a study program specializing in technology-enhanced learning (TEL). The goal of this group was to envision and experiment with the use of learning technologies with students in school settings. Hence, these students use also in their own studies multiple tools and technologies (e.g. personal mobile devices/tablets, social media, games) for individual access, manipulation and analysis of information as well as for communication, sharing and joint knowledge construction with peers. In comparison to group B, group A utilized the phenomenon-based approach more thoroughly and participated only minimally in traditional lectures. Another dimension that was more present in group A was collaborative 'teachership.' The aim in this program is to model collaborative teaching for students by coaching and supervising them as a team of teacher educators. In distinguishing the two groups, we called group A the "Technology" group.

Group B consisted of 12 students following a program focusing on STEM-related themes, especially in science and mathematics. This group relied on the inquiry-based curriculum but also participated in lectures more than group A. Although this group had an emphasis on communities of teachers, they were not given a model of collaborative teachership in their own studies. They had only one teacher at a time guiding their studies. We called this group the "Inquiry" group.

Measures

To assess the pre-service teachers' CPS skills from different perspectives, two measures were combined. First, a PREP21 self-report questionnaire was used. A set of questions based on the work of Wang et al. (2009), also applied as part of the PISA 2015 background questionnaire, was created to measure dispositions towards cooperation, negotiation and guidance. In this approach, these student dispositions are defined as general attitudes towards collaboration, collaborative problem solving and teamwork. Dispositions refer, thus, to students' broader attitudes, beyond any particular collaborative learning situations or contexts. Accordingly, these dispositions are supposed to predict students' performance in collaborative problem-solving activities (OECD 2017). Also, obtaining a better understanding of teamwork as a set of skills and dispositions provides the grounds for deeper exploration of how students may acquire these skills and how instruction could be better designed to assist students in developing and applying these skills in professional settings (Hughes and Jones 2011).

The items referring to students' dispositions towards collaboration, collaborative problem solving and teamwork were scored on a 7-point Likert-type scale, from 1 (not at all true of me) to 7 (very true of me). The subscales were based on responses to a PREP21 survey of a larger sample (N = 263) of Finnish pre-service teachers. For the internal consistency of measured subscales, Cronbach alpha was used. The reliabilities were measured as ($\alpha = 0.74$) for the Cooperation subscale and ($\alpha = 0.75$) for the Guidance and Negotiation subscales. These can be considered adequate reliabilities of scale (Nunnally 1978). First, negotiation is seen as a central element of teamwork, because an individual needs to negotiate and adjust his/her actions according to the surrounding group. The Negotiation subscale comprises variables related with the ability to listen to others, flexibility and openness to others' thoughts and ideas. *Negotiation* was measured with six items: "I am a good listener"; "I enjoy seeing my classmates be successful"; "I take into account what others are interested in"; "I am flexible when working with a team"; "I enjoy considering different perspectives"; "I am open to all sorts of opinions". The subscale of *Guidance* includes the teacher education students' dispositions towards their skills to guide and mentor their other team members. The disposition of guidance was measured with six items: "I like to be in charge of groups or projects"; "I enjoy sharing ideas"; "I convince others to see things my way"; "I enjoy exchanging ideas"; "I like convincing peers"; "I enjoy bringing a team together". The subscale of *Cooperation* includes teacher education students' dispositions towards working together as a team. Cooperation was measured with four items: "I prefer working as part of a team to working alone"; "I find that teams make better decisions than individuals"; "I find that teamwork raises my own efficiency"; "I enjoy cooperating with peers".

In addition to the survey of dispositions towards collaboration and teamwork, an assessment portal, ATC21S, was used to assess the students' skills over the course of CPS activities. Each pair of students completed one bundle of five assessment tasks over a period of 90 min. Group A completed Laughing Clowns, Plant growth, Balance, Olive oil and Game of 20. For Group B, Game of 20 was replaced by Small pyramids. These tasks have been described by Care et al. (2015). They are complex game-like tasks, mainly in the science and math domains, related both to curriculum content and to generic skills. The participating pairs proceeded well in the assessment. All of them could either enter or finish the last task (Game of 20 or Small pyramids). Moreover, in the ATC21S portal, students' completion of the assessment tasks yielded log file data. The data generated were captured in a process stream data file, and patterns in these data were automatically coded as indicators of the CPS elements (Adams et al. 2015; Hesse et al. 2015). Furthermore, the tasks captured social and cognitive components of students' CPS skills. Each of the skills could thus be scaled based on the actions taken by the students, which were collected as process data, together with the online chat discussions that took place while performing CPS tasks.

The scoring itself took into consideration students' actions as they moved through the tasks. The process data consisted of distinct keystrokes and mouse events that indicated exploration of the task environment, such as typing, clicking, dragging, cursor movements, hovering time and action sequences, all of which explicitly demonstrated students' thinking processes and skill levels. The log file data from the assessment tasks were processed by the Assessment Research Centre of the University of Melbourne. All of the user actions and chat messages were recorded and time-stamped. The files generated for the automatic records of student-task interactions are referred to as session log files (Adams et al. 2015). Next, MySQL database architecture was used to record the interactions within the task environment. The scoring engine then automatically coded and scored data to produce reports for teacher and student use. Figure 7.1 provides an example of the reports on social and cognitive skills retrieved from the portal. This particular student (fifprr0002a) was estimated at a Level 5 for her cognitive skills and a Level 6 for her social skills.

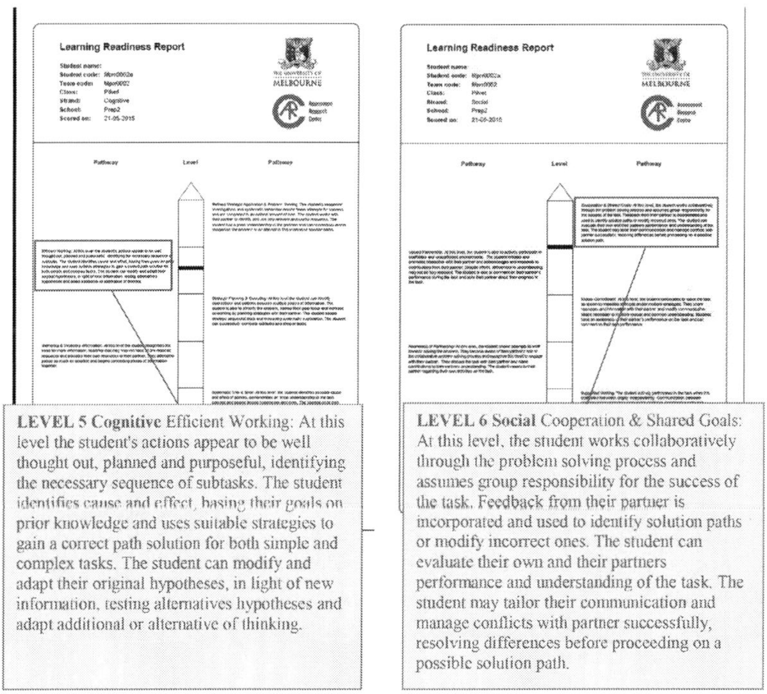

Fig. 7.1 Learning readiness reports from ATC21S™ portal: cognitive and social skills

Table 7.1 Range of WLE scores in the ATC21S portal corresponding to the learning readiness levels

Level of learning progression	WLE range social 2D1	WLE range cognitive 2D2
1	Below −1.3	Below −3.5
2	−1.3 between −0.7	−3.5 between −0.8
3	−0.7 between −0.5	−0.8 between 0.5
4	−0.5 between 0.3	0.5 between 1.7
5	0.3 between 1.5	1.7 between 2.1
6	above 1.5	above 2.1

Data Analysis

Scores on respondents' skill level estimates were firstly drawn from the ATC21S assessment portal by utilising the Rasch modelling on the ConQuest™program (Wu 2007), a multi-aspect test software. All analysis was performed with ConQuest™, using a Partial Credit model with Guass-Hermite Quadrature estimation with 15 nodes. These skill level estimates were then used to create the skill level reports. In accordance with the procedures of Rasch modelling, the average of the task scores was set to zero and the difficulty of the item was presented as an estimate describing the level of the students based on their results on the bundle of tasks they had completed. Each student received a Weighted Likelihood Estimate score (WLE), which could vary from −4 to 4 on both social and cognitive dimensions. The report displays are based on the Weighted Likelihood Estimate scores (WLE) distributed on different levels of learning progression, presented in Table 7.1.

The participants were analysed as two separate groups based on their study group. SPSS v 22 was then used to investigate confidence intervals (using T-tests), descriptive statistics and correlation in the whole set of data and between the two groups. The statistical significance of mean differences was tested using one way analysis of variance. Due to the small sample size, the correlations were calculated with non-parametric Spearman's rho. We used general criteria to interpret the correlation coefficients: 0.10–0.29 for weak, 0.3–0.49 for moderate, 0.5–0.69 for strong, and above 0.7 for very strong associations between variables (c.f., Cohen 1988).

Results

The descriptive statistics for the scores received from the ATC21S assessments and PREP21 questionnaire dispositions for all participants are presented in Table 7.2. The ATC21S WLE scores are presented separately for social and cognitive skills. Pre-service teacher students' social skills were reported with a mean of 1.92 (SD = 0.65), which falls in the highest level of learning progression: Level 6. Their

Table 7.2 Descriptive statistics, 95 % confidence interval of difference, Spearman's rho

Measured skills		Descriptive						One sample T-test			
		Items	Scale	Min–max	*M*	*SD*	*CI*	1	2	3	4
1	WLE Social	1	−4–4	0.71–3.85	1.92	0.65	[1.64, 2.19]				
2	WLE Cognitive	1	−4–4	−0.39–3.38	1.62	1.02	[1.19, 2.05]	0.57**			
3	GUIDANCE	6	1–7	4.0–6.67	5.32	0.65	[5.05, 5.60]	0.19	0.17		
4	COOPERATION	6	1–7	2.25–7.0	5.25	1.24	[4.72, 5.78]	0.15	−0.13	0.48*	
5	NEGOTIATION	4	1–7	3.33–6.83	6.08	0.75	[5.77, 6.40]	0.57**	0.00	0.41*	0.57**

$N = 24$. **$p < 0.01$, *$p < 0.05$

cognitive skills were reported with a mean of 1.62 (SD = 1.02), which falls in Level 4 of learning progression. The level of social skills was fairly consistent at the very top level, but cognitive skill levels varied and were overall at lower level compared to social skills. The dispositions from the PREP21 questionnaire were at a rather high level. The mean of *Guidance* was 5.32 (SD = 0.65), the mean of *Cooperation* was 5.25 (SD = 1.24) and the mean of *Negotiation* was the highest, at 6.08 (SD = 0.75) on a scale of 1 to 7. Due to the small sample size, and the fact that the sample responses were not normally distributed, correlations were calculated with non-parametric Spearman's rho. *Negotiation* correlated significantly and positively ($r = 0.57$) with the ATC21S social skills WLE score. ATC21S cognitive skills WLE score did not have statistically significant correlations on any measured variables. The disposition variables also correlated significantly with each other. Negotiation correlated strongly ($r = 0.57$) with cooperation and moderately ($r = 0.41$) with guidance. Also cooperation correlated moderately ($r = 0.41$) with guidance.

Due to the small number of respondents, it was also possible to examine each student's scores and dispositions individually, based on their study groups. Table 7.3 presents these individual measures separately. The WLE scores were indicated as levels of learning readiness based on Rasch modeling of the item difficulties. There were no significant differences in the mean scores between the two groups of pre-service teachers. Still, group A "Technology" scores were more consistent, with lower standard deviations on both social and cognitive WLEs when compared to group B "Inquiry". Group A students also generally indicated slightly higher dispositions than group B students. But only on negotiation was the difference statistically significant ($p < 0.05$), where the group A mean was 6.40 and the group B mean was 5.76. When Social skills WLE are associated with negotiation dispositions, it can be interpreted that students from both groups utilized their negotiation capacity well in the social processes of collaborative problem solving. When examining the dispositions on individual level, it is possible to recognise that four students from group B indicated their negotiation dispositions below 6 and two below 5. In group A, only one student's dispositions were below 6. When examining the results of individual student ID 5a, it can be seen that her social skills WLE were measured on the lowest level (1.29) in group A. When examining the results of individual students from group B it can also be seen that student ID 21a had reported her dispositions as rather low on cooperation (3.00) and negotiation (3.33), which are actually the lowest ratings of all. Her skills were also measured as the lowest with ATC21S. In this particular case the ATC21S measurement and student's own dispositions met exceptionally well. Still, this particular students' pair ID 21b had very high ratings on the portal, where both her social and cognitive skills were measured at the very top level. Despite her high measured skills, her dispositions did not indicate high expectations regarding her skills on teamwork and collaboration when compared to other high scoring students. The only clear difference, when compared to her pair 21a, was that her dispositions on negotiation were clearly higher (4.67). This indicates that negotiation dispositions were clearly associated with this student's measured social skills.

Table 7.3 Individual portal scores and dispositions

Group A technology						Group B inquiry					
ID	Soc WLE (level)	Cog WLE (level)	COOP	GUID	NEGO	ID	Soc WLE (level)	Cog WLE (level)	COOP	GUID	NEGO
Mean (SD)	1.97 (0.42)	1.54 (0.63)	5.71 (1.02)	5.49 (0.59)	6.40* (0.31)		1.86 (0.84)	1.70 (1.32)	4.79 (1.30)	5.17 (0.69)	5.76* (0.97)
2a	1.77(6)	1.93(5)	4.00	5.00	6.00	19a	1.22(5)	0.11(3)	5.50	4.83	6.17
2b	2.19(6)	1.51(4)	6.00	6.00	6.67	19b	1.79(6)	1.36(4)	4.50	5.50	6.33
3a	2.58(6)	1.28(4)	7.00	5.50	6.83	20a	1.52(6)	3.38(6)	5.00	5.33	5.33
3b	2.14(6)	1.66(4)	5.50	5.83	6.50	20b	1.86(6)	3.31(6)	5.25	5.00	5.83
4a	2.25(6)	1.93(5)	6.25	4.33	6.33	**21a**	**0.71(5)**	**−0.39(3)**	**2.25**	**4.50**	**3.33**
4b	2.14(6)	1.80(5)	5.75	6.17	6.17	**21b**	**2.07(6)**	**3.19(6)**	**3.00**	**5.00**	**4.67**
5a	**1.29(5)**	**0.81(4)**	**5.50**	**5.00**	**5.83**	22a	3.85(6)	3.38(6)	6.25	6.67	6.33
5b	1.86(6)	0.85(4)	7.00	5.00	6.67	22b	1.41(5)	1.02(4)	6.00	5.50	6.17
6a	1.94(6)	1.54(4)	6.00	6.33	6.67	23a	1.67(6)	1.45(4)	4.00	4.67	6.17
6b	1.62(6)	2.50(6)	6.00	5.83	6.33	23b	1.31(5)	0.95(4)	6.75	5.83	6.33
7a	1.35(5)	0.38(3)	6.00	5.67	6.17	24a	3.05(6)	1.81(5)	4.50	4.00	6.33
7b	2.54(6)	2.32(6)	3.50	5.17	6.67	24b	1.86(6)	0.91(4)	4.50	5.17	6.17

Note. *the mean difference between groups A and B is statistically significant $p < 0.05$

Discussion and Conclusions

Recent developments in technology-enhanced assessments have made it possible to evaluate complex performance such as collaborative problem solving more effectively. In this study, we used the ATC21S to assess teacher education students' collaborative problem-solving skills and a PREP21 self-report instrument to measure more general collaboration and teamwork dispositions. The results indicate that the current level of collaborative problem-solving skills among these students is generally high; measured levels of social skills were especially high, as compared to cognitive skills. Social skills were also connected positively with collaboration and teamwork dispositions – in particular with negotiation. However, the cognitive skills scores did not correlate with teamwork and collaboration dispositions. This indicates that the social aspect of collaborative problem solving is probably the key for success in these kinds of shared tasks.

The respondents were representing two different study groups with slightly different implementation of their study programs. Group A "Technology" focused particularly on technology-enhanced learning, and group B "Inquiry" followed the STEM-related program. Common to both of these programs is that they apply collaborative modes of studying. It can be assumed that these students have been trained to be more familiar with productive forms of collaboration and collaborative problem solving than an average group of students. As compared to group B, group A had a slightly stronger focus on phenomenon-based curriculum, with hardly any lectures in their studies. Furthermore, they also received a model of collaborative teaching as they were coached and supervised by a team of teacher educators.

Group A "Technology" had consistently higher results on social skills when compared to group B "Inquiry". Both groups had higher social skills than cognitive skills, but there were no significant mean differences between the groups. The finding that negotiation had statistically significant and positive correlation with social skills WLE scores measured by ATC21S supports the assumption that there is an empirical connection between these two independent measures.

Given the adaptations that a society based on knowledge and competence demands from school pedagogy, it must be remembered that teacher education needs to be adjusted to meet the challenges. Pre-service teachers have a central role in developing twenty-first century learning practices and promoting skills such as collaborative problem solving in future schools. In Finland, autonomy is typical for the teaching profession, which also means that teachers often work too independently, sometimes alone. As the skills to solve complex, cross-curricular problems in teams become more important in our society, teachers should acquire these skills also by themselves. In general, the adoption of new pedagogical innovations has been unsuccessful, primarily because too little attention has been paid to teacher's' own learning processes (Lieberman and Pointer Mace 2008). Thus, we argue that the task of teacher education is to guide these processes.

Pre-service teachers are themselves the result of traditional school culture, which strongly influences their assumptions regarding good teaching models (i.e., favouring models featuring a traditional teacher-led approach) (Mäkitalo-Siegl et al. 2011;

Schratzenstaller 2010; Webb and Mastergeorge 2003). We believe that pre-service teacher education could be a powerful means of sparking long-term change in the field. To create change in schooling, pre-service teachers first need to learn how to adapt to the new learning culture. One of the specific aims of the PREP21 project is to outline the analysis and pedagogical designs regarding students' collaborative problem solving skills and the related pedagogical practices in pre-service teacher training programs. Based on this experimental study it can be inferred that skills needed in successful collaborative problem solving measured by ATC21S benefit from collaborative practices of instructional methods in teacher training. Using this web-based portal to measure collaborative problem solving in the pre-service teacher education context was the first pilot in advancing the assessment of students' complex skills. It can be concluded that these tasks are welcome and well suited to pre-service teacher training.

In research to follow, we will apply ATC21S assessments in the context of teacher education on a wider scale, in which the assessment session is followed by debriefing of students' scores. With larger numbers of respondents, we will examine the interesting associations between teamwork dispositions, self-assessment and ATC21S. In addition, by monitoring the performance of students during the tasks by applying online measures of their performance (e.g. by capturing screen activity) and combining it with subjective data (e.g. cued retrospective interviews) (see Pöysä-Tarhonen et al. 2016) we might be able to better understand the individual differences monitored over the course of this study.

Acknowledgements We would like to thank Mrs. Anne Martin for her help on the data collection of the study. We would also like to thank the lecturers of teacher training, in whose classes the portal assessment took place. This study has been funded by the Academy of Finland (project no 273970).

References

Adams, R., Vista, A., Scoular, Awwal, N., Griffin, P., & Care, E. (2015). Automatic coding procedures. In P. Griffin & E. Care (Eds.), *Assessment and teaching of 21st century skills. Methods and approach* (pp. 115–132). Dordrecht: Springer.

Binkley, M., Erstad, O., Herman, J., Raizen, S., Ripley, M., Miller-Ricci, M., & Rumble, M. (2012). Defining 21st-century skills. In P. Griffin, B. McGaw, & E. Care (Eds.), *Assessment and teaching of 21st century skills* (pp. 17–66). Dordrecht: Springer.

Care, E., Griffin, P., Scoular, C., Awwal, N., & Zoanetti, N. (2015). Collaborative problem solving tasks. In P. Griffin & E. Care (Eds.), *Assessment and teaching of 21st century skills. Methods and approach* (pp. 85–104). Dordrecht: Springer.

Cohen, J. (1988). *Statistical power analysis for the behavioral sciences* (2nd ed.). New Jersey: Lawrence Erlbaum.

Häkkinen, P., Järvelä, S., Mäkitalo-Siegl, K., Ahonen, A. K., Näykki, P., & Valtonen, T. (2017). Preparing teacher students for 21st century learning practices: A framework for enhancing collaborative problem solving and strategic learning skills. *Teachers and Teaching: Theory and Practice, 23*(1), 25–41. http://dx.doi.org/ 10.1080/13540602.2016.1203772.

Hesse, H., Care, E., Buder, J., Sassenberg, K., & Griffin, P. (2015). A framework for teachable collaborative problem solving skills. In P. Griffin & E. Care (Eds.), *Assessment and teaching of 21st century skills. Methods and approach* (pp. 37–56). Dordrecht: Springer.

Hughes, R. L., & Jones, S. K. (2011). Developing and assessing college student teamwork skills. *New Directions for Institutional Research, 149*, 53–64. http://dx.doi.org/10.1002/ir.380.

Kong, S. C., Chan, T. W., Griffin, P., Hoppe, U., Huang, R., Kinshuk, & Yu, S. (2013). E-learning in school education in the coming 10 years for developing 21st century skills: Critical research issues and policy implications. *Educational Technology and Society, 17*(1), 70–78.

Krokfors, L., Kangas, M., Vitikka, E., & Mylläri, J. (2010). Näkökulmia tulevaisuuden koulupedagogiikkaan [Insights into future school pedagogy]. In R. Smeds, L. Krokfors, H. Ruokamo, & A. Staffans (Eds.), *InnoSchool – välittävä koulu. Oppimisen verkostot, ympäristöt ja pedagogiikka* (pp. 51–85). Espoo: Aalto yliopisto.

Lieberman, A., & Pointer Mace, D. H. (2008). Teacher Learning: The key to educational reform. *Journal of Teacher Education, 59*(3), 226–234.

Mäkitalo-Siegl, K., Kohnle, C., & Fischer, F. (2011). Computer-supported collaborative inquiry learning and classroom scripts: Effects on help-seeking processes and learning outcomes. *Learning and Instruction, 21*(2), 257–266. http://dx.doi.org/10.1016/j.learninstruc.2010.07.001.

Niemi, E. K. (2012). Opettajakysely. In E. K. Niemi (Ed.), *Aihekokonaisuuksien tavoitteiden toteutumisen seuranta-arviointi 2010 [Evaluation of the fulfilment of cross-curricular themes], Koulutuksen seurantaraportit 2012:1* (pp. 19–39). Helsinki: Opetushallitus.

Norrena, J. (2013). *Opettaja tulevaisuuden taitojen edistäjänä: "jos haluat opettaa noita taitoja, sinun on ensin hallittava ne itse"* [Teacher enhancing the skills for the future: "If you are going to teach them, you have to know them yourself"] (Jyväskylä Studies in Computing, Vol. 169). Jyväskylä: University of Jyväskylä.

Nunnally, J. C. (1978). *Psychometric theory*. New York: McGraw-Hill.

OECD. (2017). *Draft PISA 2015 collaborative problem solving framework*. Retrieved from http://www.oecd.org/pisa/pisaproducts/Draft PISA 2015 Collaborative Problem Solving Framework.pdf

Pöysä-Tarhonen, J., Care, E., Awwal, N., Häkkinen, P., & Ahonen, A. (2016). Tracking student teachers' technology-enhanced collaborative problem solving: Combining objective assessment data with subjective verbal reporting. In C.-K. Looi, J. Polman, U. Cress, & P. Reimann (Eds.), *Transforming learning, empowering learners: The 12th International Conference of the Learning Sciences (ICLS) 2016* (Vol. 2, pp. 839–842). International Society of the Learning Sciences. https://www.isls.org/icls/2016/docs/ICLS2016_Volume_2.pdf

PREP21. (2015). Prep21 Blog. Preparing teacher students for 21st century learning practices. Retrieved from https://prep21.wordpress.com/about/.

Schratzenstaller, A. (2010). The classroom of the past. In K. Mäkitalo-Siegl, J. Zottmann, F. Kaplan, & F. Fischer (Eds.), *Classroom of the future: Orchestrating collaborative spaces* (pp. 15–39). Rotterdam: Sense Publishers.

Van Aalst, J. (2013). Assessment in collaborative learning. In C. E. Hmelo-Silver, C. A. Chinn, C. K. K. Chan, & A. O'Donnell (Eds.), *The international handbook of collaborative learning* (pp. 280–296). New York: Routledge.

Wang, L., MacCann, C., Zhuang, X., Liu, O. L., & Roberts, R. D. (2009). Assessing teamwork and collaboration in high school students: A multimethod approach. *Canadian Journal of School Psychology, 24*(2), 108–124. http://dx.doi.org/10.1177/0829573509335470.

Webb, N. M., & Mastergeorge, A. (2003). Promoting effective helping behaviour in peer-directed groups. *International Journal of Educational Research, 39*(1–2), 73–97.

Wu, M. L., Adams, R. J., & Wilson, M. R. (2007). *ACER ConQuest version 2.0: Generalised item response modelling software*. Melbourne: ACER Press.

Chapter 8
A Twenty-First Century Skills Lens on the Common Core State Standards and the Next Generation Science Standards

Kathleen B. Comfort and Michael Timms

Abstract The changing natures of technology, competition in the global job market, and college and career readiness have impacted the skills and knowledge that young people need to be successful in today's global economy (Trilling B, Fadel C, Royal society for the encouragement of arts, manufactures and commerce journal. A game of skills. What talents do young people need to thrive in the 21st century?, 2012). In the United States, the *Common Core State Standards* (CCSS) and the *Next Generation Science Standards* (NGSS) provide an opportunity to transform education standards to be more aligned with the needs of today's world. By the end of 12th grade, all students should possess sufficient knowledge of science to engage in public discussion of related issues, be careful consumers of scientific and technological information related to their everyday lives, and have the skills to enter a career of their choice, including but not limited to careers in STEM (NRC, A framework for K-12 science education: practices, crosscutting concepts, and core ideas. The National Academies Press, Washington, DC, 2012b). The National Research Council's (NRC) *Science Framework for K-12 Science Education* (2012b) lays out an agenda that can begin to reshape what students need to know and be able to cultivate as twenty-first century leaders in science and citizenship. Furthermore, it has become evident that strong linkages between twenty-first century skills and scientific and engineering practices will provide insight into deeper learning of STEM content and to certain clusters of twenty-first century skills (NRC, Education for life

K.B. Comfort (✉)
WestEd, Redwood City, CA, USA
e-mail: kcomfor@wested.org

M. Timms
Australian Council for Educational Research, Melbourne, Australia

E. Care et al. (eds.), *Assessment and Teaching of 21st Century Skills*, Educational Assessment in an Information Age,
DOI 10.1007/978-3-319-65368-6_8

and work: developing transferable knowledge and skills in the 21st century. The National Academies Press, Washington, DC, 2012a).

Introduction

The world has changed dramatically over the last century, and experts maintain that this change is as big as the shift from the Agriculture Age to the Industrial Age more than 350 years ago. This time, the shift is from an Industrial Age to an Information and Knowledge Age where information, knowledge, expertise, and innovation are increasingly the main engines of our economy (Trilling and Fadel 2009, 2012). In today's digital age, jobs migrate around the globe and land with highly skilled individuals. It is more important than ever to equip young people with twenty-first century skills and to ensure that they can apply these skills to real-world challenges (Trilling and Fadel 2012). A recent Gallup study of Americans aged 18–35 found that "those with high 21st century skill development are twice as likely to have higher work quality compared to those who had low 21st century skill development" (Gallup 2013, p. 4).

Current research is showing that the trend in demands for twenty-first century skill competencies is clearly growing. The labor market demand for increased years of schooling has risen noticeably over the past four decades (NRC 2012a). The labor market now requires that students attain levels of mastery across multiple areas of skills and knowledge that were previously unnecessary for individual success in education and the workplace (NRC 2012a). The global economy's need for different worker competencies has considerably shifted over time with blue collar jobs declining from nearly one-third of all jobs in 1979 to only one-fifth of all jobs in 2009. White-collar jobs, such as administrative support positions, were also noted to seriously decline within this same time period (Autor et al. 2008). According to Levy and Murnane (2004) the demand is growing for expert thinking (non-routine problem solving) and complex communication competencies (non-routine interactive skills). They predict that in the future, jobs requiring low or moderate levels of competencies will continue to decline, and recommend that schools teach twenty-first century skills such as complex communication and non-routine problem solving to all students (Levy and Murnane 2004). However, current research shows that students are not learning twenty-first century skills because teachers are not teaching them (Saavedra and Opfer 2012).

While we recognize that the teaching and learning of twenty-first century skills is a global issue that spans the curriculum, in this chapter, we explore it through the lens of STEM education in the USA as a case study that we hope will be of general relevance to other countries and subject areas.

Why Students Are Not Learning Twenty-first Century Skills

The dominant approach to compulsory education in much of the world is still the transmission model through which teachers transmit factual knowledge to students through lectures and textbooks (RAND 2012; Schleicher 2012). Students have the opportunity to learn information through the transmission model, but typically do not have much practice applying the knowledge to new contexts, communicating it in complex ways, using it to solve problems, or using it as a platform to develop creativity (RAND 2012). Experts agree that this is not the most effective way to teach twenty-first century skills (Boix-Mansilla and Jackson 2011; Schwartz and Fischer 2006; Tishman et al. 1993). A second obstacle to students' development of twenty-first century skills is that they do not learn them unless they are explicitly taught, and these skills are not typically taught in separate stand-alone courses. Most teachers do not have sufficient experience teaching twenty-first century skills to have developed the deep expertise needed to train others.

In the United States, the Common Core State Standards (CCSS) in Mathematics and English language arts (NGA and CCSSO 2010 a, b) and the Next Generation Science Standards (NGSS States 2013) established high expectations for K-12 education. The CCSS prepares students to be lifelong learners in a technology-driven world. While the English language arts standards place greater emphasis on the use of text evidence to support complex, real world thinking, the mathematics standards encourage deeper understanding of core concepts and the use of skills and knowledge to solve real-world problems (NGA and CCSSO 2010b).

The Next Generation Science Standards (NGSS) integrate scientific disciplinary core ideas with scientific and engineering practices and crosscutting concepts. At the core of the intersection is a new definition of what it means to be competent in science. This new definition requires students to engage in arguments, develop and use models, explain phenomena, and prove a position based on evidence (NRC 2012b). Since literary skills and mathematics are essential to building understanding and knowledge in science, the CCSS are closely linked to the NGSS (NGSS Lead States 2013). The Venn diagram of Fig. 8.1 shows the relationship and convergences found in the student practices for CCSS for English language art and mathematics and the NGSS scientific and engineering practices (Lee et al. 2013).

The changing natures of technology, competition in the global job market, and college and career readiness have impacted the skills and knowledge that young people need to succeed in today's global economy. It is more important than ever to equip young people with twenty-first century skills to ensure that they can apply these skills to real world challenges (Trilling and Fadel 2012). Survival and success will require students to possess sufficient aptitude in critical thinking and problem solving, collaboration across networks, and curiosity and imagination (Wagner 2010).

Over the last decade, several efforts have been underway in the U.S. to incorporate twenty-first century skills in various educational efforts. The Partnership for Twenty-First Century Skills (P21), in conjunction with states and business partners, has designed and implemented tools and resources for twenty-first century skills

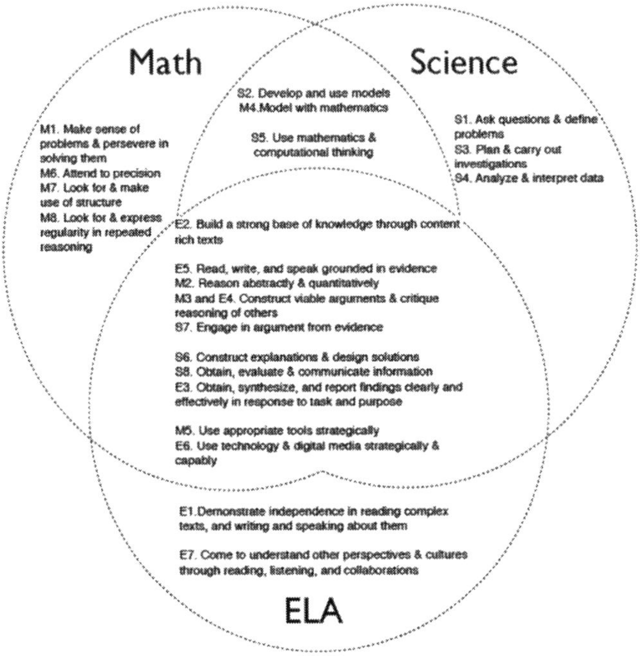

Fig. 8.1 Relationship and convergences of student practices in CCSS English Language Arts, Mathematics and NGSS Science

learning in sixteen states (P21 2009). The international ATC21S—Assessment and Teaching of Twenty-First Century Skills—was also implemented in the US. Despite the implementation of new standards and the work of P21 and ATC21S, the teaching and assessing of twenty-first century skills is minimal in US schools.

However, in light of the integration of scientific and engineering practices, crosscutting concepts, and disciplinary core ideas in the NRC Framework and the translation of this content into the Next Generation Science Standards (NGSS), instructional practices should start to shift from transmission models to more constructive models. This shift in instructional practices should enable students to build on existing mental models and learn in real-world, authentic environments in which they can apply their knowledge meaningfully (Trilling and Fadel 2012). As of December 2016, eighteen states have adopted NGSS as their state standards, and state departments of education, school districts, state science organizations (e.g., California Science Teachers Association) and national science organizations (e.g., the National Science Teachers Association) have begun developing and implementing summer institutes, web seminars, short courses, face-to-face conference lectures and workshops for teachers, all designed to build an understanding of the NGSS and provide a pathway for incorporating the standards into classroom instruction.

Importance of Twenty-first Century Skills to STEM Education

Success in the global workplace will require increased performance in the STEM disciplines. Employers are increasingly seeking STEM skills as a source of innovation and growth (Cisco 2008). In the U.S., STEM is a prominent focus and education policy priority of both public and private sectors. In Honorable Timothy Bishop's address to the U.S. House of Representatives on the importance of STEM education, he stated that a STEM workforce has become increasingly central to U.S. economic competitiveness and growth, and that it is widely recognized that STEM education must be a national priority if we are to continue to succeed in an increasingly global economy (Bishop 2013). In concert, The National Research Council's (NRC) Science Framework for K-12 Science Education (2012b) lays out an agenda that can begin to reshape what students need to know and be able to cultivate as twenty-first century leaders in science and citizenship (NRC 2012b). Furthermore, it has become evident that strong linkages between twenty-first century skills and scientific and engineering practices will provide insight into deeper learning of STEM content and to certain clusters of twenty-first century skills (NRC 2012a).

As the foundation for the NGSS, the NRC Framework identifies key scientific ideas and practices all students should learn by the end of high school. The Framework is based on a rich and growing body of research on teaching and learning in science, as well as on nearly two decades of efforts to determine foundational knowledge and skills for K-12 science and engineering (NRC 2012b, p. 2). The three major dimensions of the Framework include: (1) Scientific and Engineering Practices, (2) Crosscutting Concepts, and (3) Disciplinary Core Ideas. At the core of the intersection of the three dimensions is a new definition of what it means to be competent in science. This new definition no longer describes competence as what students simply know, can do or understand; but instead requires students to engage in arguments, develop and use models, or explain, justify and/or prove a position based on evidence (NRC 2012b). The eight practices include: asking questions (science) and defining problems (engineering); developing and using models; planning and carrying out investigations; analyzing and interpreting data; using math, information and computer technology, and computational thinking; constructing explanations (science) and designing solutions (engineering); engaging in argument from evidence; and obtaining, evaluating and communicating information. The eight practices do not operate in isolation; they intentionally overlap and interconnect. For example, the practice of asking questions may lead to modeling or planning and carrying out an investigation, which in turn may lead to data interpretation and discourse (NGSS Lead States 2013).

In the NRC report, *Education for life and work: Developing transferable knowledge and skills in the twenty-first century* (2012a), Pellegrino maintains that the area of greatest overlap between the framework and twenty-first century skills is found in the scientific and engineering practices. He states that this overlap provides insight into the meaning of "deep" in deeper learning and into certain clusters of

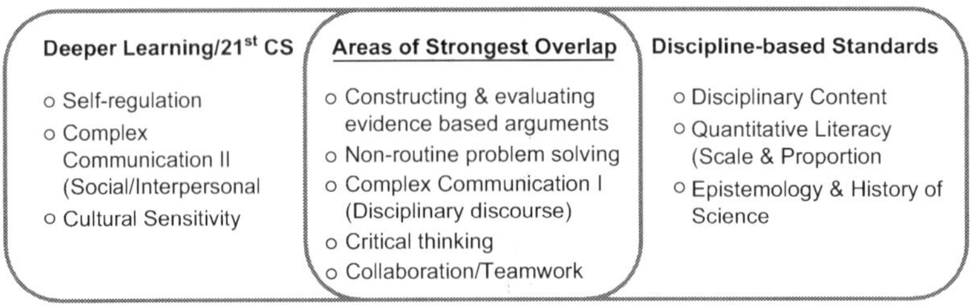

Fig. 8.2 Overlap between the science standards framework and twenty-first century skills

twenty-first century skills, especially those categorized as cognitive. Figure 8.2 illustrates Pellegrino's findings for the overlap (or intersection) between the science standards framework and twenty-first century skills (NRC 2012a).

In particular, critical thinking, collaborative problem solving, constructing and evaluating evidence-based arguments, systems thinking, and complex communication are all strongly supported in the NRC Framework (2012b) and construed as central and indispensable to the disciplines of science and engineering. Within the domain of interpersonal skills, the NRC Framework provides strong support for collaboration and teamwork. A prevalent theme throughout the Framework is the importance of understanding science and engineering as norm-governed enterprises conducted within a community, requiring well-developed twenty-first century skills for collaborating and communicating (NRC 2012b, p. 27).

According to Wallace et al. (2004), one way to gauge scientific practice, critical thinking and collaborative problem solving is through writing. When students engage in the process of science writing, their ideas progress from vague notions to more complex understandings (Keys et al. 1999); and writing to enhance learning becomes more powerful when combined with collaborative peer discussion (Chen et al. 2013).

Using Augmented Reality Games to Support Learning

Questions arise about how learning activities in the classroom might be structured to promote the development of twenty-first century skills, and some researchers have begun to address this issue. For example, Bressler (2014) has shown that collaborative mobile learning games are effective at supporting collaborative peer discourse and problem solving. According to Sanchez and Olivares (2011), learning games positively impact the development of collaboration skills; and students enjoy playing collaboratively because it encourages discussion among players (Sharritt 2008). Research is also showing that collaborative mobile augmented reality (AR) games developed for science learning have the potential for promoting scientific learning and practices (Squire and Klopfer 2007), and scientific literacy (Squire and Jan 2007). Other researchers have found AR games designed to put students in different roles during gameplay allow students to engage in the processes of scientific inquiry (Dunleavy et al. 2009) and argumentation (Mathews et al. 2008).

To illustrate how learning activities might need to change it is informative to take a more detailed look at a study by Bressler (2014) that investigated the scientific writing and collaborative discourse and problem solving of two teams of eighth-grade students: one team (treatment) played a mobile AR game, and a second team (control) participated in a similar, non-game based activity. The researcher investigated the following questions:

1. How do communication responses of game teams compare to those of control teams?
2. How do scientific practices of game teams compare to those of control teams?
3. How are treatment groups different when discourse is analyzed at the team level?

Participants in the study included eighth-grade students in a middle school in the state of Pennsylvania in the US representing a diverse urban area with low-income households. The researcher used a continuum of above average mathematics scores, average mathematics scores and below average mathematics scores to randomly assign both treatment and control students to a collaborative group/team consisting of three to four students.

The science activity in the study consisted of a pre-existing eighth-grade curriculum unit on mystery powders. Conducted over a 3–5-day period, the mystery powder activity engaged small collaborative groups of students in six scientific practices as defined by the NRC Framework. The six practices included:

Practice 1: Asking questions and defining problems.
Practice 3: Planning and carrying out investigations.
Practice 4: Analyzing and interpreting data.
Practice 6: Constructing explanations.
Practice 7: Engaging in argument from evidence.
Practice 8: Obtaining, evaluating, and communicating information.

Students in the three treatment groups engaged in a mobile augmented reality game played on iPads with quick response (QR) codes located throughout the school. As treatment students moved throughout the school they scanned the QR codes to gain information, interviewed people to access additional information, and deciphered codes to answer questions. The game was played in collaborative teams of three to four students with specific roles including: social networker, techie, photographer or pyrotechnician. Based on their role, each student in a team was provided with different pieces of information as they progressed through the game. To solve the mystery, students in a team had to collaborate and work together, sharing different pieces of information needed to solve the problem.

Students in the three control groups were also assigned roles and different pieces of information and worked in collaborative teams. Instead of engaging in a mobile augmented reality game on an iPad, the control groups had to solve the problem by conducting a hands-on laboratory investigation. Students in both treatment and control teams developed hypotheses and conducted basic physical and chemical tests to analyze data and determine the nature of the mystery powder. Student collaborative discourse and responses for both treatment and control students were audio recorded and transcribed, and the researchers also took notes and photographs to document student interactions.

The researchers engaged in two levels of coding. The first level was based on a review of the literature on communication responses and scientific practices. Barron (2003) reported that when collaborative teams were more engaged and on task, the teams significantly provided more engaged responses than teams that did not collaborate successfully. The second level of coding was based on close reading of the transcripts and coded independently by two individual readers using a rubric. The rubric graded written responses on a Likert-style scale ranging from 0 to 4 points where insufficient responses were scored a "0" and exemplary responses were scored a "4." The student responses were captured from items representing the six practices embedded in the mystery powder activity. Students were scored on responses to nine open-ended explanations with a possible score range from 0 to 36.

Student responses that were captured in team conversations were coded as Accept, Discuss, and Reject (Barron 2003, p.7). According to the researchers (Bressler 2014): Accept was defined as when a student agreed with the speaker, supported the idea, or proposed a next step; Discuss was defined as when a student questioned an idea, asked for clarification, or challenged an idea with new information; and Reject was defined as when a student rejected an idea or interacted in any way that would not facilitate further discussion.

When the researchers compared the three communication response types—Accept, Discuss, and Reject—between the treatment (mobile AR game on iPad) and control teams (hands-on labs) they found different patterns of communication responses:

- The treatment teams had *moderate* to *low* levels of Reject responses and control teams had *moderate* to *high* levels of Reject responses.
- The treatment teams had *moderate* to *high* levels of Accept responses and control teams had *moderate* to *low* levels of Accept responses.
- The treatment teams had *high* or *very high* levels of Discuss responses and control teams only had *moderate* levels of Discuss responses.

According to Barron (2003), Accept and Discuss responses are categorized as engaged responses, and Reject responses are categorized as non-engaged responses. According to their findings, the researchers reported that the treatment teams produced a fairly high level of engaged responses, and the control teams produced a fairly high level of non-engaged responses.

Student discourse, transcribed in team conversations and in student written responses, was coded to align to the NRC (2012b) scientific practices. For each practice, the researchers defined the type of dialog that would qualify to represent that specific practice. They categorized occurrences of practices into levels of low (1–4 occurrences), moderate (5–8 occurrences), high (9–14 occurrences), and very high (over 14 occurrences) for each scientific practice. When the researchers compared the scientific practices between treatment (mobile AR game on iPad) and control teams (hands-on labs), they found different usage patterns of scientific practices during team conversations. For Practice 1: defining problems, the treatment teams revealed a stronger understanding of describing a problem and understanding how to create a hypothesis; while the control teams revealed a basic understanding of describing a problem and a very basic understanding of how to create a hypothesis. For Practice 3: planning the investigation, the control teams demonstrated a better understanding of the plan needed to determine the identity of the mystery powders than the treatment teams. For Practice 4: interpreting data, while both treatment and control teams showed high levels of occurrences, the treatment teams provide observations that were more specific and substantive than the control teams. For Practice 6: constructing explanations, while both treatment and control teams demonstrated only a basic understanding, the researchers found that the higher achieving treatment teams constructed explanations about both the game narrative and the science content, focusing more on this practice. The higher achieving control team only explained the science content. For Practice 7: arguing with evidence, multiple treatment team members demonstrated the ability to both argue with evidence more than once during conversations, and to make evidence-based arguments, while not all control team members demonstrated this practice. For the control team members that did exhibit this practice, the researchers found that they only revealed it at the end of the activity, and only one of the three control teams had multiple members demonstrating the practice. The researchers concluded that findings for team conversations showed that treatment teams revealed a greater ability to engage in practices that the control teams (Bressler 2014).

In regards to findings for student written responses for items in the activity coded to the NRC scientific practices, the researchers found that the treatment teams defined the problem in an exemplary capacity; exhibited a developing understanding of how to write a hypothesis; showed an exemplary ability in how to interpret data with detailed and specific observations; and their discourse about data was more explicit and substantive than the control teams. The researchers also found that student responses from both treatment and control teams revealed a low-level capacity for planning investigations and a range of capabilities for constructing an argument in writing. The researchers suggest that more data are needed to draw conclusions about the connection between team discourse and students' ability to construct explanations and draw conclusions between data in their writing (Bressler 2014).

Overall results from this study conclude that collaborative games hold promise for promoting effective collaborative practice by scaffolding and supporting student discourse during gameplay (Bressler 2014). AR games offer learning experiences that promote critical thinking and support scientific practices. This study showed that the treatment students participating in the AR games had greater levels of scientific practices in their conversations than the control teams that only engaged in a hands-on lab. The treatment teams also demonstrated that scientific knowledge could be advanced through student collaboration (Bressler 2014). While the results of this study hold great promise for the intersection of twenty-first century skills and scientific practices, important twenty-first century skills such as critical thinking and collaboration are poorly taught and poorly assessed, particularly in science education (Bressler 2014).

Teacher Professional Development and Twenty-first Century Skills

As noted earlier, the dominant approach to education is the transmission model through which teachers transmit factual knowledge to students by means of lectures and textbooks (RAND 2012). Students do not learn twenty-first century skills unless they are explicitly taught, and these skills are not taught in separate stand-alone courses. Most teachers lack sufficient experience teaching twenty-first century skills to develop the deep expertise needed to train others.

The *Common Core State Standards* and the *Next Generation Science Standards* demand major conceptual shifts in curriculum, instruction and assessment. These new standards were intentionally designed to address college and career readiness through the lens of twenty-first century skills. They require students to exhibit critical thinking, problem solving, and other twenty-first century skills to demonstrate their under- standing of concepts and apply this understanding to real-world scenarios (NGA and CCSSO 2010a, b; NRC 2012b). If students are to master the twenty-first century skills needed to thrive in a global economy, teachers must be provided opportunities to learn how to explicitly teach twenty-first century skills. Student learning of twenty-first century skills requires twenty-first century teaching (Adamson and Darling-Hammond 2015).

In order to begin to address the major paradigm shifts in the new standards, and provide teachers with opportunities to learn how to teach twenty-first century skills, next generation professional development must:

- Model the explicit teaching of twenty-first century skills in different content areas
- Provide opportunities for teachers to practice the teaching of twenty-first century skills in their content areas with students
- Provide coaching for teachers as they learn to teach twenty-first century skills
- Provide opportunities for teachers to learn how to assess twenty-first century skills and to review student work
- Provide opportunities for teachers to learn how twenty-first century skills fit into their curriculum and instruction and how to evaluate resources for teaching twenty-first century skills
- Help teachers learn how to discuss twenty-first century skills with parents and other stakeholders
- Provide communities of learners among teachers for sharing experiences, strategies and resources

According to Bellanca (2014), the professional development of teachers is one of the most important areas to address in today's educational system. She maintains that teachers are being bombarded with 1 or 2-day lectures on how to implement new reform mandates, and there is no way of knowing if they are implementing what they are learning or if they have actually learned anything. She argues that deep change is needed in teacher professional development to advance student learning of twenty-first century skills and that 'band aids' or quick fixes will not work.

Research shows that high quality professional development can have a powerful effect on teacher skills and knowledge and on student learning and achievement if it is sustained over time, focuses on core content, and is embedded in the work of professional learning communities that support improvements in teachers' practice (Gulamhussein 2013; Darling-Hammond et al. 2009). Research also shows quality professional development is intensive, sustained, well defined, and strongly implemented (Garet et al. 2001; Guskey 2003); is based on a carefully constructed and empirically validated theory of teacher learning and change (Ball and Cohen 1999; Richardson and Placier 2001); addresses core content and pedagogy (Gulamhussein 2013; Weiss and Pasley 2009); and promotes effective curricula and instructional models based on a well-defined and valid theory of action (Cohen et al. 2002; Hiebert and Grouws 2007; Rossi et al. 2004). Effective professional development addresses concrete challenges in teaching and learning, and specific content, rather than abstract educational principles or teaching methods taken out of context (Darling-Hammond et al. 2009). Teachers are more likely to try out practices that have been modeled for them (Gulamhussein 2013; Penuel et al., 2007; Snow-Renner and Lauer 2005; Desimone et al. 2002), and they judge learning opportunities more valuable when they are hands-on, build on their own content knowledge, and provide strategies for teaching the content to their students (Gulamhussein, 2013).

Conclusion

The changing natures of technology, competition in the global job market, and college and career standards have impacted the skills and knowledge young people need to be successful in today's global economy. In the US, the *Common Core State Standards* (CCSS) and *Next Generation Science Standards* (NGSS) provide an opportunity to transform education to be aligned with the needs of today's world. By the end of high school, all students should possess sufficient knowledge of science to engage in public discussion of related issues, be careful consumers of scientific and technological information related to their everyday lives, and have the skills to enter a career, including, but not limited to STEM (NRC 2012b).

An emerging body of research suggests that twenty-first century skills—e.g., adaptability, complex communication/collaboration skills, non-routine problem solving skills, self-management/self-development, and systems thinking—are increasingly valuable across a wide range of jobs in the national economy (NRC 2010).

Success in the global workplace will require increased performance in the STEM disciplines. Employers are increasingly seeking STEM skills as a source of innovation and growth (Cisco 2008). It is widely recognized that STEM education must be a national priority for countries that wish to thrive in an increasingly global economy (Bishop 2013). In concert, The National Research Council's (NRC) *Science*

Framework for K-12 Science Education (2012a) lays out an agenda that can begin to reshape what students need to know and be able to cultivate as twenty-first century leaders in science and citizenship (NRC 2012a). Furthermore, it has become evident that strong linkages between twenty-first century skills and scientific and engineering practices will provide insight into deeper learning of STEM content and to certain clusters of twenty-first century skills (NRC 2012a).

Pellegrino's study (NRC 2012b) concludes that the greatest overlap between the framework and twenty-first century skills is found in the scientific and engineering practices; and that this overlap provides insight into the meaning of "deep" in deeper learning and into certain clusters of twenty-first century skills, especially non-routine problem solving and complex communication which are construed as central and indispensable to the disciplines of science and engineering.

Very little research exists on twenty-first century skills. Despite widespread interest in twenty-first century skills, little empirical evidence exists that these skills can be taught or learned. In addition, there is little evidence currently that such learning, where it may occur, influences achievement outcomes of students in their subject or discipline areas. These issues are not dissimilar to those identified in the literature on generalisability of higher order skills (NRC 2012a), but go beyond this issue to the application of such skills beyond the context in which they are initially embedded.

A two-prong approach is needed to ensure that all students have access to learning and utilizing twenty-first century skills. First, further research is needed to investigate (a) the degree to which selected twenty-first century skills can be taught and learned within K-12 science education, (b) which models of instruction might influence student learning outcomes, and (c) the degree to which these different models of teaching might enhance learning outcomes for students. Second, once a clear picture emerges from the research, sustainable professional development for teachers in how to teach twenty-first century skills will be needed to ensure that teaching practice changes.

References

Adamson, F., & Darling-Hammond, L. (2015). Policy pathways for 21st century skills. In P. Griffin & E. Care (Eds.), *The assessment and teaching of 21st century skills: Methods and approach* (pp. 293–310). Dordrecht: Springer.

Autor, D. H., Katz, L. F., & Kearney, M. S. (2008). Trends in US wage inequality: Revising the revisionists. *The Review of Economics and Statistics, 90*(2), 300–323.

Ball, D. L., & Cohen, D. K. (1999). Developing practice, developing practitioners: Toward a practice- based theory of professional education. In L. Darling-Hammond & G. Sykes (Eds.), *Teaching as the learning profession: Handbook of policy and practice* (pp. 3–32). San Francisco: Jossey Bass.

Barron, B. (2003). When smart groups fail. *Journal of the Learning Sciences, 12*(3), 307–359.

Bellanca, K. (2014) Professional learning experiences: There is no quick fix. Http://p2.org/news-events/p21blog/1422-professional-learning. 27 May, 1(4), No. 14.

Bishop, T. (2013). Recognizing the Importance of STEM Education. In Congress.gov. http://beta.congress.gov/members.

Boix Mansilla, V., & Jackson, A. (2011). *Educating for global competence: Preparing our youth to engage*. New York: CCSSO, Asia Society.

Bressler, D. (2014). Better than business-as-usual: Improving scientific practices during discourse and writing by playing a collaborative mystery game. double helix. *Journal of Critical Thinking & Writing, 2*, 1–13.

Chen, Y.-C., Hand, B., & McDowell, L. (2013). The effects of writing-to-learn activities on elementary students' conceptual understanding: Learning about force and motion through writing to older peers. *Science Education, 97*(5), 745–771.

Cisco (2008). Equipping every global leader for the 21st century. ://newsroom.cisco.com/feature content;jsessionid=68602DD6F8BFD10FFDDC55815F165989?type=webcontent&articleId=4323028.

Cohen, D. K., Raudenbush, S., & Ball, D. L. (2002). Resources, instruction, and research. In F. Mosteller & R. Boruch (Eds.), *Evidence matters: Randomized trials in education research* (pp. 80–119). Washington, DC: Brookings Institution.

Darling-Hammond, L., Chung Wei, R. A., Richardson, A. N., & Orphanos, S. (2009). *Professional learning in the learning profession: A status report on teacher development in the United States and abroad*. Oxford: National Staff Development Council.

Desimone, L. M., Porter, A. C., Garet, M. S., Yoon, K. S., & Birman, B. F. (2002). Effects of professional development on teachers' instruction: Results from a three-year longitudinal study. *Educational Evaluation and Policy Analysis, 24*, 81–112.

Dunleavy, M., Dede, C., & Mitchell, R. (2009). Affordances and limitations of immersive participatory augmented reality simulations for teaching and learning. *Journal of Science Education and Technology, 18*.(1 February, 7–22.

Gallup (2013). 21st century skills and the workplace; A 2013 Microsoft Partners in Learning and Pearson Foundation Study. http://www.gallup.com/poll/162818/21st-century-skills-linked-work-success.aspx.

Garet, M. A., Porter, A. C., Desimone, L., Birman, B., & Suk Yoon, K. (2001). What makes professional development effective? Results from a national sample of teachers. *American Educational Research Journal, 38*(4), 915–945.

Gulamhussein, A. (2013). *Teaching the teachers: Effective professional development in an era of high stakes accountability*. Alexandria: Center for Public Education.

Guskey, T. R. (2003). What makes professional development effective? *Phi Delta Kappan, 84*(10), 748–750.

Hiebert, J., & Grouws, D. A. (2007). The effects of classroom mathematics teaching on students' learning. In F. K. Lester (Ed.), *The second handbook of research in mathematics education*. Reston: New Age and National Council of Teachers of Mathematics.

Keys, C. W., Hand, B., Prain, V., & Collins, S. (1999). Using the science writing heuristic as a tool for learning from laboratory investigations in secondary science. *Journal of Research in Science Teaching, 36*(10), 1065–1084.

Lee, O., Quinn, H., & Valdés, G. (2013). Science and language for english language learners in relation to next generation science standards and with implications for common core state standards for english language arts and mathematics. *Educational Researcher, 42*(4), 223–233. doi.10.3102/0013189X13480524.

Levy, F., & Murnane, R. J. (2004). *The new division of labor: How computers are creating the next job market*. Princeton: Princeton University Press.

Mathews, J., Holden, C., Jan, M.-F., Martin, J. (2008). *Sick at South Shore Beach: A place-based augmented reality game as a framework for building evidence-based arguments*. Paper presented at the Proceedings of the 8th international conference on International conference for the learning sciences – volume 3, Utrecht, The Netherlands.

National Governors Association Center for Best Practices, & Council of Chief State School Officers. (2010a). *Common core state standards for english language arts and literacy in history/social studies, science, and technical subjects*. Washington, DC: National Governors Association Center for Best Practices, & Council of Chief State School Officers.

National Governors Association Center for Best Practices, & Council of Chief State School Officers. (2010b). *Common core state standards for mathematics*. Washington, DC: National Governors Association Center for Best Practices, & Council of Chief State School Officers.
National Research Council. (2010). *Exploring the intersection of science education and 21st century skills: A workshop summary*. Washington, DC: The National Academies.
National Research Council. (2012a). *Education for life and work: Developing transferable knowledge and skills in the 21st century*. Washington, DC: The National Academies.
National Research Council. (2012b). *A framework for K-12 science education: Practices, crosscutting concepts, and core ideas*. Washington, DC: The National Academies.
NGSS Lead States. (2013). *Next generation science standards: For states, by states*. Washington, DC: The National Academies.
Partnership for 21st Century Skills (P21) (2009). *Framework for 21st century learning*. Tucson. http://www.p21.org/storage/documents/P21_Framework.pdf.
Penuel, W., Fishman, B., Yamaguchi, R., & Gallagher, L. (2007). What makes professional development effective? Strategies that foster curriculum implementation. *American Educational Research Journal, 44*(4), 921–958.
RAND Corporation. (2012). In A. R. Saavedra & V. Darleen Opfer (Eds.), *Teaching and learning 21st century skills: Lessons from the learning sciences*. Santa Monica: RAND Corporation.
Richardson, V., & Placier, P. (2001). Teacher change. In V. Richardson (Ed.), *Handbook of research on teaching* (4th ed., pp. 905–994). Washington, DC: American Education Research Association.
Rossi, P. H., Lipsey, M. W., & Freeman, H. E. (2004). *Evaluation: A systematic approach* (7th ed.). Thousand Oaks: Sage Publications.
Saavedra, A., & Opfer, D. (2012). Learning 21st—century skills requires 21st—century teaching. *Kappan, 94*(2), 8–13.
Sánchez, J., & Olivares, R. (2011). Problem solving and collaboration using mobile serious games. *Computers & Education, 57*(3), 1943–1952.
Schleicher, A. (Ed.). (2012). *Preparing teachers and developing school leaders for the 21st century: Lessons from around the world*. Paris: OECD.
Schwartz, M., Fischer, K. (2006). Useful metaphors for tackling problems in teaching and learning. *Wiley: About Campus, 11*, 2–9. doi:10.1002/abc.154
Sharritt, M. J. (2008). Forms of learning in collaborative video game play. *Research & Practice in Technology Enhanced Learning, 3*(2), 97–138.
Snow-Renner, R., & Lauer, P. (2005). *Professional development analysis*. Denver: Mid-continent Research for Education and Learning.
Squire, K. D., & Jan, M. (2007). Mad city mystery: Developing scientific argumentation skills with a place-based augmented reality game on handheld computers. *Journal of Science Education and Technology, 16*(1), 5–29.
Squire, K., & Klopfer, E. (2007). Augmented reality simulations on handheld computers. *Journal of the Learning Sciences, 16*(3), 371–413.
Tishman, S., Jay, E., & Perkins, D. N. (1993). Teaching thinking dispositions: From transmission to enculturation. *Theory Into Practice, 32*, 147–153.
Trilling, B., & Fadel, C. (2009). *21st century skills: Learning for life in our times*. San Francisco: Wiley & Sons Inc.
Trilling, B., & Fadel, C. (2012). Royal society for the encouragement of arts, manufactures and commerce journal. *A game of skills. What talents do young people need to thrive in the 21st century?*
Wagner, T. (2010). *The global achievement gap: Why even our best schools don't teach the new survival skills our children need and what we can do about it*. New York: Farrar, Straus and Giroux.
Wallace, C., Hand, B., & Prain, V. (2004). *Writing and learning in the science classroom*. Dordrecht: Kluwer.
Weiss, I. R., & Pasley, J. D. (2009). *Mathematics and science for a change: How to design, implement, and sustain high-quality professional development*. Portsmouth: Heinema.

Chapter 9
Teaching Twenty-First Century Skills: Implications at System Levels in Australia

Claire Scoular and Esther Care

Abstract The question surrounding teaching of twenty-first century skills is no longer why, but instead how. In this regard, there are many unknowns including teacher training, resources, and impact. To address these unknowns, research needs to focus on: What is the skill set educators need to teach the skills? How do they teach the skills? And, what are the implications of doing so? A necessary step in this endeavour is to identify clear definitions of the skills, and develop assessment tools to measure them. Training for educators to interpret the demonstration of skills at varying stages of ability needs to occur. Once skills are better understood, then instructional materials and guided examples of successful implementation can be provided. This chapter presents three examples from Australia of implemention in this emerging area. These examples vary in their approach and their perspectives, ranging across three systems; a professional body, an educational institution, and industry. The goal for each is the same – to support educators to find and implement effective methods to teach the skills.

Introduction

Increasingly, the workforce seeks employees who have strong abilities in problem solving, teamwork, oral and written communications, leadership, managing others, and system thinking (World Economic Forum 2016; World Bank 2016). In the twenty-first century, education institutions are expected to do more to ensure that students leave schools and higher education with the skills they need to be productive workers and citizens (Holtzman and Kraft 2011). Research has highlighted the shifting workplace requirements and the change that is required in education and training to equip the emerging workforce with the skills required for the twenty-first century (Binkley et al. 2012).

C. Scoular (✉) • E. Care
University of Melbourne, Melbourne, VIC, Australia
e-mail: c.scoular@unimelb.edu.au

E. Care et al. (eds.), *Assessment and Teaching of 21st Century Skills*,
Educational Assessment in an Information Age,
DOI 10.1007/978-3-319-65368-6_9

The changes from the twentieth to twenty-first century direct the skills required of the emerging workforce (Autor 2015). There are many challenges facing educators when we consider not only how to define these skills, and teach them, but also our capacity to measure and monitor the skills. Researchers consider collaboration, communication, metacognition, and problem solving as some of the main pillars of cognitive learning (O'Neil et al. 2004; World Economic Forum 2015). Yet there are few assessments of such skills that are usable in the classroom (Care and Kim 2018). In particular, student ability to apply their learning and transfer understanding to real-life environments, or their ability to work as part of a group are not consistently assessed as part of the curriculum (Dede 2010).

Defining Twenty-First Century Skills

In order to teach a skill, we need to be able to identify how it might be demonstrated. Educators need examples of student performance across low to high levels of proficiency to be able to identify behaviours in the classroom. A challenge for educators is making sense of the many frameworks for twenty-first century skills. The skills themselves have been labelled by several names including twenty-first century skills, general capabilities, soft skills, non-cognitive skills, and transversal competencies. Notwithstanding these differences, there appears to be a general consensus on the most critical skills – which typically include problem solving, critical thinking, collaboration, information literacy, technology literacy and creativity (Griffin et al. 2012; O'Neil et al. 2004; OECD 2009; Trilling and Fadel 2009).

It is important to note that while twenty-first century frameworks are relatively recent, the skills themselves are not 'new skills'. However, these 'newly important' skills have not been specifically addressed in education, assessment, and curriculum spaces in previous centuries (Larson and Miller 2011). Students need to be equipped not only to absorb and use information but to produce, analyse and consume information in both offline and online environments, engaging with a variety of technologies.

A challenge facing educators is which skills to focus on and when. There is no concensus on which skills should be taught before others, at what age students can begin learning the skills, or whether some are foundational skills. It is possible some skills are more relevant to certain disciplines, for example, teaching literacy within English, numeracy within Maths, and problem solving within Science. However, this does not necessarily mean that skills cannot be taught across several disciplines.

Australia's General Capabilities

Educators globally are recognising the shift in skill requirement and have begun to incorporate twenty-first century skills into curricula. Australia has specifically addressed the need for assessing and teaching skills through the Australian

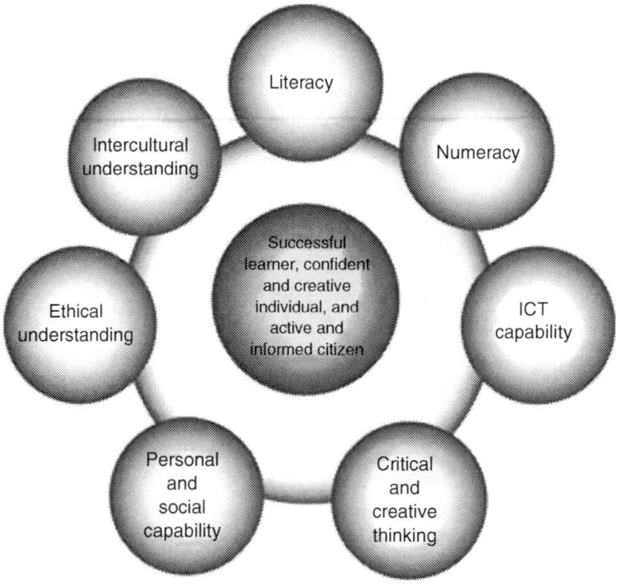

Fig. 9.1 ACARA's seven general capabilities (2013)

Curriculum, Assessment and Reporting Authority's (ACARA) development of the General Capabilities (ACARA 2013). These seven general capabilities are educational goals to develop every student as a "successful learner, confident and creative individual, and active and informed citizen". Along with literacy and numeracy, the capabilities include ICT capability, critical and creative thinking, personal and social capability, ethical understanding and intercultural understanding (Fig. 9.1).

These capabilities sit in alignment with the curriculum and are addressed explicitly in the content of the key learning areas. ACARA view these general capabilities as integrated across the existing discipline areas and referenced across three cross-curriculum priorities: Aboriginal and Torres Strait Islander histories and culture, Asia and Australia's links with Asia, and sustainability. ACARA demonstrates this cohesion of capabilities, disciplines and priorities as a grid (Fig. 9.2) stating that "co-curricular and extra-curricular activities could also support the development of the general capabilities just as they support students' acquisition of the knowledge, understanding and skills in each of the learning areas" (McGaw 2013).

ACARA's online presentation of the Australian curriculum allows for the filtering of disciplines, topics and years based upon the general capability under review. This enables educators to view relevant suggestions for integration in their teaching. ACARA also provides documentation addressing each of the capabilities within each of the disciplines by year level. Although the general capabilities have been formally adopted at policy level, there is little information to date concerning imple-

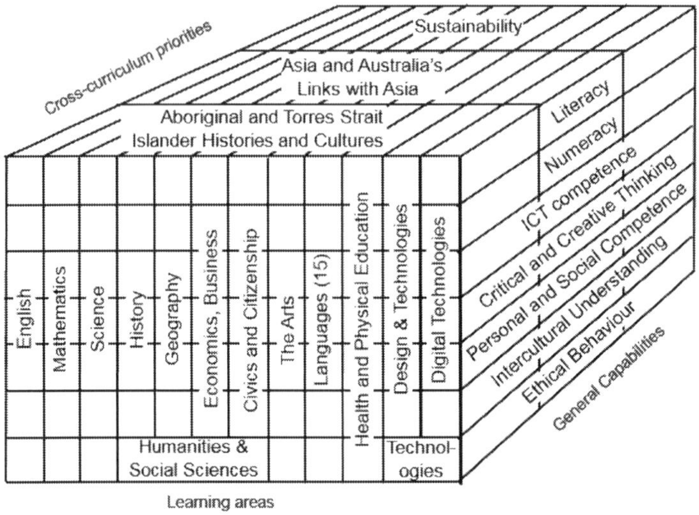

Fig. 9.2 The structure of the Australian curriculum

mentation of teaching these capabilities. Notwithstanding the online availability of materials and guidelines, the capabilities do not receive the same attention in the classroom as the key learning areas. Klenowski and Carter (2016) draw attention to lack of preparation time for implementation of new curricula, and in particular discuss the question of which areas in schools take responsibility for cross-disciplinary reforms such as those introduced by ACARA.

Training for Educators

Although there is an expectation that teachers will teach these skills, the pedagogical implications of so doing have not been deeply considered in the pre-service teacher education sector. It is important for higher education programs to provide sufficient opportunities for pre-service teachers to learn how to teach the skills. Unlike key learning areas, there is no mainstream program of education focused on development of skills in the higher education sector. There are programs supported by learning and teaching offices in some universities which are designed primarily to address deficits in student skills. These include programs to develop writing and language skills, for example, as well as programs to develop 'career skills'. Many universities identify graduate skills as priorities to be addressed in the design and development of courses. However, this identification is not accompanied by an acknowledgement that these skills might comprise an area of development in their own right, if they are to be articulated across disciplines. The need arises for teacher

Table 9.1 Summary of three case studies

Case study	Coordinator	Focus
1	Professional industry body	Development of a teacher resource pack; teaching twenty-first century skills explicitly
2	Higher education institution	Teacher professional development training
3	School based	Integration of interdisciplinary subjects

education to address the skills area in order to equip pre-service teachers with the capabilities such that they can develop the skills in their primary and secondary school students upon their entering the workforce.

The three case studies outlined in this chapter focus on improving education of twenty-first century skills but each adopt a different strategy (Table 9.1). The case studies involved schools in the State of Victoria, Australia, and were facilitated by researchers at the Assessment Research Centre at the University of Melbourne.

The research presented in these case studies was developed from the work of the Assessment and Teaching of 21st Century Skills (ATC21S) project and adopted its assessment tools. The tools include sets of collaborative problem solving (CPS) tasks designed for two students to work together on different devices. Student communications via an embedded chat box and their actions in the task are recorded in a log file. The behaviours identified in the log files are then coded, scored and mapped onto a framework for CPS developed by Hesse et al. (2015). The assessments produce reports which indicate student estimated ability level in CPS. The reports are designed to enable teachers to plan targeted intervention for students to develop the social and cognitive skills that characterise CPS. For more detailed information about the assessments see Care et al. (2015).

Case Study One: Explicit Teaching of Skills

The first case study was managed by a professional body, Pearson Australia, which developed and implemented a resource pack (titled 'Destination Imagination') to assist in teaching skills explicitly. Destination Imagination began in North America as an after-school non-profit organisation running challenges and tournaments to foster skills. Due to the growing demand for classroom based resources and teacher professional development in relation to the skills and the changing expectations of the curriculum, Pearson Canada and Destination Imagination (DI) collectively developed a classroom edition. The classroom resource was designed to guide teachers through open-ended classroom activities that engage students and develop their skills. The pack includes 50 instant and 15 team challenges built for the regular classroom environment at grades 3–9 (North American grades) that students work through in groups. The focus is to bring resources into a changing education system that prepares the students, not only for what to learn, but for how to learn both individually and with others (Destination Imagination 2013). The challenges are problem solving activities with a particular focus on supporting the development of creativity, critical thinking, communication, and collaboration skills. These four skills were derived from the Learning and Innovation strand of the Partnership for twenty-first Century Skills framework which states that "creativity, critical thinking, communication and collaboration is essential to prepare students for the future" (Partnership for 21st Century Skills 2011).

The purposes of the DI materials and ATC21S assessment tools are closely aligned, enabling implementation of a pilot project combining both resources. The pilot, led jointly by researchers at the University of Melbourne and learning architects at Pearson Australia, targeted the deepening of students' twenty-first century skills as demonstrated through collaborative problem solving (CPS). The purpose of the pilot was twofold, investigating the potential for localisation and alignment of the DI materials within the Australian curriculum, as well as allowing for validation and use of the assessments developed by the ATC21S project. The pilot addressed how efficient DI is in developing the skills of students and changing teacher practice within the context of the Australian curriculum. The ATC21S assessment tools were used as a pre and post measure of student progress with the DI materials serving as the intervention in between.

There are many ways in which the ATC21S and DI approaches are aligned. DI acknowledges that a jigsaw approach to CPS is a resourceful one (Destination Imagination 2013). A jigsaw approach provides each collaborator in a group with a specific task or resource that is necessary for solving the problem. This approach recognises that, just as in the world external to the classroom, each collaborator can bring a different perspective, expertise or information to problem solution. This perspective is central to definition of CPS identified by the ATC21S project. A second alignment between ATC21S and DI is the philosophy that task completion is a limited indicator of performance, and that building capacity, about knowledge building, and progressing in learning are also critical. DI challenges are presented at varying levels of ability and teachers are encouraged to assess student needs and differentiate their instruction accordingly. DI provides self and peer student assessments providing information on their perceived learning after completing a challenge. The reports and developmental learning progressions provided by ATC21S on completion of the assessment tasks, provide information about a student's estimated level of ability on a developmental continuum that can guide ongoing instruction and intervention. Both DI and ATC21S propose that student feedback should be immediate in order to reach maximum effectiveness.

An example of a DI task is The World Canvas which can be undertaken over a series of lessons. Students are divided into teams and asked to design a project to meet a need in the community. They must work with community partners and draw on critical thinking, collaboration, communication and creativity skills to complete their challenge successfully. DI have linked these tasks to the Arts, English Language and Social Studies curriculum. Table 9.2 demonstrates how the activities and behaviours specified in the challenge can be measured using the Hesse et al. (2015) CPS framework developed in the ATC21S project.

Table 9.2 Mapping of the Hesse et al. (2015) CPS framework onto a DI challenge

The World Canvas challenge activities	Hesse et al. (2015) CPS skills
Identify a need in the community and carry out a project to address it	Problem analysis
Analysing and synthesis information	Resource management
Ask questions	Collecting information
Evaluate your work	Self evaluation
Generate range of ideas to complete goals	Goal setting
Communicate with different audiences for different purposes	Audience awareness
Communicate well with others	Interaction
Remain flexible and willing participants	Tolerance for ambiguity
Compromise with others to achieve the project goals	Negotiation

Participants

Two classes of Year 8 students (44 total) between 13 and 14 years old who were enrolled in a secondary school in rural Victoria participated in the project. Four teachers and one coordinator were involved in the professional development activities and implementation of the pilot. The teachers were all graduates of accredited pre-service teacher training institutions and were registered with the Victorian Institute of Teaching. Their years of teaching varied from 3 to 40 years, and all were female.

Procedure

At the start of the study, teachers involved in the pilot completed professional development activities delivered collaboratively by Pearson and the University of Melbourne. One activity involved training on the use of the DI resources. Another activity involved training on the administration of the ATC21S assessments and interpretation of the reports. In addition, teachers were trained on the definition of CPS and its composite skills, as well as the expected behaviours that would demonstrate varying levels of proficiency.

At the beginning of the school year, all students involved in the pilot completed a set of the ATC21S assessments measuring their CPS skills. Reports for each student were distributed to the teachers to assist in their planning for intervention. Students underwent re-assessment at the end of the school year using an equivalent set of ATC21S assessments. In between the two assessments, one class were taught lessons integrating the DI materials including explicit teaching of the skills. The teachers used the DI materials in eight lessons across the subject areas of English, History, Science and Maths. The other class served as a control group, and were taught regular lessons.

Results

An increase in student ability level was used to identify the impact of the DI teaching resources. The student ability level was generated by the ATC21S CPS assessment tool and presented to teachers in a report which identified each student at one of six levels on the CPS developmental progression. Student growth was identified as a student progressing to a higher level from the pre-assessment to the post-assessment.

Over the 8 month period between assessments, of the students in the experimental condition who were exposed to the DI teaching resources, 47% progressed one student ability level, while the remaining 53% remained at the same level. In the control condition, in which students experienced regular classes, 33% of students progressed one student ability level, while the remaining 67% remained at the same level. It should be noted that students in both conditions may have progressed in student ability within level, but growth was only considered for reporting purposes if they moved into the next level since this was thought to indicate a qualifiable change in proficiency. There were no cases in which students appeared to decrease in proficiency level.

Overall, a greater number of students increased in proficiency in the experimental class compared to those in the control class, although the small sample size should be noted. It appears that explicit teaching may be beneficial for student skills development. Currently, there is no research evidence concerning expected growth rates in such skills, or the degree to which growth might typically be expected due to natural maturation. This pilot also provided feedback from teachers about the practicalities of implementing such resources in the classroom. This feedback was collected during a face to face focus group with teachers, initially audio recorded, and then transcribed. The feedback can be summarised into themes of planning, resources and content, and use.

Planning

Teachers met six times over the 8 month period to plan lessons and select and discuss which challenges each would complete and when. They also attended two professional development sessions each 2 h in duration. These sessions were designed to familiarise teachers with the skills and the materials. Teachers fed back that these sessions were useful, but that longer and more detailed training was needed. Specifically, teachers identified a need for case examples, videos of students at varying levels of ability, and how to assess using rubrics and progressions.

Resources and Content

Many teachers selected the challenges based on the availability of resources required to carry them out. All teachers reported that they were more likely to select challenges that required fewer resources or none at all. Teachers reported that localisation of resources would be critical for wider use of the DI classroom materials in Australia, since these were not linked closely enough to the curriculum. This made it difficult for teachers to integrate the challenges into their curriculum-aligned lessons. Another issue highlighted was the physical space available was limited and impacted on student ability to complete the challenges as they were initially intended. This issue is a significant one, not only for this specific application, but in the context of calls for teachers to change pedagogical practices toward more active and participatory models. It is associated with issues of classroom design and use of technologies in the classroom.

Use

Teachers found the student performance evaluations useful and used these regularly. However, teachers were not able to use 'reflections' strategies as much as they would have liked. Reflections materials were designed to be completed by students at the end of a challenge to allow them to evaluate the skills they applied and any learning that took place. Many teachers stated that there was sufficient lesson time for completion of the challenges but no time left to complete a reflection activity, which they felt would have contributed significantly to student learning.

Summary

The outcomes from this pilot indicate that more time needs to be allocated if skills teaching, learning and reflection are to take place. In addition, to assist educators to teach the skills, teaching needs to be aligned, if not embedded, within existing curricula and lesson plans. Increased emphasis on metacognition as one aspect of ACARA's critical and creative thinking makes clear the perceived centrality of these processes to development of general capabilities. Professional learning for teachers in this area is critical and there is demand from educators to undertake training in relation to teaching twenty-first century skills.

Case Study Two: Embedding the Skills within Existing Curriculum

The second case study focused on professional development training conducted by the University of Melbourne and consisted of aligning and embedding skills within the existing curriculum. This option could be considering the most appealing given the already demanding workload for teachers and the extensive curriculum already established. The approach was tested by conducting professional development with teachers in two schools with focus on the nature of the target skills and followed by workshops to develop lesson plans. This pilot was conducted across 2013–2014 school years.

Participants

This pilot involved two groups of Year 8 teachers from two secondary schools Victoria, Australia (four teachers from each school). The schools have a similar profile in that they are located in metropolitan areas, co-educational, independent and support Kindergarten to Year 12 students. The schools made the decision to conduct the pilot with Year 8 students given the planned inclusion of CPS assessments in PISA 2015, which targets the same age group. Teaching experience in the group ranged from 6 to 40 years and the teachers specialised across Science, Geography, Mathematics, English, Social Studies and Religious Studies key learning areas. In total 262 students were involved in this pilot across the two schools.

Procedure

The ACT21S CPS assessment tools were administered to all Year 8 students at the start of their school year. The ATC21S project team then conducted professional development workshops with the teachers. The first workshop included refinement of skill definitions, reporting materials and the developmental progressions for collaboration and problem solving skills. The student reports from the initial assessment were reviewed to assist teacher understanding of the learning progressions of student proficiency. The second workshop consisted of lesson plan development. The skills under review were mapped to the ACARA curriculum documentation. More specifically, opportunities to teach collaboration were sought from the documentation surrounding the 'personal and social responsibility' general capability. Opportunities to teach problem solving were sought from the documentation surrounding the 'critical and creative thinking' general capability. This supported teachers to identify subject topics in which to integrate the skills. In interdisciplinary groups with the researchers, teachers identified existing lesson plans in which to embed collaboration and problem solving skills. At the end of the school year, a third workshop was held to discuss and review the implementation of the lessons.

Results

The expectation is that teaching the skills across disciplines should allow students easier transfer of skills across their key learning areas. Teachers would benefit from collaborating with teachers from other subjects, not just in their teaching of the skills but in their observations and assessment of them. Sharing collected and recorded evidence, and justification of the interpretation of that evidence, would provide teachers with guidelines for identification of whether the students apply the skills across subjects.

Reports from teachers indicated that the embedding of skills into existing lessons of traditional curriculum was an effective method for teaching the skills. They reported that using this method initially required more time to prepare lessons, but over time this decreased. Four teachers reported that they found themselves teaching the skills explicitly even in lessons where this had not been planned. Teachers also reported that students responded positively and engaged effectively when the skills were taught explicitly. The self-conscious involvement of students in their own skill development was thought by teachers to enhance the learning.

Examples of a History and a Science lesson are provided. The collaborative problem solving construct includes five major strands, the first three (participation, perspective taking and social regulation) are identified as social, and the second two (task regulation and knowledge building) are identified as cognitive. Tables 9.3 and 9.4 identify in simple terms how the student lesson behaviours map onto these five strands within a History and Science lesson respectively.

Example History Lesson

1. Previous lesson plan: Students read about different poets, pick their favourite and write an essay about the historical period in which the poets were alive. Students are provided with eight fact sheets about different poets.
2. New lesson plan: Each student in the class is given a different poet to research. Students have to act out their character and communicate with one another to gather sufficient information about the historical period relevant to their poet, in order to expand and consolidate their research. Students then write about the different poets they meet within same period.

Table 9.3 Example History lesson mapped to the five strands

CPS strand embedded	Behaviour in lesson
Participation	Asking other students questions
Perspective taking	Writing about poets from those poets' assumed perspectives given their era
Social regulation	Responding to questions from other students appropriately
Task regulation	Only talking with students who were acting as poets from the time period they were researching
Knowledge building	Linking the different poets together in relation to time period

Table 9.4 Example science lesson mapped to the five strands

CPS strand embedded	Behaviour in lesson
Participation	Asking other students questions about their animals to determine if it's the same species
Perspective taking	Adapting their picture into a presentation for their peers that is easily communicated
Social regulation	Reflecting on their own performance and participation during group work in an informal way
Task regulation	Accurate information about their animal and which species it belongs to
Knowledge building	Learning lots of information from other people

Example Science Lesson

1. Previous lesson plan: Students write an essay about a species of animal.
2. New lesson plan: Each student chooses an animal to research and draw. They share with one another the animals they have chosen, then form groups with other students of the same species of animal and create a larger picture incorporating all of the species and general knowledge about the species as a whole. Students present species as groups and self-assess their performance.

Summary

This approach appears a logical and practical method of providing opportunities for teachers to teach the skills alongside the existing curriculum. Teachers were generally supportive of this approach, given that it does not remove or override the context of existing lessons, but merely adapts these. Modifying or developing lessons which synthesise skills and subject content may take teachers time to master, but once they have done so the approach can easily be integrated into practice. Situating the twenty-first century skills as a vehicle for the subject content during lessons reinforces the learning outcomes of importance and makes for a sustainable approach. It is no longer sufficient for students to acquire subject-level mastery, they also need to work with others, solve problems, and think critically. Lessons can be reorientated to elicit these skills as well as subject knowledge.

Case Study Three: Developing Interdisciplinary Subjects in Which to Teach the Skills

The third case study was conducted by a secondary school which was implementing interdisciplinary subjects to teach the skills. The state government school had identified that many of their educators were teaching skills such as collaboration and problem solving and decided to formalise the teaching. The school reached the conclusion that to achieve different outcomes in their students, such as improved performance of skills, they needed to teach in a different way. To do so the school developed interdisciplinary inquiry based subjects across the curriculum.

The interdisciplinary subjects involved the gradual release of responsibility to students for their own learning. At the start of the subject students were highly scaffolded and explicitly taught. As they moved through the subject, they moved to conduct their own inquiries and linked their own skill development to outcomes in other subjects. Initially, the school drew on external experts to guide the process but over time, a culture of learning between teachers within the school was cultivated. Now most professional development surrounding twenty-first century skills occurs within the school. This allows teachers to learn from one another, and most importantly frees up time to observe one another and demonstrate strategies for teaching the skills. Perhaps most critically in teaching these skills, is that the principal supports exploration when it comes to trying different strategies and approaches to teaching.

The interdisciplinary approach began in Year 7. Five lessons a week brought together the subjects of Science, Social Studies, and English to teach critical thinking, collaboration and problem solving skills explicitly. The interdisciplinary approach aimed to encourage curiosity and exploration of information as well as collaboration, based on the principle that these can enhance deeper understanding of key concepts and trigger additional curiosities. As students progressed through Years 8–10 these concepts were reinforced with continued interdisciplinary activities. Students were encouraged to be metacognitive and reflect on their thinking and development.

Participants

The trial involved approximately 600 students across Years 7–10, ages 12–15, at a government secondary school in Victoria, Australia. The design included assessment of all students at these year levels within the school.

Procedure

This implementation was longitudinal, from 2014 to 2017. Each student from Years 7–10 was assessed at the beginning and end of their school year using the ATC21S CPS assessment tools. The curriculum leader at the school generated and collated the ATC21S reports of student CPS ability at each point in time. Teachers were also provided with a report for the whole class, which provided guidance about how to cluster students within the class for future teaching.

Results

The ATC21S reports were used not only for the assessment of student ability, but also to serve as a learning tool. The curriculum leader reported that it appeared some students develop skills such as collaboration and problem solving quite naturally but other students need and benefit from explicit teaching of the skills. Data from the assessments informed how teachers shaped the activities undertaken in the interdisciplinary subjects. The teachers from the school reported that the assessments provided them with data about their students' ability that they would not otherwise obtain, and from a teaching perspective this allowed them to provide interventions to students that were appropriate to their current ability level. The nature of the CPS assessments allowed students to consider how they thought about problems, not simply what they knew; and the teachers at the school were able to translate these processes back into the interdisciplinary subjects. After the ATC21S assessments were administered at the start of the school year, the teachers audited the collaborative and problem solving tasks already in their interdisciplinary curriculum and adjusted these based on the report data. These tasks included: group work or conflict resolution sessions; learning style and personal learning activities to highlight strengths and weaknesses in a group; ICT tools to support collaboration; explicit teaching of problem solving and critical thinking such as logic and reasoning activities; peer and self-evaluation in group work; and small group dynamic activities that required students to solve small problems collaboratively.

Assessing the students after the students undertook their interdisciplinary subject, allowed comparison from the baseline data such that teachers could evaluate the impact of the interdisciplinary approach. The evidence of learning outlined in the ATC21S reports allowed teachers to evaluate the skills students demonstrated and those that they might need to teach more. One of the benefits of the interdisciplinary approach and integration of assessments of twenty-first century skills was reporting activities and outcomes back to parents, enhancing the perspective that the skills are teachable and assessable, and are important.

The school reported that while initially only intending to focus on student outcomes, the process of developing, teaching and evaluating the twenty-first century skills-orientated activities in the interdisciplinary subject provided space for the teachers to develop their own twenty-first century skills. The nature of interdisciplinary working encouraged cross-disciplinary collaboration among teachers. The school is now highly regarded nationally for its interdisciplinary focus and provides professional development to other schools to support similar teaching approaches.

The school reported positive progress in the use of interdisciplinary subjects, but also identified the gap in knowledge about how the skills relate to one another. For example, they noted that many students were proficient at problem solving but struggled to work with others collaboratively. Similarly, some students collaborated well with others but did not perform as well when there were cognitive demands surrounding a task. The school recommended that the skills be taught from an earlier age, preferably in primary school in the belief that if lower level proficiencies can be taught from a younger age this may provide a stronger foundation for students to understand and develop the skills when they reach secondary school.

Discussion

The findings from these case studies demonstrate that implementation of twenty-first century skills inside the classroom can be aligned with existing teaching approaches and curriculum. The schools and teachers involved recognised the value of teaching and assessing the skills but were faced with several challenges. Teachers found that they had not been adequately prepared to teach the skills and consequently lacked confidence in implementing lessons or strategies that focuses on the skills. Teachers commented that they were uncertain of the expected outcomes in comparison to traditional lessons. This is reasonable given that there is no research evidence concerning what levels of skills outcomes should be expected, and there are no specifications of learning outcomes that are aligned with available assessments. Despite the varied nature of the case studies presented, the feedback from each was generally positive and there was a demand for activities of a similar nature. In integrating a broader range of skills into the curriculum at school level, the best strategy for integration will likely depend on the resources and support provided within each school. What was common in each of these successful case studies, was that each had school leadership support and teacher commitment.

The promulgation by ACARA that general capabilities are both valued in and necessary for student education and later working life, requires action at three levels. First, teachers who are responsible for student education need to be equipped to broaden their discipline-specific expertise. Second, teacher training institutions need to acknowledge the implications of this global demand on the basic education sector, and provide appropriate pre-service training. Third, the university sector, which is equally responsible for equipping students for the world of work, needs to identify how it will provide the teaching and learning experiences to achieve this.

In-Service Education for Teachers in the Basic Education Sector

There is a challenge for the basic education sector in adopting strategies and approaches that do not impact negatively on the already demanding workload of teachers. While teachers involved in these case studies acknowledged that twenty-first century skills are important, in all three cases the traditional curriculum took priority. In order to implement teaching and learning of the skills through the curriculum, sustainable methods to manage increasingly interactive pedagogical methods need to be adopted. For example, explicit teaching needs to occur across disciplines allowing easier transfer of the skills. This would require teachers to collaborate with teachers of other subjects, in order to understand the different ways in which the skills may enhance learning areas. Of course, in order to achieve this, teachers themselves need to be conscious of the skills, understand what they "look like" at different levels of sophistication, and understand how to develop them. It could be beneficial for teachers to have hands-on experience learning and applying twenty-first century skills in a manner similar to how students will use them to learn and how they are used in the workforce (Luterbach and Brown 2011).

Higher Education Sector Training of Teachers

In order to equip pre-service teachers to assess and teach the twenty-first century skills, the higher education sector needs to update its teacher training courses. Currently secondary school pre-service candidates in particular are required to demonstrate specific knowledge in the discipline area or "method" in which they are to specialise and teach – for example they will have a 3 or 4 year major in Science in order to teach Science, or in Mathematics similarily. General teacher preparation typically addresses some history of education, pedagogical practices, and perhaps assessment. Following the Australian curriculum, it is now necessary to equip pre-service teachers with knowledge and expertise in the general capabilities such that they can develop the skills in their primary and secondary school students.

The higher education is as subject to global trends and imperatives as the basic education sector. In the twenty-first century, higher education institutions are expected to do more to ensure that students leave colleges and universities with the skills they need to be productive workers and citizens (Holtzman and Kraft 2011) over and above specific vocational skills. In some countries, such as Malaysia, it is now a requirement that general skills or capabilities be embedded into higher education curriculum in order to address employability issues. As stated by Yassin et al. (2008) the biggest challenge facing higher education institutes is to develop employability skills, enhance knowledge and ensure graduates are valuable to employers. The introduction of generic skills to the higher education curriculum is one way to address this challenge. Within Australian higher education institutes, the general capabilities are reflected somewhat variably in practice, although they are ubiquitously reflected in graduate outcome statements of universities from the highest to lowest ranked. Many universities identify graduate skills as priorities to be addressed in the design and development of courses and subjects. However, this identification is not accompanied by requirements to include explicit teaching of these, nor by acknowledgement that such skills might not be in the repertoire of a majority of current academic staff.

Summary

Students need to be equipped not only to absorb and use information but to produce, analyse and consume information in both offline and online environments, engaging with a variety of advancing technology options. While the general capabilities in Australia have been formally adopted at policy level, there is little information concerning teaching these capabilities (Clarence and Comber 2011) or which departments within a school should take responsibility (Klenowski and Carter 2016). Online materials and guidelines have been provided by ACARA but the capabilities do not receive the same attention as the key learning areas. There is a presumption that teachers have the capacity to teach the skills, and therefore, there is a presumption that they have sufficient understanding of the skills to do so. Educators need to identify teaching strategies that challenge and support their students when it comes to developing twenty-first century skills (Bergom et al. 2011). To this degree, it is the responsibility of pre-service teacher education providers to provide this capacity.

The case studies mentioned in this chapter provided opportunities to trial assessment and teaching materials of twenty-first century skills and gain valuable feedback from stakeholders (students and educators) about the efficacy and viability of those resources. It also strengthened collaboration between the education and research sectors and industry, all of which have shared interest in bridging the gap between curriculum and twenty-first century skill development. The studies are testament to the fact that integration of twenty-first century skills in the basic education sector is in its infancy, and draw attention to the lack of systemic planning for implementation. Although the online resources provided by ACARA are impressive, this provision has not been accompanied by large scale in-service education, nor by changes in the curriculum of pre-service education.

References

Australian Curriculum, Assessment and Reporting Authority (ACARA) (2013). *General capabilities in the Australian curriculum*. Retrieved from http://www.australiancurriculum.edu.au/GeneralCapabilities/Pdf/Overview.

Autor, D. H. (2015). Why are there still so many jobs? The history and future of workplace automation. *Journal of Economic Perspectives, 29*(3), 3–30.

Bergom, I., Wright, M. C., Brown, M. K., & Brooks, M. (2011). Promoting college student development through collaborative learning: A case study of "Hevruta". *About Campus, 15*(6), 19–25.

Binkley, M., Erstad, O., Herman, J., Raizen, S., Ripley, M., & Rumble, M. (2012). Defining 21st century skills. In P. Griffin, B. McGaw, & E. Care (Eds.), *Assessment and teaching 21st century skills*. Dordrecht: Springer.

Care, E., & Kim, H. (2018). Assessment of 21st century skills: The issue of authenticity. In E. Care, P. Griffin, & M. Wilson (Eds.), *Assessment and teaching of 21st century skills: Research and applications*. Dordrecht: Springer.

Care, E., Griffin, P., Scoular, C., Awwal, N., & Zoanetti, N. (2015). Collaborative problem solving tasks. In P. Griffin & E. Care (Eds.), *Assessment and teaching of 21st century skills: Methods and approach* (pp. 85–104). Dordrecht: Springer.

Clarence, K., & Comber, B. (2011). General capabilities as a way in to planning. *Practically Primary, 16*(3), 6–8.

Dede, C. (2010). Comparing frameworks for 21st century skills. In J. Bellanca & R. Brandt (Eds.), *21st century skills: Rethinking how students learn* (pp. 51–76). Bloomington: Solution Tree Press.

Destination Imagination. (2013). *Destination imagination: Classroom edition, supporting 21st century learning*. Toronto: Pearson Canada.

Griffin, P., McGaw, B., & Care, E. (2012). *Assessment and teaching of 21st century skills*. Dordrecht: Springer.

Hesse, F., Care, E., Buder, J., Sassenberg, K., & Griffin, P. (2015). A framework for teachable collaborative problem solving skills. In P. Griffin & E. Care (Eds.), *Assessment and teaching of 21st century skills: Methods and approach* (pp. 37–56). Dordrecht: Springer.

Holtzman, D. M., & Kraft, E. M. (2011). Skills needed in the 21st century workplace: A comparison of feedback from undergraduate business alumni and employers with a national study. *Business Education & Administration, 3*(1), 61–76.

Klenowski, V., & Carter, M. (2016). Curriculum reform in testing and accountability contexts. In D. Wyse, L. Hayward, & J. Pandya (Eds.), *Handbook of curriculum, pedagogy and assessment*. London: Sage.

Larson, L. C., & Miller, T. N. (2011). 21st century skills: Prepare students for the future. *Kappa Delta Pi Record, 47*(3), 121–123.
Luterbach, K. J., & Brown, C. (2011). Education for the 21st century. *International Journal of Applied Educational Studies, 10*(2), 14–32.
McGaw, B. (2013). *Developing 21st century competencies through disciplines of knowledge*. Paper presented at an International Symposium on Education and 21st Century Competencies, Muscat, Sultanate of Oman, 22–24 September 2013, organized by the Oman National Commission for Education, Culture and Science. Retrieved from https://acaraweb.blob.core.windows.net/resources/Developing_21st_century_competencies_Prof_Barry_McGaw.pdf.
O'Neil, H. F., Chuang, S., & Chung, G. K. W. K. (2004). Issues in the computer- based assessment of collaborative problem solving. *Assessment in Education, 10*, 361–373.
Organisation for Economic Co-operation and Development (2009). Problem solving in technology-rich environments: A conceptual framework. *OECD Education Working Paper No. 36*. Retrieved from http://hdl.voced.edu.au/10707/52482.
Partnership for 21st Century Skills (2011). *Learning and innovation skills*. Online article. Retrieved from http://p21.org/overview/skills-framework/60.
Trilling, B., & Fadel, C. (2009). *21st century skills: Learning for life in our times*. England: Wiley.
World Bank. (2016). *World Development Report 2016: Digital dividends*. Washington, DC: World Bank. doi:10.1596/978-1-4648-0671-1. Retrieved from: http://documents.worldbank.org/curated/en/896971468194972881/pdf/102725-PUB-Replacement-PUBLIC.pdf.
World Economic Forum. (2015). *New vision for education unlocking the potential of technology*. Geneva: World Economic Forum in collaboration with The Boston Consulting Group. Retrieved from http://www3.weforum.org/docs/WEFUSA_NewVisionforEducation_Report2015.pdf.
World Economic Forum. (2016). *New vision for education: Fostering social and emotional learning through technology*. Geneva: World Economic Forum in collaboration with The Boston Consulting Group. Retrieved fromhttp://www3.weforum.org/docs/WEF_New_Vision_for_Education.pdf.
Yassin, S., Hasan, F. A., Amin, W., & Amiruddin, N. (2008). *Implementation of generic skills in the curriculum*. Edith Cowan University International Conference. Retrieved from http://ro.ecu.edu.au/cgi/viewcontent.cgi?article=1053&context=ceducom.

Chapter 10
Initiatives and Implementation of Twenty-First Century Skills Teaching and Assessment in Costa Rica

María Eugenia Bujanda, Leda Muñoz, and Magaly Zúñiga

Abstract Costa Rica's trajectory in the implementation of twenty-first century skills teaching and learning is strongly linked to the decision the country took in the late 1980s to introduce computers in the public education system with the intent to develop student's capacity to think logically, to solve problems with creativity and to work together with others. More recently, the Ministry of Education launched a series of curriculum reforms directed towards making the learning more relevant and attractive for the students and to develop social and personal competencies that have not been part of the generally expected learning outcomes. These reform efforts were complemented and supported by Costa Rica's participation in the Assessment and Teaching of twenty-first century skills project (ATC21S), leading the Latin American Chapter of this international research project. Nevertheless, the systematic introduction of the teaching and assessment of twenty-first century skills throughout the education system faces profound challenges that revolve around the design and effective implementation of a curriculum able to develop the knowledge, skills and dispositions that our students will need to possess to lead a productive and wholesome life in the modern world.

In the late 1980s, with the creation of the National Program of Educational Informatics, Costa Rica turned itself into a case study for many scholars and policymakers when the government made the decision to incorporate technology in primary schools to introduce the students to programing as a way to develop high-order intellectual and social skills. Since then, competencies such as problem solving, critical thinking, creativity or collaboration have been part of the learning outcomes pursued by the National Program of Educational Informatics, with the intention to prepare students, and the country as a whole, for the requirements of new technology and the connected knowledge based society and economy. The Program installed

M.E. Bujanda (✉) • L. Muñoz • M. Zúñiga
Omar Dengo Foundation, San José, Costa Rica
e-mail: maria.bujanda@fod.ac.cr

E. Care et al. (eds.), *Assessment and Teaching of 21st Century Skills*,
Educational Assessment in an Information Age,
DOI 10.1007/978-3-319-65368-6_10

computer labs, first in elementary schools then in high-schools, all over the country, where students used programming software like *Logo*, *Microworlds* and more recently others like *Scratch* and *Alice*, to explore abstract concepts, solve problems and make creative programmed objects on topics related to curricular contents.

Nevertheless, this visionary policy in the field of technology and education waited more than 15 years to see a corresponding transformation in the overall approach to teaching and learning in the curriculum. In 2006, the Ministry of Education launched a multi-year reform program called *Ethics, aesthetics, and citizenship*, aimed at strenghethening skills in these key twenty-first century domains and promoting more meaningful, effective and at the same time participatory learning environments in the schools. In 2012, important changes were introduced in Mathematics and Spanish, all directed to improving students' reasoning, argumentative, and problem solving skills, as well as more basic reading comprenhension skills. These initial reforms have lead during the 2014–2018 administration to a whole curriculum reform called *Education for a new citizenship*. This initiative has adopted the twenty-first skills framework generated by ATC21S as a guide for the formulation of student learning profiles for each school cycle, from pre-school to upper secondary education.

A vital point in these reforms was the change in the assessment methodologies – a change that has started but has not yet been completed. A very significant impulse for the advancement of the approaches and tools existing in the country for the assessment of twenty-first century skills was its participation in ATC21S, as described below. In the following sections, we explore in detail our country's main initiatives to promote the learning and the assessment of twenty-first century skills, and we end by acknowledging the challenges our system still faces.

Implementation of Twenty-First Century Skills Teaching in Costa Rica

The National Program of Educational Informatics

The National Program of Educational Informatics (PRONIE, by its Spanish acronym) was established in 1988, as a joint effort of the Ministry of Public Education and the Omar Dengo Foundation. Its general aim is to develop twenty-first century skills in the students and to contribute to the advancement of Costa Rican public education, through innovative and technology-supported educational projects. Currently, the Program includes primary and secondary schools all over the country, with an average coverage of more than 83% of students, from pre-school to secondary level (more than 617,000 students).

Regarding the role of technology in education, the vision that has oriented PRONIE's initiatives has been informed by a set of aspirations in four development domains (Fallas and Zúñiga 2010), as follows:

In the *individual* domain, the purpose is to promote cognitive and social development and to take advantage of the potential of computers as an amplifiying tool of people's capacities to make, collaborate and think.

In the *educational* domain, the Program seeks to contribute to the improvement of the quality of the Costa Rican education through its technological modernization and the adoption of new pedagogical models oriented to the active construction of knowledge and to the enrichment of the curriculum.

In the *social* domain, it aims to democratizing the access to high quality educational opportunities and help overcome the social gap existing both within the country (among rural and urban areas) and with regard to other countries.

In the domain of *economic development*, the goal is to prepare for the country's transition into a more competitive development model, and so enabling a more favourable integration in the international economy.

Laboratories Where You Can Think, Create and Collaborate Through Learning to Program Computers

With the above mentioned aims in mind, PRONIE made its way into the curriculum through computer laboratories established first in primary schools and then also in secondary schools. The computer lab was conceived as an open, creative and playful learning environment, where children engage in challenging and interesting activities with technology in weekly periods of two lessons (80 min) attended by an Educational Informatics teacher together with their own grade teacher. Despite having a formal learning program, with objectives to reach and a well-established and sound methodology, the implementation of PRONIE has been such that the computer lab has kept certain elements that bring it close to nonformal learning environments. From its outset, the computer lab's learning program has revolved around children learning to program computers, as a way to enhance their capacities to think, create, communicate, and so to gain deeper insights on curricular contents.[1] Notwithstanding, PRONIE has expanded its initial educational offer beyond programming to include science, robotics, entrepeneurship and citizenship programs, among others.

All these educational proposals have in common a constructivist, student-centered approach to learning, reflecting its diverse and rich methodological derivations: project based learning in some cases, inquiry based learning in others, and design based learning in some others (Muñoz et al. 2014).

---

[1] The first programming software used was *Logo*, created by Seymour Papert. In the 1990s, *MicroWorlds*, a modern version of Logo, was introduced, with the same purpose of allowing children to explore, design, create and build their own learning projects. Today, several other pieces of software are being used, such as *Scratch* and *Alice*. Together with these programming environments, the computers are equiped with an array of educational software, accessible both locally and on line: office applications, project management, video calls, image, video and audio editing, drawing, web design, etc.

The continuous thinking and monitoring of teaching and learning in the computer labs led to the development of a more precise framework of the Program's expected learning outcomes both for elementary and secondary education. Drawing on PRONIE's theoretical model of the social appropriation of digital technologies (Fundación Omar Dengo 2006), a set of student performance standards in digital technology enhanced learning (www.fod.ac.cr/estandares) were drawn up to make explicit what the program expected the children to know and to be able to do with digital technologies with regard to problem solving, productivity and civic engagement and communication, at the end of each school cycle[2] (Fundación Omar Dengo 2009).

In addition, a set of didactic guideliness that explained how to put into practice a project in each school year in order to reach the proposed standards, was developed. These guidelines were specially designed to support those teachers who struggle most with the complexities of a student centered and technology enriched classroom environment. They also sought to help newly qualified teachers, with the expectation that as they become more experienced and skilled, they will be able to design their own learning projects. Meanwhile, best performing teachers were trained in the use of diverse methodologies and in the design of learning situations aimed at supporting students' learning in problem solving and programming.

Now, as we approach the third decade of the twenty-first century and are promoting an increased presence and use of technology inside and outside our schools, PRONIE is enriching and refining the computer lab's pedagogical model and purpose. We are envisioning the emergence of a new knowledge area, no longer restricted to a physical facility, that draws on the long experience of Costa Rica in the teaching of programming and the use of technologies to promote students' high-order capacities, and at the same time looks into new and exciting perspectives as computing, engineering, and digital arts learning spreads internationally.

PRONIE's updated learning proposal, currently being field tested, is oriented to the development of computational thinking. It will promote the students' capabilities to create, solve problems, produce, and express themselves, all through the appropriation of advanced computer practices, as well as fundamental computing and programming concepts. The learning domains that it encompass are: (1) concepts, operations, and components of computational systems, including fundamental computing concepts; (2) problem solving with programming; (3) construction of physical artifacts and robots; and (4) data modelling and representation. The didactics stretch the more common approach of learning by doing to learning by making, with the incorporation of opportunities to explore fabrication and physical computing, in the context of projects that challenge students' imagination and application, while strengthening their technical knowledge and skills.

This approach to learning conceives of children as makers and creators and is based on Papert's *constructionism*, both an intellectual culture (as he would name it) and an educational methodology characterized by the attitude of *getting it to happen*

[2]The cycles comprise three school years: pre-school (4–6 years of age), first cycle (7–9 years of age), second cycle (10–12 years of age), third cycle (13–15 years of age) and fourth cycle (16–18 years of age).

(Papert 1999), that is, building something with the commitment of making it work. The focus is on subjecting own constructions to the test of reality (if they do not work, the challenge is to understand why and overcome the obstacles); they can be shown, shared and discussed with other people; and best of all, they may provide, in the course of construction, the opportunity to discover and appropriate powerful ideas and concepts (Papert 1980, 1996, 1999). In this sense, *constructionism* relates to learning by making, "an idea that includes but goes far beyond the idea of learning by doing" (Papert 1999, p. VIII).

These pedagogical perspectives that nurtured PRONIE's educational vision have been revisited by practitioners of the so-called *maker movement* (Fishman and Dede 2016); they have also been enhanced and enriched by fabrication and physical computing technologies such as 3D printing, microprocessors, wearable computing, e-textiles, *smart* materials, and new programming languages (Libow and Stager 2013). "The maker movement supplies classrooms with ideas, tools, and constructive materials to expand the breadth, depth, and range of potential projects, the primary unit of classroom experiences" (Stager 2015, p. 4).

Computers in the Classroom Building Curricular Content Knowledge and Developing Twenty-First Century Skills

In addition to the revision and enrichment of the computer labs proposal, PRONIE has made significant efforts to promote the use of digital technologies in the regular classroom. With the aim of enriching learning in key subject areas and developing the strategic skills needed today, a wide array of projects has been implemented since 2011 with different academic emphases and equipment schemes. The idea behind these implementations has been to not tie the country to a unique model but to leave space for the evolution of technology and pedagogy as time progresses, and in recognition of the different contexts in which schools operate.

Three main approaches have been explored: (1) one-to-one laptop programs, aimed at facilitating ubiquous access to technology to elementary and secondary students in rural areas specially handicapped by the digital gap, thus allowing students in such areas to experience the potential of the computer as a personal tool for learning, production and creation; (2) laptop cart programs, installed at both primary and secondary schools, with a focus in the reinforcement of research, reasoning and creative skills in subjects like language, mathematics and science; and (3) classroom computers programs, particularly in preschools, directed at enabling the transversal use of technology proposed for that school level.

The vision of these iniatives regarding the role of mobile technology in support of the curriculum is that technology amplifies and deepens our students' capacity to build knowledge together with others and to apply it. As well as making classroom learning more personally meaningful, dynamic and attractive for students, PRONIE sees it as a powerful tool serving the kind of learning most needed for today's and tomorrow's world: ubiquious, connected and self-managed learning.

Recent National Curriculum Reforms

Between 2006 and 2014 the Costa Rican Ministry of Public Education conducted several partial curriculum reforms to the learning objectives, contents and methodologies of several subjects. These reforms shared a common paradigm called by Leonardo Garnier, the Minister of Education at that time, *subversive education*. By this he meant an education for autonomy, self-efficacy and creativity, with a strong emphasis on the development of ethical, civic and aesthetic values. These initial reforms in selected subjects paved the way for a comprehensive curriculum reform launched in 2015 by Sonia Marta Mora, current Minister of Education. The new curriculum is based on a student learning outcomes framework informed by ATC21S's conception of twenty-first century skills. The two stages of the recent national curriculum reforms are described in the following sections.

Initial Curriculum Reforms

The Ministry of Education started its reform program in 2006 launching the *Ethics, aesthetics, and citizenship* program, which stimulated profound transformations in subjects such as Civics, Music, Fine Arts, Physical Education, Industrial Education, and Home Education. These areas were considered to offer an easier pathway to spearhead the conceptual and methodological changes needed towards a more student-focussed and competence based teaching. The reforms also included a series of extracurricular activities in the arts and sports (such as the *Student Festival of Arts*, the *Student Sport Games)*, and a refreshed program of student government, among others.

The goal of these reforms was to develop students' basic knowledge, skills and values associated with a healthy personal and collective identity and character: moral reasoning, civic deliberation, responsible decision making, art and music appreciation, self-managemnt, relationship management, etc.

Methodologically, the new curriculum was based on project based learning. Students had to solve problems, analyse and discuss topics of interest for the group, produce work that requires mobilizing and combining different sources of information, carry out field trips to observe and help explain different phenomena, create artwork, among others.

Within this set of initial reforms, two of the main academic subjects, Spanish and Mathematics, also underwent a major revision. The spirit of these amendments was to strenghthen the students's capacity to think in and make effective use of the essential languages of all times: the oral and written language and the mathematical language.

In Spanish, new approaches to literacy learning were instituted, recognizing that no significant advance can be made in more complex thinking-based skills, unless the students have a good command of the essential tools and substance of thinking, which is language itself: the basic ability to understand what they listen to and read, and also to say and write what they wish to convey. According to the Ministry of Education's diagnosis, Costa Rican students needed to strengthen their capacity to express themselves logically and to produce an original line of thought, connecting correctly their premises to their conclusions, without illogical leaps, contradictions, fallacies or inconsistencies (Ministerio de Educación Pública 2014).

In consequence, a new focus on developing skills such us arguing about opinions, sympathizing, disagreeing, etc., was also introduced. In Primary Education, the *Piensa en Arte/Think Art* program was initially piloted in 2007 in several schools, in Spanish classes, as a way to foster critical and rational thinking via the employment of art as a pedagogical resource. The program was adapted from the Piensa en Arte methodology developed by the Fundación Cisneros and the Colección Patricia Phelps de Cisneros in Venezuela, based on the *visual thinking curriculum* of the Museum of Modern Art in New York (MoMA). By 2014, with the help of the Asociación AcciónArte (http://accionarte.wix.com/accionarte), the program had reached almost every primary school in the country (Ministerio de Educación Pública 2014).

The implementation of *Piensa en Arte/Think Art* in Spanish classes in primary schools, gave way to the learning of logical thinking in secondary education, also as part of the Spanish program of study. In 2009, a review process explored how to complement the study of linguistic rules (i.e., grammar) with the universal rules of logic understood as the theory of formal and informal inference. The goal was to help students learn not only the correct or incorrect uses of language, but also the validity or invalidity of the assertions being made. This would increase their ability to express themselves coherently and fluidly, upon valid reasoning, and to analize critically the messages they receive. The expectation was that making this learning part of the subject of Spanish would favor the transfer of these new thinking skills to other domains.

Finally, in Mathematics an overall reform was launched in 2012 focused on increasing the Costa Rican students' mathematical competence, conceived as the capacity to use mathematics to understand and act upon in different real contexts, and to overcome the historical tradition of failure and fear towards the subject that many students in our country experience.

The new methodology was based on a constructivist approach, where learning stems from the students' early and active involvement with problems, associated with their own physical, social and cultural environment, or at least easily imaginable by them, advancing from the concrete towards the abstracte.

Subsequent Whole Curriculum Reform

Recognizing the need to rethink the ultimate learning goals of the educational system within the new knowledge and innovation based society, the Ministry of Education launched in 2015 a whole curriculum reform called *Education for a new citizenship*. The aim of the initiative was to leverage the change process driven by the first set of reforms and move towards a global curriculum transformation focused on the development of twenty-first century skills and the reinforcement of three core themes: citizenship for sustainable development, global citizenship with a national identity, and digital citizenship with social equity (Ministerio de Educación Pública 2015).

In order to guide the elaboration of new learning profiles that could serve as the basis for the curriculum development process, ATC21S's twenty-first century skills framework (Binkley et al. 2012) was selected. Consequently, its suggested set of skills grouped in four broad categories was adopted with a minor adaptation:

- **Ways of thinking:** critical thinking, systemic thinking, learning to learn, problem solving, creativity and innovation
- **Ways of living in the world:** global and local citizenship, personal and social responsibility, healthy living styles, life and career.
- **Ways of relating with others:** collaboration, communication.
- **Tools to be part of the world:** appropriation of digital technologies, information literacy.

A learning profile for each school cycle[3] was developed with the specification of expected learning outcomes for each of the above mentioned skills. This work was very much nourished, among other sources, by the skill indicators that were published by the ATC21S Latin American Chapter (Fundación Omar Dengo 2014). As of June 2017, five programs of study (English, French, Science, Social Studies and Spanish) have been redesigned under the new learning outcomes framework based on twenty-first century skills.

Implementation of Twenty-First Century Skills Assessment in Costa Rica

Participation of Costa Rica in ATC21S

The participation of Costa Rica in ATC21S was a key event in its trajectory towards the development of systems and tools capable of assessing twenty-first century skills. Costa Rica hosted the Latin American Chapter of this project, at the request of the Inter-American Development Bank (Banco Interamericano de Desarrollo) and with support of Intel Latin America, Microsoft Latin America, and the Costa Rica-United States Foundation for Cooperation.

Locally, the project was implemented by the Costa Rican Ministry of Public Education and the Omar Dengo Foundation, with the mandate of validating the tools developed by the global project for the measurement of twenty-first century skills and contributing to their contextualization for Latin American countries.

Together with Australia, Finland, Netherlands, Singapore and the United States of America, Costa Rica took part in the fieldwork needed for the development of the assessment tasks. This involved translating first all tasks and instructions contained in the modules of the assessment platform to standard Spanish and the localisation of the two tasks developed to assess the skill *Learning through Digital Networks* (Bujanda and Campos 2015). The localisation process entailed the ad hoc production of web resources in Spanish, owing to the difficulty of finding resources in this language equivalent to those used in the original version of the tasks in English. This detailed translation and localisation of the tasks allowed Costa Rica to contribute to the four processes of task concept check, cognitive laboratory, pilot and trial leading to their final calibration.

The psychometric properties of the tasks in Costa Rica were similar to those in other countries, indicating that these tasks can be completed in Costa Rica with little or no language, cultural, or country specific bias. Differences in the difficulty of the items were minor or non-existent. Out of 150 items, only two were more difficult for Costa Rica than other countries, while two items were easier for Costa Rica than other countries.

The Latin American Chapter is generally considered to have made a special contribution to understanding how linguistic and cultural differences affect the assessment of skills and competencies in the twenty-first century. Subsequently, the Latin American Chapter of ATC21S focused its work on the elaboration of materials and further resources to support teachers to teach and assess twenty-first century skills. An online platform was created to allocate the following resources (www.fod.ac.cr/competencias21):

- An interactive book on how to teach and assess twenty-first century skills (Fundación Omar Dengo 2014).
- A collection of videos showing good practices being implemented by Costa Rican teachers
- A resource bank

Of particular interest is the synthesis made by the Latin American Chapter of the key elements that characterize an assessment in accordance with the development of twenty-first century skills, formulated as practical teaching and assessing guidelines and illustrated with examples of how Costa Rican teachers are implementing them (Fundación Omar Dengo 2014):

- **Assessing content and skills comprehensively**. This involves implementing performance based assessment strategies, which require students to demonstrate what they can do by executing activities that require them to put in practice and combine their knowledge, skills and dispositions. The assessment criteria should provide evidence of progress both in knowledge and skills and attitudes (see the video of English teacher Alberto González, from *Jacinto Ávila Araya* Primary School in Palmares, Costa Rica: https://www.youtube.com/watch?v=5G19dAKVUQk).
- **Assessment for learning**. Whereas traditionally the focus has been on the *assessment of learning*, i.e. the judgement of the level of content domain obtained by the students, *assessment for learning* aims to provide the student with timely information to guide and improve her performance, as well as to encourage her persistence and self-confidence; thus, mistakes are seen as a natural part of the

learning process. A balance is therefore required between assessing learning and assessing for learning in order to gain valuable information on learning outcomes and at the same time raise the level of student learning and help students become effective life-long learners (see the video of Math teacher Greivin Calderón, from *Liceo Experimental Bilingüe de Palmares* Secondary School, in Palmares, Costa Rica: https://www.youtube.com/watch?v=0qSAFUkv_HQ).

- **Providing feedback**. Part of assessment for learning is giving students frequent and appropriate feedback on their progress and achievements. This is facilitated when intermediate products or milestones are established that allow for students to learn in a timely manner whether they are on the right track or they have things to correct or improve (see the video of Math teacher Jessica Mora, from *Liceo San Nicolás de Tolentino* Secondary School in Cartago, Costa Rica: https://www.youtube.com/watch?v=viCJnYuNfDM).
- **Incorporating opportunities for self and peer assessment**. This entails sharing and discussing with the students the learning objectives and expected outcomes, and helping them, individually and in groups, to reflect on their experiences, assess their strengths and needs based on evidence, and plan how to progress according to criteria agreed with the teacher. After each activity, students can identify what went well, what went wrong and why. Peer assessment is also a powerful tool that strengthens collaboration and communication skills, and allows students to understand more deeply the criteria with which they themselves will be assessed (see the video of Science teacher Yorleny Castro, from *Liceo Experimental Bilingüe de Naranjo*, in Naranjo, Costa Rica: https://www.youtube.com/watch?v=YFVvKLx7TYM&index=5&list=PL9ZKNydvF4iVKAdhvR7P_6kMWIp7zw6sm).

Costa Rica participation in the ATC21S project was part of the effort to promote the reform of teaching and assessment practices through the use of technology and the development of better teaching and learning tools and approaches. For the country, being part of ATC21S has opened the possibility of having access to an innovative and validated assessment platform that will allow something that was previously challenging: the rigorous and wide scale assessment of strategic cognitive and social skills.

During the project, the participating teachers' and students' anecdotal responses to the assessment tasks were very positive. The students enjoyed the tasks, they found them both engaging and challenging. The teachers showed great interest in learning how to incorporate the assessment tasks into their subjects, and they appreciated the value of the tasks as a tool to assess the students' skills and to inform their teaching practice, but also as learning resources in themselves as well.

But perhaps more importantly, for the local team it has meant the acquisition of important insights into assessment theory and measurement practice for twenty-first century skills, and especially the opportunity to learn first-hand how standardized, performance- and computer-based assessment instruments can be constructed and validated.

The assessment platform developed by ATC21S can serve both formative purposes for individual students as well as system wide monitoring evaluation. In Costa

Rica, these opportunities have been taken advantage of to monitor how students progress in their learning of these crucial skills, and how to support them in this process.

Experiences in the Construction of New Assessment Instruments and Measurements

The introduction of twenty-first century skills in school curricula brings with it two major challenges: their systematic teaching and assessment. In the case of Costa Rica, with the implementation of PRONIE MEP-FOD, questions concerning its results in terms of learning outcomes arose from its beginning.

The initial evaluations followed two different approaches. The first consisted of quasi-experimental designs where psychometric tests of general skills, such as creativity, were applied to a sample of students participating in the program to compare their results with those of a control group. These studies provided positive results for the group of students participating in the program (Ministerio de Educación Pública 1993).

The second evaluation approach aimed at the observation and analysis of students' learning processes while collaboratively making programmed products. These studies demonstrated that with the right kind of teacher mediation, the expected problem solving processes improved through the programming activity (Zuniga 1995; Dobles and Zúñiga 1994).

Both evaluation approaches presented significant limitations. The first, due to its massive and general nature, provided limited insights to help improve the teaching practice, as the emphasis was placed on students' scores and little was reported on their learning processes. The second, by its casuistic nature, failed to account for trends in the program's outcomes as a whole.

These early evaluation efforts also faced the challenge of poor definition of expected learning outcomes, as these were formulated in very general terms without the necessary specifications for the different cycles of the education system.

The student performance standards in digital technology-enhanced learning, mentioned above,[3] were the answer to that challenge. They address the expected skills as *ICT skills for learning* (Ananiadou and Claro 2009), that is, the use of digital technologies to investigate and discriminate information, solve problems, communicate, participate, develop digital products, proceed ethically and safely, and continue learning throughout life.

Expected learning outcomes profiles were developed for each school cycle. They describe the performance in three domains expected from the students as result of their participation in the educational program involving the computer labs: *Citizenship and communication* (use of technology to participate and communicate);

[3] See www.fod.ac.cr/estandares

productivity (use of technology to create useful products and know how to use tools effectively); and *problem solving and research* (use of technology to research and create software with specific objectives collaboratively).

In 2010, PRONIE's educational proposal for computer labs was aligned to these standards, allowing progress towards the development of assessment tools that account for students' knowledge and skills in the use of ICT as tools for learning throughout life.

With the participation of Costa Rica in ATC21S, the opportunity arose to learn from the methodological process followed in this project for the development of assessment tasks able to report on students' learning outcomes and simultaneously support teaching and learning by means of building learning progressions. This knowledge has informed and re-oriented the development of assessment tools at PRONIE.

Large Scale Research to Determine Impact on Student Learning

In 2014 a first version of a test to assess PRONIE's students' knowledge associated with the safe and ethical use of ICT to research, communicate and solve problems was developed. The construction of this instrument went through the processes of conceptualization (with researchers and educators familiar with PRONIE's educational proposal), development of multiple choice items with four options, cognitive laboratories and a pilot before being trialed with a sample of 9829 students. These students were starting their seventh grade (13 year-olds) and came from primary schools participating in PRONIE's computer lab program, as well as from other schools. Having students at the same development level but with different length of exposure to this program allowed researchers to group them in three separate clusters: students with any exposure, students with less than 3 years' exposure, and students with 4–6 years' exposure (maximum).

Structural equation analysis was used to confirm the one-dimensional nature of each of the three domains that conform to the standards framework (*Citizenship and Communication*, *Productivity* and *Research and Problem Solving*).[4] Classical test theory and item response theory were used to estimate the validity and reliability of the instrument.[5] The Rasch model that allows assessment of the students' ability or skill level to answer each item, with respect to the difficulty level that the item exhibits, was also used to identify the items with greater and lesser degree of difficulty for the students. After determining each student's performance level (using the Rasch model), regression analysis was used to identify the factors that

[4] Some indicators of goodness of fit: RMSEA: 0.037 and CFI: 0.962.

[5] Reliability results: Citizenship and Communication, person reliability: 0.87 and items reliability: 1.00; Productivity, person reliability: 0.90 and items reliability: 1.00; and Research and Problem Solving, person reliability: 0.84 and items reliability: 1.00.

could best explain the students' different scores. In addition to the years of exposure to the program (the variable used to assess PRONIE' effect), the regression model considered other variables associated with sociodemographic characteristics (sex, age, place of residence, number or people living in the same household) and technology access (computer ownership, internet access and frequency of use of different devices).

The regression model showed that students with longer exposure to the computer lab's program (from 3 to 6 years) scored higher than students with less than 3 years or no exposure at all in the three assessed domains. In fact, the variable *time of exposure to PRONIE's computer lab program* was one of the variables which most affected the scores, and was the most important variable explaining the results in the *problem solving and research* domain, which proved to be the most difficult for the students (Programa Estado de la Nación 2015).

Based on results generated through the Rasch model, different performance levels in the achievement of the standards were identified. For example, between the medium and high performance levels, students are able to recognize the specific purpose of different kinds of software, understand the importance of ICT in modern society, know the criteria to navigate safely and look for valid information, recognize ethical and legal issues involved in the use of the Internet, and know how to develop digital products for a specific audience. These performance levels serve as an empirical referent to advance the construction of the learning progressions followed by the students in the development of ICT skills for learning.

Currently, the efforts are focused on generating a bank of items with different difficulty levels, associated with learning progressions for each key skill within the standards, that can be used for the development of adaptive tests for students finishing the second and the third school cycles (12 and 15 years respectively).

These adaptive tests are test administered by digital applications that present items to the students choosing them from a different levels of difficulty item bank, according to the previous student's answers; which, in theory, allows one to reduce the number of items needed to assess their performance levels. With the addition of automated scoring, these tests offer the benefit of immediate reports that can present the results in relation with the learning progressions, showing what the students already know or can do, and what they do not, that is, the proximal development zone. So, the reports will inform the teacher to know how to better lead the learning process, and provide the system administrators with aggregated outcomes to inform programatic decisions at a regional and national level.

Finally, it is expected that the assessments tasks developed by ATC21S can continue to be used in our schools as a regular tool to support the formative assessment of strategic skills such as collaborative problem solving, while fostering the teachers' discussions around the ways that they can help their students be stronger in such skills.

Challenges

Our experience has shown that the complex performances associated with the twenty-first century skills are not easily achievable learning goals. On one side, they require a certain learning environment – one that favors reflexive and collaborative knowledge construction and application through discovery, tinkering and making. This kind of teaching environment and associated pedagogical style is a challenge for our teachers, who in general are still fighting to change practices based on knowledge transmission and reproduction. Costa Rica needs to strengthen pedagogical competence as well as knowledge content mastery of its teachers. Pedagogical competence has to do with knowing how to design activities and environments that foster active and cooperative learning processes, and also how to promote and sustain an intelligent dialogue in the classroom as well as student meta-cognition. These new pedagogies require rethinking initial teacher education processes and also the model, methodology and content of continuing professional development processes, in line with recommendations derived from the national (Brenes 2010) and international literature (Timperley 2008; Wei et al. 2009).

On the other side, it is difficult to measure a general and clearly observable impact on twenty-first century skills relying only on specific and isolated programs. Whole-school or whole-curriculum approaches offer much better conditions for real change to be implemented. In this regard, the curriculum reforms conducted by the Ministry of Education in the last 11 years constitute a substantial step in the right direction. It is now necessary to secure the effective and widespread implementation of those reforms.

A strengthened school management and development model is also needed. This implies creating or strengthening at least three elements: (1) participative spaces where teachers and school leaders realize their vision and purpose for the school and work together to achieve it; (2) more precise and modern mechanisms for assessing students' learning outcomes, so that more effective school-based and whole-system monitoring mechanisms are enabled, thereby supporting decision-making and accountability at both those levels; and (3) incentives to recognize the efforts of those who are trying to improve and innovate (e.g. more resources for schools or special professional development opportunities).

Future Prospects

At present, the adoption of digital technologies in Costa Rica's society advances rapidly, and the country participates increasingly in the knowledge-collaboration global society that demands new citizens with adaptive skills. Although students are increasingly connected and own multiple devices, there are existing gaps in access and appropriation of technology for learning and production. Much of PRONIE's work of the lasts years has focused on closing those gaps, through democratizing access and appropriation capacities to use digital technologies. As a result the Program has duplicated its overall national coverage in the past 3 years.

For the future, we imagine a student population that finds in PRONIE's educational proposals supported by digital technologies, opportunities to strengthen and boost the quality and equity of the educational system, as well as complementary options for the development of individual talents and interests. These proposals would favor processes of self-learning so that cognitive, physical, and temporal frontiers are defined increasingly by the student, and not only by the educational system.

This scenario is already in construction by the Program, reinforcing and expanding the enabling platforms necessary for a gradual but dynamic enriching process, so that changes can occur in a relatively short time. These platforms will allow digital and collaborative learning of teachers, school principals and students, as well as constant interaction and production among peers and local communities, and with international partners. The regular monitoring of individual and collective progress for continuous improvement will also be facilitated, both within the framework of the current curriculum defined by the national educational system as well as by personal learning paths that students and curious learners choose to follow.

The ATC21S assessment platform is a well-timed opportunity to support this vision, in particular, the formative initiatives for individual students, as well as system-wide monitoring evaluation efforts.

References

Ananiadou, K., & Claro, M. (2009). *21st century skills and competences for new millennium learners in OECD countries. OECD education working papers* (Vol. 41). Paris: OECD Publishing. http://dx.doi.org/10.1787/218525261154.

Binkley, M., Erstad, O., Herman, J., Raizen, S., Ripley, M., Miller-Ricci, M., & Rumble, M. (2012). Defining twenty-first century skills. In P. Griffin, B. McGaw, & E. Care (Eds.), *Assessment and teaching of 21st century skills* (pp. 67–141). Dordrecht: Springer.

Brenes, V. (2010). *El desarrollo profesional de los docentes en servicio en Costa Rica: Un estudio exploratorio, Tercer Informe de Estado de la Educación.* San José: Programa Estado de la Nación. Available at: http://www.estadonacion.or.cr/files/biblioteca_virtual/educacion/003/Brenes_2010_desarrollo_profesional_docentes.pdf.

Bujanda, M. E., & Campos, E. (2015). The adaptation and contextualization of ATC21STM by Costa Rica. In P. Griffin & E. Care (Eds.), *Assessment and teaching of 21st century skills. Methods and approach* (pp. 225–256). Dordrecht: Springer.

Dobles, M. Zúñiga, M. (1994). Significaciones en el contexto escolar y actividad cognitiva. Un estudio con niñas del Programa de Informática Educativa MEP-FOD. In IIMEC (Org.), La Investigación Etnográfica en el Marco de la Investigación Cualitativa en Educación. V Simposio IIMEC, San José, Costa Rica.

Fallas, I. Zúñiga, M. (2010). Las tecnologías digitales de la información y la comunicación en la educación costarricense (Informe final). In Tercer Informe de Estado de la Educación. San José, Costa Rica: Programa Estado de la Nación. Available at: http://www.estadonacion.or.cr/files/biblioteca_virtual/educacion/003/Fallas_Zuniga_2010_TIC_Educacion.pdf.

Fishman, B., & Dede, C. (2016). Teaching and technology: New tools for new times. In D. Gitomer & C. Bell (Eds.), *Handbook of research on teaching (American Educational Research Association)*. New York: Springer.

Fundación Omar Dengo. (2006). *Educación y Tecnologías Digitales. Cómo valorar su impacto social y sus contribuciones a la equidad.* San José: Fundación Omar Dengo. Available at: http://aplicaciones02.fod.ac.cr/idrc/intro.htm.

Fundación Omar Dengo. (2009). *Estándares de desempeño para estudiantes en aprendizaje con tecnologías digitales.* San José: Fundación Omar Dengo. Available at: www.fod.ac.cr/estandares/docs/descargas/el_proyectoestandares.pdf.

Fundación Omar Dengo. (2014). *Competencias para el siglo XXI: guía práctica para promover su aprendizaje y evaluación.* San José: Fundación Omar Dengo. Available at: http://www.fod.ac.cr/competencias21/index.php/areas-de-recursos/publicacion-digital#.VWSQGM9_Oko.

Libow, S., & Stager, G. (2013). *Invent to learn: Making, tinkering, and engineering in the classroom.* Torrance: Constructing Modern Knowledge.

Ministerio de Educación Pública. (2014). *Memoria institucional 2006–2014. La educación suversiva: atreverse a construir el país que queremos.* San José: Ministerio de Educación Pública. Available at: http://www.mep.go.cr/sites/default/files/page/adjuntos/memoriainstitucional20062014pdf.pdf.

Ministerio de Educación Pública. (2015). *Educar para una nueva ciudadanía. Fundamentación pedagógica de la transformación curricular.* San José: Ministerio de Educación Pública. Available at: http://www.idp.mep.go.cr/sites/all/files/idp_mep_go_cr/publicaciones/7-2016_educar_para_una_nueva_ciudadaniafinal.pdf.

Ministerio de Educación Pública [MEP]. (1993). Evaluación del Programa de informática educativa coordinado por la Fundación Omar Dengo (internal document). San José, Costa Rica.

Muñoz, L., Brenes, M., Bujanda, M., Mora, M., Núñez, O., & Zúñiga, M. (2014). *Las políticas TIC en los sistemas educativos de América Latina: Caso Costa Rica.* Buenos Aires: Fondo de las Naciones Unidas para la Infancia (UNICEF), Programa TIC y Educación Básica. UNICEF. Available at: http://www.unicef.org/argentina/spanish/Costa_Rica_OK.pdf.

Papert, S. (1980). *Mindstorms.* New York: Basic Books.

Papert, S. (1996). An Exploration in the Space of Mathematics Educations. *International Journal of Computers for Mathematical Learning, 1*(1), 95–123. Available at: http://www.papert.org/articles/AnExplorationintheSpaceofMathematicsEducations.html.

Papert, S. (1999). What is logo? Who needs it? In Almeida et al. Logo philosophy and implementation (pp. IV–XVII). Logo Computer Systems. Available at: http://www.microworlds.com/company/philosophy.pdf

Programa Estado de la Nación. (2015). *Quinto Informe Estado de la Educación.* San José: Programa Estado de la Nación. Available at: http://www.estadonacion.or.cr/estado-educacion.

Stager, G. (2015). Guide to creating and inventing with technology in the classroom. Intel Australia. Available at: http://innovationtoolbox.intel.com.au/wp-content/uploads/2015/05/18009_IntelEdu_Guide2Making_FA_LR_singles.pdf

Timperley, H. (2008). *Teacher profesional learning and development. Educational practices series* (Vol. 18). Paris: International Bureau of Education, UNESCO; International Academy of Education. Available at: http://www.ibe.unesco.org/fileadmin/user_upload/Publications/Educational_Practices/EdPractices_18.pdf.

Wei, R. C., Darling-Hammond, L., Andree, A., Richardson, N., & Orphanos, S. (2009). *Professional learning in the learning profession: A status report on teacher development in the united states and abroad.* Oxford: National Staff Development Council. Available at: http://learningforward.org/docs/pdf/nsdcstudy2009.pdf.

Zúñiga, M. (1995). Orden simbólico y funcionamiento cognoscitivo: implicaciones de las interacciones específicas entre sujetos en el funcionamiento de las estructuras cognoscitivas de niños(as) de tercero y sexto grado, al trabajar con el lenguaje Logo, en el contexto de un laboratorio de informática educativa del PIE-MEP-FOD (Tesis de Licenciatura en Psicología). Universidad de Costa Rica. San José, Costa Rica.

Part IV
Information Communication Technologies: Their Measurement and Their Uses

Chapter 11
Learning in Digital Networks as a Modern Approach to ICT Literacy

Mark Wilson, Kathleen Scalise, and Perman Gochyyev

Abstract This chapter starts from the perspective that the current conceptualization of educational assessment is out of date, but particularly with regard to conception of information and communication (ICT) literacy. It provides a summary of the conceptual changes in the idea of ICT literacy in four main steps: a concentration of knowledge about computers and their use; a transition to a view of ICT literacy as a broad set of skills that have links to many traditional and non-traditional school subjects, accompanied by the move to technology integration in education; a second transition where ICT Literacy is expressed as progress variables that are essential tools for the design of curriculum and assessments; and finally, the impact of the "social network" perspective on ICT literacy – the critical need for building the power of virtual skills through proficiency with networks of people, information, tools, and resources. The chapter then describes the ACT21S ICT Literacy Framework, which we see as embodying the last of these stages. This includes four "progress variables" that describe student growth in sophistication in ICT Literacy, each involving several increasing levels of development. An online assessment tool to assess the dimensions of the framework is described, and examples of items and responses are given. Results from an international study of students interacting with the assessments are then displayed, including empirical versions of the progress variables, and estimates of their correlation, reliability, and fit are given. The chapter concludes with a brief summary of the findings, and a discussion of its broader implications.

M. Wilson (✉)
University of California, Berkeley, CA, USA

University of Melbourne, Parkville, VIC, Australia
e-mail: markw@berkeley.edu

K. Scalise
University of Oregon, Eugene, Oregon, USA

P. Gochyyev
University of California, Berkeley, CA, USA

E. Care et al. (eds.), *Assessment and Teaching of 21st Century Skills*,
Educational Assessment in an Information Age,
DOI 10.1007/978-3-319-65368-6_11

Information and communication technology (ICT) literacy has been seen as one of the key educational goals for the twenty-first century. For example, consider this joint statement from three information technology companies:

> The economy of leading countries is now based more on the manufacture and delivery of information products and services than on the manufacture of material goods. Even many aspects of the manufacturing of material goods are strongly dependent on innovative uses of technologies. The start of the 21st century also has witnessed significant social trends in which people access, use, and create information and knowledge very differently than they did in previous decades, again due in many ways to the ubiquitous availability of ICT. (CIM 2008, p. 1)

One can assume that this broad change will have a large influence on the personal and working lives of many people, and thus will also have large effects on the educational systems that prepare people for their lives and careers. This will include the characteristics and labels of the subjects that are taught in schools, the instruction for those new subjects (and the traditional subjects), and how education is structured. Current changes in educational policies, such as in the U.S. Common Core Standards (e.g., CCSSI 2010) and the Next Generation Science Standards (NGSS Lead States 2013), are examples of efforts to cope with these broad changes. We see the movement towards twenty-first century skills (Binkley et al. 2012), in general, and towards new forms of ICT literacy in particular, as further examples of the same thing. We begin our discussion with this initial broad definition of information and communication technology literacy: information and communication technology literacy is a set of skills associated with the use of contemporary technologies for information processing and communications. The definition is deliberately variable with respect to technological developments over time – this will involve changes both in the technologies themselves (both hardware and software), and also in the range of human activities that are facilitated by those technologies. In fact, it reaches back in time, and hence can be seen to include the use of Morse code on telegraphs, signal flags on sailing ships, handwritten letters, and even glyphs carved in stone.

The current conceptualization of educational assessment is out of date in some respects. First, in business, knowledge is applied across disciplinary boundaries in the process of dealing with real problems, but in schools the subjects are based on traditional disciplines. Second, in business, people work both alone and in groups to share complementary knowledge and skills and attain common goals – this is in contrast with the situation in schools and assessments where students are required to work on projects and take tests individually. Third, in business, workers have access to large amounts of information and to technological tools, where the task is to craft an efficient and satisfying solution, which differs strongly from the typical practice of "closed book" standardized assessment. Fourth, in business, problems are contextualized in particular situations, which are not structured to be addressed by simply recalling knowledge or working through simple algorithms, which again differs from a great deal of education in schools, but most strongly the context of standardized testing (CIM 2008). We observe that these changes in the nature of work in the workplace have led to changes in the concept of ICT literacy.

The efforts described in this chapter were grounded in the Assessment and Teaching of Twenty-first Century Skills project (ATC21S – Griffin et al. 2012; Care 2017), which was launched in 2009 as a response to these transitions in the world economy due to developments in information and communication technologies.

In conceiving ICT literacy itself as a twenty-first century skill, we view it as encompassing a range of subtopics, including learning in networks, information literacy, digital competence and technological awareness, all of which contribute to *learning to learn* through the development of enabling skills. In the global economy, learning through digital networks, and the use of digital media, is becoming increasingly important in private life, in learning, and in professional life. We predict that this aspect of learning will become even more important in the future. We see this as being true at the individual level and local or regional levels as well as at international levels. Thus, we focus the concept of *learning to learn* onto the digital domain, and arrive at the idea of *learning to learn in the context of digital networks*.

We provide a brief review of developments in the concept of ICT literacy over the last 25 years or so. We see that the concept of ICT literacy has changed a great deal during these years: from a conceptualization as a specific domain of knowledge about computers to an understanding of it as a domain-general or transversal twenty-first century skill. (Note, a full account of this was originally published in Wilson et al. 2015). The second half of the chapter gives a brief account of the ICT Literacy project itself (for more details on this see Wilson et al. 2015), and then examines selected results from the empirical study, focusing on (a) the multidimensional model of ICT Literacy, and (b) The Wright Maps for its subdimensions. We conclude with a summary and discussion of broader implications.

ICT Literacy: A History of the Concept

The concept of twenty-first century skills is one that has drawn broad support in recent years. For the ATC21S project, sets of twenty-first century skills were identified based on an analysis of 12 relevant prior twenty-first century skill frameworks drawn from a number of countries and international organizations (Binkley et al. 2012). These included the OECD and countries in Europe, North America, and Asia/Oceania. In the new framework, called "KSAVE," the ten components of the framework encompass not only skills, but as the acronym implies, knowledge (K), skills (S), attitudes (A), values (V), and ethics (E). KSAVE organizes the ten components into four conceptual groupings, ways of thinking, ways of working, tools for working, and living in the world. ICT Literacy was chosen as one of these twenty-first century skills to be examined in more detail, and exemplified in the shape of online assessments. In the paragraphs that follow, we trace the conceptual changes in the idea of ICT literacy in four main steps.

(a) First, it was seen as a concentration of core knowledge and skills about computers and their use, coalescing into the concept of ICT literacy in the early years of the field.
(b) Second, this idea transitioned to a view of ICT literacy as a broad set of skills that have links to many traditional and non-traditional school subjects, and the move to technology integration in education.
(c) Third, in a second transition, ICT Literacy was expressed as progress variables that are essential tools for the design of curriculum and assessments. The "progress" view depicts the need to understand initial ICT knowledge likely to emerge followed by a developing picture of mastery.
(d) Fourth, we consider a new view of ICT that emerged from the impact of the "network" perspective into ICT – the critical need for building the power of virtual skills through proficiency with networks of people, information, tools, and resources. Here we offer a new framework for assessing student ICT learning, based on a learning progression point of view.

A Set of Core Skills

What we now call ICT Literacy was first seen as a concentration of core knowledge and skills about computers and their use, coalescing into the concept of ICT literacy in the early years of the field. Attempts to measure ICT literacy in schools go back at least 25 years. The 1989 and 1992 Computers in Education Studies (COMPED), carried out by the International Association for the Evaluation of Educational Achievement (IEA), evaluated computer use in schools and its impact on students. These IEA studies found that, at that time, in most countries, there was a consistent increase in school computer equipment being made available as well as more teachers using computers in their lessons. However, still very few educators were participating in this trend (IEA 2014a; Pelgrum and Plomp 1991). At around the same time, research synthesized in meta-analytic studies was raising awareness about the growing importance of computers in education, and of the role that digital literacy would play in student proficiencies (Kulik 1994).

An example of a traditional framework of this kind is shown in Fig. 11.1, which is from Dallas County Community College District. The framework for their *Computer Skills Placement Test* (Dallas County Community College District 2014) consists of six parts: Basic Concepts, File Management, Information and

Basic Concepts
File Management
Information and Communication
Spreadsheets—Excel
Presentations—PowerPoint
Word Processing—Word

Fig. 11.1 Framework for the computer skills placement test questions (Dallas County Community College District)

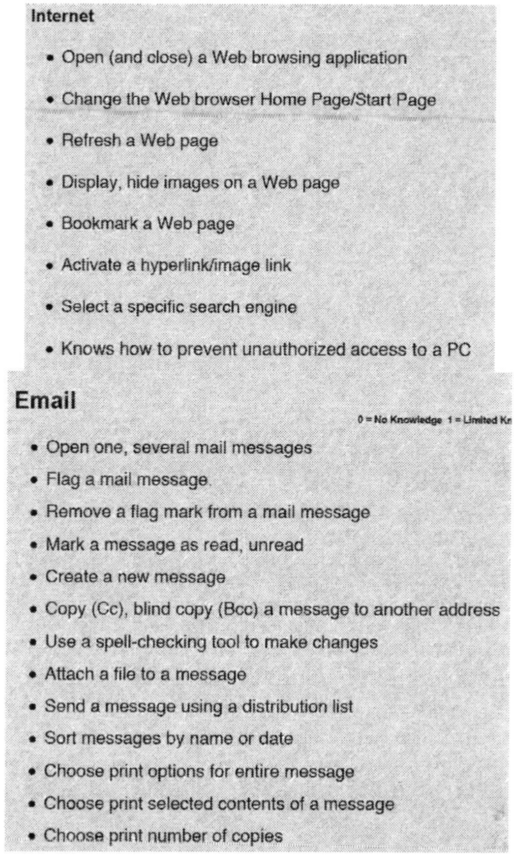

Internet

- Open (and close) a Web browsing application
- Change the Web browser Home Page/Start Page
- Refresh a Web page
- Display, hide images on a Web page
- Bookmark a Web page
- Activate a hyperlink/image link
- Select a specific search engine
- Knows how to prevent unauthorized access to a PC

Email

0 = No Knowledge 1 = Limited Kn

- Open one, several mail messages
- Flag a mail message
- Remove a flag mark from a mail message
- Mark a message as read, unread
- Create a new message
- Copy (Cc), blind copy (Bcc) a message to another address
- Use a spell-checking tool to make changes
- Attach a file to a message
- Send a message using a distribution list
- Sort messages by name or date
- Choose print options for entire message
- Choose print selected contents of a message
- Choose print number of copies

Fig. 11.2 Detail from the framework for the computer skills placement test questions (Dallas County Community College District)

Communication, Spreadsheets – Excel, Presentations – Powerpoint, and Word Processing – Word. The topics are quite tightly focused on specific ICT concepts and skills, and even specific computer software products. We chose the third topic, "Information and Communication" to focus on, as this seems more broadly based than the others (see Fig. 11.2). This section is split into two portions, Internet and Email, and each of these has a number of subtopics[1] under it: Internet has 8 subtopics, such as "Open (and close) a Web browsing application," "Bookmark a Web page," and "Knows how to prevent unauthorized access to a PC;" while Email has 13 subtopics, such as "Open one, several mail messages," "Use a spell-checking tool to make changes," and "Choose print number of copies." Again, the topics are

[1] The full list can be accessed at: https://www1.dcccd.edu/catalog/ss/transfer/CompSkillPractTest2014.pdf.

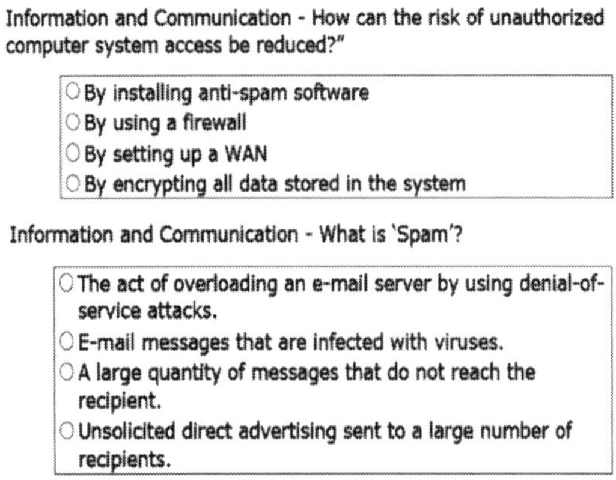
Information and Communication - How can the risk of unauthorized computer system access be reduced?"

- By installing anti-spam software
- By using a firewall
- By setting up a WAN
- By encrypting all data stored in the system

Information and Communication - What is 'Spam'?

- The act of overloading an e-mail server by using denial-of-service attacks.
- E-mail messages that are infected with viruses.
- A large quantity of messages that do not reach the recipient.
- Unsolicited direct advertising sent to a large number of recipients.

Fig. 11.3 Sample items from the computer skills placement test questions (Dallas County Community College District)

quite tightly focused on specific ICT concepts and skills. We show two of the sample items from the test in Fig. 11.3. These demonstrate the emphasis on vocabulary, knowledge and skills that are the core of traditional definitions of ICT literacy.

In 2002 the Organization for Economic Co-operation and Development (OECD) also engaged in the international work on ICT literacy. A key question of the OECD study was to examine the need for a measure of ICT literacy: was there a need to know what had been mastered by students? Or, more specifically, was there a need to understand what students know and can do, rather than simply record frequency or time duration counts of use, array of tools employed, and so forth? The resulting IILP Framework (IILP 2002) made major advances by expanding definitions of ICT competencies. Not only were the usual digital and communications tools to be included, but also the concept of "networks" or means by which students were to access, manage, integrate, evaluate and create information: these became the five components of the framework (Fig. 11.4). The overarching goal was defined as 'being able to successfully function in a "knowledge" society.'

Technical skills were required at each phase but so also were cognitive and communication skills. Not only did this include various daily life activities employing ICT, as had been described by previous usage studies, but the framework advocated for a broader understanding of the critical components of ICT literacy. This would stimulate a deeper transformation in the skills and knowledge that must be acquired. Furthermore, the framework was based on the assumption that ICT literacy was best achieved through integrated learning. Numerous researchers were beginning to agree: Kozma (2003), Jewitt (2003), and others (e.g., Ridgway and McCusker 2003; Quellmalz and Kozma 2003) called for rethinking both what digital literacy called for, and how technology could better contribute to its assessment. In other words, single ICT-focused, stand-alone curricula in information technology courses was not advocated. Rather, ICT literacy skills were described as needing to be integrated appropriately into curricula in subject matter areas. At the same time, the instructors

Access	Knowing about and knowing how to collect and/or retrieve information	Select and open appropriate e-mails from list
Manage	Applying an existing organizational or classification scheme	Identify and organize the relevant information in each email
Integrate	Interpreting and representing information. It involves summarizing, comparing and contrasting	Summarize the interest in the courses provided by the company
Evaluate	Making judgments about the quality, relevance, usefulness, or efficiency of information	Decide which courses should be continued next year, based on last year's attendance
Create	Generating information by adapting, applying, designing, inventing, or authoring information	Write up your recommendation in the form of an e-mail to the vice president of human resources

Fig. 11.4 The five components of the IILP framework

in these courses would need to be able to address IT and technical skills, or have support materials available, in order to ensure improved ICT literacy.

Transition to ICT as a Key Educational Practice

The computer or other digital device is one important means by which students engage in key educational practices to form, consolidate, elaborate and communicate domain knowledge, whether during instruction or during assessment (Ainley et al. 2014; Fraillon 2014). In this way, information and communication technologies have rapidly become for schools not so much an independent skill but an *embedded* skill, or a vehicle used by students to express and engage in their discipline specific knowledge, understanding, and skills in many schooling areas.

One way of approaching school use of digital literacy is to consider it a practice, or way of working through new tools. Friedman (2007) described such practices as a major shift toward technology that educators need to address. He discussed how it may be counter-productive to ask students to power down when they enter the school doors (as is the case in many schools, where technology such as cell phones are seen primarily as distractions from the "real" work). Rather, students should actively engage in digital literacy practices in formal learning, including using the tools, networks and body of expertise available to students virtually. This both underscores developing ICT knowledge and skills as an important practice in schools, and allows educators to teach and model appropriate use while supporting subject matter learning.

One key to assessment developments marking this evolution was the emergence of subject-matter specific technology-enhanced assessments (TEAs), more commonly referred to at the time as "computerized tests". Of course, migration from paper-and-pencil to the computer environment was expected, given greater ease of assessment delivery and data collection (Scalise and Gifford 2006; Wilson et al. 2012; Wilson and Scalise 2011). However, this movement also acknowledged the expectation of at least some familiarity with digital literacy practices in subject matter areas. This development both enhances the importance of ICT literacy, and at the same time promotes the idea of ICT literacy as a broad set of skills that underlie success in other substantive areas such a traditional school subjects, and (of course) other twenty-first century skills. Some examples of prominent efforts along these lines are the OECD PISA programs of Digital Reading assessments (OECD 2011, 2013a) and Collaborative Problem Solving assessments (OECD 2013b), the IEA Progress in International Reading Study (PIRLS) in 2016 (Mullis and Martin 2013), and the U.S. National Assessment of Educational Progress technology-based startup pilot administrations in mathematics, reading and science (US Department of Education 2010).

Of course, as the integration of ICT into subject-matter areas continued along with the move to extend the ICT frontier, the need to think of student knowledge as encompassing a *developing span* of skills grew. Earlier foreshadowed in the IILP framework, it was becoming not enough to think of digital skills as only use, or even as present or absent. The view of it as a laundry list of traits that could be checked off as mastered or not, used or not used, was showing serious shortcomings. Both the *degree* and *type* of knowledge present or absent in any given area of ICT importance was growing more important to understand. Research revealed that students might know how to log in to an online site but not how to navigate effectively or make strategic and creative use of the resources present. It became clear that it mattered significantly whether students had advanced skills, or only novice skills with some school-specific tools, such as spreadsheets and simulators. Especially, degree and type of knowledge tended to interact with the specific context.

Thus, the move to technology integration and the need for subject matter specificity of skills brought the need for a developing conception of student understanding to the fore. What does it look like to be proficient and to grow more proficient? What are detailed markers of proficiency, and how do these markers change as students grow in their skills? Key to emerge in these new efforts was the idea of collaboration as an aspect of digital literacy. The benefits of such collaboration included the contributions of student peer-to-peer engagement (Erstad 2006; Loader 2007) as well as expectations of being able to collaborate digitally.

Introduction of the Explicit Progress Variable

The next transition for ICT Literacy expressed as a movement towards progress variables, which are essential tools for the design of curriculum and assessments. The "progress" view depicts the need to understand initial ICT knowledge likely to emerge followed by a developing picture of mastery. Students are acknowledged as not one-size-fits-all in ICT literacy but moving toward increasing competency in their virtual skills, knowledge, competency, awareness, and use.

An ICT Literacy framework was developed by the Australian Council for Educational Research (ACER) and released in a national report (MCEETYA 2005). In this framework, ICT Literacy was defined as:

> The ability of individuals to use ICT appropriately to access, manage, integrate and evaluate information, develop new understandings, and communicate with others in order to participate effectively in society. (MCEETYA 2005, p. xiii)

The MCEETYA/ACER Framework includes six processes, which are similar to the five components of the IILP Framework (Fig. 11.3) – three remain essentially the same, with 'Integrate and Create' subsumed into a new one called 'Creating,' while two new ones are added, 'Communicating' and 'Using ICT Appropriately.' These processes were then examined both substantively and empirically to ascertain a deeper dimensional structure, and the result is that they were then combined into three strands: Working with Information, Creating and Sharing Information, and Using ICT responsibly. Moreover, these strands were each seen as instances of the concept of a "progress variable", explicitly acknowledging the importance of the developing view of proficiency and according it measurable characteristics (Masters et al. 1990):

> Any assessment is underpinned by a conception of progress in the area being assessed. This assessment of ICT literacy was based on a hierarchy of what students typically know and can do. It was articulated in a progress map described in terms of levels of increasing complexity and sophistication in using ICT. For convenience, students' skills and understandings were described in bands of proficiency. Each band described skills and understandings that are progressively more demanding. The progress map is a generalised developmental sequence that enables information on the full range of student performance to be collected and reported. (ACARA 2012, p. 8–9)

Although the progress variables for these three strands were also developed, the eventual use of the progress variable concept in the national tests was as a single progress variable, as shown in Fig. 11.6, which provides the *MCEETYA/ACER Framework: Digital Transformation for ICT Literacy.* Note that the "Levels" in Fig. 11.5 correspond to the "levels" and "bands" in the quotation above.

Level 1:

Students working at level 1 perform basic tasks using computers and software. They implement the most commonly used file management and software commands when instructed. They recognise the most commonly used ICT terminology and functions.

Level 2:

Students working at level 2 locate simple, explicit information from within a given electronic source. They add content to and make simple changes to existing information products when instructed. They edit information products to create products that show limited consistency of design and information management. They recognize and identify basic ICT electronic security and health and safety usage issues and practices.

Level 3:

Students working at level 3 generate simple general search questions and select the best information source to meet a specific purpose. They retrieve information from given electronic sources to answer specific, concrete questions. They assemble information in a provided simple linear order to create information products. They use conventionally recognised software commands to edit and reformat information products. They recognise common examples in which ICT misuse may occur and suggest ways of avoiding them.

Level 4:

Students working at level 4 generate well targeted searches for electronic information sources and select relevant information from within sources to meet a specific purpose. They create information products with simple linear structures and use software commands to edit and reformat information products in ways that demonstrate some consideration of audience and communicative purpose. They recognise situations in which ICT misuse may occur and explain how specific protocols can prevent this.

Level 5:

Students working at level 5 evaluate the credibility of information from electronic sources and select the most relevant information to use for a specific communicative purpose. They create information products that show evidence of planning and technical competence. They use software features to reshape and present information graphically consistent with presentation conventions. They design information products that combine different elements and accurately represent their source data. They use available software features to enhance the appearance of their information products.

Level 6:

Students working at level 6 create information products that show evidence of technical proficiency, and careful planning and review. They use software features to organise information and to synthesise and represent data as integrated complete information products. They design information products consistent with the conventions of specific communication modes and audiences and use available software features to enhance the communicative effect of their work.

Fig. 11.5 The levels of the MCEETYA/ACER framework

Social-Networking Learning Progression Perspective

In this subsection, we discuss the impact of a "social-networking" perspective on ICT – the critical need for building the power of virtual skills through proficiency with networks of people, information, tools, and resources. Here, we offer a new

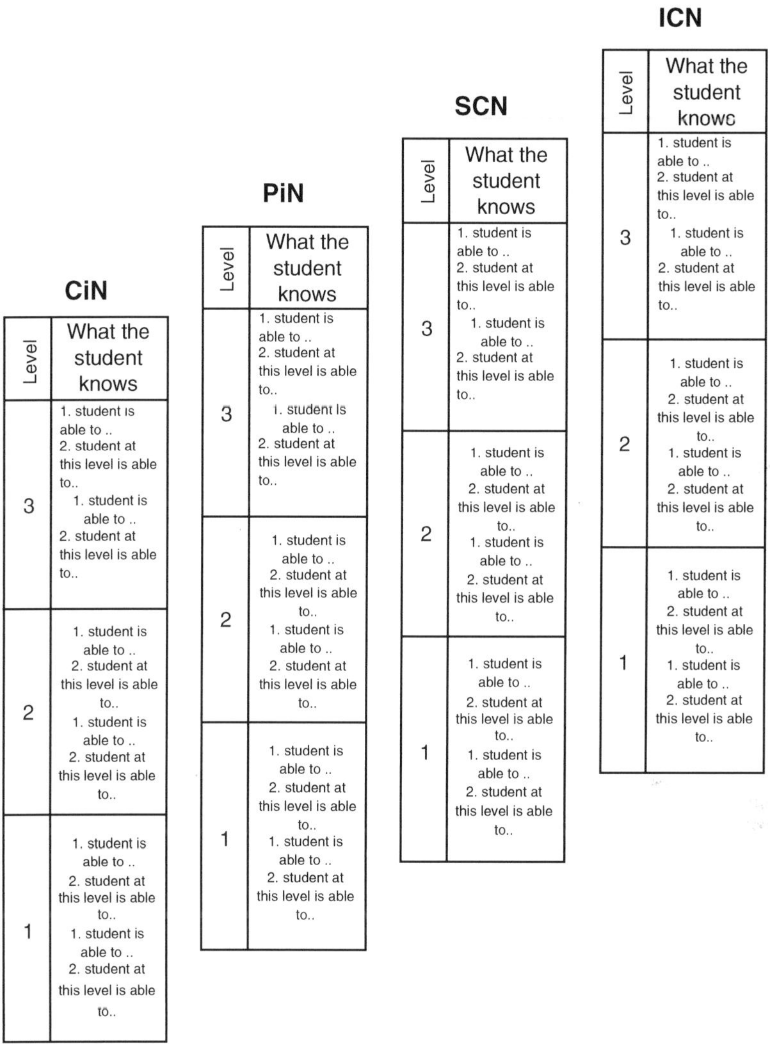

Fig. 11.6 The four strands of ICT Literacy, represented as a profile of four staggered progress variables

framework for assessing student ICT learning, based on a learning progression point of view.

As mentioned above, the ATC21S project was initiated to develop new assessments in the area of twenty-first century skills, based on the idea that new assessments could lead the way to these new subjects. Using the BEAR[2] Assessment System approach (Wilson 2004; Wilson et al. 2012), the project developed a demonstration ICT assessment. The ATC21S effort yielded a synergy of both schools of thought: collaboration and strategic solution, creation and effective application. The ATC21S methodology group described that, in order to achieve a working hypothesis of such a complex domain, one approach is to describe "dimensions of progression," or theoretical maps of intended constructs, in terms of depth, breadth and how the skills change as they mature for students (Wilson et al. 2012). For this, the ATC21S project set up an expert panel of ICT experts,[3] who turned to the research literature to inform expanded definitions of digital literacy.

Studies and research findings tapped into by the ATC21S panel of ICT experts included the areas of augmented social cognition (Chi et al. 2008), applied cognition (Rogers et al. 2007), team cognition (Cooke et al. 2007), social participation (Dhar and Olson 1989), cognitive models of human-information interaction (Pirolli 2007), technological support for work group collaboration (Lampe et al. 2010; Pirolli et al. 2010), theories of measurement for modeling individual and collective cognition in social systems (Pirolli and Wilson 1998), and topics in semantic representation (Griffiths and Steyvers 2007).

For instance, research in augmented social cognition (Chi et al. 2008) describes how the ability of a group of people to remember, think and reason together emerges. It explores how people augment their speed and capacity to acquire, produce, communicate and use knowledge, and to advance collective and individual intelligence in socially mediated environments. It is expected that augmented digital and virtual settings will be increasingly common for students to navigate in twenty-first century skills learning.

The ATC21S panel of experts then developed definitions in these areas. Here, the goal was formulation of hypotheses concerning the nature and characteristics of the developmental learning continua associated with relevant skills. Such developmental progressions, if validated, could help define the skills in such a way that they could effectively be measured, and ultimately mapped to curriculum and instruction.

Consistent with the thinking that some beliefs about the current practice of schooling are outmoded in the global working environment, the expert panel described how definitions of ICT literacy are changing. Recent workshops on a National Initiative for Social Participation (NISP), funded by the U.S. National Science Foundation (Pirolli et al. 2010) identified the need for an educational focus on learning in networks (or technology-mediated social participation). A report by

[2] Note that 'BEAR' is an acronym for "Berkeley Evaluation and Assessment Research" Center.

[3] The ICT Literacy Expert Panel consisted of: John Ainley (Chair), Julian Fraillon, Peter Pirolli, Jean-Paul Reeff, Kathleen Scalise, and Mark Wilson.

the subgroup on educational priorities (Lampe et al. 2010) recognized that learners fall into multiple categories and suggested curricular goals for K-12 and higher education. These goals included skills for information access and literacy (as a consumer), increasingly sophisticated participation (games, forums), increasingly sophisticated ability to develop social capital (e.g., find opportunities and gain support, organizing others), and "computational thinking" about social-computational functions and services such as using bots to match people and tasks or using crowdsourcing to solve problems.

These reports from the NISP, along with research from other agencies and operational examples around the world, informed the ATC21S framework development efforts. These included the National Assessment Program Information and Communications Technologies in Australia (ACARA 2012) mentioned above, Singapore's ICT Master Plans (Park 2011), the ISTE standards from the U.S. (http://www.iste.org/standards), international efforts of OECD with the Programme for the International Assessment of Adult Competencies (PIAAC, http://www.oecd.org/site/piaac/), and early planning on the IEA International Computer and Information Literacy Study (ICILS, http://www.iea.nl/icils).

These efforts identified many important and worthy ICT literacy goals for students. Clearly established in frameworks worldwide were individual *consumer* skills, or using information and tools available through technology, often on a Web 1.0 model of repositories that could be accessed over the Internet by students. Emerging trends were additionally seen around a variety of *producer* skills, in which students needed to craft, create, express, post and manage digital assets, in new ways due to the emergence of Web 2.0 technologies. Finally, it was noted that, as described in the NISP documents (e.g., Pirolli et al. 2010), the field was beginning to recognize and acknowledge the importance to education of networks, both requiring *social capital* skills of students and the ability to draw on *intellectual capital* of groups and teams. This included Web 3.0 skills of "semantics," or meaning-making through technology, with such tools as analytics, effective use and evaluation of ratings, crowd sourcing, peer evaluation, tagging and the ability to judge credibility and viability of sources.

ACT21S "Learning in Digital Networks" ICT Literacy Framework and Assessments

To make progress on this goal, the expert panel challenged itself to define, for each of these four competencies, what having "more" and "less" of the competency would look like, for students aged 11, 13 and 15. In other words, as one expert noted, "When someone gets better at it, what are they getting better at?" This might also be described as what students will know and be able to do, as well as how the field of education will recognize the ranges of skills and abilities likely to be seen if the competencies are assessed and instructed (Wilson and Scalise 2013).

For ATC21S the focus of ICT Literacy was on *learning in networks*, seen as being made up of four strands:

- Functioning as a consumer in network
- Functioning as a producer in networks
- Participating in the development of social capital through networks
- Participating in intellectual capital (i.e., collective intelligence) in networks.

The four strands are seen as interacting, as parallel developments that are interconnected.

First, functioning as a *Consumer in Networks* (CiN) involves obtaining, managing and utilizing information and knowledge from shared digital resources and experts in order to benefit private and professional lives. It involves questions such as:

- Will a user be able to ascertain how to perform tasks (e.g., by exploration of the interface) without explicit instruction?
- How efficiently does an experienced user use a PDA or other mobile device to find answers to a question?
- What arrangement of information on a display yields more effective visual search?
- How difficult will it be for a user to find information on a website?"

Second, functioning as a *Producer in Networks* (PiN) involves creating, developing, organizing and re-organizing information/knowledge in order to contribute to shared digital resources.

Third, developing and sustaining *Social Capital through Networks* (SCN) involves using, developing, moderating, leading and brokering the connectivities within and between individuals and social groups in order to marshal collaborative action, build communities, maintain an awareness of opportunities and integrate diverse perspectives at community, societal and global levels.

Fourth, developing and sustaining *Intellectual Capital through Networks* (ICN) involves understanding how tools, media and social networks operate and using appropriate techniques through these resources to build collective intelligence and integrate new insights into personal understandings.

In Tables 11.1, 11.2, 11.3, and 11.4, levels of these four strands are described as hypothesized construct maps showing an ordering of skills or competencies involved in each. At the lowest levels of each are the competencies that one would expect to see exhibited by a novice or beginner. At the top of each table are the competencies that one would expect to see exhibited by an experienced person – someone who would be considered very highly literate in ICT.

These construct maps are hierarchical in the sense that a person who would normally exhibit competencies at a higher level would also be expected to be able exhibit the competencies at lower levels of the hierarchy. The maps are also probabilistic in the sense that they represent different probabilities that a given compe-

Table 11.1 Functioning as a consumer in networks (CiN)

	Consumer in networks
Discriminating consumer	
CiN3	Judging credibility of sources/people
	Integrating information in coherent knowledge framework
	Searches suited to personal circumstances
	Filter, evaluate, manage, organize and reorganize information/people
	Seeking expert knowledge (people through networks)
	Select optimal tools for tasks/topics
Conscious consumer	
CiN2	Select appropriate tools and strategies (strategic competence)
	Construct targeted searches
	Compiling information systematically
	Knowing that credibility is an issue (web pages, people, networks)
Emerging consumer	
CiN1	Performing basic tasks
	No concept of credibility
	Search for pieces of information using common search engines (e.g. movie guides
	Knowing that tools exist for networking (e.g. Facebook)

Table 11.2 Functioning as a producer in networks (PiN)

	Producer in networks
Creative producer	
PiN3	Team situational awareness in process
	Optimize assembly of distributed contribution to products
	Extending advanced models (e.g. business models)
	Producing attractive digital products using multiple technologies/tools
	Choosing among technological options for producing digital products
Functional producer	
PiN2	Establishing and managing networks and communities
	Awareness of planning for building attractive websites, blogs, games
	Organizing communication within social networks
	Developing models based on established knowledge
	Developing creative and expressive content artifacts
	Awareness of security and safety issues (ethical and legal aspects)
	Using networking tools and styles for communication among people
Emerging producer	
PiN1	Produce simple representations from templates
	Start an identity
	Use a computer interface
	Post an artifact

Table 11.3 Developing social capital through networks (SCN)

	Developer of social capital
Visionary connector	
SCN4	Take a cohesive leadership role in building a social enterprise
	Reflect on experience in for social capital development
Proficient connector	
SCN3	Initiate opportunities for developing social capital through networks (e.g. support for development)
	Encourage multiple perspectives and support diversity in networks (social brokerage skills)
Functional connector	
SCN2	Encourage participation in and commitment to a social enterprise
	Awareness of multiple perspectives in social networks
	Contribute to building social capital through a network
Emerging connector	
SCN1	Participating in a social enterprise
	Observer or passive member of a social enterprise
	Knowing about social networks

Table 11.4 Developing intellectual capital through networks (ICN)

	Participator in intellectual capital (collective intelligence)
Visionary builder	
ICN4	Questioning existing architecture of social media and developing new architectures
	Functioning at the interfaces of architectures to embrace dialogue
Proficient builder	
ICN3	Understanding and using architecture of social media such as tagging, polling, role-playing and modeling spaces to link to knowledge of experts in an area
	Identifying signal versus noise in information
	Interrogating data for meaning
	Making optimal choice of tools to access collective intelligence
	Sharing and reframing mental models (plasticity)
Functional builder	
ICN2	Acknowledges multiple perspectives
	Thoughtful organization of tags
	Understanding mechanics of collecting and assembling data
	Knowing when to draw on collective intelligence
	Sharing representations
Emerging Builder	
ICN1	Knowledge of survey tools
	Able to make tags
	Posting a question

tence would be expected to be exhibited in a particular context rather than certainties that the competence would always be exhibited.

The levels and assessments in the ATC21S Learning in Digital Networks framework were developed using the BEAR Assessment System (BAS) approach (Wilson 2004), which takes as its first step the delineation of qualitatively different levels of performance, just as for the progress variable described above. The levels in each strand follow a similar valuing of:

- Awareness and basic use of tools
- Followed by more complex application directly relevant to teaching and learning
- With evaluative and judgmental skills emerging as experience and knowledge are gained
- Moving to leadership and ability to manage and create new approaches.

These levels within the strands may be seen as "staggered" (Fig. 11.6) in that they have not been positioned on the same fixed scale for each strand. We see them as strands of the same broad construct – ICT Literacy – but the lower levels of one strand may be equivalent to the middle or even higher levels of other strands. It should also be noted that these construct maps were developed to encompass the full range of competencies within each strand rather than the range that one might expect to be exhibited by school students at middle and secondary levels. The question of targeting assessments to match what students can do is an empirical question to be determined through consultations with teachers and cognitive laboratories with students, as well as the results of pilot and field studies.

The BEAR Center at UC Berkeley developed three scenarios in which to place tasks and questions that could be used as items to indicate where a student might be placed along each of the four strands. Each scenario was designed to address more than one strand, but there were different emphases in how the strand areas were represented among the scenarios. Where possible, they took advantage of existing web-based tools for instructional development. Just one of these is briefly described below (Wilson and Scalise 2015, shows scenario information, and includes tasks and scoring associated with scenarios).

In the Webspiration demonstration task, framed as part of a poetry work unit, students of ages 11–15 read and analyze well-known poems. Figure 11.7 shows a screen from the computer module, to give a feel for how the scenario "looks" onscreen. In a typical school context, we might imagine that the teacher has noticed that his or her students are having difficulty articulating the moods and meanings of some of the poems – in traditional teacher-centered instruction regarding literature the student role tends to be passive. Often, teachers find that students are not spontaneous in their responses to the poems, but may tend to wait to hear what the teacher has to say and then agree with what is said. To encourage students to formulate their own ideas on the poems, the ATC21S demonstration task uses a collaborative graphic organizer through the Webspiration online tool. The teacher directs the students to use Webspiration to create an idea map collaboratively using the graphic organizer tools, and to analyze each poem they read. Students submit their own

Fig. 11.7 A sample page from the Webspiration scenario

ideas and/or build on classmate thoughts. For example, a fragment of the students' chat while they were working on the graphic organizer was:

> Student 1: "it was my idea"
> Student 2: "where is?"
> Student 1: "in the middle."

Such use of networking tools and styles of communication by students is also hypothesized to occur at the PiN2 level ("Functional builder") of the Producer in Networks strand shown in Table 11.2. Here students can be seen, as stated in the scoring rubric, "using networking tools and styles for communication among people," in the process of developing creative and expressive content artifacts, in this case a collaborative graphic organizer for the analysis of a select piece of literature (poem). As the next step, students are asked to upload their work and the chat log.

Within the Webspiration task, students were asked to create a one-minute audio commentary for the poem they have found online, and also to explain how they created the audio. Note that students who are successful on this task are hypothesized to be at the highest ("Creative Producer") level of the Producer in Social Networks strand. The screen for this task is shown in Fig. 11.8.

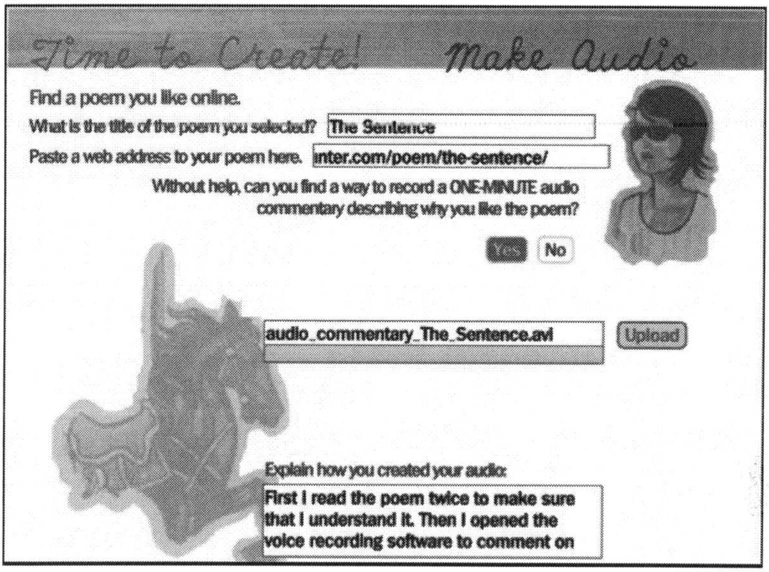

Fig. 11.8 Webspiration tool: "Time to Create!" task

Empirical Study

We selected two of the three scenarios for validation studies with middle-school students. These were (a) the science/math Arctic Trek collaboration contest and (b) the Webspiration shared literature analysis task. These were identified by participating countries as the most appropriate to study at the current time. This was because they were more aligned with the school curricula in the participating countries, which sometimes did employ mathematics simulations and online scientific quests as well as graphical and drawing tools for student use, but which infrequently used anything like cross-country chat tools. The third task (the Second Language Chat) was seen by participating countries, teachers and schools as a forward-looking and interesting scenario, but more remote from the adoption curve for school curricula.

Each of the two scenarios was presented in three forms, for 11, 13 and 15 year-olds respectively, with a subset of common items across the three forms. For a sample of 103 students in our first field test (i.e., those for whom we were able to match their login IDs for two scenarios), assessment results from the two scenarios within the overall ICT literacy domain were analyzed using a four-dimensional item response model with age groups as manifest regressors. This is a small sample for multidimensional analysis, but we see it as worthwhile to report, given the novel conceptualization of the assessments. Note that the collaboration took place within pairs or teams of students and did not use computer avatars or other pre-programmed forms of collaboration.

Before beginning the assessment on the 45-min tasks, students were provided about five minutes of directions by the assessment administrator. Students were told that they would engage in collaborative activities online and would be provided with partners. They were told that the activities were for a math/science task, for which teams were composed of four students, or for an English language literacy task, for which pairs (dyads) were assigned. In both cases, students were informed that activities were intended to provide information on how students work with the technology tools, processes, and partners provided. Students were informed they would have 45 min for one task, and that timing information would appear on the screen. Furthermore, students were encouraged to tap into assistance from their partners through the chat tools provided but told that they could not collaborate face-to-face. They also were required to restrict all collaboration and conversation to the online tools provided within the assessment environment, which does share some screen information among team members in various tools in the collaborative suite, but does not include full screen sharing. The assessment administrator remained in the room during the assessment, to answer questions and to monitor that instructions were followed. Team members and pairs were randomly assigned within classroom and students were not informed in advance of their partner(s) identities, but once beginning the task, students could communicate their identity and any other information they wished to share, through tools such as chat windows.

An initial research question was whether the plan for the four dimensions of ICT is displayed in the empirical results. That is, one can ask whether these four constructs have been successfully distinguished by the items. A typical way to test this is to ask whether a single composite construct (i.e., a unidimensional construct) could explain the results just as well as a four-dimensional construct. We fitted a single composite item response model (see Adams et al. (1997) for model equations, estimation algorithms, etc.) using ConQuest software (see Adams et al. (2012) for computation considerations, etc.) and compared the results to those for the hypothesized four-dimensional model. The overall fit statistics for the models are presented in Table 11.5.

Since the unidimensional model is nested within a multidimensional model, it is appropriate to compare the model fit using the difference in deviance (G^2), which is approximately distributed as a chi-square statistic with the difference in the number of estimated parameters as degrees of freedom. The difference in deviance between two models is 51 (3,419–3,368) with 19 degrees of freedom (22–3), and thus the multidimensional model fits this dataset significantly better than a unidimensional composite model, at the $\alpha = 0.001$ statistical significance level.

Table 11.5 Deviance and number of parameters for the two models

Model	G^2	# of parameters
Unidimensional	3419	3[a]
Multidimensional	3368	22[a]

Both models are accounting for potential differences in the latent variable between the three different grade levels using the latent regression approach

[a]Item difficulty parameters are anchored

Table 11.6 Variances and correlations from the multidimensional model

	CSN	PSN	DSC	PIC
CSN				
PSN	0.91			
DSC	0.93	0.90		
PIC	0.97	0.94	0.93	
Variance	0.74 (0.10)	0.77 (0.11)	1.75 (0.24)	1.13 (0.16)

(1) The variance from the unidimensional analysis was estimated to be 0.78 (0.11)
(2) Standard errors of the variances are shown in parentheses

Table 11.6 shows the variances and disattenuated correlations obtained from the multidimensional model. The highest correlation is between the CiN and PIC dimensions (0.97) and the lowest is between PiN and PSN (0.90). These are high correlations, and bring into question the need for a multidimensional psychometric model at this point. However, there are often high correlations among dimensions of achievement dimensions – compare for instance, the correlation of 0.86 between Science and Reading for the 2000 PISA tests (Kirsch et al. 2002) – and few educators or educational researchers would consider these two dimensions to be substantively the same dimension. Hence we continue to use the multidimensional results, as we see that there are educational differences among the dimensions, even though students are performing similarly across all four.

One way of checking if the assumptions and requirements of the model are met is to examine the weighted mean square fit statistic estimated for each item. Item fit can be seen as a measure of the discrepancy between the observed item characteristic curve and the theoretical item characteristic curve (Wu and Adams 2013). ConQuest estimates the residual based weighted fit statistics, also called infit, by comparing the observed residuals to the expected residuals by taking the ratio of the two variances and weighting down the respondents whose abilities are estimated further from the item. Ideally, infit values are expected to be close to 1.0. Values of less than one imply that the observed variance is less than the expected variance, while values of more than one imply that the observed variance is more than the expected variance. It is a common convention to use 3/4 (0.75) and 4/3 (1.33) as acceptable lower and upper bounds (Adams and Khoo 1996). Three out of the 44 items fell outside this range, all below 0.75 (at 0.68, 0.69, 0.70). This is close to the range of what might be expected by chance.

As shown in Table 11.7, the reliability estimates from the multidimensional approach using responses to both scenarios are all higher than 0.80.

Figure 11.9 shows one of the "Wright maps" (Wilson 2004) obtained from the four-dimensional model, specifically for Consumer in Social Networks. Items are vertically ordered with respect to their difficulties, and persons (cases) are vertically ordered with respect to their abilities. Each "X" on the left-hand side represents a small number of students, and the items are shown on the right-hand side using their item numbers. The locations are interpreted as follows, for dichotomous items:

(a) When a student's X matches and item location, the probability of that student succeeding on that item is expected to be 0.50

Table 11.7 Reliabilities (EAP) from the multidimensional approach

Scenario	Reliability
CSN	0.83
PSN	0.99
DSC	0.81
PIC	0.82

Reliability from the unidimensional model is estimated at 0.88

(b) When a student's X is above the item, then the probability is above 0.5 (and vice-versa), and
(c) These probabilities are governed by a logistic distribution (see Wilson 2004 for a discussion).

Where the items are polytomous, the labeling is more complex; for example, in Fig. 11.9 note that Item 5 is represented by two labels: 5.1 and 5.2. The former is used to indicate the threshold between category 0 and categories 1 and 2 (combined); the latter is used to represent the threshold between categories 0 and 1 (combined) and category 2. The interpretation of the probability is equivalent to that for a dichotomous item: that is, when a student's X matches the 5.1 location, the probability of that student succeeding at levels 1 or 2 on that item is expected to be 0.50; and similarly, when a student's X matches the 5.2 location, the probability of that student succeeding at only level 2 on that item is expected to be 0.50.

This map identifies whether there is a good coverage of abilities by items. Ideally, if permitted a sufficient number of items for each strand, the range of item difficulties would approximately match the range of person abilities. This would mean that there are items approximately matching every level of the person ability. This is true for the Consumer in Social Networks strand. Figure 11.9 also shows the "banding" of the levels for the Wright Map for the Consumer in Social Networks (indicated by the alternating grey and white regions on the graph) – that is, we have carried out a judgmental exercise to locate where the approximate transitions among the levels are located. This is accomplished by analyzing the skills needed for each item (or levels of the items, for polytomous ones), and mapping them back to the levels of the four strands. Note that not all items were useful in setting these bands – it is a continuing exercise to determine which items are best for this banding exercise. From Fig. 11.9, we can see that students in this sample have a range of abilities on this strand that spans all three hypothesized levels, from Emerging to Discriminating Consumer, although there are relatively more students in the lower levels than in the higher levels (an observation that will be repeated in other strands).

Figure 11.10 shows the banded Wright map for the Producer in Social Networks strand. For this map, we see that the highest level, Discriminating Producer, was not displayed by the items that remained after the item piloting. Hence there are only two levels that remained for inclusion in the Wright map. Also, not many items representing the lowest level – Emerging Producer – survived the piloting process. Thus, an effort needs to be made to develop new items for these two levels.

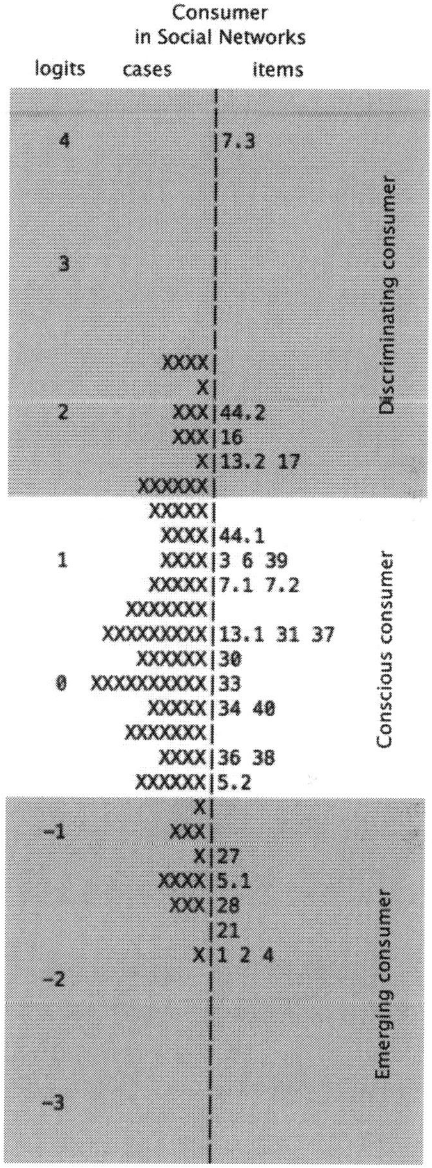

Fig. 11.9 Wright map for the consumer in social networks strand with bands representing each level

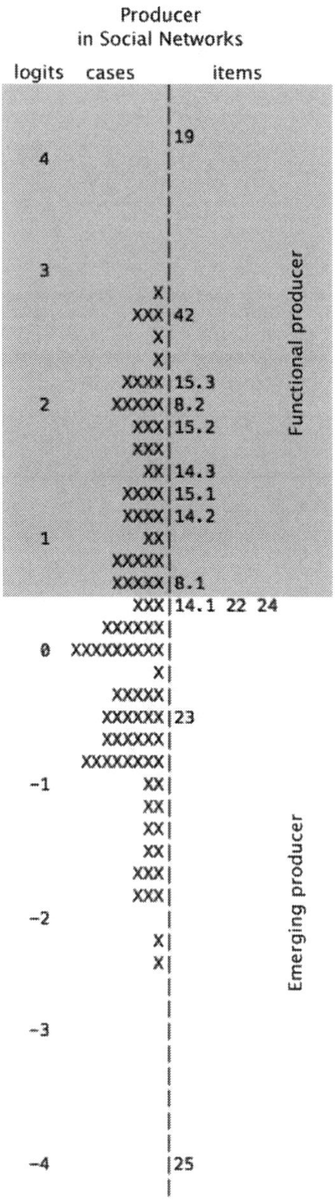

Fig. 11.10 Wright map for the producer in social networks strand with bands representing each level

We do not display a banded Wright map for the Developer of Social Capital strand, as there were only two items remaining in this strand, after items were deleted during development, both of which were aimed at measuring at third level (Proficient connector) of the construct. Thus, an effort needs to be made to develop new items for all levels of this strand.

Figure 11.11 shows the Wright map for the Participator in Intellectual Capital strand. Although all three levels are represented in the bands for this strand, both the highest and lowest are sparsely represented. Hence an effort should be made to add items at each of these levels. Again, the students are concentrated in the bottom two levels, although some are indeed at the higher levels.

Summary and Conclusion

Four steps have been used here to illustrate the trajectory of ICT literacy over approximately the last two decades. Simple early measures of computer use have morphed to include the integration of technology across educational areas and brought on a sweeping need for understanding ICT literacy as a developmental progression in student skills and thinking. We have illustrated this new understanding in the shape of (a) a four-dimensional developmental framework, including levels of sophistication within each dimension, (b) examples of online scenarios and items that can be used to assess those dimensions, and (c) empirical results that illustrate how these concepts and materials function in the real world.

Networks are groups or systems of interconnected people and resources. The ability to connect with and strategically access a vast array of people, information, tools and resources has significant and broad impact for learning and student competency. Web development has progressed through important stages, from information repository to social media to semantic environment, carrying the needs of the learner along with it.

Following this thinking we conclude that the current conceptualization of education is becoming dated, at least in some respects. Schools find their students must apply knowledge across disciplinary barriers, work effectively both alone and together, access and interact with large amounts of information, and make strategic and contextualized use of tools. Yet assessments and their associated frameworks often are missing the new trends. We still tend to measure isolated skills, and individuals working solo and stripped of augmentations such as information-rich and tool-rich access. How this compares to what we really want to teach and know is not well understood.

A new type of twenty-first century ICT literacy, which we described here, can be focused at least in part on learning and achieving goals *in networks*. While performance on any one of the four strands is not yet fully explicated, such a framework does offer new conceptualizations of the ICT literacy cognitive space. Initial efforts to address this have been reported above. We have had considerable success, with all four strands showing reliabilities higher than 0.80, and the likelihood ratio test

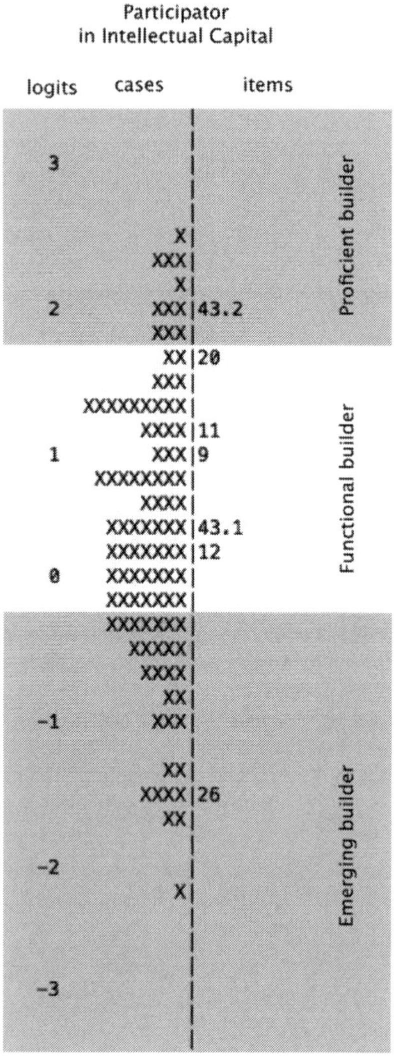

Fig. 11.11 Wright map for the participator in intellectual capital strand with bands representing each level

showing that the four strands are different in a statistical significance test. We have also found that three of the strands display content-validity according our criterion of item banding based on our construct maps (although one shows only two levels rather than three, due to a lack of higher-difficulty items that survived the stress-test of the trial) and the fourth, Developer of Social Capital, had too few items surviving to be considered for content-validity testing. The correlations among the four strands are quite high, though no higher than are correlations between, say, Mathematics and Science in large-scale testing. Clearly there will need to be more item development undertaken regarding these four strands and the novel item formats that are involved in this assessment. What are the design principles for these new assessment tasks? What are the critical implementation steps that need to be undertaken to ensure success?

Learners who are able to activate modern ICT literacy skills will need to know how to strategically and creatively interact with real people, authentic online tools, complex information, and complex virtual networks. Thus, learning in digital communities calls for also assessing in digital communities: that way we can help all learners thrive among the networks in which they must 1 day function as full and mature participants.

Educational training for this new approach to ICT literacy will involve other ideas and methods as new as those described here. There are well-established approaches for training in ICT literacy that are used with current conceptions of ICT literacy and accompanying textbooks, such as Roblyer (2004), that are very much "big-sellers" in the textbook market. Just as the technology changes described above have prompted changes in assessments, we can expect that these changes will flow into the training field as well and will be speeded by changes in the assessments (as was the intention of the technology companies mentioned in the introduction).

These developments have important consequences for assessment in other domains. In both traditional subject matter areas, as well as in other twenty-first century skills, assessments are trending towards TEAs, and this development will make ICT literacy an increasingly important area for students (and all learners, in almost any environment). The traditional importance of reading and writing (and speaking and listening) will be matched by the importance of ICT literacy. Although this does imply the need for specifically-focused ICT literacy instruction and assessment in terms of a foundation for all students, it means that more advanced instruction and assessment in those traditional subject-matter areas, and in twenty-first century skills, will need to include aspects of ICT literacy as integral components of the instructional design and the assessments.

The challenge for ICT literacy assessment is adapting to frequent and deep changes in the technology-enhanced world in which we live, as the world of work (and hence, the world of schooling) is inevitably enveloped by this technological environment. This is not just a challenge in terms of instructional materials and assessment materials, but also a challenge to the relevant professionals involved – teachers, instructional developers and assessment developers. And, in fact, it is a strong challenge also to the researchers, who, although they can stand aside from the tumult of technological change, will need to become experts in each new wave of technology, as those technologies change the educational environment.

References

ACARA. (2012). *Australian curriculum, assessment and reporting authority*. National Assessment Program, ICT Literacy, Years 6 and 10 Report 2011.

Adams, R. J., & Khoo, S. T. (1996). *Quest*. Hawthorn: ACER.

Adams, R. J., Wilson, M., & Wang, W. (1997). The multidimensional random coefficients multinomial logit model. *Applied Psychological Measurement, 21*(1), 1–23.

Adams, R. J., Wu, M., & Wilson, M. (2012). *ConQuest 3.0 [computer program]*. Hawthorn: ACER.

Ainley, J., Fraillon, J., Schulz, W., & Gebhardt, E. (2014). *Measuring changes in ICT literacy over time*. Paper presented at the National Council on Measurement in Education, Philadelphia, PA.

Binkley, M., Erstad, O., Herman, J., Raizen, S., Ripley, M., Miller-Ricci, M., & Rumble, M. (2012). Defining twenty-first century skills. In P. Griffin, B. McGaw, & E. Care (Eds.), *Assessment and teaching of 21st century skills* (Vol. 1). Dordrecht: Springer.

Care, E. (2018). Introduction: 21st century skills: From theory to action. In E. Care, P. Griffin, & M. Wilson (Eds.), *Assessment and teaching of 21st century skills: Research and applications*. Dordrecht: Springer.

Chi, E. H., Pirolli, P., Suh, B., Kittur, A., Pendleton, B., & Mytkowicz, T. (2008). *Augmented social cognition*. Palo Alto: Palo Alto Research Center.

Cisco, Intel, Microsoft (CIM). (2008). *Transforming education: Assessing and teaching 21st century skills*. Authors. Downloaded from: http://atc21s.org/wp-content/uploads/2011/04/Cisco-Intel-Microsoft-Assessment-Call-to-Action.pdf.

Common Core State Standards Initiative (CCSSI). (2010). *Common core state standards for mathematics*. Downloaded Jul 9, 2010, from http://www.corestandards.org/the-standards.

Cooke, N. J., Gorman, J. C., & Winner, J. L. (2007). Team cognition. In F. T. Durso (Ed.), *Handbook of applied cognition* (pp. 239–268). New York: Wiley.

Dallas County Community College District. (2014). *Computer skills placement test questions*. Dallas: Dallas County Community College District. Downloaded from: https://www1.dcccd.edu/catalog/ss/transfer/CompSkillPractTest2014.pdf.

Dhar, V., & Olson, M. H. (1989). Assumptions underlying systems that support work group collaboration. In M. H. Olson (Ed.), *Technology support for work group collaboration*. Hillsdate: Lawrence Erlbaum Associates.

Erstad, O. (2006). A new direction? Digital literacy, student participation and curriculum reform in Norway. *Education and Information Technologies, 11*(3–4), 415–429.

Fraillon, J. (2014). *Assessing computer and information literacy across 20 countries: The International Computer and Information Literacy (ICILS)*. Paper presented at the National Council on Measurement in Education (NCME), Philadelphia, PA.

Friedman, T. L. (2007). *The world is flat 3.0: A brief history of the twenty-first century*. New York: Picador.

Griffin, P., McGaw, B., & Care, E. (Eds.). (2012). *Assessment and teaching of 21st century skills*. Dordrecht: Springer.

Griffiths, T. L., & Steyvers, M. (2007). Topics in semantic representation. *Psychological Review, 114*(2), 211–244.

International Association for the Evaluation of Educational Achievement (IEA). (2014). *IEA completed studies: COMPED*. http://www.iea.nl/comped.html

International ICT Literacy Panel (IILP). (2002). *Digital transformation: A framework for ICT literacy*. Princeton: Educational Testing Service (ETS). http://www.ets.org/Media/Tests/Information_and_Communication_Technology_Literacy/ictreport.pdf.

Jewitt, C. (2003). Re-thinking assessment: Multimodality, literacy and computer-mediated learning. *Assessment in Education: Principles, Policy & Practice, 10*, 83–102.

Kirsch, I., de Jong, J., Lafontaine, D., McQueen, J., Mendelovits, J., & Monseur, C. (2002). *Reading for change: Performance and engagement across countries—results from PISA 2000*. Paris: OECD.

Kozma, R. (2003). Technology and classroom practices: An international study. *Journal of Research on Technology in Education, 36*(1), 1–5.
Kulik, J. A. (1994). Meta-analytic studies of findings on computer-based instruction. In E. L. Baker & H. F. O'Neil (Eds.), *Technology assessment in education and training*. Hillsdale: Lawrence Erlbaum Associates.
Lampe, C., Resnick, P., Forte, A., Yardi, S., Rotman, D., Marshall, T., & Lutters, W. (2010). Educational priorities for technology-mediated social participation. *IEEE Computer, 43*(11), 60–67.
Lead States, N. G. S. S. (2013). *Next generation science standards: For states, by states*. Washington, DC: Achieve, on behalf of the twenty-six states and partners that collaborated on the NGSS.
Loader, B. (Ed.). (2007). *Young citizens in the digital age: Political engagement, young people and new media*. London: Routledge.
Masters, G. N., Adams, R. J., & Wilson, M. (1990). Charting of student progress. In T. Husen & T. N. Postlethwaite (Eds.), *International encyclopedia of education: Research and studies* (Vol. 2, pp. 628–634). Oxford: Pergamon Press.
Ministerial Council on Education, Employment, Training and Youth Affairs (MCEETYA). (2005). *National assessment program information and communication technology literacy years 6 and 10: An assessment domain for ICT literacy*. Carlton: Curriculum Corporation.
Mullis, I. V. S., & Martin, M. O. (Eds.). (2013). *PIRLS 2016 assessment framework*. Chestnut Hill: Boston College.
OECD. (2011). Context of the PISA digital reading assessment. In *OECD PISA 2009 results: Students on line: Digital technologies and performance* (volume VI): OECD Publishing.
OECD. (2013a). *PISA 2012 assessment and analytical framework: Mathematics, reading, science, problem solving and financial literacy*. Paris: PISA, OECD Publishing.
OECD. (2013b). *PISA 2015: Draft collaborative problem solving framework*. http://www.oecd.org/pisa/pisaproducts/Draft PISA 2015 Collaborative Problem Solving Framework.pdf.
Park, J. (2011). ICT in education in Asia-Pacific. *Asia-Pacific regional forum on ICT applications*. http://www.itu.int/ITU-D/asp/CMS/Events/2011/ict-apps/s5_JPark.pdf.
Pelgrum, W. J., & Plomp, T. (1991). *The use of computers in education worldwide: Results from the IEA 'Computers m Education' survey in 19 educational systems*. Oxford: Pergamon.
Pirolli, P. (2007). Cognitive models of human-information interaction. In F. T. Durso (Ed.), *Handbook of applied cognition* (pp. 443–470). New York: Wiley.
Pirolli, P., & Wilson, M. (1998). A theory of the measurement of knowledge content, access, and learning. *Psychological Review, 105*(1), 58–82.
Pirolli, P., Preece, J., & Shneiderman, B. (2010). Cyberinfrastructure for social action on national priorities. *IEEE Computer, 43*(11), 20–21.
Quellmalz, E. S., & Kozma, R. (2003). Designing assessments of learning with technology. *Assessment in Education: Principles, Policy & Practice, 10*, 389–408.
Ridgway, J., & McCusker, S. (2003). Using computers to assess new educational goals. *Assessment in Education: Principles, Policy and Practice, 10*(3), 309–328.
Roblyer, M. D. (2004). *Educational technology in action: Problem based exercises for technology integration*. New York: Prentice Hall.
Rogers, W. A., Pak, R., & Fisk, A. D. (2007). Applied cognitive psychology in the context of everyday Living. In F. T. Durso (Ed.), *Handbook of applied cognition* (pp. 3–27). New York: Wiley.
Scalise, K., & Gifford, B. R. (2006). Computer-based assessment in e-learning: A framework for constructing: "Intermediate Constraint" questions and tasks for technology platforms. *Journal of Teaching, Learning and Assessment, 4*(6).
U.S. Department of Education. (2010). *Transforming american education, learning powered by technology national education technology plan 2010*. Retrieved from http://www.ed.gov/sites/default/files/netp2010.pdf.
Wilson, M. (2004). *Constructing measures: An item response modeling approach*. Mahwah: Erlbaum. (now published by Taylor and Francis, New York).

Wilson, M., & Scalise, K. (2011). The nature of assessment systems to support effective use of evidence through technology. *E-Learning and Digital Media, 8*(2), 121–132.
Wilson, M., & Scalise, K. (2015). Assessment of learning in digital networks. In P. Griffin & E. Care (Eds.), *Assessment and teaching of 21st century skills: Methods and approach* (pp. 57–81). Dordrecht: Springer.
Wilson, M., Bejar, I., Scalise, K., Templin, J., Wiliam, D., & Torres Irribarra, D. (2012). Perspectives on methodological issues. In P. Griffin, B. McGaw, & E. Care (Eds.), *Assessment and teaching of 21st century skills*. Dordrecht: Springer.
Wilson, M., Scalise, K., & Gochyyev, P. (2015). Rethinking ICT literacy: From computer skills to social network settings. *Thinking Skills & Creativity, 18*, 65–80.
Wu, M., & Adams, R. J. (2013). Properties of Rasch residual fit statistics. *Journal of Applied Measurement, 14*(4), 339–355.

Chapter 12
Intersecting Learning Analytics and Measurement Science in the Context of ICT Literacy Assessment

Mark Wilson, Kathleen Scalise, and Perman Gochyyev

Abstract This chapter reviews the state-of-play in overlap between learning analytics (LA), specifically data mining and exploratory analytics, and the field of measurement science. First, some basic ideas are introduced in a broad way. Then a current definition of LA is introduced, and main ideas of the area are discussed. Second, the logic of measurement science is reviewed, as instantiated through the BEAR Assessment System (BAS; Wilson, Constructing measures: an item response modeling approach. Lawrence Erlbaum Assoc, Mahwah, 2005), and illustrated in the context of an LA example. An example based in the context of ICT Literacy is presented, showing how complex digital assessments can be designed through BAS with attention to measurement science, while LA approaches can help to score some of the complex digital artifacts embedded in the design. With that background, ways are suggested through which the two approaches can be seen to support and complement one another, leading to a larger perspective. This chapter concludes with a discussion of the implications of this emerging intersection, and a survey of possible next steps.

M. Wilson (✉)
University of California, Berkeley, CA, USA

University of Melbourne, Parkville, VIC, Australia
e-mail: markw@berkeley.edu

K. Scalise
University of Oregon, Eugene, OR, USA

P. Gochyyev
University of California, Berkeley, CA, USA

E. Care et al. (eds.), *Assessment and Teaching of 21st Century Skills*,
Educational Assessment in an Information Age,
DOI 10.1007/978-3-319-65368-6_12

Learning Analytics

A popular definition of learning analytics was adopted by the Society for Learning Analytics Research in 2011:

> Learning analytics is the measurement, collection, analysis and reporting of data about learners and their contexts, for purposes of understanding and optimising learning and the environments in which it occurs.

Two other aspects should be considered: (i) how to interpret results, and (ii) how to choose data types and algorithms. It is important to reflect on the interpretation of the data analysis, over and above the results (Wilson 2005; Wilson et al. 2012, in press).

Surprisingly, this phase of interpretation is not a part of the LAK/SoLAR definition; that is "collection, analysis and reporting" does not explicitly include this critical aspect. A blind-spot like this can lead to the disastrous situation where, once results are reported, it is assumed that their meaning is self-evident.

Sound interpretation is facilitated by an evidence-based framework—an example is the four measurement principles of the BEAR Assessment System, described below (Wilson 2005; Wilson et al. 2012). In order to make useable claims about the learner, such a framework must be designed to link between the goals of the analysis back to the results (Mislevy et al. 2003; Wilson and Sloane 2000). In addition, a scientific interpretation must encompass the uncertainty, or range of error, present in the results.

This needs to have a sound evidentiary argument to support interpretations about learning and can be couched as either a posteriori (following the analysis) or a priori (in advance of the analysis). The a posteriori approach is an exploratory approach, which, for scientific purposes, will need confirmation by a second round of data collection. It is commonly called "data mining" (Papamitsiou and Economides 2014) or, sometimes, "machine learning," as well as "unsupervised learning" (Russell and Norvig 2009), in contrast to the supervised learning concept described in the next paragraph, where models are set up with theoretical structures and/or empirical data. When there is a need is to explore the patterns in the data sets in a context where not much is known, such exploratory approaches can be very useful.

In contrast, an a priori approach begins with a strong theory and/or prior empirical information, and is thus labeled as a confirmatory learning analysis. Russell and Norvig (2009) called it "supervised learning," meaning that characteristics of the LA learning algorithms such as factors, weights, and network structures, are pre-set at some level of detail, based on prior data or theory.

Measurement Approach

For our analysis we use four principles of good assessment and measurement practice which are part of the BEAR[1] Assessment System (BAS: Wilson 2005). BAS delineates techniques used in the construction of high-quality assessments (see Fig. 12.1). The four principles (Wilson 2005), expressed in the context of technology-enhanced assessments and learning (Scalise et al. 2007) are:

- Principle 1: Assessments should be based on a developmental perspective of student learning.
- Principle 2: Assessments in learning should be clearly aligned with the goals of instruction.
- Principle 3: Assessments must produce valid and reliable evidence of what students know and can do.
- Principle 4: Assessment data should provide information that is useful to teachers and students to improve learning outcomes.

In Principle 1, the concept of a developmental perspective of student learning entails that we consider how student understanding of particular concepts and skills develops over time, rather than taking a one-shot view. This perspective requires a definition of what students are expected to know at particular points in their development, incorporated into a theoretical framework of how that learning unfolds as the student makes progress.

For Principle 2, the concept of establishing a good match between what is taught and what is assessed means that the goals of learning and the assessments should be directly related. This is the opposite of the situation where teachers interrupt their

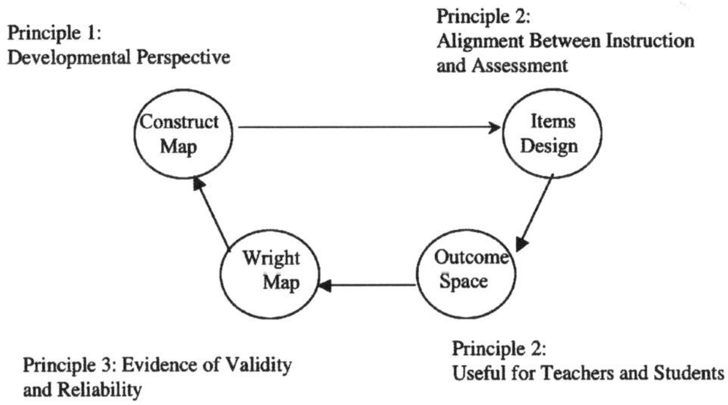

Fig. 12.1 A diagram of BAS, showing both the principles and four building blocks of measurement

[1] BEAR Center = Berkeley Evaluation and Assessment Research Center.

regular curriculum progress to "teach the test" that students will encounter on summative tests.

Principle 3 addresses issues of technical quality in assessments. Numerous technology-enhanced learning assessment procedures are gaining "currency" in the educational community by making inferences about students that are supported by evidence for the validity and reliability of those inferences. Reliability concerns the consistency of results and validity relates to whether an assessment measures what it is intended to measure. To make results useful across time and context, these issues must be addressed in any serious attempt at technology-based measures.

Principle 4 is perhaps the most critical: learning assessment systems must provide information and interpretations that are useful for improving learning outcomes. Teachers must have efficient means to explain resulting data and make appropriate inferences. Students also should be participants in the assessment process, and their assessments should be designed to encourage the development of metacognitive skills that will further the learning process. If teachers and students are to be held accountable for performance, they need a good comprehension of what students are expected to learn and of what counts as sound evidence of student learning. Teachers are then in a better position, and a more central and responsible position, for presenting, explaining, analyzing, and defending their students' performances and outcomes of their instruction.

These four principles summarize a way to understand the advantages and disadvantages of assessments, how to use such assessments, and how to apply these methods to develop new instruments or adapt old ones (Wilson 2005). These four principles match four "building blocks" (see Fig. 12.1) that make up an assessment—the construct map, the design plan for the items, the outcome space, and the statistical measurement model or algorithms to be used to compile and analyze patterns in the data.

Bringing the Two Perspectives Together

So here is the intersection of measurement technology and information technology. In the context of applying learning analytics to educational assessment, can the two perspectives work together to achieve something that is more than the sum of the two parts? To help answer this question, we next take up a brief example that incorporates the two in the context of looking at the assessment of collaborative learning in digital interactive social networks (Wilson and Scalise 2015).

The example we will use here is taken from the Assessment and Teaching of Twenty-First Century Skills project (ATC21S), and as both the project and the example have been described earlier in this Volume (Wilson et al. 2018), we will not describe them here, but assume that the reader has read that chapter.

The ATC21S demonstration scenario is conceived as a "collaboration contest," or virtual treasure hunt. The Arctic Trek scenario conceptualises social networks through ICT as an assembly of different tools, resources and people that together

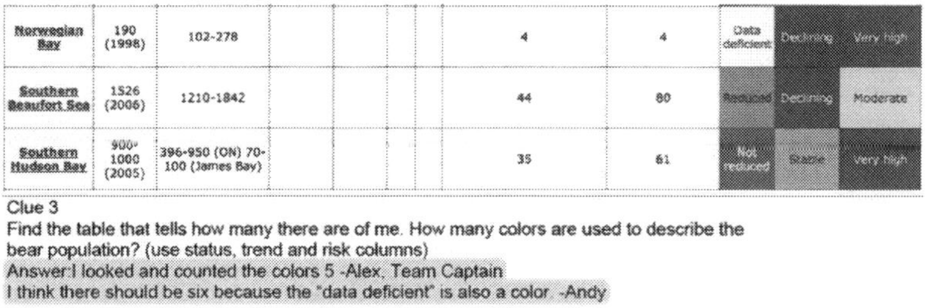

Fig. 12.2 Example of student collaborative chat in Arctic Trek task

build a community in a relevant topic. In this task, students in small teams explore tools and approaches to unravel clues through the Go North site, by visiting information about scientific and mathematics expeditions of actual scientists.

In the Arctic Trek task challenge shown in Fig. 12.2, students must identify the colors that are used to describe the bear population in the table, a part of which is shown at the top. The highlighted chat log of students at the bottom of Fig. 12.2 (which actually takes the form of a collaborative laboratory notebook) indicates that students are indeed communicating to identify what is signal versus noise in the supplied information. The colors in the text are the colors shown in the columns on the right of the table. Requiring both identifying signal versus noise in information and interrogating data for meaning, this performance can be mapped into the ICN3 level ("Proficient builder") of the ICN strand (Wilson et al. 2018). For further examples of activities and items from the Arctic Trek scenario, see Scalise (2018).

The connection between measurement science and learning analytics can be made in two ways in the context of this example. First, the statistical analysis approach used to estimate scores in measurement science is generically called a "measurement model." It serves as an algorithm to gather the results together and make inferences about learners. Other fields such as computer science that have come to learning analytics from a different historical basis often use a different vocabulary to describe such algorithms. For instance the Rasch model often used in educational assessment from a computer science perspective would be considered as an LA algorithm employing a multilayer feed-forward network (Russell and Norvig 2009) with g as the Rasch function (a semi-linear or sigmoidal curve-fitting function), in which weights (item discrimination) are constrained to one for all inputs, and the item parameters estimated are the thresholds on each item node (item difficulty).

Secondly, the critical point we want to illustrate in this section is that additional tools from learning analytics can be added to or embedded within the traditional measurement model. Below we show an example of such embedding through an automated scoring engine. The scores produced by a scoring engine can be merged into a data set to be analysed by a measurement model. As an example, some of the complex student work products from the Arctic Trek module were also analysed under a learning analytics approach called "sentiment analysis" which involves predictions of team success in the collaborative notebooks.

In this example, some notebooks that were identified to be used for a training set of the LA engine were initially handscored using traditional tools such as rubrics and exemplars. A collection of 28 hand-scored notebooks, which were the work products from approximately 112 students, provided this training set. The training set was then analysed by RapidMiner (Hofmann and Klinkenberg 2013) for the LA sentiment analysis approach.

Sentiment analysis in RapidMiner is an LA technique that aims to extract information from large full-text data sources such as online reviews and social media discussions. It can be used to interpret and optimize what is being thought, said, or discussed about a company or its products—or in this example, it is used to analyze what is being discussed in a collaborative learning situation the ATC21S Arctic Trek task.

The main idea in sentiment analysis is to classify an expressed opinion in a document, in a sentence or an entity feature, as positive or negative. In this example, "positive" means that the notebook shows some good evidence of learning in networks, based on the construct conceptualization described above. To calibrate the engine, first, both positive and negative "scores" of the task results are analysed—or in other words, a training set of scored collaborative notebooks are provided to the engine.

The engine first stems the words into root words. Then, a vector word list and a model are created. Using the training set, the model compares each word in the given notebook being considered with that of words that come under different predictions stored earlier. The notebook prediction is estimated based on the majority of words that occur under a polarity (i.e., a trend direction toward a negative or positive prediction). In this way, sentiment analysis is an artificial intelligence technique based on a "bag of words" (Russell and Norvig 2009). More sophistication can be added to the sentiment analysis data mining engine to include a variety of relationships between words, if desired, or data adjustments such as spelling corrections, "black lists" and "white lists" that are addendums or eliminations from the data dictionary, etc. An example of the sentiment analysis design window is shown in Fig. 12.3. The components of the full analysis for the Arctic Trek sentiment analysis engine used here are shown in Fig. 12.4.

Following the establishment of the training set, four additional collaborative notebooks were added to the work product data set for the sentiment analysis. These additional notebooks were not used for the sentiment analysis in the first instance. Rather, the LA engine was used to generate the prediction for each of the four notebooks. However, the four notebooks were also hand-scored in advance using the same human scoring approaches as for the other notebooks. The point was to see if the LA engine could match and even potentially add to the results generated by the hand-scoring.

Thus, this could provide some evidence that an LA sentiment analysis engine (in this case, RapidMiner) might effectively be incorporated into the measurement science approach. This could help to satisfy the measurement principle of usability by teachers and students, since an effective LA engine might eliminate some of the

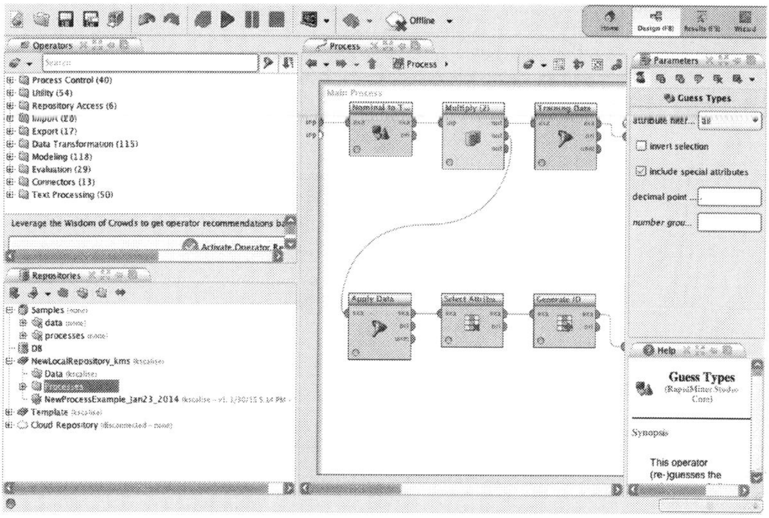

Fig. 12.3 Sentiment analysis design window for ATC21S example

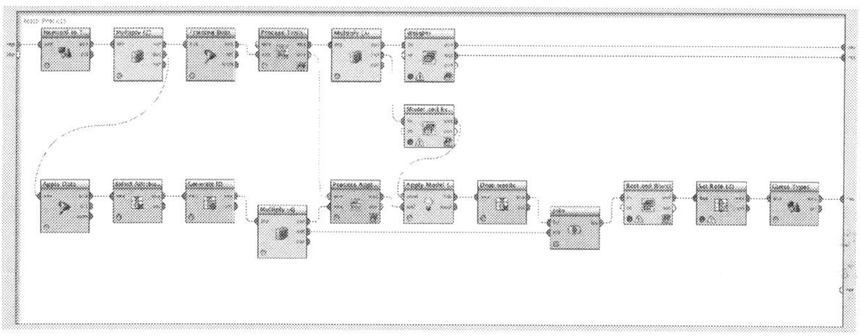

Fig. 12.4 Sentiment analysis component elements for LA engine in Arctic Trek

need for extensive hand-scoring. And, this could be applied to other, more complex learning and assessment activities.

The four notebooks selected were a small but very purposive sample for the engine to score. Only one notebook was high scoring according to the human rating (see Table 12.1). A second notebook with a low hand-score illustrated a similar level of text complexity but without as much substantively correct information and with little evidence of collaboration. Two additional notebooks were scored—they represented sparser and less correct scripts, with poor evidence of effective *learning in networks* practices, according to the construct ideas described above. All notebooks were supplied to the engine in their original formats, without editing or correction.

Table 12.1 Sentiment analysis results for Arctic Trek four notebooks

Notebook ID number	Sentiment ranking (pos/neg)	RapidMiner "Score"	Hand-score ranking and notes
A (original case number 32)	Positive	78.0	1 (only notebook of the four judged as high-scoring, illustrated strong elements of collaboration)
B (original case number 11)	Negative	46.0	2 (low-scoring notebook but with some beginner elements of collaboration; text complexity similar to notebook A above)
C (original case number 14)	Negative	39.0	3 tie (low-scoring notebook, few if any relevant elements of collaboration visible)
D (original case number 13)	Negative	35.0	3 tie (low-scoring notebook, few if any relevant elements of collaboration visible)

One caveat concerning the limitations that should be noted in advance of reporting the results is that this is a very small data set intended only to serve as an illustrative example and a larger set would be needed to provide a more formal example. Thus, this example should not be considered conclusive evidence of the sentiment engine here as being effective or ineffective for such purposes. Rather it should be considered as being illustrative of the general topic: the potential for positive interaction of measurement science and learning analytics. Typically, collaborative data sets based on teams of four result in fewer unique work products than result from individual assessments. A larger data set of 150–175 notebooks, (i.e., about 600–900 students), if composed of collaborative teams of four students per notebook, would be more desirable for training an engine. Furthermore, it should be noted that if other collaborative data sets were available, other LA techniques might be more desirable (Chi et al. 2008; Pirolli 2007, 2009; Pirolli et al. 2010; Pirolli and Wilson 1998).

A very small example of the results of the sentiment analysis is shown in Table 12.1. It shows that the LA sentiment engine in this case was able to rank the four notebooks in the same order as the hand-scoring. The highest scoring notebook was rated considerably higher than the next ranked notebook, in spite of the similar text complexity between the two notebooks. Furthermore, RapidMiner was also able to do a reasonable job of awarding "partial credit," establishing a score substantially higher for the top notebook, but also ranking the next notebook somewhat higher than the other two, as had been the case for the human ratings. The notes in the hand-score ranking column provide some interpretive context for teachers and students and could be applied to the LA results as well, and mapped to the construct information described above.

If the improvement of twenty-first century skills such as digital collaboration for learning in social networks is a goal, it is important to help teachers understand what a successful performance looks like in a collaborative digital space. In addition, providing tools that populate the intersection of measurement science and LA, as described in this chapter, can help to inform teaching so that teachers know how such skills can be effectively assessed.

Discussion and Conclusion

What Measurement Can Learn from LA

Learning Analytics has evidenced a "brave-new-world" view in taking advantage of the new sources and large scope of data that have become available in this digital age. This has hugely expanded the types and volume of data available to education, and has opened unforeseen possibilities, from moment-to-moment data collection in educational settings to fine-grained records of interactive settings, such as one-on-one conversations and classroom discussions, to the data representation of objects that were previously not available to quantitative analysis, such as syntactic and content representations of document, student products, and so forth.

Not only is it the data being collected that is changing, it is the speed of collection, and the possibility of intelligent computer-generated feedback that opens up significant possibilities for education. Educators no longer have to wait for the data analysts to spend days (or weeks) analyzing the data and preparing reports. Teachers can have effectively instantaneous feedback, once the student has responded—it is this that holds the greatest promise. The impact of classroom assessment on student success has been well documented in a classic meta-analysis by Black and Wiliam (1998). But this historic level of impact had little to do with measurement since, in the past, the classroom environment was too fast-paced for the decidedly careful pace of traditional educational measurement. Partly by virtue of its usual funding sources (policy-level decision-makers), and partly due to the lack of appropriate technology, as noted above, measurement has been focused on large-scale samples of sparse data for each sampled student. What was useful for administrative and program evaluation purposes had no place in the most important site of educational change and improvement—the classroom. While early measurement scientists often had a strong domain grounding in what they were trying to measure (e.g. psychologists trying to measure psychological traits), measurement science has become its own sub-discipline, and much of the domain expertise has been lost directly by the psychometricians (Mislevy 2016). In contrast, LA researchers have worked to build strong, diverse teams that bring domain expertise back into play in ways from which measurement science can learn. These teams can tackle much more complex work products and data streams, but only because they ensure that they have educational professionals and domain analysts for the given area of interest working on the team.

What LA Can Learn from Measurement

The discussion above notes several potential strengths of the measurement approach as a framework for LA. First, whenever someone interprets LA student performance results, they are making certain assumptions. Over many years and across a wide range of contexts, the nature of these assumptions has been considered and contested within the domain of the science of measurement. In the discussion above, we have emphasized the critical importance of having a scientific theory that is the basis for the interpretation of these results (the construct map in the context of the BAS—although, of course, there could be many other such bases). Equally, there needs to be an understanding of how the data generation model relates back to this scientific theory (this was embodied in the item design and the outcome space in the BAS). And, in order to evaluate how well the accumulated evidence relates to the hypothesised scientific construct, it is important to have a statistical model for estimation so that uncertainty can be included in the resulting outcomes (which is one aspect of the measurement model in the BAS).

In addition, Quality Control considerations need to be invoked, which are expressed in the measurement approach through the concepts of validity and reliability evidence (e.g., AERA/APA/NCME 2014), which constitute the grounds on which to be assured that the interpretations that analysts would like to make of the LA results are indeed valid.

No abundance of data (i.e., "big data"), nor frequency of responses, nor novelty of data-format, will eliminate the need for these issues to be considered and responded to. At the initial stages of implementation, it may be acceptable to ignore this need, but long practice in many different domains has told us that such ignorance is fraught with risk, not just for the Learning Analysts and their findings, but also for the students and teachers who rely on them.

What LA and Measurement Can Do Together

Perhaps even more important than what the two approaches can learn from each other is that they can benefit by working together. The small example above shows some of the overlaps and complementarities that can be seen to exist between the two approaches (with a little bit of cross-disciplinary insight). Our principal argument above is not based on necessary oppositions between the two, but rather on how they can be seen to offer ways to extend each other.

Learning Analytics and Measurement Science

Considering the discussions in this chapter, one can perceive new research directions at the intersection of LA and measurement. First, from the direction of how interactions with LA can improve and expand measurement science, we noted the following possibilities:

(a) Measurement science needs to adapt its methods to the new directions that LA takes as standard, in particular to the gathering and analysis of new types of data relating to student behaviors beyond the standard measurement science formats of the test and the questionnaire/survey—for instance to incorporate not just student "answers," but also their many steps and actions that lead to those answers.

(b) Measurement science also needs to explore the broader horizon of being able to examine real-time segments of student educational experiences—not just a single "test" event in a single classroom in a single year—by having access to the whole range of IT-enabled data that will be available regarding students. The very size of LA data sets is also a challenge to standard measurement science—the typical techniques of statistical analysis will have to give way to more flexible and faster algorithms and means of communicating results.

Second, thinking about how interactions with measurement science can improve and expand LA, one can see several possibilities. One possibility will include new LA algorithms and aggregation approaches. These are likely to be situated in data density, but they will also rely on more pattern finding and probably noisier patterns, with more construct irrelevant variance, included in less structured but larger data sets. A good direction for assessing efficacious algorithms and methods of classification and feedback specifically for educational applications will be to search for methods that add to the explained variance of models already employed in measurement science. As LA matures beyond a focus on predictive validity to the establishment of well-accepted procedures for quality and the adherence to strong measurement standards, new research directions will emerge in the science of LA assessment. These are likely to include technical studies and simulations to understand and address (a) reliability and precision information for LA, (b) assessment form creation, (c) linking and equating, (d) adaptive administrations, (e) the evaluation of data-generation assumptions, and (f) the checking of data-model fit. As LA opens up more opportunities for deeper assessment of hard-to-measure constructs that are instructionally relevant, the interpretive focus of LA will become more prominent. LA will need to add expertise regarding validity evidence for the interpretation of its outcomes: measurement science has had over 100 years of experience in this, and it will be much more efficient for LA to learn from that experience than to repeat that century of effort and thinking.

Contemplating this from both sides, an important area of research emerges related to improving and informing instruction. Research questions to be asked include:

(a) How and whether teaching and feedback opportunities can enrich student learning outcomes, and
(b) Whether they can address that need for *all* students, including disadvantaged students.

Technology can help to level the playing field and close achievement gaps, but it can also further marginalize some populations.

Thus, we see a need for new research and development projects that combine the two approaches. Such projects must provide for a wide dissemination of research outcomes and products in order to reach the many widely distributed fields of application, which often do not share the same resource spaces. Joint publication of books that combine the approaches and synthesize approaches would be helpful. And advanced training programs are needed that combine the two, both for graduate students and for working professionals and academics.

In conclusion, as we enter a brave new world of digitally-extended data collection, we need to match the fearlessness of LA with the strength and re-assurance of measurement science.

References

American Educational Research Association, American Psychological Association, National Council for Measurement in Education. (AERA, APA, NCME, 2014). *Standards for educational and psychological testing*. Washington, DC: American Educational Research Association.

Black, P., & Wiliam, D. (1998). Assessment and classroom learning. *Assessment in Education: Principles, Policy & Practice, 5*(1), 7–74. doi:10.1080/0969595980050102.

Chi, E. H., Pirolli, P., Suh, B., Kittur, A., Pendleton, B., & Mytkowicz, T. (2008). *Augmented social cognition*. Palo Alto: Palo Alto Research Center.

Hofmann, M., & Klinkenberg, R. (2013). *RapidMiner: Data mining use cases and business analytics applications*. Boca Raton: CRC Press.

Mislevy, R.J. (2016). Discussion of learning analytics.

Mislevy, R. J., Almond, R. G., & Lukas, J. F. (2003). *A brief introduction to evidence-centered design, CRESST Technical Paper Series*. Los Angeles: CRESST.

Papamitsiou, Z., & Economides, A. A. (2014). Learning analytics and educational data mining in practice: A systematic literature review of empirical evidence. *Educational Technology & Society, 17*(4), 49–64.

Pirolli, P. (2007). Cognitive models of human-information interaction. In F. T. Durso (Ed.), *Handbook of applied cognition* (pp. 443–470). New York: Wiley.

Pirolli, P. (2009). *An elementary social information foraging model*. Paper presented at the CHI 2009, ACM Conference on Human Factors in Computing Systems, Boston, MA.

Pirolli, P., & Wilson, M. (1998). A theory of the measurement of knowledge content, access, and learning. *Psychological Review, 105*(1), 58–82.

Pirolli, P., Preece, J., & Shneiderman, B. (2010). Cyberinfrastructure for social action on national priorities. *IEEE Computer, 43*(11), 20–21.

Russell, S., & Norvig, P. (2009). *Artificial intelligence, a modern approach* (3rd ed.). Upper Saddle River: Prentice Hall.

Scalise, K. (2018). Next wave for integration of educational technology into the classroom: Collaborative technology integration planning practices. In E. Care, P. Griffin, & M. Wilson (Eds.), *Assessment and teaching of 21st century skills: Research and applications*. Dordrecht: Springer.

Scalise, K., Bernbaum, D. J., Timms, M. J., Veeragoudar Harrell, S., Burmester, K., Kennedy, C. A., & Wilson, M. (2007). Adaptive technology for e-learning: Principles and case studies of an emerging field. *Journal of the American Society for Information Science and Technology, 58*(14), 001–015.

Wilson, M. (2005). *Constructing measures: An item response modeling approach*. Mahwah: Lawrence Erlbaum Assoc.

Wilson, M., & Scalise, K. (2015). Assessment of learning in digital networks. In P. Griffin & E. Care (Eds.), *Assessment and teaching of 21st century skills: Methods and approach* (pp. 57–81). Dordrecht: Springer.

Wilson, M., & Sloane, K. (2000). From principles to practice: An embedded assessment system. *Applied Measurement in Education, 13*(2), 181–208.

Wilson, M., Bejar, I., Scalise, K., Templin, J., Wiliam, D., & Torres Irribarra, D. (2012). Perspectives on methodological issues. In P. Griffin, B. McGaw, & E. Care (Eds.), *Assessment and teaching of 21st century skills*. New York: Springer.

Wilson, M., Scalise, K., Gochyyev, P. (in press). ICT literacy – learning in digital networks. In R. W. Lissitz, & H. Jiao (Eds.), *Technology enhanced innovative assessment: Development, modeling, and scoring from an Interdisciplinary perspective*. Charlotte: Information Age Publisher.

Wilson, M., Scalise, K., & Gochyyev, P. (2018). ICT literacy in digital networks. In E. Care, P. Griffin, & M. Wilson (Eds.), *Assessment and teaching of 21st century skills: Research and applications*. New York: Springer.

Chapter 13
How Can the Use of Data from Computer-Delivered Assessments Improve the Measurement of Twenty-First Century Skills?

Dara Ramalingam and Raymond J. Adams

Abstract Technology is continuing to change the way we live. Given its centrality to our lives, it is not surprising that its use in educational assessment has been increasing, and has been an important focus of education assessment research in recent years. While the initial motivation for computer-delivered assessments was gains in assessment efficiency, this chapter demonstrates that computer delivery can enhance validity and reliability through the capture of process data. When an assessment is computer-delivered, every interaction of the test-taker with the environment may be recorded as process data. The use of process data holds much promise for providing previously inaccessible insights into not just *whether* a student solved a task, but *how* they did so. Further, it is the processes that contribute to twenty-first century skills that are likely to be amenable to direct targeting in terms of teaching and learning. However, collecting large amounts of information in the absence of a plan for its analysis and use is unlikely to lead to useful outcomes. Through item response theory analysis of process data collected in the Digital Reading Assessment included as part of the 2012 cycle of the Programme for International Student Assessment (PISA), this chapter illustrates how process data that relates to the way a student navigates the problem space can be used to improve validity and reliability. By fitting alternative item response models to the data, it is shown that measurement can be improved by using process data if a clear connection is made between these data and theories of developing competence in the domain of interest.

D. Ramalingam (✉) • R.J. Adams
Australian Council for Educational Research, The University of Melbourne, Melbourne, VIC, Australia
e-mail: Dara.Ramalingam@acer.edu.au

E. Care et al. (eds.), *Assessment and Teaching of 21st Century Skills*, Educational Assessment in an Information Age,
DOI 10.1007/978-3-319-65368-6_13

The Importance of Computer-Delivered Assessments

Technology is fundamentally changing the way we live, the way we gather and organise information, the way we work, and the way we interact. Access to computers and the Internet has grown rapidly in recent years, with Internet use almost trebling between 2005 and 2015 (International Telecommunications Union 2015). In some countries, access is near universal. Recent data from large international surveys suggest that students have high levels of access to computers both at home and at school: across OECD countries participating in the Programme for International Student Assessment (PISA), for example, on average, 71.7% of students reported using a desktop, laptop, or tablet computer at school (OECD 2014).

Computers are used in schools for a variety of purposes. For example, they might be used purely as a delivery system for instruction, or a tool for accessing resources. They might also be used specifically for the purpose of acquiring skill and knowledge in ICT (Crawford and Toyama 2002; Cuttance and Stokes 2001; Kozma 2003). Also, computers are increasingly being used to deliver assessments (Quellmalz and Pellegrino 2009).

The initial rationale for the use of computer delivery of assessments was the gains in efficiency: if scoring and reporting could be automated, or testing made adaptive, assessments could be delivered more cheaply, feedback could be given virtually instantaneously, and testing could be more targeted (Bennett et al. 1999; Lord 1980). However, more recently, the potential of computer-delivered assessments to give insight into previously inaccessible processes has been acknowledged as possibly of even greater importance (Ridgway and McCusker 2003). Certainly, the new forms of data capture made possible by computer delivery of assessments provide a major opportunity for researchers to explore both the nature of any skills being assessed, and concomitantly, how these might best be measured. A focus on the processes and sub-skills that comprise broader twenty-first century skills is likely to lead to improved teaching and learning. If these sub-skills are better understood, then they can be targeted in teaching, resulting in better application of these important skills across a broad range of situations and environments. In practice, however, using information from assessments to make statements about the component sub-skills of a broader domain can be difficult, not least because those involved in framework and assessment development do not always consider such issues prior to the development of assessment materials.

In the case of paper-based assessments, what is collected is the final product of a test-taker's thinking or work. In form, this product might be their choice of response to a multiple-choice item, or an extended written response, but, regardless of form, the final product can offer only limited insight into the thought process and steps that led to the final product: it is not possible to have, in every case, students show their working, and to use this in allocating a score to a response. As a consequence when an assessment is paper-based, it is very difficult to make valid observations about the process a student made use of in reaching their final conclusion. In contrast, when an assessment is delivered via computer, every interaction of the test-taker with the environment may be recorded, making it possible to collect far more information than has previously been possible (Baker and Mayer 1999; Chung and Baker 2003; Schacter et al. 1999). While it is a simple matter to capture human-computer interactions such as mouse clicks, the dragging and dropping of an item from one place to another or the selection of an item in a drop-down menu – sometimes called 'process data' (Zoanetti 2010) – the significance of the methodological advances this data collection suggests should not be underestimated. In particular, this data capture has the potential to give insights as to the processes followed by students in reaching their final response to an assessment item. In general, there are three kinds of process data. First, we can think about the type of interaction that the student has with the material. At the most general level, this includes mouse clicks. Depending on the assessment, it might also include such interactions as mouse down/up rollover actions, dragging and dropping an item from one place on the screen to another, choosing an option from a drop-down menu or entering text. Second, we can consider the frequency of interaction. This is related to, but different from the first category. Knowing that a student clicked on a particular button or link gives us one kind of information. Knowing that they clicked on the same button multiple times may give us a different kind of information. A third kind of process data involves time. Each individual action completed by a student has a time stamp, making it possible to examine both the total time taken to complete an item, and the time taken to complete individual steps within an item (Ramalingam et al. 2017).

Opportunities to Make Processes Visible

Collectively, these process data represent a wealth of new information: the implication of this enhanced ability to collect a new range of data is that it is now possible to observe processes directly, rather than being limited to inferring them, and it is possible to do so unobtrusively. There is an opportunity, using process data made available through computer delivery, to address the inherent difficulty in making statements about the processes that inform twenty-first century skills. However, the analysis and interpretation of process data is not straightforward (Williamson et al. 2006; Zoanetti and Griffin 2017). Planning for such analyses should involve deep consideration of the link between assessment design and evidence about proficiency (for examples of frameworks that can be used to assist in this process, see Mislevy et al. 2006; Wilson and Scalise 2006). More generally, process data are best understood where a connection to cognitive theories of task demand has been made (Pelligrino et al. 2001).

The increase in computer delivery of assessments has seen a proliferation of new, 'complex' item types, and a focus on the challenges of how to interpret, score, and analyse the data resulting from these (Williamson et al. 2006). Less focused on, but arguably even more important, is exploration of the ways in which the computer delivery of assessments might enable improvements to the scoring and analysis of simpler item formats, such as multiple-choice. Multiple-choice items have long been used in educational testing because they enable efficient assessment, and are easy to administer and score. These advantages, particularly in the context of large-scale testing programs, are significant. The focus of this chapter is on how process data can be used to improve measurement in simple items. In particular, where a link between an indicator derived from process data and a theory of developing competence has been made, there is the possibility of directly including such indicators in scoring. This approach has several major advantages. Chief among them is that we obtain a far more comprehensive assessment of twenty-first century skills. It suggests a sharp focus for future work, in which the capture and measurement of sub-skills that contribute to complex twenty-first century skillsets can be a direct and intentional focus throughout the process of assessment development.

An Example of the Use of Process Data from the PISA Digital Reading Assessment

Examples in this chapter come from secondary analyses of the log-file data produced from the computer-delivered assessment of reading from OECD's PISA 2012 cycle (known as the digital reading assessment). In total, nearly 60,000 students from 32 countries completed this assessment (OECD 2012a). For each student participating in these assessments, a log file was generated, containing a complete record of that student's interactions with the system.

Including Indicators Derived from Process Data in Scoring

The importance of linking assessment data explicitly to theories of developing competence has been well emphasised (Mislevy et al. 2006; Pelligrino et al. 2001). In the case of large-scale assessments, conceptual frameworks exist to guide assessment development (see for example, OECD 2009a, 2012b) and make the link between theory and assessment design clear. In this discussion, one variable that is explicitly included in the framework for PISA digital reading that can be constructed from process data is introduced, and models that show how this indicator might be used in scoring are outlined.

Items in the PISA Digital Reading Assessment are set in a simulated web environment with multiple, linked, websites or web pages. The conception of digital reading for the purposes of PISA is that digital reading is one kind of reading. It requires the same skills as print reading, and at the same time, makes new and different demands on readers. Broadly, it is conceived as having two components: text processing and navigation.[1] The text processing component involves decoding and

[1] This explicit acknowledgement that digital reading has two components raises the possibility that digital reading should be viewed as a multidimensional, rather than a unidimensional construct. Detailed comment on this issue is beyond the scope of this chapter, but a series of analyses undertaken suggested that the use of a unidimensional model (used in the analyses reported in this chapter) was appropriate.

comprehension of the text – this aspect of digital reading constitutes the common ground between digital and print reading. The navigation component involves making choices about how to move through a hypertext environment by predicting the likely content of links and then enacting one's choice of pathway by clicking on links, scrolling, or using tabs (Mendelovits et al. 2012). Although analogous skills exist in paper-based reading, in PISA, these navigation skills are only included in the digital reading assessment. Further, the nature of navigation in the digital realm is different to that in print reading. Within print text a natural order of reading is suggested by the page and chapter structure of books, and a primarily linear approach is taken to the presentation of information. In contrast, when reading hypertext, readers must select their own pathway through a text. When they engage with hypertext, readers must create their own text through actively choosing which links to click on in relation to their goals for reading (Barab et al. 1996; OECD 2009b; Reinking 1997; Rouet and Levonen 1996).This process of constructing one's own text from a set of material can be challenging because it requires engagement and reflection. Nonetheless, the ability to navigate effectively is critical to the ability to engage in successful digital reading. Given the dramatic increase over the last two decades in particular, in the amount of reading that takes place online (International Telecommunications Union 2016), navigation can be considered an important twenty-first century sub-skill.

The requirement for navigation within the PISA digital reading items is best illustrated through an examination of the demands inherent in the items. The publicly-released unit 'Seraing' (OECD n.d.)[2] consists of three items relating to a common set of stimulus materials.[3] In the first item, the starting page is the page on which the target information is located, so there is no need to navigate beyond the starting page. In the second and third items within the unit, being able to answer the question correctly is dependent on successfully navigating to the page (or pages) containing the target information.

The second item in the unit is the present focus, for the purposes of illustration. In this item, there is more than one pathway that can be followed to locate the target information. The item begins on the home page for Seraing (Fig. 13.1a). The first step is to follow the instruction to 'Find the page for the Seraing Community Cultural Centre'. In this case, there are two possible ways to do this – either by clicking on the prominent link 'Community Cultural Centre' in the middle of the homepage, or alternatively, using the dropdown menu that appears when 'services' is clicked (Fig. 13.1c).

Either of these options will take students to the Community cultural centre home page (Fig. 13.1b). At this point, there are, again, two possibilities. The item asks students to locate the film that will be shown in the first week of November. They may either link 'date' with 'November' to click on 'Programme by date', or they may make a link between 'film' and 'event type' to click on 'Programme by event type'. If they choose to click on 'Programme by date' their next page will give the

[2]This material has been publicly released.

[3]This unit can be viewed at the website cbasq.acer.edu.au

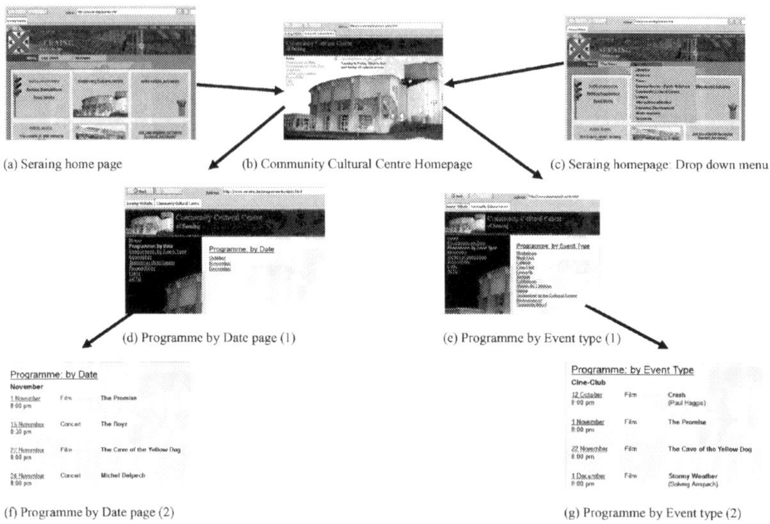

Fig. 13.1 Alternate pathways for reaching the target information for Seraing, item 2. (**a**) Seraing home page, (**b**) Community cultural centre homepage, (**c**) Seraing homepage: drop down menu, (**d**) Programme by date page *1*, (**e**) Programme by event type *1*, (**f**) Programme by date page *2*, (**g**) Programme by event type (2) (Reproduced from OECD n.d.)

options 'October', 'November' and 'December' (Fig. 13.1d), whereas if they click on 'Programme by event type', a set of 12 options will appear, one of which is 'cine-club (Fig. 13.1e)'. Clicking on 'November' in the first pathway, and 'cine-club' in the second will take students to a final page, containing the target information (Fig. 13.1f, g respectively).

It is clear that navigation is central to the demand of this item, consistent with the definition of digital reading in the PISA framework. At present, however, it is the case both in this item and more generally that while the text processing component of digital reading is directly assessed in the PISA digital reading items the navigation component is assessed only indirectly.

For example, a typical multiple-choice item in this assessment, such as the item detailed above, might involve finding information by navigating to the page containing the answer. Scoring of such items only involves examination of whether the student chose the correct multiple-choice option. The text processing component of digital reading is being assessed through student's selection of the correct answer – that is, there is an assumption that if the correct answer was chosen, it is most likely that the student could comprehend the text. The navigation component is being assessed only indirectly – we make an assumption that if the correct option was chosen, the student must have navigated to the page (or pages) containing the target information. However, this may not be the case: it is of course entirely possible that a student did not navigate to the required page/s, but nevertheless managed to correctly answer the question through guessing. The possibility of guessing has always been an issue in multiple-choice items. The advent of computer delivery offers an opportunity to address this concern in relation to navigation: when an assessment is computer-delivered, it is a trivial matter to record the student's entire path – every page they visited. It is no longer necessary to make an assumption that a student visited the required pages – through examination of the log-file constructed as they complete the assessment, we can now know for certain whether or not the needed pages were visited.

It is for this reason that for the purposes of this work, a relatively simple indicator of navigation behaviour was constructed for use in scoring. While it would be possible to construct indicators of navigation behaviour that take into account exactly which pages were visited, and in which order, to address the issue of guessing, one only needs to know whether or not a student visited the page/s containing the target information.

Construction of such a variable involves several steps. The first is to identify the page (or pages) that contain the target information. The second step is to detail all possible pathways that enable students to access the target page(s). In some cases, it is possible to access the target page from many other pages. Since, in the case of the present, simple indicator of navigation behaviour, we are interested only in *whether* a student accessed the target page(s) (not *how* they did so), it is necessary to exhaustively list the possible ways that the target page can be accessed. In the case of the item described, only two expected pathways were outlined. However, the unit structure is such that many other pathways are possible, which might include using any or all of the hyperlinks contained within each page of the unit, the tabs that appear once more than one website is open, and the back and forward browser buttons.

A complication in defining this indicator is introduced by the assessment structure of items within units. The PISA digital reading items are grouped in units, where a unit is a set of items based around a common set of stimulus materials, in this case, a set of linked websites or web pages. In the digital reading units, all stimulus material is available throughout the unit. Thus while in some cases students are explicitly directed not to take into account any information from a page beyond their given starting page, exploration is not precluded. The significance of this in relation to this work is that it is possible for students to have obtained the information needed to answer a given item in the course of exploration completed during a previous item. In light of this issue, for the purposes of the present work, the definition of 'reaching the target page/s' took into account student's actions in any previous items in the unit – that is, if a student did not visit the target page for item 2 in the course of completing item 2, but did visit this target page when completing item 1, they would still be deemed to have reached the target page.[4]

[4] Defining navigation so that exploration in a previous item is included in the definition of whether the target page has been visited potentially introduces dependency issues. Detailed exploration of this form of dependency (and potentially others) is beyond the scope of this chapter, but a series of tests of the level of dependency between items suggested that this was not an issue in the current work.

Having identified whether or not the target page was accessed, a variable was constructed that combined whether or not the item was answered correctly, and whether or not the target page was reached. In a simple multiple-choice question, there are four possible categories for this variable:

1. The item was answered correctly and the target page was reached
2. The item was not answered correctly, but the target page was reached
3. The item was answered correctly, but the target page was not reached
4. The item was not answered correctly, and the target page was not reached.

Clear links to the variables outlined in the PISA framework for digital reading (OECD 2011) are suggested through this categorisation. If we take correctness of response as a proxy for text processing skill, in general, students in category 4 display neither text processing nor navigation skills. Students in category 3, it can be demonstrated, must have guessed the correct answer, so they, too, show neither text processing nor navigation skills. Students in category 2 display navigation skills, but lack text processing skills, while students in category 1 show both navigation and text processing skills.

The description above suggests an expectation about the order of the categories: one would expect the hierarchy in terms of ability to be in the order that the categories are listed, with students in category 1 having the highest ability, followed by those in category 2, then those in categories 3, and 4. The set of digital reading items were examined by running three different models in ACER ConQuest, a computer program that allows data analysis using a range of item response models (Adams et al. 2015).

Evaluation of the Models

The first model, which was used with a view to exploring the hierarchy of the responses, was Bock's nominal response model (Bock 1972). In this model a score is estimated for every response category, with that estimated score indicating the relative merit that should be assigned to that response.

The Bock model uses the multivariate logistic function to model category response functions (CRFs) for each of the response categories of an item, denoted as c where $c = 0,1,2..,m$, and m is the number of possible response categories for a given item. The Bock model describes each item using two parameters, namely:

λ_{ih} = the slope associated with category h of item i., and

ζ_{ih} = the intercept associated with category h of item i.

Under the Bock model, the probability of a given response category is expressed as in Eq. 13.1.

$$P_{ic}(\theta) = \frac{e^{(\lambda_{ic}\theta + \zeta_{ic})}}{\sum_{h=0}^{m} e^{(\lambda_{ih}\theta + \zeta_{ih})}} \tag{13.1}$$

To run this model the four response categories outlined above were used. Although there is an expectation about the order of the categories, in this model no assumptions are made about the merit that should be assigned to each response category. Using this exploratory model therefore allows expectations about the order of categories to be tested.

The second model was Wilson's (1992) Ordered Partition model which requires the a-priori assignment of integer scores to each of the response categories. The mathematical formulation of the Ordered Partition model is given below, with Eq. 13.2 being taken directly from Wilson (1992). If X_{ni} is a random variable describing the response of person *n* to item *i*, the probability of person *n*, with ability θ_n selecting response *k* is given in Eq. 13.2.

$$P\left(X_{ni}=k\right)=\frac{e^{\left[\theta_n\beta_i(k)-\xi_{ik}\right]}}{\sum_{h=1}^{K_i}e^{\left[\theta_n\beta_i(h)-\xi_{ih}\right]}} \tag{13.2}$$

In Eq. 13.2, ξ_{ik} is a parameter for item i associated with response category k, and ξ_{ik} is constrained so that $\xi_{i1}=0$. In Eq. 13.2, $\beta_i(k)$ is a function defining the scoring for item *i* and response *k*. It is this function that leads to the defining feature of the Ordered Partition model. β_i can be defined at the level of each item, and more than one response may map to a given level.

This model was run for the purposes of comparison. In this model navigation behaviour was not taken into account in scoring: the same four response categories were used as in the Bock model, but in this case two possible scores were assigned, based on correctness of response only. Scoring for each of the four categories outlined above was as follows: 1,0,1,0. One implication of these scoring rules is that equivalent credit is given to students in categories (1) and (3) outlined above, which means that students who, it can be demonstrated have guessed the correct answer, are given the same credit as those who navigated to the target page and answered correctly. With the benefit of process data, these scoring rules appear inadequate – those who guessed the answer receive credit – however this is the standard approach to scoring that has been, and is, used in the absence of process data.

Finally, a Partial Credit scoring model was estimated (Masters 1982). As with the Ordered Partition model this model requires the a-priori assignment of scores to each of the response categories, but unlike the Ordered Partition model the Partial Credit model requires the assignment of a unique score to each response category. The Partial Credit model is used when correctness of response is defined by more than one category. The set of item parameters in this model set out ordered pairs of the possible adjacent categories of response to a given item. The parameters then describe the difficulty of the higher category in the pair. In the Partial Credit model, X_{ni} is an integer random variable taking a value between 0 and m_i, where m_i is the maximum category for item *i*.

As explained by Berezner and Adams (2017), if the probability of a response of *t* by person *n* to item *i* is denoted by $P_{ni,t}(X_{ni}=t;\,\theta_n,\delta_{it})$, then the Partial Credit model can be written as Eq. 13.3:

$$\frac{P_{ni,t}}{P_{ni,t-1}+P_{ni,t}}=\frac{\exp(\theta_n-\delta_{it})}{1+\exp(\theta_n-\delta_{it})} \tag{13.3}$$

Assuming the constraint $\sum_{m_i}^{t=0} P_{ni,t}=1$

To fit this model, two of the four response categories outlined above were collapsed into one category so that three response categories remained, with scores '0', '1' and '2'. These rules were consistent with the ordering of categories suggested by the results of the exploratory Bock model (the first model described) but, perhaps more importantly, were developed with reference to the construct of digital reading so that interpretation of the results could be linked to developing proficiency. In general, for items where navigation was required, the scoring categories for this model collapsed categories 3 and 4 outlined above, so that students who neither answered correctly, nor reached the target page were combined for the purposes of scoring, with those who, it can be demonstrated, guessed the answer to the question – that is, students who guessed their response received no credit for it, regardless of whether it was correct or incorrect. Categories 1 and 2 remained separate so that those who reached the target page, but did not answer correctly received partial credit for showing some skill in navigation. Full credit was reserved for those students who both reached the target page and answered correctly.

In this work, a multi-step process was used to consider how process data might best be used. The first step was exploratory (the Bock model). Although a clear expectation existed as to what the relative ability of students in different categories would be, work making use of vast volumes of process data is still in its infancy, and exploratory techniques are of value. They are of most value, though, when they can be followed up with confirmatory work. The inclusion of navigation directly in a Partial Credit model for scoring digital reading items acts as such confirmation. The scoring rules developed for the new model including navigation were both consistent with the exploratory work, and grounded in the PISA framework for digital reading, which acknowledges navigation as a critical element of reading in the digital medium. As shown, where the use of process data can be grounded in knowledge of developing competence in a domain, we can use newly-available information to better assess the construct of interest, an opportunity to improve the validity of the assessment.

Comparison of the Bock model with each of the other two models took place through a comparison of reliability, and a comparison of the qualitative properties of the models. The outcome of the comparison of reliability is shown in Fig. 13.2. The model with the highest reliability is the Bock model, but the Partial Credit model has a substantially higher reliability than the Ordered Partition model. The practical effect of higher reliability is that including navigation in scoring reduces the uncertainty in the estimate of the ability of the student (Adams 2005; Mislevy et al. 1992). The difference in reliability between the Ordered Partition model and the Partial Credit model is important, as it suggests that the model in

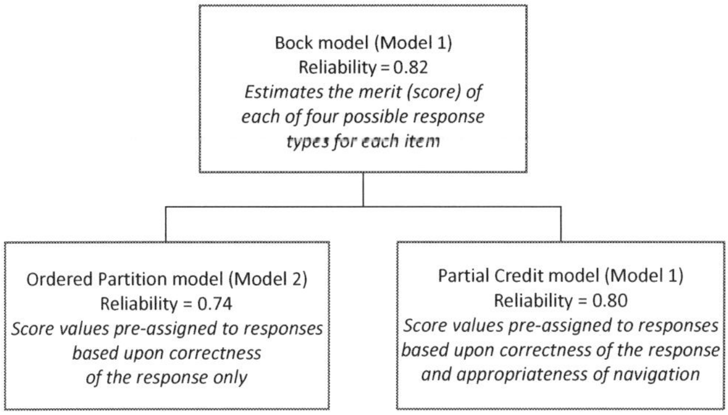

Fig. 13.2 Comparison of the Bock model, Ordered Partition model and Partial Credit model

which navigation is included in scoring is an improvement on the model in which it is not. This constitutes an illustration of the value of process data when it is used with appropriate consideration of the nature of the construct being assessed.

The Importance of Process Data

The advent of computer-delivered assessments has made possible the collection of a wealth of new kinds of data. This discussion has used a specific indicator to illustrate how process data might be used to improve construct validity. The focus in this chapter has been on the capture of processes – the essence of twenty-first century skills – and on how the capture of such data allows more comprehensive assessment of a target domain. More broadly, however, considerations around data capture have strong implications for the teaching and learning of twenty-first century skills, since more comprehensive assessment, and a better understanding of target constructs will ultimately enable better targeting skills of importance in the twenty-first century in the classroom.

Navigation behaviour in general, and whether a student visited the target page, in particular, is an example of an indicator derived from process data which can be used to improve measurement. It is also an example of a critical sub-skill contributing to the broader twenty-first century skill of digital reading. In hypertext environments, the ability to navigate between and within web pages is critical to successfully achieving one's goals because unlike in paper-based texts, the structure of information is not linear. The examination of navigation behaviour via process data exemplifies exploitation of data that are (a) only accessible when an assessment is computer-delivered and (b) critical to an important twenty-first century skill. By including this measure in scoring, validity is enhanced in two ways. First, in including such measures in scoring, we are able to assess directly something that is defined in the framework as part of the construct, but which was previously only assessed indirectly. Including navigation in scoring, then, broadens what is being assessed so that the assessment more accurately represents the construct. Second, using process data about navigation behaviour can isolate the group of students that answered correctly, but did not visit the target page. These students can only have guessed the answer to the item. Since this is the case, it is expected that these students will be of a lower ability than those students who both answered correctly, and visited the target page/s. If these two groups can be treated differently in the item analyses, we are better taking into account our expectations about the link between navigation behaviour and ability.

This work illustrates the importance of careful consideration of how any indicators derived from process data are related to proficiency. While new kinds of information have great potential to offer insight, it is imperative that a plan for their analysis be in place, preferably one that shows precisely how the data being used is connected to theories of developing competence in the domain of interest. It is in this way that these data can be used to improve measurement, and ultimately, to allow better teaching and learning of twenty-first century skills.

References

Adams, R. J. (2005). Reliability as a measurement design effect. *Studies in Educational Evaluation, 31*(2–3), 162–172.

Adams, R. J., Wu, M. L., & Wilson, M. R. (2015). *ACER ConQuest: Generalised item response modelling software (Version 4)*. Melbourne: Australian Council for Educational Research.

Baker, E. L., & Mayer, R. E. (1999). Computer-based assessment of problem solving. *Computers in Human Behavior, 15*(3–4), 269–282.

Barab, S. A., Bowdish, B. E., Young, M. F., & Owen, S. V. (1996). Understanding kiosk navigation: Using log files to capture hypermedia searches. *Instructional Science, 24*(5), 377–395.

Bennett, R. E., Goodman, M., Hessinger, J., Kahn, H., Ligget, J., Marshall, G., & Zack, J. (1999). Using multimedia in large-scale computer-based testing programs. *Computers in Human Behavior, 15*(3–4), 283–294.

Berezner, A., & Adams, R. J. (2017). Why large-scale assessments use scaling and item response theory. In P. Lietz, J. C. Cresswell, K. F. Rust, & R. J. Adams (Eds.), *Implementation of large-scale education assessments* (pp. 323–356). Hoboken: Wiley.

Bock, R. D. (1972). Estimating item parameters and latent ability when responses are scored in two or more nominal categories. *Psychometrika, 37*, 29–51.

Chung, G. K., & Baker, E. L. (2003). An exploratory study to examine the feasibility of measuring problem-solving processes using a click-through interface. *Journal of Technology, Learning, and Assessment, 2*(2).

Crawford, V., & Toyama, Y. (2002). Assessing the educational technology proficiency of students and educators – A review of current policy, practice, and research – Final Report. SRI Project 11061. Retrieved 29 May, 2003, from http://www.sri.com/policy/ctl/pdfs/Task2_FinalReport3.pdf.

Cuttance, P., & Stokes, S. (2001). *School innovation: Pathway to the knowledge society*. Canberra: Department of Education Science and Training.

International Telecommunications Union. (2015). ITU World Telecommunication/ICT Indicators database. Retrieved July 7, 2015, from http://www.itu.int/en/ITU-D/Statistics/Pages/stat/default.aspx.

International Telecommunications Union. (2016). ITU World Telecommunication/ICT Indicators database. Retrieved November 22, 2016, from http://www.itu.int/en/ITU-D/Statistics/Pages/stat/default.aspx.

Kozma, R. (Ed.). (2003). *Technology, innovation, and education change: A global perspective: A report of the Second Information Technology in Education Study (SITES) Module 2*. Eugene: International Society for Technology in Education.

Lord, F. M. (1980). *Applications of item response theory to practical testing problems*. Hillsdale: Erlbaum.

Masters, G. N. (1982). A Rasch model for partial credit scoring. *Psychometrika, 47*(2), 149–174.

Mendelovits, J., Ramalingam, D., & Lumley, T. (2012). *Print and digital reading in PISA 2009: Comparison and contrast*. Paper presented at the Annual Conference of the American Educational Research Association (AERA), Vancouver.

Mislevy, R. J., Beaton, A. E., Kaplan, B., & Sheehan, K. M. (1992). Estimating population characteristics from sparse matrix samples of item responses. *Journal of Educational Measurement, 29*, 133–161.

Mislevy, R. J., Steinberg, L. S., Almond, R. G., & Lukas, J. F. (2006). Concepts, terminology and basic models of evidence-centred design. In D. M. Williamson, I. I. Bejar, & R. J. Mislevy (Eds.), *Automated scoring of complex tasks in computer-based testing* (pp. 15–48). Mahwah: Lawrence Erlbaum.

OECD. (2009a). *PIAAC problem solving in technology rich environments: Conceptual framework*. Paris: OECD.

OECD. (2009b). *PISA 2009 assessment framework: Key competencies in reading, mathematics and science*. Paris: OECD.

OECD. (2011). *PISA 2009 results: Students on line: Digital technologies and performance (Volume VI)*.

OECD. (2012a). *PISA 2009 Technical Report PISA* Retrieved from http://dx.doi.org/10.1787/9789264167872-en

OECD. (2012b). *PISA 2012 main survey problem solving framework*. Paris: OECD.

OECD. (2014). *PISA 2012 results: Creative problem solving: Students' skills in tackling real-life problems* (Vol. V). Pisa: OECD Publishing.

OECD. (n.d.). PISA computer-based sample items. Retrieved July 22, 2012, from cbasq.acer.edu.au.

Pelligrino, J., Chudowsky, N., & Glaser, R. (Eds.). (2001). *Knowing what students know: The science and design of educational assessment*. Washington, DC: National Academy Press.

Quellmalz, E. S., & Pellegrino, J. W. (2009). Technology and testing. *Science, 323*(5910), 75–79.

Ramalingam, D., McCrae, B., & Philpot, R. (2017). The PISA 2012 assessment of problem solving. In B. Csapó & J. Funke (Eds.), *The Nature of problem solving: Using research to inspire 21st century learning* (pp. 75–91). Paris: OECD Publishing.

Reinking, D. (1997). Me and my hypertext: A multiple digression analysis of technology and literacy (Sic). *The Reading Teacher, 50*(8), 626–643.

Ridgway, J., & McCusker, S. (2003). Using computers to assess new educational goals. *Assessment in Education: Principles, Policy & Practice, 10*(3), 309–328. doi:10.1080/0969594032000148163.

Rouet, J.-F., & Levonen, J. J. (1996). Studying and learning with hypertext: Empirical studies and their implications. In J.-F. Rouet, J. J. Levonen, A. Dillon, & R. J. Spiro (Eds.), *Hypertext and cognition* (pp. 9–23). Hillsdale: Erlbaum.

Schacter, J., Herl, H. E., Chung, G. K. W. K., Dennis, R. A., & O'Neil, H. F., Jr. (1999). Computer-based performance assessments: A solution to the narrow measurement and reporting of problem-solving. *Computers in Human Behavior, 15*(3–4), 403–418.

Williamson, D. M., Bejar, I. I., & Mislevy, R. J. (2006). Automated scoring of complex tasks in computer-based testing: An introduction. In D. M. Williamson, I. I. Bejar, & R. J. Mislevy (Eds.), *Automated scoring of complex tasks in computer-based testing* (pp. 1–13). New Jersey: Laurence Erlbaum Associates.

Wilson, M. (1992). The ordered partition model: An extension of the partial credit model. *Applied Psychological Measurement, 16*, 309–325.

Wilson, M., & Scalise, K. (2006). Assessment to improve learning in higher education: The BEAR assessment system. *Higher Education, 52*(4), 635–663.

Zoanetti, N. (2010). Interactive computer based assessment tasks: How problem-solving process data can inform instruction. *Australasian Journal of Educational Technology, 26*(5), 585–606.

Zoanetti, N., & Griffin, P. (2017). Log-file data as indicators for problem-solving processes. In B. Csapó & J. Funke (Eds.), *The nature of problem solving: Using research to inspire 21st century learning* (pp. 177–191). Paris: OECD Publishing.

Chapter 14
Next Wave for Integration of Educational Technology into the Classroom: Collaborative Technology Integration Planning Practices

Kathleen Scalise

Abstract Technology integration planning (TIP) practices are yielding many emerging examples of effective ICT practice in schools. This chapter will explore and evaluate some best practices on a recently emerging trend in schools: the use of digital collaboration that brings together groups of students into learning networks. This chapter exemplifies the approach with a case study analysis of a sample of collaborative science notebooks from the Assessment and Teaching of Twenty-First Century Skills (ATC21S) project. How, when, and why such technology is being infused into education as digital literacy moves forward will be explored, using the case study. One approach to a systematic process for the effective inclusion of technology is to identify skills that students need to master to support a virtual skill or practice, such as digital collaboration. Here the TIP case study example helps teachers answer key questions about how to assess and evaluate collaborative work online, and how to employ such techniques in the classroom.

Sarah Brown Wessling, an English language arts teacher selected as U.S. National Teacher of the Year in 2010, likes to foster collaborative work in her classroom (Nelson 2010). She has students write together over the computer. They log onto laptops, compose essays in collaborative word processing documents, share their creative ideas together, and peer-edit their final work products online.

Wessling's approach is an example of one of the latest waves of technology integration planning (TIP) in the classroom: digital collaboration. She is using TIP to implement English language arts educational writing standards for 9th and 10th graders in her state. According to the educational standards, her students of about age 14 and 15 must be able to use technology to produce, publish, and update shared writing products online (Wessling 2012). They must be able to access and compose

K. Scalise (✉)
University of Oregon, Eugene, OR, USA
e-mail: kscalise@uoregon.edu

E. Care et al. (eds.), *Assessment and Teaching of 21st Century Skills*,
Educational Assessment in an Information Age,
DOI 10.1007/978-3-319-65368-6_14

documents collaboratively over the internet, and are expected to grow over time in their ability to manage and negotiate working together effectively in a virtual environment. By 12th grade, students in Wessling's state should be able to include new arguments or information in their shared writing in response to ongoing feedback, and show skills in reaching a common understanding and a shared presentation product with other students.

With the onset of Web 2.0 and 3.0 – the social and semantic webs – a next wave for integration of educational technology into the classroom is occurring. It is bringing collaboration and shared meaning-making through technology environments increasingly into learning environments (Evergreen Education Group 2014). Some teachers are beginning to include student-to-student online collaboration in their technology integration practices, and some research projects are examining useful methodologies for incorporating evaluation, assessment and reflection of the approaches (Wilson et al. 2012, 2014).

For many teachers, the idea of teaching twenty-first century standards such as digital collaboration is challenging (Partnership for 21st Century Skills & American Association of Colleges of Teacher Education 2010; Schrum and Levin 2014). Teachers ask how they should go about helping students build these skills, and wonder what a successful performance looks like in a collaborative digital space. They want to know how such skills can be effectively assessed, and whether and how students should be expected to improve over time. Instructors have a lot of experience recognizing more traditional work products in the classroom, but sometimes don't know if they can effectively recognize increasing student proficiency in an area such as digital collaboration.

In this chapter, as a case study, we examine one of the collaborative work products from the Assessment and Teaching of Twenty-First Century Skills (ATC21S) project. ATC21S is an alliance launched by Cisco, Intel, and Microsoft and including government, schools, and university partners across numerous countries. Goals include encouraging the development of twenty-first-century learners and enhancing the skills of the workforce of tomorrow (Griffin et al. 2012).

For the case study discussed here, a digital collaboration in an ATC21S science and mathematics activity is examined (Wilson and Scalise 2012). The case study introduces ways of viewing and interpreting collaborative performances online. It discusses some key attributes of successful digital collaboration that are easy for teachers to recognize in classroom work products.

Digital Collaboration as a Twenty-First Century Skill

One key topic that teachers ponder in digital collaboration is how to effectively evaluate collaborative work in an online setting (McFarlane 2003). They often feel they are good at evaluating work products in their subject matter areas, for instance they can "grade" and provide feedback for language, math or science competencies in a given assignment. But what factors might they tap as indicators of growing student proficiency in collaborative online digital literacy more generally (Wilson et al. 2012)? Without help in choosing or developing indicators, it can be difficult for teachers to gauge how they are helping students improve in this type of educational practice.

Digital literacy as a domain encompasses a wide range of subtopics, including learning in networks, information literacy, digital competence and technological awareness, all of which contribute to learning to learn through the development of enabling skills (Wilson and Scalise 2012). For the ATC21S project, sets of twenty-first century skills were identified based on an analysis of 12 relevant frameworks drawn from a number of countries and international organizations around the world (Binkley et al. 2012). These included the OECD and countries in Europe, North America, Asia and Australia.

For the ATC21S case study discussed here, the focus is on a digital literacy portion of the framework. Called *learning through digital networks*, the digital literacy domain for ATC21S is comprised of four strands of a learning progression, or a set of progressively more proficient levels. The four strands are:

- Functioning as a consumer in networks;
- Functioning as a producer in networks;
- Participating in the development of social capital through networks;
- Participating in intellectual capital in networks.

Each of the four strands has indicators and levels of proficiency. The first strand, Consumer in Networks (CiN), involves obtaining, managing and utilizing information and knowledge from shared digital resources and experts in order to benefit private and professional lives.

The second strand, functioning as a Producer in Networks (PiN) involves creating, developing, organizing and re-organizing information/knowledge in order to contribute to shared digital resources.

The third strand, developing and sustaining Social Capital through Networks (SCN), involves using, developing, moderating, leading and brokering the connectivities within and between individuals and social groups in order to marshal collaborative action, build communities, maintain an awareness of opportunities and integrate diverse perspectives at community, societal and global levels.

The fourth strand, developing and sustaining Intellectual Capital through Networks (ICN), involves understanding how tools, media, and social networks operate, and using appropriate techniques through these resources to build collective intelligence and integrate new insights into personal understandings. An outline of the fourth strand, including indicators of increasing levels of sophistication, is shown in Table 14.1. This strand is shown in detail because it is the focus of the Case Study section of this chapter.

Given the broad reach of these four strands, planning for technology integration practices (TIP) that support collaboration cannot be the domain of any one subject matter area. Rather, examples of effective technology integration strategies are to be found across many content areas. These include language arts/foreign languages, mathematics/science, social studies, art/music, physical education/health, and special education.

Thus, one way of approaching school use of digital literacy is to consider it a practice, or way of working, across domains through new tools (Scalise 2014).

Table 14.1 Developing intellectual capital through networks (ICN)

	Participator in intellectual capital (collective intelligence)
ICN4	Visionary builder
	Questioning existing architecture of social media and developing new architectures
	Functioning at the interfaces of architectures to embrace dialogue
ICN3	Proficient builder
	Understanding and using architecture of social media such as tagging, polling, role-playing and modeling spaces to link to knowledge of experts in an area
	Identifying signal versus noise in information
	Interrogating data for meaning
	Making optimal choice of tools to access collective intelligence
	Sharing and reframing mental models (plasticity)
ICN2	Functional builder
	Acknowledges multiple perspectives
	Thoughtful organization of tags
	Understanding mechanics of collecting and assembling data
	Knowing when to draw on collective intelligence
	Sharing representations
ICN1	Emerging builder
	Knowledge of survey tools
	Able to make tags
	Posting a question

Friedman describes such practices as a major shift toward technology that educators need to consider (2007). He discusses how it may be counter-productive to ask students to power down or give up their social media when they enter the school doors. To extend this thinking and consider how it can be applied, teachers using technology integration practices should actively engage in digital literacy practices in formal learning, including using the tools, networks and bodies of expertise available to students virtually (Scalise 2013). This both underscores developing ICT knowledge and skills as an important practice in schools and allows educators to teach and model appropriate use while supporting subject matter learning.

Yet there are important interactions between ICT and the given subject matter domain in which it is to be applied. Therefore, teachers preparing to move to novel digital formats need to examine how the formats and tools may be useful for teaching in their areas of interest.

Applying the Concept of TIP to Digital Collaboration in the Classroom

When considering digital literacy objectives, it is important to consider the technology integration that is done by educators in schools (Roblyer 2006). Technology integration for education is often defined simply as using technology as a tool for teaching and learning (Barron et al. 2003). Scholars in recent years have described ICT literacy as often best achieved through integrated learning with technology rather than stand-alone (Ridgway and McCusker 2003; Somekh and Mavers 2003). In integration, technology use is embedded in subject matter areas, authentic tasks, real-world problems or other applications. By contrast, when taught in stand-alone instruction, the focus will typically be more on learning a tool than on its application. Kozma, Jewitt and others have called for rethinking both what digital literacy calls for, and how technology can better contribute to its teaching and assessment (Kozma 2003; Quellmalz and Kozma 2003).

For technology integration planning in the classroom, best practices include understanding how, when, and why technology can be infused into education to improve learning outcomes. Poor technology integration planning can result in too much technology in the classroom instead of too little. For instance, using technology for its own sake, rather than strategically to support specific learning outcomes, can lead to overuse and become a problem in some schools. Scaffolded hands-on experiences with technology and modeling of technology between teachers helps to bring about more effective technology integration planning.

Roblyer describes technology integration planning or TIP for teachers as encompassing five phases (2004):

- Phase 1: Determine the relative advantage of using technology
- Phase 2: Decide on objectives and assessments
- Phase 3: Design technology integration strategies
- Phase 4: Prepare the instructional environment to support successful use of technology
- Phase 5: Evaluate and revise the integration strategies to improve the experience and the learning outcomes for students

How to Know What to Look for

Key to the process of both teaching and assessing student performance in the area of digital collaboration is gaining an understanding of what student patterns of proficiency look like as they develop. By using indicators of proficiency, it should be possible to contrast teams showing evidence of more and less advanced skills. For instance, indicators can include what practices the members of a team employ for effective collaboration and what they elicit from others during the process of learning in networks.

Collaboration as a face-to-face instructional strategy in classrooms has a long history in schools. Extensive research literature is available on collaboration and is documented in prior ATC21S publications (Binkley et al. 2012), so will not be further discussed here except to say that collaboration is prominent in most twenty-first century frameworks. Descriptions of digital collaboration in twenty-first century frameworks often mimic team-based structures of the twenty-first century workplace (Dede 2010). The benefits of digital collaboration are described as including tapping collective intelligence and building shared understandings. They include the contributions of student peer-to-peer engagement, participation, mentoring, and feedback (Erstad 2006; Loader 2007).

In addition, expectations of being able to collaborate digitally are becoming more prominent. Technologies incorporating social media have made large strides in the personal and work worlds. For instance, Facebook has been a topic social networking application on the web for some time. It brings together communities who participate in information sharing. The tool is often used for joint social planning at small scale or large. Pinterest is a different type of high usage social media tool. It allows users to readily tag, assemble and share various items they discover on the web. By contrast, the more ephemeral Snapchat at the time of the publication of this chapter was considered one of the top social media tools among millennials, who reached adulthood around the year 2000. Snapchat incorporates a concept of information privacy by allowing users to share images that will automatically expire in a short period and therefore not persist over time. In the work world, work tools that involve a type of social media include information sharing platforms, such as Yammer, but also more internal types of tools such as Zoom or WebEx for collaborative meetings, Adobe Connect for large group conferencing combined with small group breakouts, and SharePoint, Igloo and other shared workspaces and virtual collaboration suites.

Specific characteristics of successful digital collaboration vary by age, work product, subject matter area, need, and other contextual factors. However, some essential attributes can be identified. First, team performance in collaboration varies at least in part due to the proficiency of the team constituents, and the members of the team. Secondly, teachers often find strikingly similar characteristics of individual performance when students are placed into a variety of different groupings. Students can return to the same or similar roles and behaviors again and again. Finally, some strategies and learning interventions can be taught to improve student collaboration. Then the roles that students repeat when *learning through digital networks* may become more efficacious as well.

Use of Digital Collaboration in the Classroom

Teachers use digital collaboration in the classroom today in many different ways. Sarah Brown Wessling, whose teaching work is described at the beginning of this chapter, asks her students to compose on Google Docs, an online editing platform in which all the authors of a document can share access to the document so that they can write simultaneously (Wessling 2012). Students grouped into teams of three or four work on individual laptops. They sit together in table groups. They can speak together face-to-face and discuss the developing shared writing in person, but they also compose over the computer together for both draft and final documents. The online environment affords a variety of virtual tools, such as for annotation, tagging, and version tracking.

Wessling observes that she knows her students will need to be able to manage these skills in productive ways in their later lives. This will involve collaboration skills such as turn-taking, affirmation, constructive critique, and etiquette. She describes how anyone who has tried to write collaboratively knows it can be difficult. For her students who are new to collaboration, writing can seem both personal in content and idiosyncratic in structure. She believes the online platform makes student thinking more visible to each other as they compose. Wessling also likes that she can log in and leave comments and suggestions for the groups as their work develops. The students can share the feedback and ponder solutions together.

In comments in response to Wessling's report, which can also be seen on the Teaching Channel (Wessling 2012), other teachers using Google docs describe having groups of three to four students create a play script following the selection of a passage from a novel. One teacher asks students to follow up their reading efforts by writing a depiction of what the characters might do next, in a drama or comedy. Students write, discuss, and edit collaboratively throughout the process of creating.

Another teacher responding to Wessling's examples describes using collaborative tools for second language acquisition. She has students start with moving the text of an article they are studying in a new language into a collaborative tool, Lingro.com, then employs the tool to give students glossaries and expand vocabulary in the new language. Students can hyperlink words and leave the tags behind for teammates.

Science, math and social studies teachers are quick to point out that it is not only language collaborations that can serve to create a TIP advantage and support learning objectives. Other online tools readily support better outcomes in their fields as well. Some of these teachers employ shared presentations, in which students organize an outline and "jigsaw" together the slides of their collective work, followed by peer review, mock presentation and refinement within the team before a large group presentation.

Another powerful tool described by these teachers was the use of collaborative spreadsheets for shared data collection, analysis and the display of quantitative thinking. Also, visualization tools online are employed at the start of a unit for mind mapping, concept generation, and brainstorming for posing questions.

These examples show teachers working through Phases 1–3 of the TIP process. The teachers are identifying a TIP rationale for the relative advantage of the digital collaboration, deciding on some objectives and ways to elicit learning evidence through the process, and they have designed some technology integration strategies they intend to employ. They have also had to work through Phase 4, by setting up the learning environment.

For Phase 5 – evaluating and reframing their approaches as needed – teachers see themselves as helping students participate in authentic ways in which adult work is done today in many contexts. In this way, teachers say, they help students leverage their learning time. Embracing "learning to learn" as a twenty-first century skill is an objective for the teachers, and all adult learners, as well as for the students. Phase 5 is seen as an opportunity to take a precious moment for reflection.

Some researchers see the digital divide as encompassing both student and teacher. Does each teacher have the ability to bring technology effectively into the classroom? Can each teacher help his or her students effectively process the digital world? If a teacher feels bombarded by technology and is hesitant to deploy it, students in the classroom may experience fewer or less successful opportunities to learn. This is rapidly developing as a new type of digital divide for digital collaboration.

For instance, teachers ask with regard to classroom management: is there an effective way to hold students accountable for staying on-task during digital collaboration? This involves being able to observe and facilitate digital collaboration in the classroom, of course, but also effectively assess and evaluate the results.

Teachers say that effective tools for collaboration during learning allow them to see how each student has contributed to the group project. This can be done through viewing revision histories in some tools, or through annotations that the interface marks directly on the screen. Teachers describe how students can be seen identifying themselves, marking their writing and questions with information annotations.

Teaching for meaningful learning has many facets, including the arranging of effective learning environments (Barron and Darling-Hammond 2008; National Research Council 2000; Roblyer 2006). Some administrative tools allow portfolios to be collected for the classroom, and shared with parents and caregivers. One such product is Edmodo, which allows students to have all their collaborative documents "appear" in virtual "backpacks" for a variety of assembly purposes. Parents and caregivers can log in to view student progress, sign off on student work, or even to be allowed to collaborate if desired by teachers, for instance in a writer's workshop approach that involves collecting writing comments from a range of readers.

Case Study: Digital Collaboration in the ATC21S Arctic Trek Science Notebooks

One potential mechanism for the assessment of student ability in the learning network aspect of ICT literacy is to model assessment practice through a set of exemplary classroom materials. An ATC21S module that has been developed for this purpose for students aged 11–15 is the "Arctic Trek" scenario, based on the Go North/Polar Husky information website (www.polarhusky.com), a project established by the University of Minnesota. The Go North website is an online adventure learning project based around arctic environmental expeditions.

The Arctic Trek scenario, the opening screen of which is shown in Fig. 14.1, views social networks through ICT as an aggregation of different tools, resources and people that together build community in areas of interest. Through a series of screens, the tour through the site for the ATC21S demonstration scenario is conceived as a "collaboration contest," or virtual treasure hunt. In this task, students in small teams ponder problems and use tools and approaches to unravel clues through the Go North site, via touring scientific and mathematics expeditions of actual sci-

Fig. 14.1 Opening screen of the ATC21S Arctic Trek scenario, a collaborative digital literacy task in a science and mathematics content area

entists. For examples of activities and items from the Arctic Trek scenario, see Wilson and Scalise (2012).

The Arctic Trek task includes the use of a collaborative science lab "notebook" shared by teams of four students in the classroom. The notebook focuses especially on the developing and sustaining Intellectual Capital through Networks (ICN) portion of the ATC21S framework. The notebook allows groups to "construct" a collaboration online. Note that no face-to-face collaboration opportunities are made available in the Arctic Trek scenario, so the notebook itself is a collaborative work product.

The collaborative notebook was employed in trials of the Arctic Trek task in four countries. Using either a Microsoft OneNote document or a collaborative Google document online, student teams were provided with a link in the Arctic Trek activity and a "secret code" to login into their shared document online with their assigned team members. They then had an "open canvas" or mostly blank collaborative work space. The unstructured nature of the approach meant that each team could employ the tool in the manner that they thought best and student work across the team could be evaluated for attributes capturing how effectively the team itself decided to employ their opportunity to collaborate.

To identify attributes to help interpret the collaborative performances seen, Arctic Trek notebooks representing a purposive range of performance were sampled from the ATC21S project. The notebooks were reviewed by methods of integrative research to gather a set of core ideas for patterns seen in the student work. These represented both some common ground and some divergent characteristics by which teachers could recognize important attributes of the ICN performance in the collaborative artifact.

Methods of integrative research (Jackson 1980) include sampling the relevant materials and then representing the characteristics of their evidence. Miles and Huberman's approaches to data reduction and display were used (Miles and Huberman 1994). The purpose of the work was to clarify what information might shed light on interpreting more and less successful collaborative work products, so ordered tabular displays such as shown in Fig. 14.2 were used.

The purposive sample here consisted of nine notebooks representing a range of performance. They were analyzed and coded for attributes that teachers could recognize in distinguishing the range of performance seen in the collaborative work products. Twelve attributes were identified, as shown in Fig. 14.2. These helped describe the phenomena of interest, and were identified as readily recognizable by teachers.

Such pattern codes are often identifiable when ideas repeat in the student work products, and themes or meaningful trends in performance begin to emerge. Thematically, the twelve attributes progress from indicators of ICN1 to ICN3 in the ATC21S intellectual capital strand.

As shown in Fig. 14.2, the twelve attributes ranged from, at initial levels, accessing the digital tool being used for collaboration, making attempts to identify team members, posing initial questions and sharing simple answers, to, at more intermediate levels, working on at least some types of role allocation, planning strategies and sharing thinking for the collaborative process to, at the highest level, participating in effective evidence sharing, systematic execution, flexible adjustment and analysis during the activities and attempting to come to a shared understanding on tasks across the team.

Notebook ID	Accessed Tool	Team ID Attempts	Pose Ques Attempts	Answ Share Attempt	Role Plan Attempt	Evid Share Attempt	Role Plan Complete	Systematic Player ID	Player Number Used	Supports ID Author	Shared Evidence Eval	Answers Reconciled	Total Attributes	Percent Achieved
4	1	1	1	1	0	0	0	0	0	0	0	0	4	33%
8	1	1	1	1	0	0	0	0	0	0	0	0	4	33%
7	1	1	1	1	0	0	0	0	0	0	0	0	4	33%
1	1	1	1	1	1	0	0	0	0	0	0	0	5	42%
9	1	1	1	1	1	1	0	0	0	0	0	0	6	50%
5	1	1	1	1	0	1	0	0	0	1	0	0	6	50%
3	1	1	1	1	1	1	1	1	1	0	0	0	9	75%
2	1	1	1	1	1	1	1	1	1	1	1	0	11	92%
6	1	1	1	1	1	1	1	1	1	1	1	0.5	11.5	96%

Fig. 14.2 Table showing attributes achieved for the nine case study notebooks sampled. Note. Teachers can use simple data displays like this as rubrics for student teams to self-evaluate their collaboration efforts

The 12 attributes identified were analyzed by subject matter experts and then sorted using a cognitive diagnostic technique of ordering from "easier" attributes to "harder", based on sample numbers in which the attributes appeared, with ranking of "ties" by subject matter experts. Figure 14.2 shows the sorting of attributes in the columns, and the sorting of notebook performances from low to high in the rows. A zero in the table indicates that the attribute was not present in the notebook; a one indicates that the attribute was present. The fairly regular pattern on the diagonal of zeros and ones in the table indicates that teams with lower performing notebooks tended to consistently display the same few attributes while higher performing teams compiled both more attributes, and higher level attributes on the ICN strand.

Initial proficiency shown by student teams in the notebook case study sample indicated, as described in Fig. 14.2, the ability to access the collaborative space, begin to identify team members, and attempt to pose at least some initial questions and answers to the team. In the nine notebooks sampled, all teams were able to progress this far in their shared efforts. These indicators are at the ICN1 level of the framework.

Two teams were additionally able to extend to a mid-range of collaboration that involved establishing at least some partial roles or turn-taking in the collaborations and employing the ability to share not only their initial questions and answers but some of the evidence and evaluation that the team collected or completed in their information foraging during the task. These indicators are at the ICN2 level of the framework.

Three teams at the higher performing range of proficiency seen on the 12 attributes of Fig. 14.2 showed more systematic and complete progress in employing intellectual capital effectively. Their role-planning efforts were more thorough and showed evidence of being carried out as agreed upon. This included, at times, making adjustments during the task. The teams independently developed ways to systematically identify contributions from different team members and engaged in evidence reconciliation. This included identifying signal versus noise in information, interrogating data for meaning and sharing aspects of mental models during visualizations of scientific data.

As illustrative examples, three of the notebooks in the case study sample above are used to show how teachers can explore some degree of "benchmarking" for digital collaboration work products. The three notebooks again represent a range of the performance shown in Fig. 14.2, with one selected from each of ICN1 to ICN3. These notebooks are shown in Fig. 14.3 below and in Fig. 14.4 and Fig. 14.5 in the Appendix to this chapter.

Example 1 in Fig. 14.3 is an excerpt from Notebook ID 4. This notebook is at the lower end of the collaborative range seen here but still showed performance of value in the task because it established the foundations of collaboration. Teachers can help such students by pointing out what they are already doing effectively as well as continuing to work with them to build additional understandings. Achieving four of the twelve attributes listed in Fig. 14.2, the team's notebook shows proficiencies within the first level, or ICN1 of the ATC21S digital literacy "intellectual capital" strand. Students correctly access the collaborative tool, make simple efforts to identify their team members ("who is this?"; "yes it is me!!"), and begin to pose some initial but relevant questions and answers to each other ("you go which website???", "i will click 3. now u post ur ans. so I can copy for what they ask.").

is it2???
i saw black and grey... ya maybe but i thought also got white?
yup
u go which website???
i go to polar bear populations because the hint asked me 2.
i think is 3 cos' in one of the clue they also say which on the map got white polar bear...
i will click 3. now u post ur ans. so i can copy for what they ask .but we must explain.... i try my best ok?
i oso
i havent go to tat Question yet.yupppppy
i keep pressing wrong thing
orh...
come on give me a answer
my answer is 3. Then i will do my research to accompany my answer.

who is this?

naila and verretta. r u esan?
we r doing some research..
yes it is me!!

Fig. 14.3 An excerpt from Notebook ID 4. This notebook is at the lower end of the collaborative range but still showed performances to be reinforced in student digital collaboration, such as accessing a collaborative tool, identifying team members, and posing relevant questions and answers

In one part of the task, students are expected to find colors that are used to describe the bear population in an online table. Requiring both identifying signal versus noise in information and interrogating data for meaning, a fully successful performance on the "color" task can be mapped into the ICN3 level ("Proficient builder") of the ICN strand (Wilson and Scalise 2012) but partial credit is also possible. On the color question, the team using Notebook 4 as shown in Fig. 14.3 do not review the correct representation, so their color interpretation is far from correct. Yet they still show evidence of attempting to share their thinking at a level appropriate to ICN1. They post simple questions about the color arrangement they believe they have correctly selected, and they puzzle together about some initial answers. However, their postings include little or no evidence to support their thinking, and the team members do not evaluate shared results or attempt strategic thinking across the group to resolve discrepancies ("i saw black and grey… ya maybe but I thought also got white"; no additional commentary following on this topic following the discrepant comment).

By the end of the task, this team shows some basic success in accessing and using a digital tool for collaboration, establishes the beginning of an ability to "tag" the identity of a fellow team member, and is successful in posting some relevant questions and answers digitally. Team members also show some degree of frustration in their attempts to collaborate. For instance, answers are posted without explanation or evidence: "but we must explain," one student tries to correct the group; "i try my best ok?" another student responds. Another student reverses the temporal order of answer and evidence supplied, telling the team, "my answer is 3. then i will do my research to accompany my answer."

In Example 2 in Fig. 14.4 in the appendix, from Notebook ID 9, the students achieve six of the twelve attributes in Fig. 14.2. The team here is emerging into behaviors of the next level of the intellectual capital strand of the framework, ICN2. The team shows somewhat more knowledge than Team 4 about the mechanics of collecting and assembling data together in a digital collaboration, and of knowing when to draw on collective intelligence. These are some of the attributes of ICN2. For instance, they make attempts at some role planning, which Team 4 did not do. "We need to decide who will do what task," one student says; "ok do you want to decide," a teammate replies. Other data collection planning comments include "Can I pick what I want to do?" and "i would like to do the coloring task."

However, the members of Team 9 never systematically agree on or execute the planning decisions as a whole. So while this team is moving beyond ICN1 and into ICN2, its members are just beginning to master the skill set of more strategic collaboration efforts (at the emerging levels, sometimes alternatively called cooperation in the research literature). These students also begin to acknowledge multiple perspectives by sharing evidence and not just answers across the team during their information foraging. On the color task, one student reports, "i chose four because the graph showed four colors to show the living conditions." Another student disagrees and advances a claim with concrete details as her evidence for five colors: "They use red for declining populations. They use orange for reduced populations. They use green for not reduced populations. They use light green for stable populations. Then they use yellow for moderate." A third student on the team checks this answer, and then confirms the five-color evidence statement. The team goes on to have a lengthy discussion about other questions and activities in the task.

In Example 3 in Fig. 14.5 in the appendix, which is from Notebook ID 6, students achieve nearly all – 11.5 – of the 12 attributes identified in Fig. 14.2. Team behaviors show not only ICN2 traits, but a substantial degree of systematic effort associated with the next level of the framework, ICN3. In their responses to the "color" question, for instance, the team members identify signal versus noise in information as they come up with the answer of not just five but six colors, using codes for missing data in the task included as a source of discrepancy for advanced teams to ponder. They record their consideration of whether white could be considered a color used to represent "data deficiency" or in other words the intended missing data, along with recording the five color codes for the bear populations actually identified in the color chart.

In other answers from the team, not shown in the Fig. 14.5 excerpt because the notebook is quite extensive, the students interrogate data for meaning. They explore how the scientific expedition data indicate that the species under consideration is "on the general decrease" and "facing high risks of being endangered" but share their thinking to introduce caveats. Team members describe areas they have discovered in the reporting from the scientific expedition that are not consistent with the overall trend, like "the Gulf of Boothia, Southern Beaufort Sea and M'Clintock Channel" where "risks of future decline are low."

The students on Team 6 also show evidence of sharing aspects of their mental models with each other. They describe their visualizations of data. To do this, they effectively fit data on bear population graphs with digital tools online and describe how they "control the gradient/frequency" of the display and "the y-intercept" so

Hello? O.o We need to decide who will do what task.
ok do you want to decide

Can I pick what I want to do?
yes we have to make sure we dont end up with the same task
deose anyone no what we are suppose to be doing, because i would like to do the coloring task

ay ay hold on a sec...
i chose four because the graph showed four colors to show the living conditions.

They use red for declining populations. They use orange for reduced populations. They use green for not reduced populations. They use light green for stable populations. Then they use yellow for moderate. ~Jenia

no it's five there's a green light green orange yellow red

Fig. 14.4 An excerpt from Notebook ID 9, showing that students achieved 6 out of the 12 attributes in Fig. 14.2. The team here is entering into the second level of the intellectual capital strand of the framework, ICN2. The team shows emerging knowledge about the mechanics of collecting and assembling data together in a digital collaboration, and of knowing when to draw on collective intelligence. Team members also begin to acknowledge multiple perspectives by sharing some evidence and not just answers across the team during their information foraging

Roles
(1)David: Captain, Decoder
(2)Stephenie:Work on clue 1,2,3
(3)Xinyi: Work on clue 4,5,6
(4)Amanda: Scout, Recorder

Clues
Clue 1:
Where the white bear lives. Where on the map do polar bears live who do NOT belong to any country?
Polar bears live in North Pole

Clue 2:
Arctic Fox

Clue 3:
Answers of person:
(1)There are 5 colours of red, orange, light green, dark green and yellow with one extra colour white to represent data deficiency
(2) 5
(3) 5
(4) 5

Fig. 14.5 An excerpt from Notebook ID 6, showing that students achieved nearly all – 11.5 – of the 12 attributes identified in Fig. 14.2. Team behaviors show not only ICN2 traits, but a substantial degree of systematic effort associated with the next level of the framework, ICN3. See the text description for additional contents of the notebook. In the full transcript, of which only a portion is shown here, the team members establish and employ clear role assignments, identify signal versus noise in information, interrogate data for meaning, and share aspects of their mental models during their visualizations of the scientific data

that they can come up with, record, and share with each other the best fitting curve for the scientific data.

However, even for this team, from the reporting of discrepant opinions it is unclear whether the students always consider whether they need to reframe their thinking after consulting. The group does not appear to reach a consensus or otherwise sum up the conclusions of the team as a whole. As they move between questions, they sometimes simply report a set of different answers.

Looking ahead, especially to work settings where digital collaboration might be an important skill, the expectation is often to establish a shared product, such as a common recommendation, a report or presentation that synthesizes the knowledge of the group. Going beyond what the students exemplify in ICN3, this might be an important aspect to add to ICN4, as a distinguishing characteristic.

Conclusion

For many teachers, the idea of teaching twenty-first century skills such as digital collaboration is both exciting and challenging. Teachers want to know how to help students build such skills, which many believe will be important in the future work and lives of their students. But teachers often ask what a successful performance in digital collaboration looks like, and how they should gauge and support the learning of these skills.

This chapter has discussed results from an ATC21S case study employing digital collaboration through a shared online "notebook" in a science and mathematics activity for students aged 11–15. Using one strand of the ATC21S framework for learning through digital networks, a range of student collaboration evidence is explored through a set of purposively sampled notebook products across a range of performance.

The case study notebooks reveal a range of performance that can be described by a set of twelve attributes in digital collaboration aligned with ICN levels 1–3 of the ATC21S framework. By examining the attributes and using simple displays and tabulations of results as shown in the examples provided here, the case study illustrates ways in which teachers can readily recognize traits for building more successful digital collaboration in their student work.

As teachers increasingly embrace digital tools and collaboration in their classrooms through such technology integration planning, they will often find, as one principal observed, that students are highly engaged in the activities. This is a "win, win" when the activities can also be shown to frame a progression in the foundations of effective learning.

Appendix

Examples of excerpts from three different Arctic Trek notebooks are shown in Fig. 14.3, 14.4 and 14.5, which illustrate different ranges of performance seen in the team activities, and how teachers can recognize differences in digital collaboration performance.

References

Barron, B., & Darling-Hammond, L. (2008). How can we teach for meaningful learning? In L. Darling-Hammond, B. Barron, G. N. Cervetti, P. D. Pearson, A. H. Schoenfeld, E. K. Stage, J. T. Tilson, & T. D. Zimmerman (Eds.), *Powerful learning: What we know about teaching for understanding* (pp. 11–70). San Francisco: Jossey-Bass.

Barron, A., Kemker, K., Harmes, C., & Kalaydjian, K. (2003). Large-scale research study on technology in K12 schools: Technology integration as it relates to the national technology standards. *Journal of Research on Technology in Education, 25*(4), 489–507.

Binkley, M., Erstad, O., Herman, J., Raizen, S., Ripley, M., Miller-Ricci, M., & Rumble, M. (2012). Defining twenty-first century skills. In P. Griffin, B. McGaw, & E. Care (Eds.), *Assessment and teaching of 21st century skills* (Vol. 1). Dordrecht: Springer.

Dede, C. (2010). Comparing frameworks for 21st century skills. In J. Bellanca & R. Brandt (Eds.), *21st century skills: Rethinking how students learn* (pp. 51–75). Bloomington: Solution Tree Press.

Erstad, O. (2006). A new direction? Digital literacy, student participation and curriculum reform in Norway. *Education and Information Technologies, 11*(3–4), 415–429.

Evergreen Education Group. (2014). *Keeping pace with K-12 digital learning: An annual review of policy and practice*. Retrieved from http://www.kpk12.com/reports/.

Friedman, T. L. (2007). *The world is flat 3.0: A brief history of the twenty-first century*. New York: Picador.

Griffin, P., McGaw, B., & Care, E. (Eds.). (2012). *Assessment and teaching of 21st century skills*. Dordrecht: Springer.

Jackson, G. B. (1980). Methods for integrative reviews. *Review of Educational Research, 50*(3), 438–460.

Kozma, R. B. (Ed.). (2003). *Technology, innovation, and educational change: A global perspective*. Eugene: International Society for the Evaluation of Educational Achievement.

Loader, B. (Ed.). (2007). *Young citizens in the digital age: Political engagement, young people and new media*. London: Routledge.

McFarlane, A. (2003). Assessment for the digital age. *Assessment in Education: Principles, Policy & Practice, 10*, 261–266.

Miles, M. B., & Huberman, A. M. (1994). *Qualitative data analysis: An expanded sourcebook*. Thousand Oaks: SAGE Publications.

National Research Council. (2000). *5. Mind and brain how people learn: Brain, mind, experience, and school: Expanded edition* (pp. 114–128). Washington, DC: The National Academies Press.

Nelson, R. (2010). An interview with 2010's national teacher of the year, Sarah Brown Wessling. *Hope Foundation*. http://www.hopefoundation.org/sarah-brown-wessling-teacher-of-the-year-interview/.

Partnership for 21st Century Skills & American Association of Colleges of Teacher Education. (2010). 21st century knowledge and skills in educator preparation. http://www.p21.org/storage/documents/aacte_p21_whitepaper2010.pdf.

Quellmalz, E. S., & Kozma, R. (2003). Designing assessments of learning with technology. *Assessment in Education: Principles, Policy & Practice, 10*, 389–408.

Ridgway, J., & McCusker, S. (2003). Using computers to assess new educational goals. *Assessment in Education: Principles, Policy and Practice, 10*, 309–328.

Roblyer, M. D. (2004). *Educational technology in action: Problem based exercises for technology integration*. Upper Saddle River: Prentice Hall.

Roblyer, M. D. (2006). *Integrating educational technology into teaching*. Upper Saddle River: Pearson.

Scalise, K. (2013). Planning for transition: Evolution of next-generation assessment system designs to support ongoing improvements in measuring complex skills and constructs. CCSSO National Conference on Student Assessment: CCSSO National Conference on Student Assessment.

Scalise, K. (2014). Technology-enhanced assessments in NAEP. California Educational Research Association (CERA) Conference, Building California's Future: Strategies for Achieving Coherence among Standards, Instruction, Assessment, and Evaluation.

Schrum, L., & Levin, B. B. (2014). *Evidence-based strategies for leading 21st century schools*. Thousand Oaks: Corwin.

Somekh, B., & Mavers, D. (2003). Mapping learning potential: Students' conceptions of ICT in their world. *Assessment in Education: Principles, Policy & Practice, 10*, 409–420.

Wessling, S.B. (Producer). (2012). Google Docs in the classroom. *Grades 9–12/All Subjects/Collaboration*. Retrieved from http://www.teachingchannel.org/videos/fostering-student-collaboration

Wilson, M., & Scalise, K. (2012). *Assessment of learning in digital social networks; assessment of technology-based collaboration skills: Transforming assessment for the 21st century*. Paper presented at the American Educational Research Association, Vancouver, Canada.

Wilson, M., Bejar, I., Scalise, K., Templin, J., Wiliam, D., & Torres Irribarra, D. (2012). Perspectives on methodological issues. In P. Griffin, B. McGaw, & E. Care (Eds.), *Assessment and teaching of 21st century skills*. Dordrecht: Springer.

Wilson, M., Scalise, K., Gochyyev, P. (2014). *ICT literacy – learning in digital networks*. Paper presented at the The Fourteenth Annual Maryland Conference, Technology Enhanced Innovative Assessment: Development, Modeling, and Scoring from an Interdisciplinary Perspective, College Park, MD.

Part V
Transforming Education Systems to Integrate Twenty-First Century Skills

Chapter 15
Curricular and Implementation Challenges in Introducing Twenty-First Century Skills in Education

Nienke Nieveen and Tjeerd Plomp

Abstract In this chapter we report on our search for ways of increasing the chances that learners indeed will have the opportunity to acquire twenty-first century skills. We examine the implications of introducing these skills in education with the usage of three curriculum-related 'lenses' each of which will be applied to one of the three levels in education: the classroom level, the school level and the system level. As introducing twenty-first century skills will be a process of change at all three interconnected levels, we – from the perspective of a systemic curriculum implementation approach – discuss guiding principles for increasing the chances for successful implementation of these skills in education.

To be able to participate in our fast-changing society and professions as well as for personal growth and well-being, it is expected that citizens will need digital literacy, critical thinking, creativity, and several other skills. Consequently, present-day schools and teachers need to assist learners and students in acquiring these 'twenty-first century skills'. Recently, much has been written about the need for these skills and efforts have been put in specifying and operationalizing the consequences for teaching and learning. Within this context, Binkley et al. (2012) warn us that without a certain depth of detail, these (sometimes national) statements of twenty-first century aims and goals are unlikely to be reflected in the actual learning experiences of students. Their conclusion is that the lack of careful curriculum design (or re-design) may result in apparently valuable developments at the national level, but a lack of accomplishment at the level of teaching and learning in schools.

N. Nieveen (✉)
SLO Netherlands Institute for Curriculum Development, Enschede and TU/e Eindhoven University of Technology, Eindhoven, The Netherlands
e-mail: n.nieveen@slo.nl

T. Plomp
University of Twente, Enschede, The Netherlands

E. Care et al. (eds.), *Assessment and Teaching of 21st Century Skills*, Educational Assessment in an Information Age,
DOI 10.1007/978-3-319-65368-6_15

This warning is taken as a starting point for this concluding chapter to this volume in which we report on our search for ways of increasing the chances that learners indeed will have the opportunity to acquire twenty-first century skills. We examine the implications of introducing these skills in education through three curriculum-related 'lenses' for three levels in education: the classroom level, the school level and the system level. As introducing twenty-first century skills will be a process of change, we will – from the perspective of a systemic curriculum implementation approach – also discuss some guiding principles for increasing the chances for the successful implementation of these skills in education.

Perspective on Twenty-First Century Skills

As a result of globalization, technological advances and the rise of the knowledge economy in the previous century, professions and society have changed fundamentally. These changes have resulted in the need to prepare learners for jobs that are no longer stable, but dynamic and permanently changing, and to prepare them to become responsible citizens in a society with an overload of information, technological challenges and an expectation to participate actively in social media. In his analysis of the implications of the knowledge society for education, Anderson (2008) identifies two major forces: greater intercultural interaction made possible by global electronic networks; and an economic system in which knowledge functions as a commodity. He concludes that the demands of the knowledge society require from young people (particularly those entering the work force) skills like knowledge construction; adaptability; finding, organizing, retrieving information; information management and ICT utilization; critical thinking and teamwork. It is obvious that these skills are much broader than just the learning and use of ICT.

These and other implications of the new age have been thoroughly analyzed and discussed in the first volume of this series (Griffin et al. 2012). Moreover, several authors (Binkley et al. 2012; Thijs et al. 2014; Voogt et al. 2012) and institutions and organizations (e.g. European Union 2006; OECD 2004) have listed frameworks of twenty-first century skills or lifelong learning skills. The ATC21S project summarized these skills (Binkley et al. 2012) into four categories:

- Ways of Thinking: Creativity and innovation, critical thinking, problem solving, decision making; learning to learn, metacognition
- Ways of Working: Communication, collaboration (teamwork)
- Tools for Working: Information literacy – including research on sources, evidence, biases, etc.; ICT literacy
- Living in the World: Citizenship – local and global; life and career; personal and social responsibility – including cultural awareness and competence.

Obviously, these statements do not reflect the actual learning experiences that students need in order to master them, nor do they provide references to how to teach or assess these objectives. Therefore, to enable next steps, the ATC21S project designed for each skill operational definitions in terms of the following three categories (Binkley et al. 2012):

- Knowledge (K): the required knowledge or understanding for each of the skills
- Skills (S): the required abilities and processes for each skill
- Attitudes/Values/Ethics (AVE): the behaviors and aptitudes that students exhibit in relation to each of the ten skills.

The resulting KSAVE model provides teachers and schools with a more specific set of objectives of what students or learners need to demonstrate when they master a particular skill.

A renewed curriculum at the school level and the ones at the classroom level need to reflect a balance between knowledge and skills that have been traditionally valued and those that are considered necessary in the current and future society. For school leaders and teachers it is a challenge to decide on the approach for incorporating twenty-first century skills in the curriculum of their school and classrooms. At the core, the following three approaches can be distinguished (Voogt et al. 2012). The skills can:

(a) *Be added* to the already existing school curriculum as new subjects or as new content within traditional subjects;
(b) *Be integrated* as cross curricular competences that both underpin the subjects of school curriculum and place emphasis on the acquisition of wider key competences; or
(c) Become part of a *new curriculum* in which the traditional structure of school subjects is transformed and schools are regarded as learning organizations.

An important premise taken by the ATC21S project was that it would be a mistake to think that good education for the information age may consist of 'traditional' education expanded with the teaching of information and communication technology (ICT). As a consequence of technological developments in the previous century, professions and society have changed so fundamentally, that there must be consequences for education. This has been thoroughly analyzed and discussed in the first volume of this series (Griffin et al. 2012). In the remainder of this chapter, we elaborate on the consequences of integrating twenty-first century skills as cross curricular competences. Linking these twenty-first century skills with subjects is not a trivial enterprise nor a one-off event at the school and the classroom level. For instance, teachers may consider twenty-first century skills as competing additions, especially when they are used to focus their teaching on the subject-related goals and objectives of their courses.

Integrating twenty-first century skills in the curriculum refers to a process demanding fundamental changes at all levels, i.e., at the classroom, the school and the system levels. In this chapter, we elaborate on the major consequences at these three levels using various curricular lenses. We begin with the implications at the classroom level, followed by the school level and the system level, as we believe that the needs and demands at the classroom level should determine changes at the school and system level.

Implications at the Classroom Level

Addressing twenty-first century skills as cross-curricular competences has major consequences for the curriculum at the classroom level. In order to consider these consequences, we use the lens of the *curricular spider's web*, proposed by Van den Akker (2003), representing the relevant components of a curriculum (Fig. 15.1). In this view, the rationale or vision of learning can be seen as the core component of a curriculum. Changes to this core presuppose changes to all other aspects of the curriculum, such as the aims and objectives, learning activities, teacher role, materials and resources and assessment.

The metaphor of the spider's web emphasizes the vulnerable nature of a curriculum. Although a spider's web is relatively flexible, it will most certainly rip if certain threads are pulled at more strongly or more frequently than other ones. In the remainder of this section, we synthesize the major consequences of the integration of twenty-first century skills in the classroom based on the work of scholars in this field (Anderson 2008; Binkley et al. 2012; Dede 2010; Gipps and Stobart 2003; Kozma 2011; Scardamalia et al. 2012; Voogt 2003; Voogt and Odenthal 1997; Voogt and Pelgrum 2003).

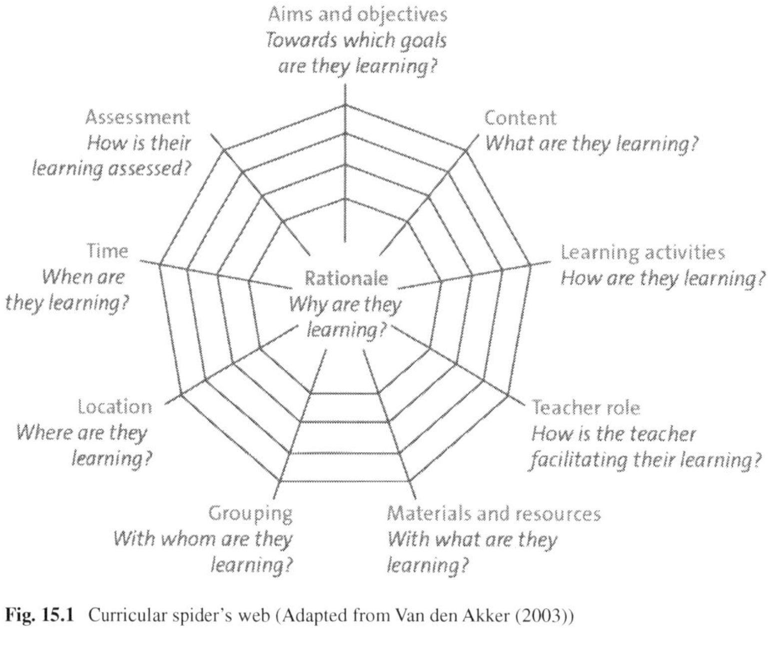

Fig. 15.1 Curricular spider's web (Adapted from Van den Akker (2003))

Rationale

When relating the integration of the twenty-first century skills to the metaphor of the curricular spider's web, it becomes clear that we are discussing aims and objectives here and not so much the rationale itself. The question of *why* these skills are important needs to get specific attention – a well phrased rationale provides direction for the renewal. In the introduction of this chapter, we pointed to the rationale by referring to the fast-changing society and professions due to globalization and technological developments.

Aims and Objectives

The rationale implies new aims and objectives that have to be dealt with: learners need to acquire twenty-first century skills, such as problem solving skills, independent learning skills and creativity. The KSAVE model refers to these, and Binkley et al. (2012) provide elaborations for these skills.

Content

As twenty-first century skills are 'empty' in themselves, it will be necessary to teach them linked to the core subjects in the curriculum. In addition, students need to be able to understand relations between concepts instead of being able to just reproduce facts. Authentic problems should have a clear place in the curriculum.

Assessment

New assessments have to be realized linked to the new aims and objectives. Instead of measuring the extent to which students are able to reproduce knowledge to respond to standard problems, assessment should measure students' ability to apply knowledge in realistic settings. Consequently, closed formats of assessment need to be supplemented with more open formats, such as portfolio and performance assessment (Gipps and Stobart 2003). Also more emphasis must be placed on formative assessment, instead of the current focus on summative assessment. See for example the work of the Assessment Reform Group in the UK (ARG 2010; Kozma 2011).

Learning Activities

First of all, the character of twenty-first century skills is such that learning can no longer be seen as the pure transfer of knowledge and skills, but it has to be viewed as a process in which students actively develop their knowledge and skills. It is imperative to enable learners to become more active and to give them more responsibility for arranging their own learning process, in particular because learning needs to continue after leaving school. With reference to the characteristics of education in an information society, Voogt (2003) presented expectations for the pedagogical approaches relevant for teaching and learning of twenty-first century skills by using the words 'less' and 'more' (Table 15.1). The table indicates that education nowadays is searching for a new balance between 'traditional' and 'emerging' pedagogies.

Teacher Role

It is obvious that all developments discussed so far also have an influence on the role of the teacher. Encouraging and supporting active learning needed to acquire these skills implies that learning processes have to be organized in such a way that learners learn - with the help of teachers as professional 'coaches' – how to become more or less the architect of their own learning process. Voogt and Odenthal (1997) give

Table 15.1 Overview of pedagogy in the industrial versus the information society

Aspect	Less 'traditional pedagogy'	More 'emerging pedagogy'
Active	Activities prescribed by teacher	Activities determined by learners
	Whole class instruction	Small groups
	Little variation in activities	Many different activities
	Pace determined by the program	Pace determined by learners
Collaborative	Individual	Working in teams
	Homogeneous groups	Heterogeneous groups
	Everyone for him/herself	Supporting each other
Creative	Reproductive learning	Productive learning
	Apply known solutions to problems	Find new solutions to problems
Integrative	No link between theory and practice	Integrating theory and practice
	Separate subjects	Relations between subjects
	Discipline-based	Thematic
	Individual teachers	Teams of teachers
Evaluative	Teacher – directed	Student – directed
	Summative	Diagnostic

Adapted from Consequences of ICT for aims, contents, processes and environments of learning (p. 222), by J. Voogt, 2003, Dordrecht, The Netherlands: Kluwer. Copyright 2003 by Springer Science + Business Media Dordrecht (Adapted with permission)

an example of picturing the changing roles of teachers, such as: teachers focus on interests and needs of individual students, they actively create a rich learning environment for students, and they support the learning process of students actively and interactively (give direct feedback, stimulate reflection, evaluate progress).

Materials and Resources

Integrating twenty-first century skills will also impact the need for less structured sources of information and a variation in ICT use. In this context, Dede (2010) refers to the world-to-the-desktop interface, which provides access to distributed knowledge and expertise across space and time through networked media.

Location

Location of learning proves to be a less neutral factor than was often supposed. Learning may take place anywhere inside or outside the school building. The boundaries between the school and the outside world need to fade. It is expected that students will spend less time in the classroom and the school. According to Voogt and Odenthal (1997) the physical environments within and outside the school need to be suitable for learning individually and in small groups. Learning increasingly will become flexible in location, meaning that students will not use the specific locations in the same manner.

Grouping

As indicated before, teaching and learning methods need to move towards meeting the needs of individual learners. This will have consequences for grouping, i.e., with whom will learners learn. Learning increasingly needs a community-centered approach that enhances students' collaborative construction of meaning via different perspectives on shared experiences.

Time

Finally, time is a classical object of curriculum discussions; this will be even more the case where time to be spent on twenty-first century skills will be at the expense of other ('traditional') aims and objectives. A key question related to implementing twenty-first century skills becomes how the scarce amount of time will be distributed across domains and learning tasks. Moreover, it should be discussed how to allocate time where learning becomes flexible.

Summary

In sum, a careful and coherent approach to the integration of twenty-first century skills in the curriculum at the classroom level, considering all curricular components, is needed to increase chances for success and sustainable implementation. The lens of the curriculum spider's web illustrates the familiar expression: every chain is as strong as its weakest link.

Implications at the School Level

Especially for schools and teachers who take a subject-based approach towards the curriculum, the implications of integrating twenty-first century skills at the classroom level are substantial. Moreover, successful and sustainable school-based renewal needs synergy and productive relations between curriculum development, professional development of teachers, and school organization development. Consequently, schools that change their local curriculum towards embedding the twenty-first century skills as cross curricular competences also need to consider the consequences for teachers' professional development and school organization development. In this section, we present the challenge at the school level with a second lens, namely to accomplish a sustainable interrelationship between these three developments (Fig. 15.2).

Curriculum Development

Schools that change their local curriculum towards embedding the twenty-first century skills as cross curricular competences need to reconsider the components of the curricular spider's web at the school level. Taking into account the policy

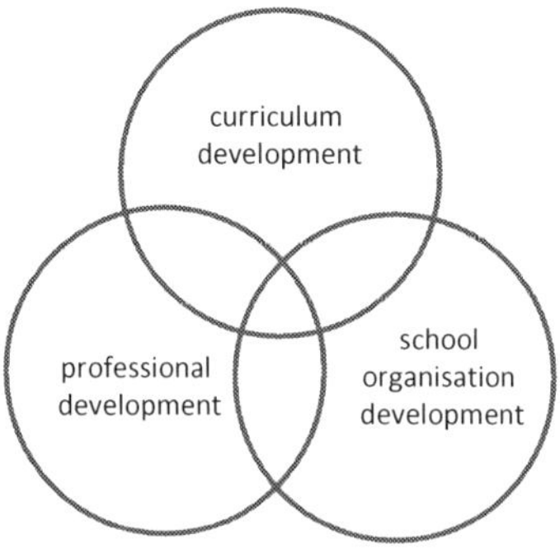

Fig. 15.2 Three interrelated developments at the school level

guidelines, they have to address many questions, such as: What is the school's main rationale for the renewal? What learning strands and assessment strategies throughout several school years will support learning the skills? What are consequences for the layout of the school? Without a shared image of the renewal, collaborative action of school leadership and teachers is not likely to occur. Clarification of the various components of a curriculum is especially valuable and needed when trying to understand and anticipate the challenges that come with implementing twenty-first century skills in the school-wide curriculum. The spider's web metaphor illustrates that the curricular components of the renewal need to form a coherent set. In other words, and using a metaphor taken from Fullan (2007), the implementation process is like a 'meal' and not a 'menu' from which one may choose any number of components.

Professional Development

Major curriculum changes at the school and classroom level imply a need for change on all three dimensions of the teaching-learning processes as suggested by Fullan (2007): new pedagogies (e.g. students working more independently with the teacher in a different role), new materials (e.g. educational software, open source, web-based materials), and – very important – teachers who may need to alter their beliefs about what they think is good education and what should be taught and how. According to Fullan (2007) the complexity of educational change increases when more of these dimensions are involved. As integrating twenty-first century skills do pertain to all three dimensions, there will be "no curriculum development without teacher development". Accordingly, several authors convincingly recommend putting teachers-as-learners in the forefront of curriculum change (e.g., Black and Atkin 1996; Putnam and Borko 2000). The potential means of professional learning can be sorted into four categories that should preferably be combined in the process of professional development (Kwakman 2003): reading and observing (in order to collect new knowledge and information); experimenting (as an intentional effort of teachers to try something new within the classroom); reflection (as a prerequisite to recognize and change routine behavior); and collaboration (to provide teachers with support for learning and feedback and to bring about new ideas and challenges). Moreover, according to Skilbeck (1998) and underlined in more recent studies (Handelzalts 2009; Huizinga 2014), there is great potential in encouraging teachers to be involved more fully in school-based curriculum development processes. *Teachers-as-designers* in local curriculum development helps improving the quality and relevance of what is taught and will strengthen teachers' professionalism. Furthermore, teachers' participation in such design processes contributes to developing ownership, an important factor for sustaining school-wide changes.

School Organization Development

Creating and implementing local curriculum change is not an easy task, even for teachers who appreciate the change. Part of the problem is that most teachers teach alone in isolated classrooms without having the opportunity to reflect together on their teaching practices, bring in new perspectives, discuss new ideas, give each other feedback on improvement efforts. In order to move away from their customary isolation, teachers need to collaborate. Little (1990) suggests that schools that aim at curriculum change need teachers who work together on the renewal and reflect on and learn from their experiences. Advocates of 'professional learning communities' have offered comparable arguments (e.g. Hord 2004; Lieberman and Miller 2004; McLaughlin and Talbert 2001). Moreover, collaboration of teachers seems crucial for schools that are working towards more coherence in the overall curriculum. For schools that are integrating twenty-first century skills, teacher collaboration is needed to lead to meaningful connections between topics or skills that are usually addressed in different subject areas.

In order to support the collaborative work of teachers in teacher design teams, the school context should become a powerful environment (Nieveen et al. 2005). This means that schools should foster a *culture* that addresses collaboration and accountability in a meaningful way. Teachers' collaborative work needs to be encouraged, and, according to Hargreaves (2003), there should also be agreements that this joint work consistently focuses on improving teaching and learning and for solving whole-school problems. Moreover, deep and sustainable change calls for a form of distributed leadership (Hargreaves 2003; McLaughlin and Talbert 2001). Here leaders spread responsibility and ownership for community values throughout the school (for instance by giving substantive roles to department chairs and working groups).

Moreover, *structures* within a school should foster this kind of school culture. This means for example that teacher teams need to have scheduled time to design and learn together, have a suitable workplace for joint work, are buffered from outside disruptions, are (made) aware of knowledge resources and opportunities for learning inside and outside school, have budget to work on these opportunities, and are enabled to negotiate different understandings about practice. When it comes to the integration of twenty-first century skills, investments in the ICT infrastructure will be needed. From an early stage on, the renewal needs coordination by organizing cross-over structures and diverse and regular communication to all staff in the school about decisions being made, developments in the process, and progress made.

Summary

In sum, schools need curricular leaders (teachers and school leaders) who take responsible ownership of the curriculum and who encourage others to strive for design decisions that fit the overall choices. Continuing professional development of teachers in pedagogical matters as well as in becoming cooperative designers requires a cooperative school culture and a supportive infrastructure. Change processes that integrate these reciprocal developments are in the heart of the model introduced in Fig. 15.2.

Implications for the Wider Educational System

As schools are not functioning in an empty space when integrating twenty-first century skills, it is important to pay attention to the wider context of schools. For considering this, we use the lens illustrated in Fig. 15.3. The model illuminates the notion that curriculum change at the school and classroom level may benefit from several sources in the wider educational system: direction and facilitation from the system level (top-down), space for teachers to take initiatives (bottom-up), and lateral support (from aside) e.g. from support agencies, textbook publishers, teacher education and professional learning communities (Hargreaves and Shirley 2009; Kuiper et al. 2013). In this section, we discuss these sources.

Top-Down Direction and Facilitation

Curriculum change benefits from a shared vision about the needs for and affordances of twenty-first century skills, preferably based on careful deliberation between relevant parties in society and on what to prioritize in the curriculum at the national level. A clear and shared vision or rationale offers a joint and better defined sense of direction about what the goals and contents 'of most worth' to teach, learn and assess are (Millar and Osborne 1998). Moreover, Kozma (2011) argues that

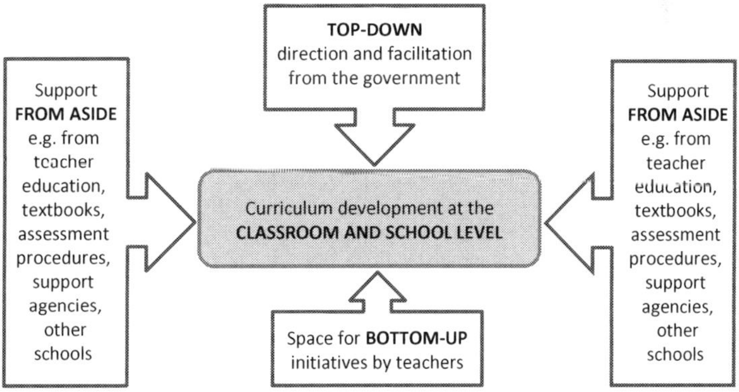

Fig. 15.3 Curriculum change and the wider educational system: influences from three directions (Adapted from Kuiper et al. 2013. Adapted with permission from SLO)

Table 15.2 Typology of curriculum representations (Van den Akker 2003)

Intended	Ideal	Vision (rationale or basic philosophy underlying a curriculum)
	Formal/Written	Intentions as specified in curriculum documents and/or materials
Implemented	Perceived	Curriculum as interpreted by its users (especially teachers)
	Operational	Actual process of teaching and learning (also: curriculum-in-action)
Attained	Experiential	Learning experiences as perceived by learners
	Learned	Resulting learning outcomes of learners

polices from the top should be formulated in such a way that they give direction to and facilitate the changes needed at the school and classroom level.

Building on the work of Goodlad et al. (1979) and van den Akker (2003) presents a typology of curriculum representations (Table 15.2) pointing out that traditionally the *intended* domain refers predominantly to the influence of curriculum policy makers and curriculum developers (in various roles), the *implemented* curriculum relates especially to the world of schools and teachers, and the *attained* curriculum has to do with the students.

With Table 15.2 one can illustrate that policies can facilitate change in schools, but do not guarantee its implementation and impact in practice. At the level of the intended curriculum, policy makers may decide what schools should teach and learners should learn, and these decisions might be elaborated in curriculum documents and materials that are meant to support schools. But at the level of the implemented curriculum, the intended curriculum will be interpreted in the schools and teachers will organize the processes of teaching and learning. Oftentimes the interpretations and translations by schools and teachers deviate from the intentions of policy makers. Moreover, the actual teaching and learning processes may deviate from the intentions, which may result in learning experiences and outcomes (the attained curriculum) that do not reflect the original intentions. Kozma (2011) points to the danger that policies – if not formulated in a way that they will have system-wide impact on school structures and classroom practices – become merely symbolic acts to which schools and teachers respond only in a symbolic way by making only superficial changes.

The approach governments take in guiding changes vary. With regard to this, two extremes have been distinguished by Kuiper et al. (2013). At the one extreme, curriculum *regulation* reflects a government's intention to prescribe the curriculum at the input level in terms of goals and contents and at the output level in terms of modes of assessments and examinations and surveillance by the inspection and governance. Those prescriptions usually imply a fidelity approach (Fullan and Pomfret 1977) to implementation in which the room for school-specific curricular choices is restricted. At the other extreme, curriculum *deregulation* reflects a government's intention to refrain from prescription and control at the input and output level. Here an enactment approach would fit, stimulating school-based curriculum decision-making. A mutual adaptation approach to implementation suits situations that lie in between these two extremes. Here the government provides clarity about the basic ideas and directions underlying the curriculum change, and provides details in the form of (several alternative) exemplifications that can help schools and teachers adjust to the change. However, at the same time, this approach leaves room for schools and teachers to make suitable on-site modifications, which is seen as an important issue because of the differing circumstances facing schools and teachers.

As curriculum regulation from the top varies from one country to the other, countries also show differences in the amount of space for teachers' initiatives and in the kind of supportive actions from aside by support agencies, textbook publishers, teacher education, etc. (Nieveen et al. 2014). In our view a mutual adaptation approach to curriculum implementation would be most beneficial when looking at the changes that are needed when integrating twenty-first century skills and looking at the contextual differences of schools. In this approach, the curriculum renewal process is seen as "a two-way street": adjustments of schools and teachers will feed the intentions at the national level, for instance to improve the relevance and practicality of curriculum frameworks at the national level. Moreover, in this approach *all* components in the education system have to be addressed, including the support provided by teacher professional development, assessment procedures, textbooks, etc. In the next two sections, we elaborate on the implications of a mutual adaptation approach for the space for bottom-up initiatives of teachers and the support from aside.

Space for Bottom-Up Initiatives by Teachers

In accordance with the mutual adaptation approach to be applied at the system level, the guidance from national curriculum policy should leave room for site-specific interpretations and choices. This means that next to their teaching and managerial duties, teachers and school leaders will be involved in planning, developing, and implementing their local curriculum. In order to ensure the development of good quality curricula at the school and the classroom level, teacher teams and school leadership need to have several capabilities (Huizinga 2014; Nieveen and Van der Hoeven 2011), such as subject matter expertise, pedagogical content knowledge including coaching skills for teaching twenty-first century skills, communicative skills, change skills. However, the school team also needs to have curriculum design capacity in their midst, referring to capacities to analyze, construct and evaluate (drafts of) the new curricula and using a helicopter view to make sure that all curriculum components are coherent and that the renewal matches the vision of the school, the learning strands of a subject, needs of the learners, etc. The need for curriculum design capacity has been recognized broadly and must receive special attention at the system level in order to be able to live up to the expectations of a school-wide curriculum change that places much emphasis on the twenty-first century skills (Marsh et al. 1990; Priestley and Biesta 2013; Law and Nieveen 2010).

Next to the need for curriculum design capabilities, other issues arise when considering bottom-up initiatives. For instance, change is not an event, but a process and reality shows that in general it takes 5–10 years to fully implement school-based curriculum innovations (Nieveen et al. 2014). Because of the complexities already described, integrating twenty-first century skills will not be an exception. The question is how to ensure that school leaders and teachers remain motivated to complete these innovations successfully. The process oftentimes will be challenged, for instance by personal shifts in school management and/or teachers or by external pressure from the school board, parents, and/or the inspectorate, who are determined to see "good" results as time passes. A key aspect here is to encourage cooperation and support between all involved in the renewal (between teachers, between teachers and school leaders, between schools and their school board, between schools and parents, within networks of schools, teacher education institutes and support agencies, etc.). In this way schools and teachers will be supported to create a curriculum that fits their local context.

Support from Aside

From the point of view of the schools and teachers who are working on curriculum renewal, support may come from many group of actors, such as text book publishers, assessment developers, teacher educators, support agencies, school boards, to name a few. When reflecting on the challenges of integrating twenty-first century skills at the classroom and the school level, these types of lateral support are crucial. Kozma (2011) argues that transformational change is needed in all components of the system, including the groups who are responsible for lateral support. This also underpins the relevance and importance of the fact that the ATC21S project not only has been focused on the KSAVE model on identifying the twenty-first century skills, but that the project also attended to suggestions for continuing professional development, teaching and learning materials, and assessment procedures associated with these skills. Resources should be made available from the system level to advance lateral support that connects the policy intentions to changes that need to be made in schools and classrooms (Cohen and Hill 2001).

In conclusion, the integrating of twenty-first century skills at the classroom and school level needs to be considered as a change *process* with all complexities that are associated with it. For that reason, this type of renewal needs to be embraced and supported by the entire educational system. It needs direction and facilitation by an inspiring and coherent policy vision. The lateral support for schools and teachers should be transformed in such a way that these connect the policy intentions with needs that accompany site-specific curriculum decision-making. One of the major challenges that comes with this systemic curriculum renewal approach is that it should safeguard room for teachers' initiatives to act upon their local contexts. This stimulates the question: How much guidance, specification, and exemplification (provided by the different partners in the system) is effective without endangering the local curricular space of schools and teachers? As the essence of curriculum implementation is established by the efforts of teachers (Hargreaves and Fullan 2012), top priority needs to be the building of curriculum design capacity of teach ers and school leaders, and to assist networks of schools in sharing good practices.

Integrating Twenty-First Century Skills in Education: Guiding Principles for the Change Process

We have considered the implications of integrating twenty-first century skills in the curriculum at classroom level, the school level and the system level, using three different curriculum-related lenses. We set out for a mutual adaptation approach towards implementing this major curriculum change. A strong point of this approach is its emphasis on creating a spirit and culture of encouragement for all involved in the curriculum change process. Although there are no recipes for integrating twenty-first century skills in the curriculum, we propose five guiding principles for the change process (Nieveen and Plomp 2017):

- Implementation process is a learning process for all involved
- Implementation needs freedom within boundaries
- Implementation needs time to evolve
- Implementation efforts form a meal not a menu
- Implementation needs care for the old and encouragement for the new

The last principle: when it comes to the awareness that implementation is a learning process of all involved, the notions of 'care' and 'courage' (Plomp et al. 1996) are of help. Paraphrasing their line of reasoning, Plomp et al. argue that in the course of implementing an innovation in the schools, both 'care' and 'courage' are concepts that have to be taken into account. On the one hand, a program of change should not be exclusively aimed at what has to be realized in future, but has to take care of the existing practice as well. On the other hand, 'courage' should not be mistaken for an attitude that neglects the values of the existing education system. Where ultimately, 'new' needs to replace 'old', schools cannot and must not focus all attention and resources entirely on the future and ignore the demands of the existing system. A balance between 'new' and 'old' is needed. It requires care and attention out of respect for the people and for what has been achieved and out of trust that professionals and their organizations will be able to change. Both concepts of care and courage and the relative attention for these in the course of time are depicted in Fig. 15.4.

As change is a process, we must realize that the transformation to new forms of education will start while the 'old' still exists. New or emergent practices may compete for the same sources as the existing ones. As more people become involved in

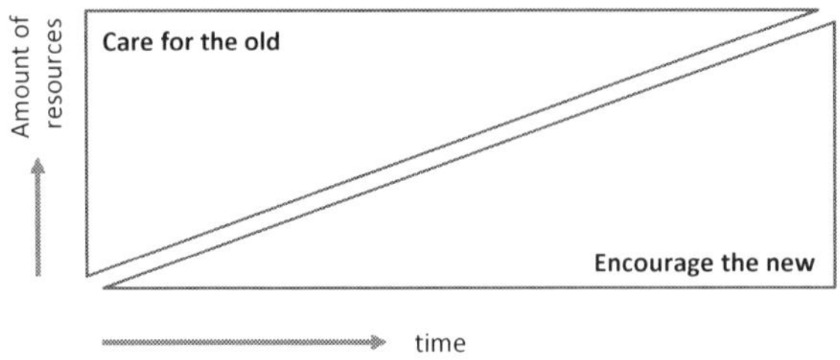

Fig. 15.4 'New' replaces 'old'

these emergent practices, the consequences for the existing practice will gradually become clear and this may cause resistance. Without a program of action to help these emergent practices to flourish, the existing practice will have the tendency to continue, the more so when the existing interests benefit from continuation of the status quo.

In reality different schools may decide for different emphases in the processes of curriculum change they decide to embark on. This implies that across schools the balance between what is traditionally valued and what is considered important for the future may have many different representations. It is important that schools work on their own processes of implementing twenty-first century skills starting from a vision of how they see schooling in a future society. This also means that direction and facilitation from the top, and lateral support from aside need to value variation, as well as need to provide enough guidance in order to keep the change within the intended boundaries.

Such a careful process goes well together with the suggestions in this chapter for curriculum (re)design work at the classroom level, the school level and the system level and the interconnectedness of these layers. To initiate an emergent practice, it takes creativity and endurance, and it takes courage to maintain the intention of replacing existing practices. In this context, 'care' means also preparing people and their organizations for transformation, building confidence and strength for 'the leap into the future'.

References

Anderson, R. (2008). Implications of the information and knowledge society for education. In J. Voogt & G. Knezek (Eds.), *International handbook of information technology in primary and secondary education* (pp. 5–22). New York: Springer.

ARG Assessment Reform Group UK (2010). About ARG. http://assessment-reform-group.org/ downloaded 11 June 2013.

Binkley, M., Erstad, O., Herman, J., Raizen, S., Ripley, M., & Rumble, M. (2012). Defining 21st century skills. In P. Griffin, B. McGaw, & E. Care (Eds.), *Assessment and teaching of 21st century skills* (pp. 17–66). Dordrecht: Springer.

Cohen, D., & Hill, H. (2001). *Learning policy: When state education reform works*. New Haven: Yale University Press.
Black, P., & Atkin, J. M. (Eds.). (1996). *Changing the subject: Innovations in science, mathematics, and technology education*. London: Routledge.
Dede, C. (2010) Comparing frameworks for 21st century skills. In J. Bellanca & R. Brandt (Eds.), *21st century skills* (pp. 51–76). Bloomington: Solution Tree Press.
Union, E. (2006). Recommendation of the European Parliament and of the council on key competences for lifelong learning. *Official Journal of the European Union, L394*, 10–18.
Fullan, M. (2007). *The new meaning of educational change*. New York: Teachers College Press.
Fullan, M. G., & Pomfret, A. (1977). Research on curriculum and instruction implementation. *Review of Educational Research, 47*(2), 335–397.
Gipps, C., & Stobart, G. (2003). Alternative assessment. In D. Stufflebeam & T. Kellaghan (Eds.), *International handbook on educational evaluation* (pp. 549–576). Dordrecht: Kluwer Academic Publishers.
Goodlad, J. I., Klein, M. F., & Tye, K. A. (1979). The domains of curriculum and their study. In J. I. Goodlad et al. (Eds.), *Curriculum inquiry: The study of curriculum practice* (pp. 43–76). New York: McGraw-Hill.
Griffin, P., McGaw, B., & Care, E. (Eds.). (2012). *Assessment and teaching of 21st century skills*. Dordrecht: Springer.
Handelzalts, A. (2009). *Collaborative curriculum design in teacher design teams*. Doctoral thesis. Enschede: University of Twente.
Hargreaves, A. (2003). *Teaching in the knowledge society: Education in the age of insecurity*. New York: Teachers College Press.
Hargreaves, A., & Shirley, D. (2009). *The fourth way: The inspiring future for educational change*. Thousand Oaks: Corwin.
Hargreaves, A., & Fullan, M. (2012). *Professional capital: Transforming teaching in every school*. New York: Teachers College Press.
Hord, S. (2004). *Learning together, leading together: Changing schools through professional learning communities*. New York: Teachers College Press.
Huizinga, T. (2014). *Developing curriculum design expertise through teacher design teams*. Doctoral thesis. Enschede: University of Twente.
Kozma, R. B. (2011). A Framework for ICT Policies to Transform Education. In UNESCO (2011). *Transforming Education: The Power of ICT Policies* (pp. 19–36). Paris: UNESCO.
Kuiper, W., Nieveen, N., & Berkvens, J. (2013). Curriculum regulation and freedom in the Netherlands: A puzzling paradox. In W. Kuiper & J. Berkvens (Eds.), *Balancing curriculum regulation and freedom across Europe. CIDREE Yearbook 2013* (pp. 139–162). Enschede: SLO.
Kwakman, K. (2003). Factors effecting teachers' participation in professional learning activities. *Teaching and Teacher Education, 19*(2), 149–170.
Law, E. H.-F., & Nieveen, N. (Eds.). (2010). *Schools as curriculum agencies: Asian and European perspectives on school-based curriculum development*. Rotterdam: Sense publishers.
Lieberman, A., & Miller, J. (2004). *Teacher leadership*. San Francisco: Jossey-Bass.
Little, J. W. (1990). The persistence of privacy: Autonomy and initiative in teachers' professional relations. *Teachers College Record, 91*, 509–536.
Marsh, C., Day, C., Hannay, L., & McCutcheon, G. (1990). *Reconceptualizing school-based curriculum development*. Bristol: Falmer Press.
McLaughlin, M. W., & Talbert, J. E. (2001). *Professional communities and the work of high school teaching*. Chicago: The University of Chicago Press.
Millar, R., & Osborne, J. F. (Eds.). (1998). *Beyond 2000: Science education for the future*. London: King's College London.
Nieveen, N., Handelzalts, A., Van den Akker, J. (2005). *Teacher design teams in view of school-based curriculum development*. Paper presented at AERA annual meeting, Montreal, Canada.
Nieveen, N., & Van der Hoeven, M. (2011). Building the curricular capacity of teachers: Insights from the Netherlands. In P. Picard & L. Ria (Eds.), *Beginning teachers: A challenge for edu-*

cational systems. CIDREE Yearbook 2011 (pp. 49–64). Lyon: ENS de Lyon, Institut français de l'Éducation.

Nieveen, N., & Plomp, T. (2017). *Five guiding principles for curriculum change*. Enschede: SLO.

Nieveen, N., Sluijsmans, L., & Van den Akker, J. (2014). Encouraging curriculum change in the Netherlands: The next episode. In F. Nyhamn & T. N. Hopfenbeck (Eds.), *From political decisions to change in the classroom. CIDREE Yearbook 2014* (pp. 162–183). Oslo: The Norwegian Directorate for Education and Training.

OECD. (2004). Lifelong learning. Observer. February, 1–8. Retrieved 30 June 2005 from http://www.oecd.org/dataoecd/17/11/29478789.pdf

Plomp, T., Ten Brummelhuis, A., & Rapmund, R. (1996). *Teaching and learning for the future, Report of the Committee on Multimedia in Teacher Training [COMMITT] to the Netherlands Minister of Education*. The Hague: Sdu.

Priestley, M., & Biesta, G. J. J. (Eds.). (2013). *Reinventing the curriculum: New trends in curriculum policy and practice*. London: Bloomsbury Academic.

Putnam, R. T., & Borko, H. (2000). What do new views of knowledge and thinking have to say about research on teacher learning? *Educational Researcher, 29*(1), 4–16.

Scardamalia, M., Bransford, J., Kozma, B., & Quellmalz, E. (2012). New assessments and environments for knowledge building. In P. Griffin, B. McGaw, & E. Care (Eds.), *Assessment and teaching of 21st century skills*. Doredrecht: Springer.

Skilbeck, M. (1998). School based curriculum development. In A. Hargreaves, A. Lieberman, M. Fullan, & D. Hopkins (Eds.), *International handbook of educational change* (pp. 121–144). Dordrecht: Kluwer Academic Publishers.

Thijs, A., Fisser, P., & Van der Hoeven, M. (2014). *21e eeuwse vaardigheden in het curriculum van het funderend onderwijs. [21st century skills in primary and secondary education curriculum]*. Enschede: SLO.

Van den Akker, J. (2003). Curriculum perspectives: An introduction. In J. van den Akker, W. Kuiper, & U. Hameyer (Eds.), *Curriculum landscapes and trends* (pp. 1–10). Dordrecht: Kluwer.

Voogt, J. M. (2003). Consequences of ICT for aims, contents, processes and environments of learning. In J. van den Akker, W. Kuiper, & U. Hameyer (Eds.), *Curriculum landscapes and trends* (pp. 217–236). Dordrecht: Kluwer.

Voogt, J. M., & Odenthal, L. E. (1997). *Emergent practices geportretteerd: Conceptueel raamwerk. [Emerging practices portrait: Conceptual Framework]*. Enschede: University of Twente.

Voogt, J., & Pareja Roblin, N. (2012). A comparative analysis of international frameworks for 21st century competences: Implications for national curriculum policies. *Journal of Curriculum Studies, 44*(3), 299–321.

Voogt, J. M., & Pelgrum, W. J. (2003). ICT and the curriculum. In R. B. Kozma (Ed.), *Technology, innovation and educational change: A global perspective. A report of the IEA Second Information Technology in Education Study, Module 2*. Eugene: International Society for Technology in Education.

Made in the USA
Monee, IL
12 August 2021

5753c8f8-9679-46de-91db-45e416090e36R01